JimSmith
2022

PACIFIC CARRIER WAR

OSPREY
PUBLISHING

PACIFIC
CARRIER WAR

CARRIER COMBAT FROM PEARL HARBOR TO OKINAWA

MARK E. STILLE

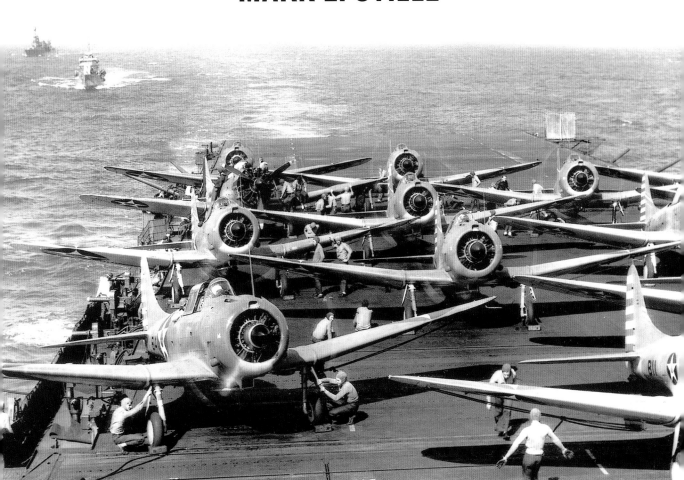

OSPREY PUBLISHING
Bloomsbury Publishing Plc
Kemp House, Chawley Park, Cumnor Hill, Oxford OX2 9PH, UK
29 Earlsfort Terrace, Dublin 2, Ireland
1385 Broadway, 5th Floor, New York, NY 10018, USA
E-mail: info@ospreypublishing.com
www.ospreypublishing.com

OSPREY is a trademark of Osprey Publishing Ltd

First published in Great Britain in 2021

ISBN: HB 9781472826336; PB 9781472826374; eBook 9781472826350; ePDF 9781472826343; XML 9781472826367

21 22 23 24 25   10 9 8 7 6 5 4 3 2 1

Cover design, Art Direction and layout by Stewart Larking (Osprey)
Maps by www.bounford.com
Index by Zoe Ross
Printed and bound in India by Replika Press Private Ltd.

Osprey Publishing supports the Woodland Trust, the UK's leading woodland conservation charity.

To find out more about our authors and books visit **www.ospreypublishing.com**. Here you will find extracts, author interviews, details of forthcoming events and the option to sign up for our newsletter.

CONTENTS

INTRODUCTION

It would be an exaggeration to say that the Pacific War was decided by the five carriers that fought during the conflict, but perhaps not much of an exaggeration. At the start of the war, both sides still largely believed that a decisive battle between the Imperial Japanese Navy (IJN) and the United States Navy (USN) would be determined by a climactic clash of battleships. This view was not universally held within each navy, as shown by the Japanese creation of an independent carrier force – the First Air Fleet – in April 1941, and prewar American experimentation with independent strike groups built around carriers. Both sides recognized the importance of naval air power, and both had built very different carrier forces.

Facing a numerical disadvantage created by the interwar system of naval treaties and Japan's industrial inferiority, the IJN created a carrier force based on achieving a qualitative edge over the USN. This edge was created by establishing a cadre of highly trained aviators – the most highly trained in the world – and designing aircraft capable of striking at longer ranges than their American counterparts. Creation of the First Air Fleet was a force multiplier since, by the summer of 1941, it combined six fleet carriers into a single operational entity. This ability to mass naval air power was a game changer, as demonstrated at Pearl Harbor and other places during the opening months of the war. Had the Japanese maintained the cohesion of the First Air Fleet during this initial period, the history of the war would have turned out much differently.

As the Japanese massed naval air power, the Americans still operated carriers singly. Some American admirals saw the benefits of massing multiple carriers into a single task force, but most preferred to keep them separated to avoid detection and destruction. Operating singly, or even in pairs, American carriers lacked the striking power of the First Air Fleet. Also impacting their striking power was the short range of American carrier aircraft and the almost total ineffectiveness of the standard torpedo bomber and its torpedo.

The IJN's carrier force had a predictable run of successes in the first few months of the war. Their apparent smashing victory at Pearl Harbor was followed

OPPOSITE This photograph shows a group of Helldivers and Avengers on their way to attack the First Mobile Fleet on the afternoon of June 20, 1944. The shorter-ranged Helldivers suffered heavily on this mission. Of the 51 that participated in the attack, four were lost in combat and 39 were lost operationally for an overall loss rate of 84 percent. (Naval History and Heritage Command) by more success at Rabaul, the Dutch East Indies, Darwin, Australia, and finally by a massive raid into the Indian Ocean. However, the only time during the war that the Japanese operated all six of their prewar fleet carriers in a single formation was at Pearl Harbor. This lack of concentration gave the Americans an opportunity to defeat the First Air Fleet piecemeal. The First Air Fleet was set up for destruction by bad operational planning by the most overrated admiral of the war – Yamamoto Isoroku – not by a lack of tactical prowess.

At the battle of the Coral Sea, American Admiral Chester Nimitz aggressively sought an opportunity to engage the Japanese carrier force. The appearance of American carriers in the South Pacific in March 1942 forced the Japanese to send carriers to the region to protect any further advances. To cover his next operation, Yamamoto allocated only two fleet carriers and a light carrier to seize Port Moresby. For his part, Nimitz was prepared to send all four of his operational carriers to the South Pacific, but the raid on Tokyo held up two carriers, leaving only two to deal with the massive Japanese incursion into the Coral Sea. The resulting first carrier battle was a very confused affair with both sides having and wasting opportunities to launch an all-important first strike. When the preliminaries were over, both sides finally struck the other's main carrier force on May 8, 1942. The exchange was deadly, but the prewar notion that carriers were extremely vulnerable to air attack was proven incorrect. One American fleet carrier was sunk, and another damaged. Japanese losses were much heavier. The light carrier was sunk, one of the fleet carriers bombed and heavily damaged, and the second fleet carrier had its air group so attrited that it was considered by the Japanese to be incapable of operations. Thus, of the 11 IJN carriers operational before the battle, only eight remained available for the next, and most famous, carrier battle.

The battle of the Coral Sea was just a preface to Yamamoto's major operation the following month. This operation was targeted on Midway Atoll but was actually focused on annihilating Nimitz's remaining strength in a decisive battle. Through a series of astoundingly bad decisions, the remaining four Japanese fleet carriers were actually outnumbered at the point of contact against Nimitz's three fleet carriers and the many aircraft stationed on Midway. Using exquisite intelligence, and insightfully positioning their carriers where they could strike the Japanese, the Americans pulled off the only successful ambush during any of the war's carrier battles. Despite major issues in coordination and communication that threatened to derail Nimitz's ambush, fate placed the Americans' most powerful weapon, their dive-bombers, over the Japanese carriers at the point they were most vulnerable. The result was the bombing of three carriers within the span of minutes, all of which later sank. A single remaining Japanese fleet carrier acquitted itself well, heavily damaging an American carrier that was later finished off by an American submarine, before it was also sunk. The battle of Midway was not the kind of decisive battle that Yamamoto was planning for. At its conclusion, the IJN's offensive power in the Pacific was blunted. But it was not the end of the IJN's carrier force, as is often suggested.

Following their victory at Midway, the Americans were quick to seize the strategic initiative in the Pacific. To protect the sea lines of communication between the United States and Australia, and to begin the counteroffensive to recapture Rabaul, which had become the main Japanese bastion in the South Pacific, American attentions turned to the South Pacific. The hastily prepared first American offensive of the entire war selected the island of Guadalcanal in the southern Solomons for invasion because the Japanese were building an airfield there. Control of this airfield was critical to the outcome of the campaign, which stretched to six months and extracted heavy losses from both sides.

During the campaign, the Americans used their carriers to defend against major Japanese efforts to recapture the island. There were only two carrier battles over the span of six months. In the first, the battle of the Eastern Solomons, carrier forces of equal size fought a very cautious and indecisive battle. In the process, Yamamoto's first poorly planned attempt to throw the American invasion force off the island was defeated. The second carrier battle was the result of the largest Japanese effort of the campaign to retake the airfield with a land offensive and then destroy American naval forces around the island. This encounter, the battle of Santa Cruz, is the least well understood of the war's carrier battles. It was also the only time during the war that the Japanese carriers gained a clear victory. However, in doing so, Japanese aircraft losses were so high they were unable to follow up their victory. Throughout the battle, control of the airfield on Guadalcanal was the path to victory. The Japanese were never able to suppress the airfield for any extended period to allow them to move large ground forces to the island and supply them for an offensive to capture the airfield. Carriers on both sides played supporting, but important, roles during the Guadalcanal campaign.

Both carrier forces were exhausted after Guadalcanal. For the next 18 months, the Japanese tried to rebuild their carrier force. This effort was unsuccessful in many areas. Japanese industry only completed a single purpose-built carrier during this period and failed to design and produce carrier aircraft with dramatically better performance than those that had populated the IJN's flight decks at the start of the war. Even more difficult was the process of training new aviators with anything like the skills of those from the beginning of the war. This reflected the heavy losses from the four carrier battles in 1942 and the subsequent commitment of the rebuilt carrier air groups into the defense of the central and northern Solomons in the second half of 1943. Most of all, the IJN proved unable to harness new technologies to the same degree as did the USN. For the last carrier battle of the war in June 1944, the IJN fought with an inferior version of the force with which they had begun the war.

While the Japanese tried to rebuild their carrier fleet for another attempt to fight a decisive battle, the Americans produced a carrier force much more powerful and capable than had ever before been seen in any of the world's oceans. This was demonstrated in a series of campaigns from late 1943 until the battle of the Philippine Sea in mid-1944. When the last carrier battle was fought following the American invasion of Saipan, the outcome was preordained. Not only did the USN possess a marked numerical and qualitative advantage, but its new carrier doctrine was able to defeat a massive Japanese initial blow, something that had been impossible in 1942. Philippine Sea was the most crushing loss for the IJN of any carrier battle during the war; it was even more decisive than Midway since, after the battle, the Japanese no longer had any ability to build a viable carrier force to contend with the next American advance.

That next advance came at Leyte in the Philippines four months later. Yet again, the IJN made plans for a decisive battle. This time the state of the IJN's carrier force made it suitable only as a decoy force. The centerpiece of the plan to turn back the American invasion fell upon the IJN's still-powerful force of battleships and heavy cruisers. The battle of Leyte Gulf included four major actions. In one of these, a small strike from the remaining Japanese carriers attacked an American carrier task force. So weak was the strike that the Americans did not even recognize it as the final Japanese carrier strike of the war. The next day the might of the American carriers was turned on the Japanese carrier force. This was not a carrier battle, but rather a maritime execution. Without air cover, and for other reasons, the Japanese operation at Leyte was doomed to defeat. The principal vehicle to their defeat was the USN's carrier force. Over the course of three days, and in spite of poor command decisions that hamstrung its operations and effectiveness, American carriers launched the greatest number of offensive air sorties in naval history at the Japanese force of heavy combatants while still striking the Japanese carrier force and sinking every one of its four carriers. While the Japanese plan at Leyte Gulf contained a clever aspect of using its carriers as a diversion to lure the American carrier force out of position, it still resulted in such a defeat that the IJN never mounted another major operation during the war. Even these crippling losses resulted in no delay to the American advance.

After Leyte Gulf, the IJN chose to resort to suicide attacks, epitomized by the kamikaze.

These caused mayhem and death, even against well-defended American aircraft carriers, but proved unable to turn the tide against the USN or even to delay its final advance to Japan. In spite of the kamikaze threat, the USN's carrier force operated continually off Okinawa for some three months, ensuring the invasion would succeed. From there, the carriers embarked on a series of large-scale raids on the Japanese homeland. From the first raid on Japan in April 1942 with 16 army bombers launched from a single carrier, American carriers were able to mount strategic attacks with thousands of sorties over several days from almost 20 carriers. The combination of massive production of ships and aircraft, added to excellent training and a proven doctrine, all supported by logistics on an unprecedented scale, made the American carrier force a war-winning weapon. The Pacific Carrier War had come full cycle from the opening day of the conflict at Pearl Harbor.

CHAPTER 1
SHIPS, AIRCRAFT, AND MEN

THE IMPERIAL JAPANESE NAVY (IJN) CARRIER FORCE

The IJN was quick to appreciate the potential of carrier aviation, and commissioned its first small carrier in 1922. Two more large carriers followed in 1927 and 1928. Early carrier aircraft missions included scouting and spotting the fall of shot from the battle line. By the end of the 1920s, the use of fighter aircraft to cover the battle line and to gain control of the airspace over the enemy's battle line was emphasized. This largely defensive focus was due mainly to the inability of early attack aircraft to carry large payloads that compromised their ability to attack heavily armored battleships. As better aircraft and weapons were developed, Japanese carriers were increasingly seen as offensive platforms with American carriers as their principal targets. Neutralizing enemy carriers ensured air dominance over the battle area. This could be accomplished by sinking American carriers or, more easily, by wrecking their flight decks. The Japanese believed that enemy carriers were vulnerable to dive-bombing (compared to horizontal bombing) since this method offered the possibility of precision attacks. Torpedo attacks were considered necessary to sink enemy carriers and other large warships, and by the late 1930s the IJN had developed both dive-bombing and

torpedo attack tactics. Like every other component of the Imperial Navy, Japanese carriers were designed and trained for offensive warfare. In the case of carrier combat, the essential precondition for victory was to find the enemy's carriers first and launch overwhelming strikes as quickly as possible. Ideally the attacks would be executed beyond the range from which the enemy could retaliate. This doctrine explained the great Japanese emphasis on large carrier air groups composed of aircraft uniformly lighter than their opponents, giving them greater range.

Prior to the war, Japanese carriers operated as divisions in a semi-independent but strictly adjunct role to the fleet they were assigned to. As carriers were assessed to be extremely vulnerable to attack, dispersal seemed to increase their prospects of survival since only a portion of friendly carriers could be detected and attacked. In 1940 aviation advocates began to press the Commander of the Combined Fleet, Admiral Yamamoto Isoroku, to concentrate the existing carrier divisions into a single command to form an "air fleet" which could train and fight together. Concentration offered both the potential of greater offensive power by launching larger strikes with better prospects for coordinating attacks and increased defensive capabilities by massing fighters and antiaircraft fire.

ABOVE The Imperial Navy's first carrier was *Hosho*, shown here on trials in November 1923. The small island proved unsuccessful and was removed the following year, but the ship gave invaluable service as a test platform for flight operations at sea. (Yamato Museum)

Accordingly, the First Air Fleet was established in April 1941. It was commanded by a non-aviator (which was the norm in the IJN), Vice Admiral Nagumo Chuichi, and was composed of three carrier divisions: Carrier Division 1 included the large fleet carriers *Akagi* and *Kaga*; Carrier Division 2 was assigned fleet carriers *Soryu* and *Hiryu*; Carrier Division 3 possessed only the old *Hosho* and the light carrier *Ryujo*. Immediately before the war, carriers *Shokaku* and *Zuikaku* were commissioned and formed Carrier Division 5.

One important advantage exercised by the Japanese at the start of the war was their ability to mass carrier air power. The *Kido Butai* (literally "Mobile Force" but better translated as "Striking Force") was the operational component of the First Air Fleet. Unlike in the US Navy, where the carrier division served only in an administrative capacity, the carrier divisions of the *Kido Butai* were operational entities. Air groups from the division's carriers routinely trained and fought together. During multiple carrier operations, the entire strike would be commanded by one of the carrier group commanders who would direct the operations. For a major strike, one carrier division would typically contribute its dive-bomber squadrons and another carrier division its torpedo squadron. This allowed a quick launch of the strike, since all the aircraft could be parked on the flight deck without the need to spot another group of aircraft on the flight deck and prepare it for launch. Typically, the strike was accompanied by an escort of six to nine fighters from each carrier. The creation of the First Air Fleet was revolutionary in concept. It gave the Japanese the means to mass air power at any spot in the Pacific. This mass of Japanese air power comprised high-quality aircraft flown by skilled aviators which enabled the IJN to overwhelm Allied defenses early in the war.

Akagi photographed in 1939 after modernization. Assigned to Carrier Division 1, she was also the flagship of the *Kido Butai* until being sunk at Midway in June 1942. As a converted battlecruiser, she was fast, well protected, and able to embark a large air group. (Naval History and Heritage Command)

THE SHIPS

The IJN began the war with the world's largest fleet of aircraft carriers. Japanese interest in carriers began as early as 1914 and benefited from a Royal Navy mission in Japan from 1921 to 1923 to assist in naval aviation. The Washington Naval Treaty of 1922 had a great impact on future Japanese carrier design and construction. Under the treaty, total Japanese carrier tonnage was restricted to 81,000 tons compared with the US Navy's 135,000 tons. Individual ships could not displace over 27,000 tons, but the conversion of two existing capital ships was permitted with a maximum tonnage of 33,000. This position of inferiority forced the Japanese into several schemes in order to maintain numerical parity with the Americans. At the end of 1936, Japan left the naval treaty system and was thereafter free to build carriers as it desired.

The first Japanese carrier, *Hosho*, was commissioned in December 1922. This small carrier was key in the early days of carrier development but by the start of the war was of marginal utility. After participating in the Midway operation, *Hosho* was used as a training carrier for the remainder of the war.

Akagi was one of the two capital ships permitted to be converted into carriers under the terms of the Washington Naval Treaty. Converted from a battlecruiser, *Akagi* was fast and well protected with the capacity to carry a large number of aircraft. The other capital ship conversion was *Kaga*. Since *Kaga* was originally a battleship, she was slower than *Akagi* but her larger hull allowed for a greater aircraft capacity.

Kaga shown in 1936 after her major reconstruction. Note the smoke exhaust aft of the island which was angled toward the water to avoid placing smoke over the flight deck. She was the largest of the IJN's prewar carriers, having been converted from a battleship. (Naval History and Heritage Command)

Key Characteristics of Japanese Early War Carriers			
SHIP	TONNAGE (STANDARD)	MAXIMUM SPEED	AIRCRAFT CAPACITY
Hosho	7,470	25kts	11
Akagi	36,500	31kts	66
Kaga	38,200	28kts	72
Ryujo	12,500	29kts	26
Soryu	15,900	34kts	63
Hiryu	17,300	34kts	57
Shokaku, Zuikaku	26,675	34kts	72
Shoho, Zuiho	11,262	28kts	30
Hiyo, Junyo	24,140	26kts	48

Ryujo pictured underway in September 1938 after her two major rebuilds to correct stability issues. Even when these were complete, she possessed limited effectiveness because of her small flight deck, small elevators, and poor elevator placement which hindered efficient flight operations. (Naval History and Heritage Command)

After the conversion of *Akagi* and *Kaga*, the IJN only had 30,000 tons left of its treaty allotment for carrier construction. At this point the Japanese began to get imaginative. Under the terms of the treaty, carriers under 10,000 tons were exempt from tonnage calculations. Accordingly, the IJN planned to build an 8,000-ton ship able to embark 24 aircraft. Before construction began, the Japanese decided that 24 aircraft was insufficient, so the design was recast with a second hangar deck in order to embark 48 aircraft. Not surprisingly the new design came in at 12,500 tons, which not only placed it well over treaty restrictions but also created severe stability problems. *Ryujo* underwent two rebuilds before the war to correct design defects and, despite having a nominal aircraft capacity of 48, only embarked 26 at the start of the war.

The first Japanese ship designed as a carrier from the keel up was *Soryu*. She epitomized the Japanese preference for a carrier with a large aircraft capacity on a fast, light hull. *Hiryu*'s design was based on *Soryu*'s but used the extra displacement to improve protection and create a greater beam that improved stability. *Hiryu* was considered very successful and became the template for the Shokaku and the late war Unryu classes.

Just as the Yamato-class superbattleships were designed to create a qualitative overmatch against their American counterparts, the Japanese intended the same to be true for the Shokaku-class carriers (*Shokaku* and *Zuikaku*), laid down in 1937 after treaty restrictions had ended. The design was an enlarged *Hiryu* with much better protection, range, and aircraft capacity. The two ships were the best Japanese carriers of the war and superior to any other aircraft carrier in the world until the arrival of the American Essex class in 1943.

In another effort to evade treaty restrictions, the IJN launched a number of ships before the war which were designed to be easily converted into

TOP This is *Hiryu* on trials in April 1939. The extra tonnage allotted to her design produced a much more balanced ship compared with the relatively unprotected *Soryu*. *Hiryu* was the basis for the highly successful Shokaku class. Since it was easier to mass produce than the larger Shokaku class, the Japanese returned to *Hiryu*'s design in 1942 for the Unryu class, of which six ships were laid down in 1942 and 1943. However, only three Unryu-class ships were completed and none ever launched an aircraft against the Americans in combat. (Naval History and Heritage Command)

ABOVE *Soryu* photographed in January 1938 during sea trials. Her design epitomized the Japanese preference for a fast carrier able to embark a large air wing, giving it maximum offensive potential. (Naval History and Heritage Command)

ABOVE *Shokaku* was the first Japanese carrier built without regard to treaty limitations and was an unqualified success. The two ships of this class were the most powerful carriers in the world until the arrival of the USN's Essex class in late 1943. This is *Shokaku* after completion in August 1941. (Naval History and Heritage Command)

RIGHT *Zuikaku* photographed in September 1941 after completion. Of the six carriers which participated in the Pearl Harbor operation, *Zuikaku* had the longest career and was not sunk until October 1944. (Naval History and Heritage Command)

carriers when the need arose. The first two were originally intended as high-speed oilers and then were redesigned as submarine tenders. As carriers the two ships were known as the Shoho class. They proved to be useful conversions but lacked any protection and possessed a mediocre top speed. More useful were the two ships of the Hiyo class which were laid down in 1939 as large passenger liners. Conversion began in February 1941, and both ships entered service the following year. To increase speed, a hybrid propulsion system of destroyer-type boilers mated to merchant turbines was used, but this proved troublesome in service and top speed remained marginal. However, the ships were able to embark an air group of 48 aircraft.

Japanese carriers possessed marginal antiaircraft capabilities. The standard long-range antiaircraft gun was the Type 89 5-inch High-Angle Gun that equipped almost all Japanese carriers of the period. The weapon itself was adequate with fairly high elevating speeds, a high muzzle velocity, and a 51lb shell. However, the weapon was handicapped by its fire-control director, the Type 94 High-Angle Firing Control Installation. It was simply too slow to generate fire-control

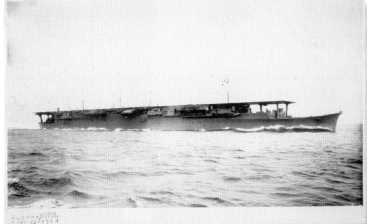

ABOVE One of the ways the Imperial Navy devised to escape treaty restrictions on carrier tonnage was to build a fleet of auxiliaries which could be quickly converted into carriers. *Shoho*, shown here in December 1941 after her conversion was completed, was the first of these ships. (Yamato Museum)

LEFT *Zuiho* was a light carrier conversion capable of embarking an air group of some 30 aircraft. She saw extensive service and was present at two of the carrier battles of 1942 and at Philippine Sea in 1944. (Yamato Museum)

BOTTOM LEFT *Junyo* photographed in Kure taking on fuel on May 3, 1944. Note the ship's large island and angled stack. Also noticeable is the mercantile lines of her hull, which betray her origin as a passenger liner. Despite her shortcomings, *Junyo* and sister ship *Hiyo* were valuable additions to the IJN's carrier fleet. (Yamato Museum) solutions on high-speed targets like American carrier aircraft. This placed the burden of shipboard air defense on the Type 96 25mm antiaircraft gun. This weapon was standard on all Japanese carriers and was fitted in both dual and triple mounts. Unfortunately for the Japanese, the Type 96 was a mediocre weapon and ineffective in its assigned role. It had an effective range of only 1,635 yards, was slow in training and elevation, had a low sustained rate of fire, and produced excessive blast and vibration which affected its accuracy. Also, its fire-control director, the Type 95 Short-Range High-Angle Director, could not handle high-speed targets. No Japanese carrier began the war equipped with radar.

THE AIRCRAFT

At the start of the war, Japanese fleet carriers were equipped with three types of aircraft which paralleled the organization of the ships' air groups. The fighter squadron was assigned the Mitsubishi A6M2 Navy Type 0 Carrier Fighter Model 21. It was generally referred to as simply the "Zero" as it will be here. Initial design specifications were issued by the IJN in 1937 with the first variant, the A6M1, taking flight in April 1939. This model was underpowered, so the next variant was given a more powerful 950hp engine and a legend was born. The A6M2 variant was the early war standard for both Japanese carrier and land-based fighter units. The designers had succeeded in meeting a very challenging set of design specifications for a long-range, maneuverable, and heavily armed fighter. The Zero was known for its strengths of unparalleled range, exceptional maneuverability, and great climb and acceleration. In a classic dogfight it was nearly invincible. However, the desire to make the airframe as light as possible came with a significant cost – both the aircraft and pilot had essentially no protection.

The A6M2 Type 0 carrier fighter was the outstanding carrier-based fighter of the early period of the Pacific War. When combined with an experienced pilot, it proved a formidable combination. (Naval History and Heritage Command)

The standard IJN early war torpedo bomber was the Nakajima B5N Navy Type 97 Carrier Attack Bomber (later given the Allied reporting name of "Kate" but referred to in this book as the Type 97). When introduced in November 1937, it was the most modern torpedo bomber in the world but by the start of the war was nearing obsolescence. The aircraft first flew in December 1939; the standard version at the start of the war was the B5N2 Navy Type 97 Carrier Bomber Model 12. With its decent top speed of 235mph and the reliable Type 91 aerial torpedo, the B5N2 proved to be a formidable ship killer. As was the case for the Zero, the Type 97 lacked protection for the crew and the fuel tank. Its defensive armament of a single 7.7mm machine gun fitted in the rear of the cockpit was very weak. In addition to carrying a single Type 91 torpedo, the aircraft could carry 1,764 pounds of bombs to attack maritime or land targets.

Rounding out Japanese carrier air groups was the Aichi D3A1 Navy Type 99 Carrier Bomber Model 11. This aircraft was the standard Japanese dive-bomber at the start of the war and remained so into 1943. It was later given the Allied reporting name of "Val" but will be referred to in the book as the Type 99. It was a superb dive-bombing platform and was very maneuverable. In fact the Type 99 sank more Allied ships than any other Japanese aircraft, although this was more due to the fact it enjoyed its successes early in the war against minimal Allied fighter opposition and because it was piloted by top-notch aviators. Performance of the Type 99 was mediocre, with a top speed of only 240mph and the ability to carry only one 551lb bomb. Like the IJN's other front-line carrier aircraft, the Type 99 was unable to endure substantial battle damage.

TOP The Type 97 carrier attack plane was a formidable ship killer by virtue of its primary weapon, the Type 91 air-launched torpedo. It had a 529lb warhead and a top speed of 42 knots. (Naval History and Heritage Command)

ABOVE The Type 99 dive-bomber was ungainly in appearance with its fixed landing gear, but it was a steady bombing platform and took a heavy toll of Allied shipping during the first period of the war. (Naval History and Heritage Command)

CARRIER AIR GROUP ORGANIZATION AND TACTICS

The air group of each Japanese carrier was permanently assigned to the ship. Fleet carriers carried three squadrons: a fighter, a dive-bomber (carrier bombers to the Japanese), and torpedo bomber (carrier attack in IJN parlance). At the start of the war, fighter squadrons were equipped with 18 Zeros. These were typically divided into two nine-aircraft *chutai*, one to accompany strike aircraft on offensive missions and the other to perform air defense patrols. The Japanese mounted standing combat air patrols (CAPs) with a division of three fighters. The lack of radar forced the remaining Zeros to stand alert on the flight deck ready to scramble if warning came of approaching enemy aircraft. This system might have worked if clear visibility permitted the carriers' escort to provide warning since the Zero possessed the ability to climb quickly to interception altitude, but it was also a source of potential disaster if adequate warning was not available. This system was further handicapped by the lack of reliable radios in the Zeros, which made airborne direction of the fighters all but impossible.

The carrier bomber squadron comprised 18 Type 99s on the smaller fleet carriers and 27 Type 99s on the *Kaga* and the two Shokaku-class carriers. The light carriers did not carry dive-bombers. The Japanese assessed that a typical 18-aircraft dive-bomber squadron would be effective against an American carrier but would suffer heavy losses in the process. Of the 18 aircraft, five or six were expected to score hits and eight would be shot down. Unlike most Japanese prewar assessments, this one turned out to be essentially correct. Type 99 pilots had achieved a high level of proficiency before the war led by Lieutenant Takahashi Sadamu, who devised tactics calling for the dive-bomber to approach its target head-on at some 10,000 feet. The head-on approach was preferred, but if the wind was greater than 30 knots the best approach was keeping the wind at the tail of the dive-bombers to reduce wind drift. If several dive-bomber sections were involved, they attacked from several different angles. In the attack run, the Type 99s formed an echelon formation, went to full throttle, and began a 10-degree dive. When the lead pilot judged the target was close enough, he led the formation into a 65-degree dive. The bomb was typically released at about 2,000 feet above the target, but more experienced pilots often pressed their attack lower in an effort to guarantee a hit.

The carrier attack squadron on fleet carriers flew the Type 97. *Soryu* and *Hiryu* carried 18 Type 97s at the start of the war and the larger fleet carriers carried 27. Light carriers carried a smaller number of Type 97s. Japanese torpedo attack tactics called for the Type 97s to approach the target head-on from an altitude of between 3,300 and 9,800 feet. The aircraft went into a dive to gain speed some 10–12nm from the target and divided into groups to attack the target from both sides. This was known as an "anvil" attack and was designed to catch the target broadside no matter which way it turned. The Type 91 torpedoes were dropped from an altitude of 160–330 feet at a speed of 140–162 knots with distance to the target typically 2,600–4,000 feet.

In addition to devoting much effort to perfecting the individual forms of attack, the Japanese also gave priority to coordinating these attacks into a single operation. The thinking was that it might be possible for the enemy to defend against either dive-bombing or torpedo attacks, but if these were conducted closely together the enemy defenses would be overwhelmed. In such an operation, fighters would sweep the airspace over the target of defending fighters and then strafe the enemy carriers. These were immediately followed by dive-bombers and then torpedo bombers. Such a closely sequenced attack was very difficult to achieve since it required precision timing and favorable tactical circumstances. Only the most skilled and aggressive air groups had a chance of achieving a coordinated attack.

LEADERSHIP

The Combined Fleet had been under the command of Admiral Yamamoto since September 1939. Yamamoto was a complex figure who is given credit for unusual insight (for a Japanese officer) into the United States and for being a far-sighted aviation advocate. In reality, he was an orthodox thinker who still adhered to the notion that a decisive battle could decide a war, and his attack on Pearl Harbor was a gross misjudgment of the American character. Though he supported naval aviation, he still promulgated strategy with the battleship at its center. He was both stubborn and impulsive, as the Pearl Harbor attack and the methods he used to get it approved demonstrated. Once the veneer of brilliance associated with the Pearl Harbor attack is justly removed, Yamamoto led the Combined Fleet to defeat in almost every battle it fought until his death in April 1943.

Vice Admiral Nagumo was the commander of the *Kido Butai* since its inception in April 1941. He had no aviation experience when he took command of the *Kido Butai* as his expertise was in torpedoes. His command style was traditional for the Imperial Navy where it was common for the commander to accept staff recommendations after the staff experts had reached consensus. Given Nagumo's total unfamiliarity with aviation matters, he relied

TOP Admiral Yamamoto Isoroku assumed command of the Combined Fleet in 1939 and was the IJN's principal command figure up until his death in April 1943. In spite of his reputation as a great admiral, principally due to his ill-considered Pearl Harbor attack, he guided the IJN to disaster at Coral Sea, Midway, and Guadalcanal even when possessing numerical and qualitative superiority. (Naval History and Heritage Command)

ABOVE The IJN's most experienced carrier task force commander was Vice Admiral Nagumo Chuichi who led the *Kido Butai* at Midway and at the two carrier battles during the Guadalcanal campaign. His combat record was marked by indecisiveness and more than his share of bad luck. (Naval History and Heritage Command) heavily on his chief of staff, Rear Admiral Kusaka Ryunosuke, his air operations officer, Commander Genda Minoru, and his senior strike leader, Commander Fuchida Mitsuo. Nagumo was cautious by nature and Fuchida thought him too conservative and unwilling to take the initiative. On the other hand, Nagumo's carrier division commanders were known for being aggressive. Rear Admiral Yamaguchi Tamon commanded Carrier Division 2 and had a background similar to Yamamoto's. He was an air power advocate and also commented on Nagumo's lack of boldness. Rear Admiral Hara Chuichi was in command of Carrier Division 5. He was a surface warfare officer but was known for his fiery temperament.

THE UNITED STATES NAVY (USN) CARRIER FORCE

The USN was a pioneer in naval aviation, being the first to launch an aircraft from a ship in 1910 and the first to recover an aircraft aboard a ship the following year. This early lead slipped during World War I, and the first American carrier was not funded until 1919. Like the other navies with carriers in the interwar period, American carriers were initially focused on supporting the battle fleet. Gradually the role of the carrier became offensively focused, assisted by the development of dive-bombing and aircraft capable of carrying torpedoes.

Just like the IJN, the USN assessed that carriers would be unable to withstand significant damage. This drove the doctrine to destroy enemy carriers as quickly as possible. To maximize their offensive potential, American carriers were designed to operate large air groups, and the number of aircraft that each carrier could

Langley pictured around 1932 with the majority of her air group. Experiments on *Langley* confirmed that it was possible to operate large numbers of aircraft on even a small deck and that they could be quickly launched. (Naval History and Heritage Command)

The USN's first three carriers photographed in Bremerton, Washington around 1930. The immense size of the converted battlecruisers *Lexington* and *Saratoga* compared with the diminutive *Langley* is striking. (Naval History and Heritage Command)

operate was enhanced by the practice of keeping many aircraft on the flight deck (instead of the hangar deck), a practice called a "deck park." Open unarmored hangars facilitated the quick launch of large numbers of aircraft.

Throughout 1942 American carrier strike doctrine was less mature than that practiced by the IJN. In a combat scenario, American carriers launched a morning and afternoon search by dive-bombers. If a target was located, a strike was launched as soon as possible with every available dive-bomber and torpedo plane. The fighter squadron was usually divided, with half providing strike escort and the other half assigned to CAP. American strike doctrine remained focused on the operations of a single air group. Japanese carriers operated as part of a division or several divisions that made the generation of large strikes routine, but American carriers were usually formed into a task force around a single carrier, which meant that strikes were conducted by single air groups. When launching a strike, the entire air group could not be accommodated in a single deckload, so a large strike required two separate deckloads. This created a potentially long launch cycle, as the first deckload waited overhead for the second deckload to be spotted and launched. Once launched, different aircraft speeds and altitudes precluded a joint formation. The separate squadrons would usually proceed in loose order to the target, hopefully not losing contact with each other along the way. There was no attempt to coordinate multiple air groups from different carriers even if they were going after the same target.

Further complicating the task of American strike planners was the short ranges of their aircraft. The Dauntless squadrons charged with conducting scouting missions flew out as far as 325nm, carrying a 500lb bomb to strike anything they found. Strike missions were much more limited in range. In the strike role, the Dauntless dive-bomber had a doctrinal strike radius of up to 275nm with a 500lb bomb and some 200nm with a 1,000lb bomb load. Torpedo bombers were limited to a range of 175nm with a torpedo loaded. The strike range of the Wildcat was also about 175nm since no auxiliary fuel tanks were used at this point of the war.

THE SHIPS

The first American carrier was a converted collier. Named *Langley*, she was commissioned in March 1922 for the purpose of conducting experiments on how to operate aircraft from a ship at sea. In this capacity, *Langley* was an unqualified success. *Langley* was converted to a seaplane tender in 1936–37 and served until she was sunk by air attack on February 27, 1942.

The success of *Langley* paved the way for the two ships of the Lexington class. The Washington Naval Treaty permitted the conversion of capital ships of up to 33,000 tons, and the converted Lexington-class battlecruisers needed another clause allowing an additional 3,000 tons for air and torpedo defense additions. When completed, *Lexington* and *Saratoga* were the biggest carriers in the world until the Japanese converted the third Yamato-class superbattleship into a carrier in 1944 and named her *Shinano*. The Lexington class's long hull produced high speed, but the ships were known for their poor maneuverability. They carried a large air group, which was a primary design emphasis for all American carriers. Both were fitted with a large antiaircraft battery of 5-inch/25 guns, 1.1-inch quadruple guns, and soon after the war began, a large number of single 20mm guns. Both were equipped with radar before the war began.

This is *Lexington* off Hawaii in 1932. Note the ship's huge stack, separate small island for navigation and command and control, and the enclosed hangar deck. The turrets fore and aft of the island and stack contain 8-inch guns reflecting the fear that the ships were vulnerable to attack from enemy cruisers. Most importantly, note the large number of aircraft on the flight deck which became a staple on American carriers. (Naval History and Heritage Command)

Just as the IJN devised methods to make the most out of its Washington Naval Treaty carrier tonnage, the USN tried different designs to maximize the number of carriers in service. *Ranger* was the first American carrier designed as such from the keel up. Her design displaced 13,800 tons, which meant the 69,000 tons remaining after the conversion of *Lexington* and *Saratoga* would be sufficient for five ships. Ultimately the design was a failure since the hull proved too small for adequate protection, internal compartmentation, and machinery to develop a speed over 29.5 knots which was judged to be inadequate for fleet operations. Because of her vulnerability, *Ranger* was never committed to combat operations in the Pacific.

This photo of *Ranger* in late 1936 hints at the ship's light construction. (Naval History and Heritage Command)

Key Characteristics of American Carriers			
SHIP	TONNAGE (STANDARD)	MAXIMUM SPEED	AIRCRAFT CAPACITY
Lexington, Saratoga	36,000	32kts	90
Ranger	14,500	29.5kts	76
Yorktown, Enterprise, Hornet	19,576	33kts	90
Wasp	14,700	29.5kts	72
Essex class	27,500	33kts	100
Independence class	14,300	31kts	34

TOP This is *Yorktown* just after being commissioned in 1937. Note the enlarged island compared with earlier American carriers and the hangar deck roller curtains which could be opened to increase flexibility during flight operations. (Naval History and Heritage Command)

ABOVE This fine shot of *Hornet* is from October 1941, around the time she was commissioned. When the USN wanted to build another carrier after being released from treaty tonnage restrictions, it defaulted to the Yorktown-class design with minor modifications. (Naval History and Heritage Command)

The heart of the American carrier fleet during 1942 was the Yorktown class, which comprised three ships – *Yorktown*, *Enterprise*, and *Hornet*. The design was developed with the benefit of fleet experience from the ships already in service. The Yorktown class was very successful and formed the basis for the even more successful Essex class.

After the failure of *Ranger*, the USN decided to use its remaining carrier tonnage for a couple of 20,000-ton ships which could correct the primary defect with *Ranger* – her lack of protection (*Hornet* was built after the expiration of the Washington Naval Treaty and was actually completed to a slightly different design). The extra tonnage was used to provide the ships with a 4-inch-deep side armor belt protecting key areas and a side protective system for defense against torpedoes. The ships were designed with a large hangar which allowed them to operate up to 90 aircraft. A large island was incorporated into the design which enhanced command and control. The powerful machinery produced a top speed of 33 knots, but the placement of the two engine rooms close together was a major design defect since one well-placed torpedo could knock out all propulsive power.

All ships in the class were fitted with a powerful antiaircraft battery including the first 5-inch/38 guns mounted on a carrier. The quadruple 1.1-inch mount was also carried, and after the war began a large number of 20mm single guns were added. The numbers and types of antiaircraft guns evolved throughout 1942 and the war. For example, *Enterprise* carried eight 5-inch/38 guns, four quadruple 1.1-inch mounts, and 32 single 20mm mounts at Midway, and by November of the same year this had been improved to eight 5-inch/38 guns, four quadruple 40mm mounts, and 46 single 20mm guns. By the end of the war, she retained the same number of 5-inch/38 mounts but added a total of 54 40mm guns (in 11 quad and five twin mounts) and 16 twin 20mm mounts. All Yorktown-class ships carried radar at the start of the war.

With its remaining 14,700 tons of carrier construction, the USN tried to duplicate the best features of the Yorktown class on a smaller hull. The effort was only marginally successful. The result was a slightly improved version of *Ranger* but with the continuing problem of lack of protection and a mediocre top speed. When completed, the ship came in over its design limit and suffered from stability problems in service. Nevertheless, *Wasp* did carry a large air group and a heavy antiaircraft battery. In January 1942, *Wasp* was equipped with radar.

American carriers were fitted with three types of antiaircraft weapons. Five-inch guns provided long-range protection against aircraft, 1.1-inch quadruple mounts, and later the iconic 40mm Bofors quad mount provided intermediate protection, and the Oerlikon 20mm gun provided close-in defense. American naval fire control against air attack was the most advanced in the world, and combined with the excellent weapons detailed above, USN carriers and other ships possessed the highest level of protection against air attack available.

Older carriers were fitted with the 5-inch/25 gun which dated back to 1921. It was still a useful weapon and had an effective range of 7,000 yards. Beginning with the Yorktown class, American carriers were fitted with the excellent 5-inch/38 dual-purpose gun, the most successful gun of its type of the war. It was notable for its accuracy, barrel life, and rate of fire. A well-trained gun crew could fire 15 rounds per minute or more. The 5-inch/38 was originally mated with the Mark 33 fire-control system that was self-contained with its own rangefinder and capable of handling targets up to 320 knots and diving aircraft up to 400 knots. In action though, the Mark 33 had problems generating target solutions quickly enough. Beginning with *Hornet* (and later refitted on *Enterprise* and *Saratoga*), American carriers received the Mark 37 director. This was the best long-range fire-control director of the war and was able to quickly generate solutions on 400-knot targets or aircraft in a 250-knot dive. Its effectiveness was further enhanced with the integration of radar. A four-gun 5-inch/38 battery under Mark 37 control was effective out to 10,000 yards.

The last of the USN's treaty carriers was the *Wasp,* built to a unique design to use the last 14,700 tons of carrier tonnage. This profile view shows her to be a cross between design features of the unsuccessful *Ranger* and the very successful Yorktown class. (Naval History and Heritage Command)

As dive-bombing was recognized as a threat, the USN devised means for close-in protection. Initially this was provided by large numbers of .50-caliber machine guns, but these were inaccurate and fired a small shell that was unable to knock down approaching aircraft. In early 1942 the 20mm Oerlikon gun was fitted aboard carriers and all other combatants. This was an excellent weapon with a high rate of fire and was effective out to about 1,000 yards. Guidance was provided with tracers and ring sights, but the arrival of the Mark 14 gyro-sight made the weapon much more effective. During the 1942 carrier battles, the 20mm was the most effective weapon against attacking Japanese aircraft. Intermediate antiaircraft protection was a problem at the start of the war since the only weapon available was the 1.1-inch machine cannon. This was a four-barreled weapon with a theoretical rate of fire of 140 rounds per minute, per barrel. The weapon was not a success because of maintenance issues and a propensity to jam in combat. As soon as it was available, the Bofors 40mm gun replaced the 1.1-inch mount. However, it was only available in small numbers in 1942.

Yorktown was the first American carrier to receive radar in July 1940. Early war radars, primarily the CXAM and the CXAM-1, were generally reliable in service. Depending on a number of factors, most notably atmospheric conditions, contact on a formation of aircraft flying at 10,000 feet was possible at 80nm or against single aircraft at half that range. Altitude was not provided, though experienced operators could discern some indication of the height of approaching aircraft which made fighter direction much more effective.

THE AIRCRAFT

At the start of the war, American carriers embarked three types of aircraft. The standard carrier fighter was the Grumman F4F Wildcat. In April 1942, the F4F-4 version was introduced that incorporated several important features, including folding wings, six wing-mounted .50-caliber machine guns, factory-installed armor, and a self-sealing fuel tank. These features added more weight that affected climb and maneuverability. Compared with the more famous Zero, the Wildcat was much slower to climb and possessed significantly less range. The Wildcat did have superior survivability and armament. It was outclassed in a dogfight with a Zero, but once American fighter pilots learned to exploit its ruggedness and speed in a dive the Zeros could be defeated with proper tactics.

The Douglas SBD Dauntless is probably the best-known American carrier aircraft of the war. It was a modern aircraft having been introduced in 1939. The standard 1942 version was the SBD-3, which had a twin .30-caliber machine gun for the rear gunner, improved armor, and self-sealing fuel tanks. In addition to the rear guns, the Dauntless carried two cowl-mounted .50-caliber machine guns. One 1,000lb bomb could be carried on the centerline with smaller bombs under the

BELOW The standard American carrier fighter going into the war was the Grumman F4F-3 Wildcat like the two aircraft pictured here from VF-3 in April 1942. Though outclassed by the Japanese Zero fighter in some respects, the Wildcat had important strengths which its pilots learned to capitalize on. (Naval History and Heritage Command)

LEFT The Douglas SBD-3 Dauntless was the standard American dive-bomber at the start of the Pacific War and remained so through 1943. It was also the most numerous aircraft on American carriers since it equipped two of the air group's four squadrons. Given the issues with the Devastator torpedo bomber, the Dauntless constituted the primary striking power of the American carriers in 1942. (Naval History and Heritage Command)

The Grumman TBF-1 Avenger became the standard USN carrier-based torpedo bomber by the start of the Guadalcanal campaign in August 1942. An Avenger is shown launching a Mark XIII torpedo; the weapon's unreliability limited the Avenger's ship-attack capabilities. (Naval History and Heritage Command)

wings. The Dauntless was a very successful dive-bomber by virtue of its ruggedness, stability in a dive, and large bomb load. It did suffer from a mediocre top speed of 255mph and non-folding wings that reduced the number of aircraft that could be embarked on a carrier. It remained in service until mid-1944. Compared with its Japanese counterpart, the Type 99, the Dauntless was a superior aircraft.

While the Dauntless was a superior dive-bomber and the Wildcat a respectable fighter, the standard torpedo bomber in American carrier air groups at the start of the war was nearly ineffective. Introduced in 1937, the Douglas TBD Devastator was slow (top speed 206mph), possessed limited protection, and had a very short combat range. If this was not bad enough, the Devastator was forced to employ the unreliable Mark XIII torpedo that had to be dropped from 120 feet or less and not above 100mph if there was any hope of it running a true track to the target. These limitations made the Devastator exceedingly vulnerable. Replacing the Devastator after June 1942 was the Grumman TBF-1 Avenger. The Avenger was a much better aircraft than its predecessor with its top speed of 271mph, three defensive machine guns, incredible ruggedness and increased combat radius (260nm). The Avenger served for the remainder of the war and became the most produced carrier strike aircraft in history. The only problem with the Avenger was its dependence on the Mark XIII; in 1942 the Avenger often carried four 500lb bombs for maritime strikes instead of a torpedo.

CARRIER AIR GROUP ORGANIZATION AND TACTICS

American carrier air groups were composed of four squadrons. The fighter squadron was equipped with 18 F4F Wildcat fighters. Two squadrons were equipped with the Dauntless dive-bomber. One of these was given a scouting function and the other dedicated for bombing, but in practice both squadrons performed virtually identically. Dive-bombing squadrons possessed between 16 and 21 aircraft. The torpedo squadron was assigned 12–18 TBD Devastator aircraft. In the early war period, USN carriers had a permanently assigned air group. Each of the assigned squadrons carried the hull number of the ship it was assigned to. For example, *Lexington*'s fighter squadron was numbered VF-2, her dive-bombers VB-2, her scout bombers VS-2, and her torpedo squadron VT-2. The air group commander usually was assigned his own dive-bomber; when the Avenger entered service, air group commanders typically flew it.

Dive-bombing was originally pioneered by the USN, and American naval aviators were well trained in the use of this tactic at the start of the war. On a strike

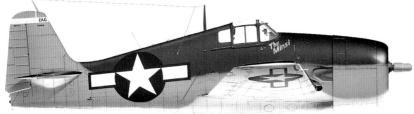

US NAVY AIRCRAFT

These profiles represent some of the leading aircraft found on US carriers. From top to bottom: Grumman F4F-4 flown by Lt Cdr John Thach, USS *Yorktown*, June 4, 1942; Grumman F6F-3 flown by Cdr David McCampbell, USS *Essex*, June 19, 1944; SBD-3 flown by Lt Richard Best, USS *Enterprise*, June 4, 1942; TBF-1 from VT-8, USS *Saratoga*, September 1942; TBD-1 flown by Lt Cdr Eugene Lindsey, USS *Enterprise*, June 4, 1942.

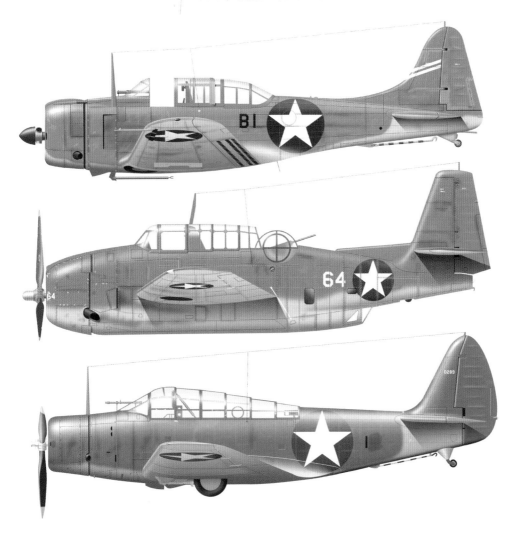

mission, escorting Wildcats were charged to clear the way for the dive-bombers. A standard dive-bombing profile began with a shallow dive from 20,000 feet followed by a steep dive from 15,000 to 12,000 feet. The dive was made at the angle of 65–70 degrees and would be pressed to 1,500–2,000 feet above the target before the bomb was dropped. A dive-bombing squadron was divided up into several six-aircraft divisions so that they could attack a target from different directions to overwhelm its defenses. The best direction to attack a target was along its longitudinal axis since this presented as large a target as possible. This explains the favorite evasion tactic of Japanese ships under air attack – by using a circular maneuver they presented dive-bomber pilots with a constantly changing target axis.

Admiral Chester Nimitz oversaw the Pacific Fleet during all five carrier battles. He wielded the Pacific Fleet's carriers with considerable aggressiveness, which set the stage for the carrier clashes at Coral Sea and Midway. (Naval History and Heritage Command)

Since torpedo bombers were so vulnerable, the ideal tactic was to conduct a coordinated attack with the dive-bombers to split the target's defenses. As described above, the Devastator was forced to conduct an attack at very low speed because of the limitations of the Mark XIII torpedo. As with the IJN, the preferred tactic was an anvil attack with aircraft attacking from both bows simultaneously so that whatever direction the target maneuvered it would be exposed. If the pilot judged his approach correctly, the torpedo would enter the water 1,400 yards from the target. With the introduction of the Avenger and modifications to the Mark XIII, torpedo attacks in 1944 were made from 800 feet at a speed of 260 knots. By 1944 American torpedo bombers were proven ship-killers, but in 1942 this was not the case.

LEADERSHIP

Admiral Ernest J. King was the final arbiter of American naval strategy during the war. He began his career in surface ships and submarines but was an early transfer to naval aviation in 1926. After Pearl Harbor he was appointed Commander-in-Chief US Fleet and in March 1942 became Chief of Naval Operations. These promotions gave him ultimate authority over all naval strategy and operations. He was a strong advocate of offensive operations in the Pacific in spite of the official "Germany First" strategy that defined the Pacific as a secondary theater. He was responsible for the first American counterattack of the war at Guadalcanal.

Effective December 31, 1941, the Pacific Fleet was under the command of Chester W. Nimitz. In April he also assumed command of Pacific Ocean Areas, which was divided into three areas. At first Nimitz had to contend with King's meddling, but by April 1942 he gained his balance and let his innate aggressiveness show. Nimitz was a calm and determined leader who inspired confidence in his men. He was able to pick capable subordinates and then empower them to get the job done.

At the start of the war, the Pacific Fleet's senior carrier commander was Vice Admiral William F. Halsey. Halsey had transferred to aviation in 1934. Most American admirals were aggressive, but Halsey was the most aggressive by far. As will be seen throughout this narrative, this aggression often bordered on foolhardiness. In spite of his seniority, Halsey did not exercise tactical command during any of the carrier battles of 1942. Through much of 1942, the most experienced American carrier admiral was Frank J. Fletcher. He had no aviation experience before the war, having spent his career as a surface warfare officer. At the start of the war it was not uncommon for non-aviators to command carrier task forces; in fact, this was commonplace through November 1942. Fletcher is a controversial figure since he was accused of passivity during and after the war. He only took risks after judging that his action could exact a greater toll from the enemy. It is also fair to point out that, after spending the first nine months of the war continually at sea, Fletcher was fatigued by August 1942 and did exhibit a notable lack of aggression.

When Halsey was laid up with a skin condition before Midway, he recommended Rear Admiral Raymond Spruance as his replacement. Spruance was also a non-aviator but had a calculating mind and was known for his intellect. After Midway, he became Nimitz's chief of staff before being selected for greater responsibility. The last non-aviator to exercise overall command of an American carrier task force in battle was Rear Admiral Thomas C. Kinkaid. Though he had a reputation as a clear thinker, he did not perform well as a carrier task force commander.

Going into the war, the Pacific Fleet's senior carrier commander was Vice Admiral William Halsey. In spite of this, he did not exercise tactical command of a carrier task force for any of the 1942 carrier battles. (Naval History and Heritage Command)

CHAPTER 2
THE FIRST SIX MONTHS

The Japanese planned a series of attacks at the beginning of the war. The *Kido Butai* was allocated to the attack against the main Pacific Fleet base at Pearl Harbor. Such an operation was thought impossible by the Americans and extremely risky by all but a few Japanese. Before the attack the power of massed carriers was only theoretical. After the attack was completed, the nature of naval war was changed. The expected war between opposing battle lines would never happen. Instead the Pacific War became a carrier war.

JAPANESE PLANNING FOR THE PEARL HARBOR ATTACK

For almost two decades the IJN had been planning a defensive war against the USN which would culminate in a decisive battle in the Western Pacific near Japanese home waters. Admiral Yamamoto was not happy with such a passive approach, so he transformed Japanese naval strategy. Yamamoto believed that the opening blow had to shatter American morale and force the Americans to the negotiating table. This concept provided the strategic framework for the attack on Pearl Harbor.

The means of Yamamoto's crushing attack was the *Kido Butai*, which had the range and striking power to deliver a shattering blow at the onset of hostilities.

The idea of attacking the Pacific Fleet in Pearl Harbor was not original to Yamamoto. As early as 1927, war games at the Japanese naval war college included a raid against Pearl Harbor with two carriers. American naval officers also saw the possibilities of such an attack. In 1929, they provided a practical demonstration of the suitability of carriers for such an operation when two American carriers conducted a surprise attack on the Panama Canal in the USN's annual fleet exercise. In 1936, the Japanese naval war college again explored a Pearl Harbor attack, and in 1938 the annual US fleet exercise featured an attack on the base by a carrier.

However promising an attack on Pearl Harbor appeared in theory, both sides saw it as a risky operation. The defenses of the base were thought to be formidable, and the striking power of the fragile carriers was still unproven. Without the energy and determination of Yamamoto there would never have been a Pearl Harbor attack. According to Vice Admiral Shigeru Fukudome, the chief of staff for the Combined Fleet, Yamamoto first broached the Pearl Harbor attack in March or April of 1940. In the late fall of 1940, after the completion of the Combined Fleet's annual

ABOVE *Kaga* is pictured steaming through heavy North Pacific seas en route to attack Pearl Harbor. The decision to take the northern route subjected the task force to a rough passage but minimized the potential of detection. (Naval History and Heritage Command)

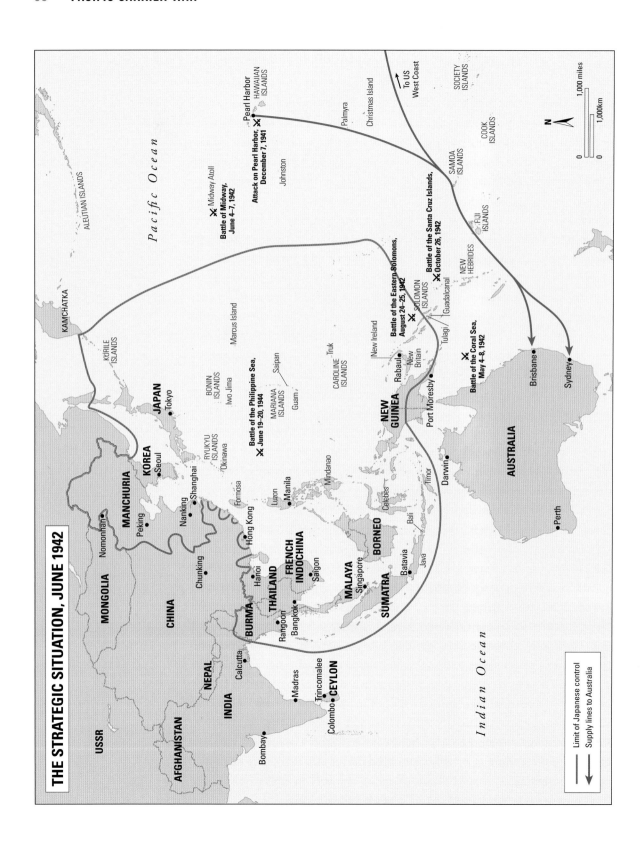

THE STRATEGIC SITUATION, JUNE 1942

USSR

AFGHANISTAN

MONGOLIA

Nomonhan

MANCHURIA

Peking

KOREA
Seoul

Shanghai

Nanking

JAPAN
Tokyo

NEPAL

INDIA

CHINA

Chunking

Calcutta

Bombay

Madras

Trincomalee
Colombo CEYLON

BURMA
Rangoon

THAILAND
Bangkok

Hanoi

FRENCH
INDOCHINA

Saigon

Formosa

Hong Kong

Luzon
Manila

RYUKYU
ISLANDS
Okinawa

MALAYA
Singapore

SUMATRA

Batavia
Java

Bali

BORNEO

Celebes

Mindanao

Timor

Indian Ocean

Perth

Darwin

AUSTRALIA

Brisbane

Sydney

NEW
GUINEA

Port Moresby

Battle of the Coral Sea,
May 4–8, 1942

Rabaul
New
Britain

New Ireland

Tulagi   Guadalcanal

SOLOMON
ISLANDS

Battle of the Eastern Solomons,
August 24–25, 1942

Battle of the Santa Cruz Islands,
October 26, 1942

NEW
HEBRIDES

FIJI
ISLANDS

SAMOA
ISLANDS

NEW
CALEDONIA

CAROLINE
ISLANDS

Truk

MARIANA
ISLANDS
Guam

Saipan

Battle of the Philippine Sea,
June 19–20, 1944

BONIN
ISLANDS
Iwo Jima

Marcus Island

KAMCHATKA

KURILE
ISLANDS

ALEUTIAN ISLANDS

Pacific Ocean

Battle of Midway,
June 4–7, 1942

Midway Atoll

Attack on Pearl Harbor,
December 7, 1941

Pearl Harbor
HAWAIIAN
ISLANDS

Johnston

Palmyra

Christmas Island

To US
West Coast

SOCIETY
ISLANDS

COOK
ISLANDS

Bombay

N

1,000 miles

1,000km

0

0

Limit of Japanese control

Supply lines to Australia

maneuvers, Yamamoto instructed Fukudome to have Rear Admiral Onishi Takijiro study a Pearl Harbor attack under the utmost secrecy. Onishi was the chief of staff of the land-based 11th Air Fleet but was an air-power advocate and a noted tactical expert and planner. In a letter dated January 7, 1941, Yamamoto ordered Onishi to study the proposal. This letter was followed by a meeting between Yamamoto and Onishi on January 26 or 27, when Yamamoto explained his vision. In February Onishi brought Commander Genda into the planning process and gave him seven to ten days to complete a study of the problem. Genda assessed that the operation would be difficult but not impossible. On or around March 10, Onishi presented an expanded draft of Genda's plan to Yamamoto along with his assessment. When the First Air Fleet was formed on April 10, 1941, it became the focal point for future planning of the Pearl Harbor attack.

The chief of staff of the First Air Fleet, Rear Admiral Kusaka, was officially informed of the planning effort in late April. At this point Kusaka outlined the plan to his boss Vice Admiral Nagumo. Nagumo thought that problems with refueling the strike force on the way to Hawaii and the unlikelihood of gaining surprise made the plan's success nearly impossible. Kusaka also began to have doubts, so ironically, as the planning evolved, the officers charged with the execution of the operation were the most dubious about it.

Nagumo and Kusaka were not the only ones to have doubts about Yamamoto's brainchild. The most serious opposition came from the Naval General Staff who had responsibility for formulating overall Japanese naval strategy. In particular, the chief of the Naval General Staff, Admiral Nagano Osami, was unimpressed by the plan. He believed the Hawaii operation was simply too risky and that the *Kido Butai*'s carriers were needed to support the thrust into Southeast Asia. But with war becoming more likely, Nagano agreed to have the plan examined at the annual war game scheduled for September.

When the war game (actually a controlled staff study to examine various courses of action) commenced, the first iteration was a disaster for the Japanese. Nagumo's force was discovered before it had a chance to launch its attack. When the attacking force reached Pearl Harbor, it met determined American resistance and inflicted only minor damage. American air raids sank two of Nagumo's four carriers. In the second iteration, Nagumo adjusted his approach further to the north and his time of arrival to avoid American searches. This gained the necessary surprise and produced much different results. American losses were assessed to be four battleships, two carriers, and three cruisers sunk, and another battleship, one carrier, and three cruisers were damaged. Japanese aircraft losses were assessed to be light. When the Americans located Nagumo's force, air attacks accounted for one Japanese carrier sunk and another damaged. The exercise demonstrated the operation to be feasible but also highlighted the importance of gaining surprise. However, the participants could not agree on the number of carriers to allocate to the operation. The Naval General Staff wanted to retain some carriers for operations in Southeast Asia, so only three or four carriers were allocated to the Hawaii attack. At the end of the conference, Nagano and the rest of the Naval General Staff still thought the operation too risky. This was confirmed again at a September 24 conference. Upon learning of the Naval General Staff's continued resistance, Yamamoto became intent on bringing the matter to a head.

An October 13 Combined Fleet table exercise was used to refine aspects of the Hawaii operation and to synchronize it with the Southeast Asia offensive. Only three carriers were assigned to the Pearl Harbor attack (*Kaga*, *Zuikaku*, and *Shokaku*) because they had the range to reach Pearl Harbor without refueling; *Akagi*, *Soryu*, and *Hiryu* were allocated to support the Southeast Asia operation. The following day there was a review during which all the admirals present were invited to speak. All but one opposed the Hawaii operation. At the end of the session, Yamamoto declared that as long as he was Commander of the Combined Fleet, Pearl Harbor would be attacked. Though this made his intentions clear to his commanders, Yamamoto still had to convince the Naval General Staff. On October 17, Kusaka again made the case that all six carriers were needed to attack Pearl Harbor. The Naval General Staff refused to agree. At this point, Yamamoto's patience was exhausted. The following day he sent a staff officer to gain the Naval General Staff's final approval and to address the carrier allocation issue. When the Naval General Staff remained adamant in their opposition, Yamamoto's emissary revealed that unless the plan was approved in its entirety, Yamamoto and his entire staff would resign. Facing this threat, the Naval General Staff folded. It was inconceivable that the Combined Fleet would go to war without Yamamoto. The Pearl Harbor operation was approved with all six of the Combined Fleet's large carriers involved.

As Yamamoto fought for his plan's approval, there were many operational details to work out before the attack was actually feasible. In early September Kusaka directed his staff to create an operational plan for the Pearl Harbor attack. Genda, the most important man after Yamamoto in the plan's implementation, was put in charge of the planning. He addressed the issue of what route the carriers should take to Hawaii. The southern and central routes required less fuel, but the northern route offered greater prospects for surprise. The northern route was virtually guaranteed to feature rough weather during the planned attack window, and the rough weather would make refueling more difficult. The much greater distance made multiple refuelings necessary. In spite of those drawbacks, Kusaka and Nagumo decided to use the northern route to increase the prospect of gaining surprise.

Refueling was a huge problem since only seven ships (carriers *Kaga*, *Shokaku*, and *Zuikaku*, along with the two escorting battleships and the two Tone-class heavy cruisers) had the radius to make the trip from the Kuriles to Pearl Harbor without refueling. Kusaka solved this problem by having the three shorter-range carriers carry extra fuel in 55-gallon drums. He ordered the other ships to develop and practice underway refueling. Eight tankers were allotted to support the operation (only seven actually took part). Three refueling exercises were held in November, and during the transit to the Kuriles all ships took on fuel ten times.

Kido Butai (Hawaii operation)

Aircraft carriers: *Akagi* (flag), *Kaga, Soryu, Hiryu, Shokaku, Zuikaku*
Battleships: *Hiei, Kirishima*
Heavy Cruisers: *Tone, Chikuma*
Light Cruiser: *Abukuma*
Destroyers: *Akigumo, Hamakaze, Isokaze, Kagero, Shiranuhi,*
    Tanikaze, Urakaze
Submarines: *I-19, I-21, I-23*
First Supply Group: Four tankers escorted by destroyer *Kasumi*
Second Supply Group: Three tankers escorted by destroyer *Arare*

Another huge problem facing the Japanese was how to employ torpedoes in the shallow waters of Pearl Harbor. If Yamamoto's attack was going to deliver the desired shock to the Americans, it had to sink a large number of battleships. This required torpedoes since bombs were unlikely to sink heavily armored battleships. In October, the most experienced and skilled Type 97 pilots were selected to train as torpedo bombers; the rest would train for level bombing. Experienced pilots were essential to solve the problem of torpedoes diving too deep before adjusting to a pre-set running depth in the 40-foot-deep waters of Pearl Harbor. To ensure that the torpedoes did not go below 33 feet, the Japanese modified them with a set of wooden extension fins attached to the torpedo's metal horizontal and vertical fins. The fins stabilized the torpedo after it was dropped and broke off when the torpedo entered the water. This, combined with intense training to drop the torpedo from 65 feet at 100 knots, solved the problem. The Japanese had to scramble to get the modified torpedoes ready in time. By the end of November, the Nagasaki Navy Arsenal had built a total of 120 torpedoes. The first 50 were sent to *Akagi*, *Soryu*, and *Hiryu* in mid-November, and another batch of 50 was loaded on *Kaga* and arrived at Hitokappu Bay in the Kuriles just two days before the fleet sailed for Pearl Harbor.

Another major issue was how to increase the effectiveness of level bombing. This was crucial since the Americans berthed their battleships in Pearl Harbor in pairs.

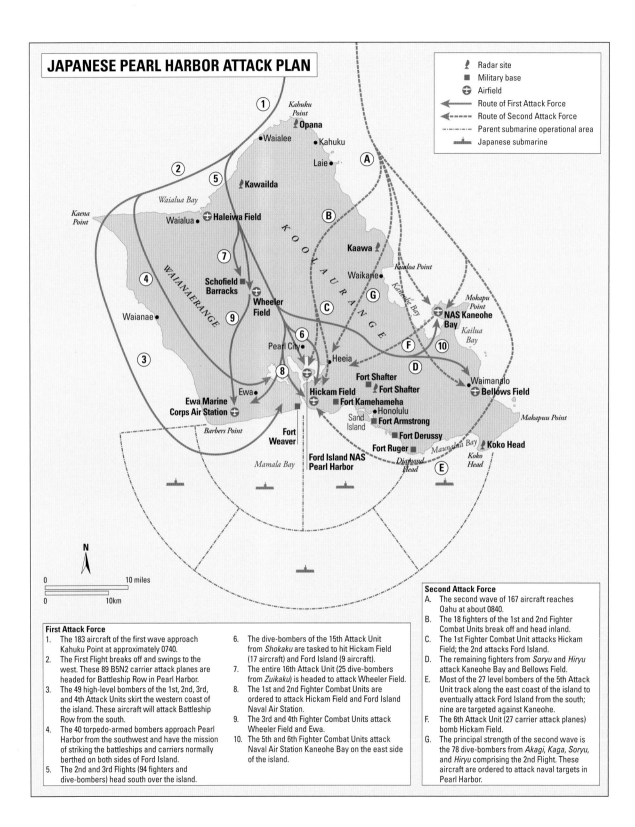

JAPANESE PEARL HARBOR ATTACK PLAN

Radar site
Military base
Airfield
Route of First Attack Force
Route of Second Attack Force
Parent submarine operational area
Japanese submarine

First Attack Force

1. The 183 aircraft of the first wave approach Kahuku Point at approximately 0740.
2. The First Flight breaks off and swings to the west. These 89 B5N2 carrier attack planes are headed for Battleship Row in Pearl Harbor.
3. The 49 high-level bombers of the 1st, 2nd, 3rd, and 4th Attack Units skirt the western coast of the island. These aircraft will attack Battleship Row from the south.
4. The 40 torpedo-armed bombers approach Pearl Harbor from the southwest and have the mission of striking the battleships and carriers normally berthed on both sides of Ford Island.
5. The 2nd and 3rd Flights (94 fighters and dive-bombers) head south over the island.

6. The dive-bombers of the 15th Attack Unit from *Shokaku* are tasked to hit Hickam Field (17 aircraft) and Ford Island (9 aircraft).
7. The entire 16th Attack Unit (25 dive-bombers from *Zuikaku*) is headed to attack Wheeler Field.
8. The 1st and 2nd Fighter Combat Units are ordered to attack Hickam Field and Ford Island Naval Air Station.
9. The 3rd and 4th Fighter Combat Units attack Wheeler Field and Ewa.
10. The 5th and 6th Fighter Combat Units attack Naval Air Station Kaneohe Bay on the east side of the island.

Second Attack Force

A. The second wave of 167 aircraft reaches Oahu at about 0840.
B. The 18 fighters of the 1st and 2nd Fighter Combat Units break off and head inland.
C. The 1st Fighter Combat Unit attacks Hickam Field; the 2nd attacks Ford Island.
D. The remaining fighters from *Soryu* and *Hiryu* attack Kaneohe Bay and Bellows Field.
E. Most of the 27 level bombers of the 5th Attack Unit track along the east coast of the island to eventually attack Ford Island from the south; nine are targeted against Kaneohe.
F. The 6th Attack Unit (27 carrier attack planes) bomb Hickam Field.
G. The principal strength of the second wave is the 78 dive-bombers from *Akagi*, *Kaga*, *Soryu*, and *Hiryu* comprising the 2nd Flight. These aircraft are ordered to attack naval targets in Pearl Harbor.

This meant that only the outer battleships were vulnerable to torpedoes; attacking the inner ships required bombs. Since the bombs carried by Japanese dive-bombers lacked the power to penetrate heavily armored battleship decks, the only viable solution was to employ Type 97s in a level bombing role with a bomb capable of penetrating battleship armor. This had its own problems since horizontal bombing at the altitude required to give the bomb enough kinetic energy to penetrate heavy armor was very inaccurate. Prior to April 1941 the Japanese were able to achieve a hit rate of only about 10 percent from high altitude. In April a new tactic was developed that had nine Type 97s drop their bombs simultaneously. This mass drop was done at the signal of the lead aircraft; accuracy improved to three-to-five hits out of the nine bombs dropped. The level bombers were ordered to drop their bombs from about 10,000 feet, since this was the minimum altitude required to pierce battleship armor and was low enough to improve accuracy. A five-plane attack group was adopted instead of the previous nine-plane group to give Genda more planning flexibility. The final hurdle facing the Japanese was to develop a bomb capable of penetrating battleship deck armor. Calculations determined that a weight of 1,764 pounds was required. To create such a bomb quickly, obsolete 16-inch shells were converted into bombs. Construction of the new bomb in the numbers required proved difficult; only 150 were available by mid-September.

Dive-bombers also had an important role to play in the attack since their 550lb bombs could penetrate the horizontal armor of relatively lightly armored aircraft carriers and cruisers. During training in the second half of 1941, dive-bombing accuracy rates reached 50–60 percent. In order to improve accuracy, dive-bomber release points were reduced to just below 1,500 feet.

The table on page 46 details how Nagumo and his staff organized the attack. In the first wave, the elite torpedo and level bombers of Carrier Divisions 1 and 2 were earmarked to destroy the battleships and carriers moored around Ford Island by a combination of 40 torpedo and 50 level bombers. The inexperienced pilots of Carrier Division 5 were used to attack bases at Ford Island, Hickam Field, and Kaneohe to cripple American air power. The second wave would arrive shortly after the first so that the Americans would have little time to recover. This strike included no vulnerable torpedo aircraft since surprise was no longer possible. Fifty-four level bombers were targeted on key airfields to complete the destruction of American air power. The heart of the second wave was the 81 elite dive-bombers from Carrier Divisions 1 and 2. Their primary targets were any carriers damaged from the first wave. The dive-bombers were ordered to complete their destruction to make any salvage impossible.

The final plan was not completed until the end of October and was still being tweaked during the transit to Pearl Harbor. On November 2 the plan was revealed

JAPANESE AIRCRAFT FROM THE PEARL HARBOR ATTACK

THIS PAGE The top profile is a Zero from *Shokaku*; the next profile is the Zero flown by Lt Cdr Itaya Shigeru from *Akagi* who was the leader of all first-wave fighters. The bottom profile is a Type 99 from *Zuikaku*.

OPPOSITE The top profile depicts a Type 99 from *Kaga*. The middle aircraft is from *Soryu* and carries a special armor-piercing 1,764lb bomb used to attack Battleship Row. The bottom aircraft is from *Hiryu* and carries a Type 91 torpedo.

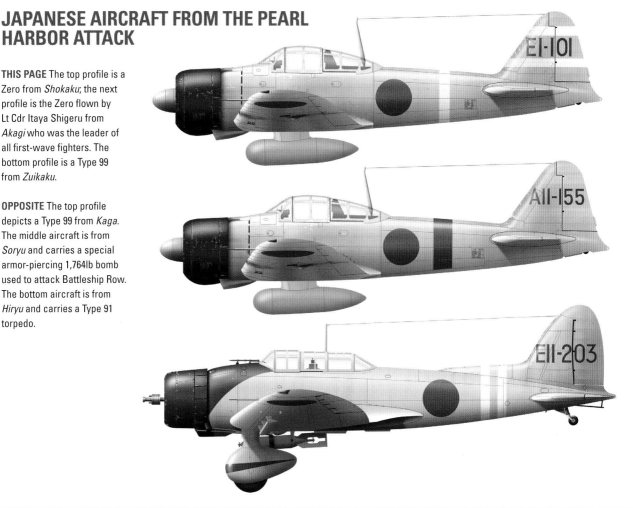

in a mass briefing aboard flagship *Akagi*. After two last weeks of exercises, on November 22 ships of the attack force departed their home ports individually or in pairs bound for Hitokappu Bay in the Kuriles. On November 24, the attack force departed for Pearl Harbor.

THE ATTACK ON PEARL HARBOR

The *Kido Butai* departed its anchorage at Hitokappu Bay at 0600 hours on November 24. During the 13-day transit to the launch point 230nm north of Oahu, through the rough waters of the North Pacific Ocean, the Japanese encountered no ships. Diplomatic efforts having failed, the message "Climb

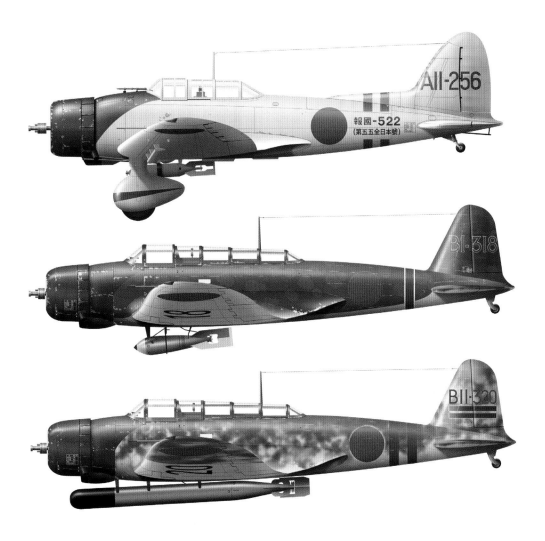

Mount Niitaka 1208" was received on December 2. This confirmed the attack would begin as scheduled on the morning of December 7. At 1130 on December 6, the *Kido Butai* changed course to 180 degrees and headed straight for Hawaii.

A reconnaissance report from the Japanese consulate in Honolulu was received aboard *Akagi* at 0150 on December 7. The report indicated that nine battleships, three light cruisers, three seaplane tenders, and 17 destroyers were present in the harbor the day before. Four light cruisers and two destroyers were in drydock. The most important aspect of the report, which was generally accurate, was that all of the Pacific Fleet's carriers and heavy cruisers were absent. A subsequent report indicated that no barrage balloons or torpedo nets were evident. On the morning of December 7, there were a total of 82 warships at Pearl Harbor. None of the Pacific Fleet's carriers

ORGANIZATION OF PEARL HARBOR ATTACK FORCE

FIRST ATTACK FORCE (FIRST WAVE)

Commander: Cdr Fuchida Mitsuo

	CARRIER	AIRCRAFT TYPE	NUMBER	TARGET
First Flight – Horizontal Bombing Force (Fuchida)				
1st Attack Unit	*Akagi*	Type 97	15	Battleship Row
2nd Attack Unit	*Kaga*	Type 97	15 (1 abort)	Battleship Row
3rd Attack Group	*Soryu*	Type 97	10	Battleship Row
4th Attack Group	*Hiryu*	Type 97	10	Battleship Row
TOTAL: 50 (49 actually attacked) All aircraft armed with a single Type 5 1,760lb bomb				
First Flight Special Group – Torpedo Force (Lt Cdr Murata Shigemaru)				
1st Torpedo Attack Unit	*Akagi*	Type 97	12	Battleship Row
2nd Torpedo Attack Unit	*Kaga*	Type 97	12	Battleship Row
3rd Torpedo Attack Unit	*Soryu*	Type 97	8	Carriers, Battleships
4th Torpedo Attack Unit	*Hiryu*	Type 97	8	Carriers, Battleships
TOTAL: 40 All aircraft armed with a single Type 91 air-launched torpedo				
Second Flight – Dive-Bomber Force (Lt Cdr Takahashi Kakuichi)				
15th Attack Unit	*Shokaku*	Type 99	27 (1 abort)	17 against Ford Island 9 against Hickam Fld.
16th Attack Unit	*Zuikaku*	Type 99	27 (2 abort)	Wheeler Field
TOTAL: 54 (51 actually attacked) All aircraft armed with a single 550lb general purpose bomb				
Third Flight – Air Control Force (Lt Cdr Itaya Shigeru)				
1st Fighter Combat Unit	*Akagi*	Zero	9	Ford Island/Hickam Fld.
2nd Fighter Combat Unit	*Kaga*	Zero	9	Ford Island/Hickam Fld.
3rd Fighter Combat Unit	*Soryu*	Zero	9 (1 abort)	Wheeler Fld./Ewa
4th Fighter Combat Unit	*Hiryu*	Zero	6	Wheeler Fld./Ewa
5th Fighter Combat Unit	*Shokaku*	Zero	6 (1 abort)	Kaneohe
6th Fighter Combat Unit	*Zuikaku*	Zero	6	Kaneohe
TOTAL: 45 (43 actually attacked) All aircraft armed with two 20mm cannon and two 7.7mm machine guns				
TOTAL AIRCRAFT IN FIRST WAVE: 189 (183 actually attacked)				

were present when the first Japanese aircraft arrived over Pearl Harbor: *Enterprise*, escorted by three cruisers and nine destroyers, was delivering a Marine fighter squadron to Wake Island; *Lexington* had departed Pearl Harbor on December 5 with three cruisers and five destroyers to deliver aircraft to Midway; and *Saratoga* was at Puget Sound, Washington, undergoing repairs. This left eight battleships, two heavy cruisers, six light cruisers, 30 destroyers, five submarines, and various auxiliaries in Pearl Harbor.

Beginning at 0530 hours on the morning of December 7, the first wave was spotted on the flight decks of the six Japanese carriers and aircraft engines began warming up. The seas that morning were some of the worst encountered on the entire transit. At 0550, the pilots manned their aircraft. The *Kido Butai* headed east at 24 knots to get sufficient wind across the deck for takeoff. The first wave

ORGANIZATION OF PEARL HARBOR ATTACK FORCE (CONT.)
SECOND ATTACK FORCE (SECOND WAVE)
Commander: Lt Cdr Shimazaki Shigekazu

	CARRIER	AIRCRAFT TYPE	NUMBER	TARGET
First Flight – Horizontal Bombing Force (Shimazaki)				
5th Attack Unit	*Shokaku*	Type 97	27	18 against Ford Island
				9 against Kaneohe
6th Attack Unit	*Zuikaku*	Type 97	27	Hickam Field
TOTAL: 54 One-half of aircraft armed with two 550lb bombs; one-half armed with one 550lb bomb and six 132lb bombs				
Second Flight – Dive-Bomber Force (Lt Cdr Egasa Takashige)				
11th Attack Unit	*Akagi*	Type 99	18	Various naval targets
12th Attack Unit	*Kaga*	Type 99	27 (1 abort)	Various naval targets
13th Attack Unit	*Soryu*	Type 99	18 (1 abort)	Various naval targets
14th Attack Unit	*Hiryu*	Type 99	18 (1 abort)	Various naval targets
TOTAL: 81 (78 actually attacked) All aircraft armed with a single 550lb bomb				
Third Flight – Air Control Force (Lt Shindo Saburo)				
1st Fighter Combat Unit	*Akagi*	Zero	9	Ford Island/Hickam Fld.
2nd Fighter Combat Unit	*Kaga*	Zero	9	Ford Island/Hickam Fld.
3rd Fighter Combat Unit	*Soryu*	Zero	9	Kaneohe
4th Fighter Combat Unit	*Hiryu*	Zero	9 (1 abort)	Kaneohe/Bellows Field
TOTAL: 36 (35 actually attacked) All aircraft armed with two 20mm cannon and two 7.7mm machine guns				
TOTAL AIRCRAFT IN SECOND WAVE: 171 (167 actually attacked)				
TOTAL ATTACKING AIRCRAFT IN FIRST AND SECOND WAVES: 360 (350 actually attacked)				

began taking off at 0600. All aircraft were off the decks within an impressive 15 minutes. Following takeoff the 183 aircraft formed a single loose formation and headed south at 0620. Immediately after the launch of the first wave, preparations began for launching the second. The same procedure was repeated, with the aircraft quickly spotted on the flight decks and their engines warmed. The fleet again turned into the wind for a second launch at 0705 and ten minutes later the aircraft began to lift off. The second wave of 167 aircraft headed south to Oahu.

Despite being picked up by three of the five operational American radars on the island, the Japanese retained surprise when only one of these stations reported its contact: a report that was quickly dismissed by the Air Defense Center at Fort Shafter. There was some confusion at 0740 when attack leader Fuchida fired one flare to indicate that surprise had been achieved and called for the more vulnerable torpedo bombers to make their attacks first. Fearing that the fighters flying above had not seen his first signal, Fuchida fired another flare. Though not part of the same signal, two flares was the signal that surprise had not been achieved. Acting on this misunderstanding, the dive-bombers and fighters rushed ahead to attack first in order to protect the torpedo planes.

This photo from May 3, 1940 gives a good orientation of the Pearl Harbor naval base. The base is full of ships as it was on the morning of December 7, 1941. There are eight battleships present along the far side of Ford Island along with *Yorktown*. Many cruisers, destroyers, and other ships are also present, most moored in groups in the East Loch located in the foreground. (Naval History and Heritage Command)

The attack by the 40 Type 97s with torpedoes was the most important part of the Japanese plan. Of the eight battleships present, five were vulnerable to torpedo attack. At 0751, the torpedo planes split up into four groups. The 24 aircraft from *Akagi* and *Kaga* looped around Hickam Field to approach Battleship Row on the eastern side of Ford Island. The remaining 16 torpedo bombers from *Soryu* and *Hiryu* came in from the west to attack the ships anchored on the western side of Ford Island. This is where the American carriers were usually moored. Even though the latest pre-attack intelligence indicated no carriers were present, no effort was made to change the basic attack plan.

Confident they had addressed the problem of employing torpedoes in the harbor, Japanese planners expected that 27 of the 40 torpedoes would hit a target.

The torpedo attack opened at 0755 hours with the 16 Type 97s from *Soryu* and *Hiryu*. In the absence of any carriers, the Japanese pilots were forced to make split decisions as to which target to attack. Chaos ensued, resulting in the expenditure of precious torpedoes against secondary targets. Six of the *Soryu* aircraft attacked the ships situated where the carriers should have been. None were worth a torpedo. Two torpedoes hit the training ship (and former battleship) *Utah*, which rolled over and sank. Another hit the old light cruiser *Raleigh* and caused severe flooding. Quick counterflooding saved the cruiser from capsizing. The other three torpedoes missed. The leader of *Soryu*'s torpedo group tried to find a more valuable target. He settled for a large target along the 1010 Pier in the Navy Yard. This was the ancient minelayer *Oglala* moored outboard of the modern light cruiser *Helena*. This torpedo ran under *Oglala* and hit *Helena* where it flooded one boiler room and one engine room. The explosion split open *Oglala*'s hull and she sank two hours later. The last *Soryu* aircraft continued toward Battleship Row. *Hiryu*'s torpedo group was less successful in handling the confusion when it became obvious no carriers were present. Four aircraft launched their torpedoes at the ships moored along the 1010 Pier but all missed. The other four joined the single remaining *Soryu* aircraft in attacking Battleship Row.

The 12 carrier attack planes from *Akagi* led the attack against Battleship Row. Genda's plan had these aircraft approach in a line-ahead formation from the same point. Battleships *Oklahoma* and *West Virginia* were directly in front of the approaching Type 97s; the first six *Akagi* torpedo planes targeted these ships beginning at 0757 and scored several hits in quick succession. The next two *Akagi* aircraft veered left to attack *California*, scoring one hit. Another aircraft attacked *West Virginia* and the final three targeted *Oklahoma*. The Japanese claimed that 11 *Akagi* carrier attack planes dropped torpedoes (one jettisoned its weapon as the result of a near air-to-air collision), and that all 11 hit one of the three battleships targeted. Interspersed among the *Akagi* torpedo bombers were the four remaining *Hiryu* aircraft. Two of these attacked *West Virginia*, and the final two targeted *Oklahoma*.

TOP LEFT The second attack wave on *Shokaku* preparing to launch. The identity of the ship is confirmed by the markings of the aircraft. Carrier Division 5 was assigned secondary targets in both attack waves because of the inexperience of its pilots. (Naval History and Heritage Command)

ABOVE A *Shokaku* Type 97 carrier attack plane takes off as part of the second attack during which it was assigned to attack airfields. (Naval History and Heritage Command)

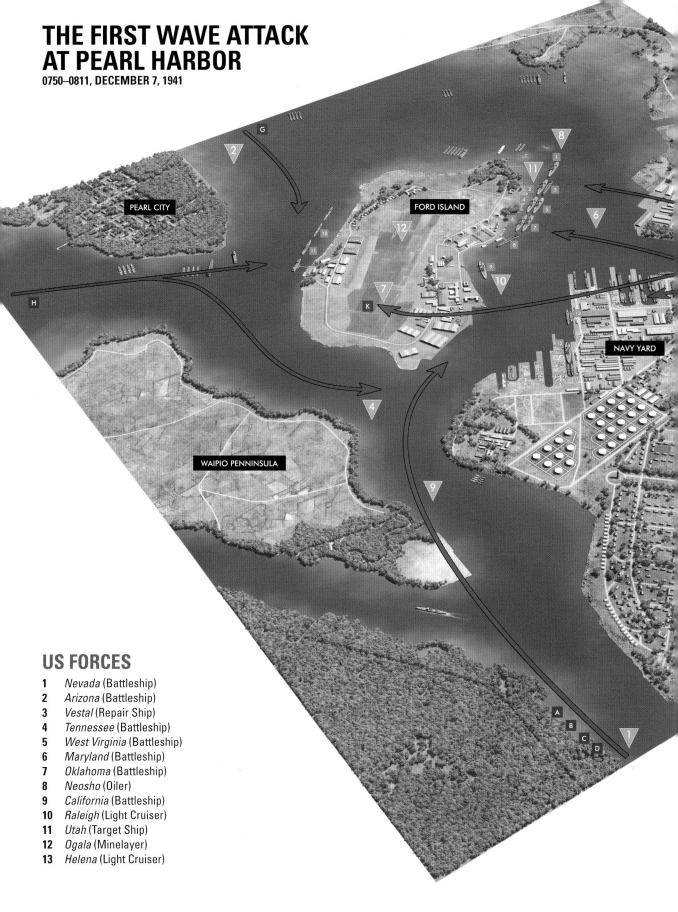

THE FIRST WAVE ATTACK AT PEARL HARBOR

0750–0811, DECEMBER 7, 1941

PEARL CITY

FORD ISLAND

WAIPIO PENNINSULA

NAVY YARD

US FORCES

1   *Nevada* (Battleship)
2   *Arizona* (Battleship)
3   *Vestal* (Repair Ship)
4   *Tennessee* (Battleship)
5   *West Virginia* (Battleship)
6   *Maryland* (Battleship)
7   *Oklahoma* (Battleship)
8   *Neosho* (Oiler)
9   *California* (Battleship)
10 *Raleigh* (Light Cruiser)
11 *Utah* (Target Ship)
12 *Ogala* (Minelayer)
13 *Helena* (Light Cruiser)

JAPANESE FORCES

FIRST ATTACK FORCE

1st Group

A 1st Attack Unit – 15 B5N2 carrier attack planes (*Akagi*)

B 2nd Attack Unit – 14 B5N2 carrier attack planes (*Kaga*)

C 3rd Attack Unit – 10 B5N2 carrier attack planes (*Soryu*)

D 4th Attack Unit – 10 B5N2 carrier attack planes (*Hiryu*)

E 1st Torpedo Attack Unit – 12 B5N2 carrier attack planes (*Akagi*)

F 2nd Torpedo Attack Unit – 12 B5N2 carrier attack planes (*Kaga*)

G 3rd Torpedo Attack Unit – 8 B5N2 carrier attack planes (*Soryu*)

H 4th Torpedo Attack Unit – 8 B5N2 carrier attack planes (*Hiryu*)

2nd Group

I 15th Attack Unit – 26 D3A1 dive-bombers (*Shokaku*)

3rd Group

J 1st Fighter Combat Group – 9 A9M2 fighters (*Kaga*)

K 2nd Fighter Combat Group – 9 A9M2 fighters (*Akagi*)

HICKAM AIRFIELD

4 **0756** – Several torpedo bombers from the 4th Torpedo Attack unit swing south along Ford Island and attack units moored at the 1010 Pier. One torpedo hits *Helena* at 0757; minelayer *Ogala* moored next to *Helena* is damaged below the waterline and later sinks at 1000.

5 **0756** – 1st and 2nd Torpedo Attack Units approach Battleship Row from the southeast.

6 **0757** – Many of the torpedoes launched against Battleship Row find their targets. The Japanese claim nine hits on *West Virginia* and *Oklahoma*; though the actual count is less, both ships sink quickly. Two torpedoes hit *California* and she eventually settles on the bottom of the harbor. *Nevada* takes a single hit, but this causes severe flooding.

7 **0757** – Nine D3A1 dive-bombers attack Ford Island, targeting hangars and parked aircraft.

8 **0803** – Torpedo hits *Nevada*.

9 **0805** – The 49 B5N2s of the 1st Group acting as level bombers begin their attack from the south.

10 **0805** – First torpedo hit on *California*.

11 **0811** – A single bomb, likely from a *Hiryu* aircraft, penetrates the forward magazine of *Arizona*, creating an explosion, which destroys the battleship and damages *Vestal* moored alongside. Other bomb hits are scored on *California*, *Maryland*, and *Tennessee*.

12 Fighter cover is provided by 18 A6M2 fighters from *Kaga* and *Akagi*, which are also tasked to strafe aircraft on Ford Island and Hickam Field.

▼ EVENTS

1 **0750** – Cdr Fuchida gives order to attack.

2 **0755** – 3rd and 4th Torpedo Attack Units commence attack on ships berthed on the west side of Ford Island. *Soryu's* torpedo bombers hit *Raleigh* once. *Hiryu's* 4th Torpedo Attack Unit scores two hits on *Utah*, which causes her to capsize at 0810.

3 **0755** – The bulk of the 2nd Group (17 D3A1 dive-bombers) attacks Hickam Field.

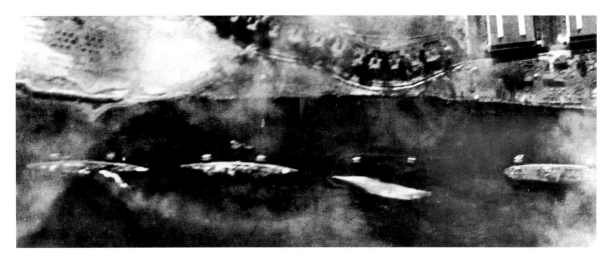

ABOVE This photograph of the western side of Ford Island, taken by a Type 97, shows the aftermath of Japanese torpedo attacks. From left to right are light cruiser *Detroit*, light cruiser *Raleigh* (listing to port after being hit by one torpedo), training ship *Utah* (already capsized after being hit by two torpedoes), and seaplane tender *Tangier.* (Naval History and Heritage Command)

MIDDLE RIGHT This remarkable photo was taken from a Type 97 bomber during the early stages of the attack. A torpedo has just hit *West Virginia* on the far side of Ford Island. *Oklahoma*, the other outboard battleship, has also been torpedoed and is listing to port. Two Type 97s are banking away from Battleship Row after launching their weapons. To the left is the western side of Ford Island with light cruisers *Detroit* and *Raleigh*, training ship *Utah*, and seaplane tender *Tangier*. *Raleigh* and *Utah* have already been torpedoed, and *Utah* is listing sharply to port. (Naval History and Heritage Command)

RIGHT Another photo taken by a Type 97 of Battleship Row early in the attack. The torpedo bombers are still attacking, but the level bomber attack has not yet begun. From lower left to right are *Nevada*, *Arizona* with repair ship *Vestal* outboard, *Tennessee* with *West Virginia* outboard, *Maryland* with *Oklahoma* outboard, oiler *Neosho* and finally *California*. *West Virginia*, *Oklahoma*, and *California* have already been torpedoed, and the first two are listing to port. Splashes from torpedo drops and torpedo tracks are visible at left and center. The heavy smoke in the distance is from Hickam Field, which was attacked by dive-bombers. (Naval History and Heritage Command)

Kaga's 12 torpedo aircraft were the last to attack. By this time the Americans had increased the volume of antiaircraft fire and the flawed Japanese approach exposed each aircraft in sequence to fire. As a result, five of the 12 *Kaga* Type 97s were shot down, making them the only torpedo aircraft to suffer this fate. Four aircraft attacked *West Virginia*, two targeted *Oklahoma*, and a single aircraft veered to the right to attack *Nevada*. The last aircraft's torpedo hit *Nevada* forward. These aircraft were joined by the final Type 97 from *Soryu*, which selected *California* and scored a hit. This aircraft was heavily damaged by antiaircraft fire, but its skillful pilot made it back to the Japanese task force where he ditched in the ocean next to a destroyer. During this phase of the attack, the Japanese claimed that eight aircraft dropped their torpedoes against three different battleships and that all eight hit their targets.

Though the Japanese claims were excessive, the attack was still deadly. In only 11 minutes, and for a cost of only five aircraft (and a sixth later forced to ditch), the torpedo bombers sank two battleships and inflicted damage leading to the sinking of two more. Added to this was the sinking of a target ship and a minelayer and damage to two light cruisers. Of the 36 torpedoes launched, it is likely that 19 hit. The carnage could have been worse if the Japanese pilots had not concentrated on *Oklahoma* and *West Virginia*. A total of 12 torpedoes were launched at *Oklahoma* and at least five hit. The ship took three torpedoes in quick succession and immediately began to heel to port. No attempt was made to counterflood, so the ship capsized in 15 minutes, accounting for heavy personnel losses of 20 officers and 395 enlisted men killed. *West Virginia* was hit by a probable seven torpedoes. Orders from quick-reacting junior officers to flood the voids on the starboard side allowed the ship to avoid capsizing. Personnel casualties were relatively light, with two officers and 103 enlisted personnel killed.

Nevada was moored at the end of Battleship Row. At 0803 hours the battleship was hit by a torpedo on her port bow which created a large hole. Burning oil from the shattered *Arizona* directly in front threatened to engulf *Nevada*, so the order was given to get underway. She began to move at 0840 and headed down the channel between the Navy Yard and Ford Island. When the second wave dive-bombers made their appearance, they found the slow-moving battleship too tempting a target to pass up.

California was positioned in the southeasternmost spot of Battleship Row. Two torpedoes hit the ship; one struck forward of the bridge below her armored belt, and the second struck under the belt in the area of Turret Number 3. Counterflooding corrected the resulting list, but a combination of poor watertight integrity and human error doomed the ship. *California* continued to slowly settle until she rested on the bottom of the harbor on December 10. Six officers and 92 enlisted men were killed.

TOP RIGHT This view of Battleship Row, taken by a Type 97, shows the early phases of the horizontal bombing attack. Ships seen are (from left to right) *Nevada*, *Arizona* with *Vestal* moored outboard, *Tennessee* with *West Virginia* moored outboard, and *Maryland* with *Oklahoma* moored outboard. A bomb has just hit *Arizona* at the stern, but she has not yet received the bomb that detonated her forward magazines. *West Virginia* and *Oklahoma* are gushing oil from their many torpedo hits and are listing to port; *Oklahoma's* port deck edge is already under water. (Naval History and Heritage Command)

RIGHT This vertical view of Battleship Row was taken right after the deadly bomb hit on *Arizona* which resulted in a magazine explosion and the ship's destruction. From left to right are *Nevada*, *Arizona* (burning intensely) with *Vestal* moored outboard, *Tennessee* with *West Virginia* moored outboard, and *Maryland* with the capsized *Oklahoma* alongside. (Naval History and Heritage Command)

The second fist of the Japanese double-punch against Battleship Row was the level bombers carrying armor-piercing 1,760lb bombs. The Japanese pilots were instructed to make as many passes as necessary to ensure accuracy. The 49 Type 97s approached Battleship Row from the south at 10,000 feet in groups of five. The primary targets were the battleships moored inboard, but these suffered widely differing levels of damage. *Maryland* was moored inboard from *Oklahoma*; of all the battleships on Battleship Row, she was the least damaged. *Maryland* was hit by a bomb on the forecastle below the waterline. A second hit the forecastle but caused little damage. *Tennessee*, moored inboard of *West Virginia*, suffered little damage during the attack. Two bombs hit the battleship; the first on the center gun of Turret Number 2, and the second penetrated the top armor of

This iconic image was taken at the moment *Arizona's* forward magazine exploded after being hit by an armor-piercing 1,764lb bomb. (Naval History and Heritage Command)

Turret Number 3 but broke apart without detonating. Moored just aft of *Tennessee* was *Arizona* with repair ship *Vestal* alongside. *Arizona* took two hits. The first hit aft on the quarterdeck. At 0806, the second struck forward, penetrating the forward 14-inch gun magazine and resulting in a cataclysmic explosion. The explosion killed 1,177 crewmen and completely destroyed the forward part of the ship. *Vestal* also took two bomb hits which created flooding and a starboard list. She got underway at 0845 and was beached nearby to keep from sinking. The destruction of *Arizona* has become the iconic moment of the entire attack and has overshadowed the overall poor results from the level bombers. The best assessment is that ten hits were scored out of 49 bombs dropped; however, of the ten hits, six failed to explode or resulted in low-order detonations.

The first of the 167 aircraft of the second wave arrived over their targets approximately 25 minutes after the last aircraft of the first wave had departed. The centerpiece of the second wave was the 78 dive-bombers from *Akagi*, *Kaga*, *Soryu*, and *Hiryu*. These were flown by the best dive-bomber pilots in the Imperial Navy. Against stationary ships in Pearl Harbor, the Japanese expected impressive results. The force was led by Lieutenant Commander Egusa Takeshige from *Soryu* who was considered to be the finest dive-bomber pilot in the Imperial Navy. Since there were no carriers present, and the 550lb bombs carried by the dive-bombers were unsuited for attacking heavily armored battleships, the prioritization plan called for attacking cruisers. However, only 17 dive-bombers attacked cruisers, while some 30 selected battleships, and as many as 16 attacked destroyers, and 12

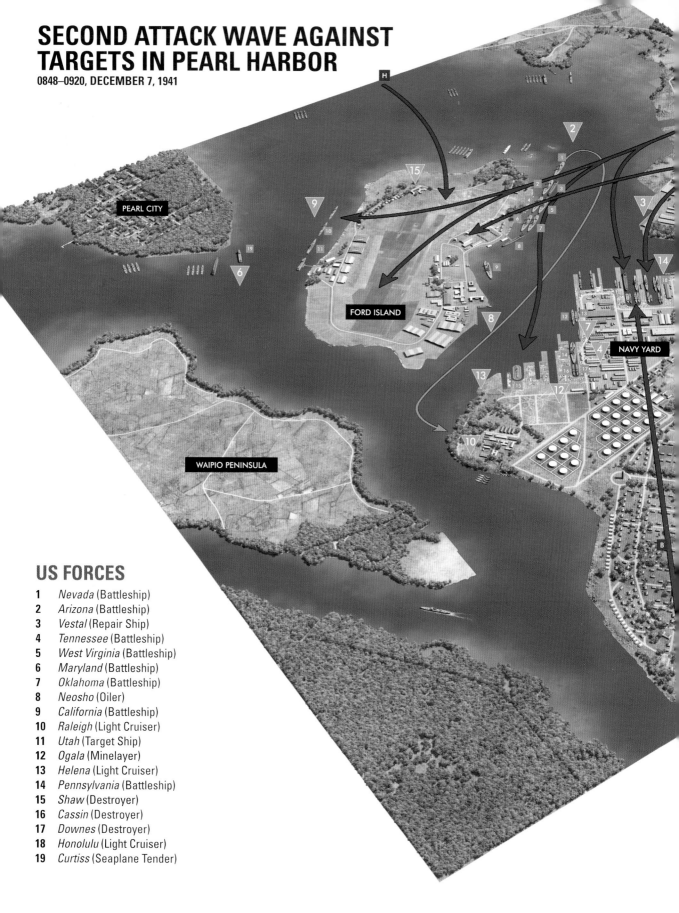

SECOND ATTACK WAVE AGAINST TARGETS IN PEARL HARBOR

0848–0920, DECEMBER 7, 1941

PEARL CITY

FORD ISLAND

WAIPIO PENINSULA

NAVY YARD

US FORCES

1   *Nevada* (Battleship)
2   *Arizona* (Battleship)
3   *Vestal* (Repair Ship)
4   *Tennessee* (Battleship)
5   *West Virginia* (Battleship)
6   *Maryland* (Battleship)
7   *Oklahoma* (Battleship)
8   *Neosho* (Oiler)
9   *California* (Battleship)
10 *Raleigh* (Light Cruiser)
11 *Utah* (Target Ship)
12 *Ogala* (Minelayer)
13 *Helena* (Light Cruiser)
14 *Pennsylvania* (Battleship)
15 *Shaw* (Destroyer)
16 *Cassin* (Destroyer)
17 *Downes* (Destroyer)
18 *Honolulu* (Light Cruiser)
19 *Curtiss* (Seaplane Tender)

JAPANESE FORCES

SECOND ATTACK FORCE

1st Group

A   5th Attack Unit – 9 B5N2 carrier attack planes (*Shokaku*)

B   6th Attack Unit – 27 B5N2 carrier attack planes (*Zuikaku*)

2nd Group

C   11th Attack Unit – 18 D3A1 dive-bombers (*Akagi*)

D   12th Attack Unit – 26 D3A1 dive-bombers (*Kaga*)

E   13th Attack Unit – 17 D3A1 dive-bombers (*Soryu*)

F   14th Attack Unit – 17 D3A1 dive-bombers (*Hiryu*)

3rd Group

G   1st Fighter Combat Group – 9 A9M2 fighters (*Akagi*)

H   2nd Fighter Combat Group – 9 A9M2 fighters (*Kaga*)

HICKAM AIRFIELD

▼ EVENTS

1 **0848** – 2nd Group approaches Pearl Harbor from the northeast. They are led by the Imperial Navy's acknowledged dive-bombing expert, Lt Cdr Egusa Takashige.

2 **0850** – Battleship *Nevada* gets underway.

3 **0850** – Fuchida sees that *Nevada* is underway and is headed for the channel entrance. He orders Egusa to attack the battleship in order to block the channel. Five quick bomb hits are scored.

4 **0857** – Dive-bombers score hits on *Pennsylvania* and two destroyers in drydock.

5 **0904** – The 5th Attack Unit arrives from the northeast and attacks hangars and aircraft on Ford Island; some aircraft attack *Pennsylvania*.

6 **0905** – A single D3A1 dive-bomber crashes into seaplane tender *Curtiss*, killing 20 crewmen and starting a fire.

7 **0907** – 5th Attack Unit hits *Pennsylvania* with 550lb bomb.

8 **0907** – *Nevada* suffers sixth bomb hit.

9 **0908** – *Raleigh* is attacked by dive-bombers; a single hit does little damage when it passes through the lightly armored ship.

10 **0910** – *Nevada* intentionally grounds on Hospital Point; she is later towed to the west side of the channel to clear the channel entrance.

11 **0910** – 27 B5N2 level bombers from *Zuikaku* commence attack on hangars and aircraft on Hickam Field. *Akagi*'s 1st Fighter Combat Unit strafes the field.

12 **0912** – 6th Attack Unit continues attack on *Pennsylvania* and other targets in the Navy Yard.

13 **0915** – Dive-bombers hit destroyer *Shaw* in floating drydock, causing fires and eventually an explosion in the ship's forward magazine.

14 **0920** – A dive-bomber scores a near miss on *Honolulu*, causing underwater damage and flooding.

15 Fighter cover for Second Attack Force is provided by 18 A6M2 fighters from *Kaga* and *Akagi*. The nine *Kaga* fighters strafe Ford Island and later use their unexpended ordnance against Wheeler Field.

attacked auxiliaries. Japanese after-action reports were inaccurate at best and misleading at worst. Using American after-action reports, it remains difficult to account for the attacks of all 78 dive-bombers. However, it is clear that the dive-bomber attack was unfocused and failed to live up to Japanese expectations.

Just as the Type 99s arrived over Pearl Harbor at about 0850, *Nevada* was spotted underway. Approximately 14–18 dive-bombers attacked the slow-moving battleship. *Nevada* was surrounded by near misses before she was hit by five bombs at 0900. At 0907 more dive-bombers arrived and scored another hit. Of these six hits, at least three struck forward of Turret Number 1 and opened holes in the bow, starting fires that soon burned out of control. The forward magazines were flooded which brought the bow down further. At 0910 *Nevada* was ordered to run aground.

The Japanese claimed that the dive-bombers added another 21 hits to targets on Battleship Row, but only *California* was actually attacked. At 0845 between one and three Type 99s attacked the battleship and scored a single hit that penetrated to the second deck before exploding and causing many casualties and a fire. The only battleship not located in Battleship Row was fleet flagship *Pennsylvania* located in Drydock Number 1. Undamaged by the first wave, she came under attack by as many as nine dive-bombers. At 0906 the battleship took a single hit that caused light damage and killed 18 officers and enlisted men. Two destroyers, *Cassin* and *Downes*, were located in the same drydock and were hit by the bombs which missed *Pennsylvania*. After a magazine explosion on *Cassin* and extensive fires, both ships became constructive losses.

At least ten Type 99s conducted attacks on the Navy Yard area presumably to hit the two heavy and two light cruisers present. Egusa himself selected heavy cruiser *New Orleans* but missed. Light cruiser *Honolulu* suffered a near miss that caused light damage, and *St. Louis* suffered three near misses but no damage. Another four dive-bombers attacked *Helena* at the 1010 Pier but missed. The only other cruiser attacked was *Raleigh*, still struggling to stay afloat from her earlier torpedo damage. As many as five Type 99s selected her for attack and at 0908 scored a hit that pierced the hull to explode outside. Despite more flooding, the cruiser did not sink.

Other attacks are hard to explain. Inexplicably several destroyers came under attack. At 0912, as many as eight dive-bombers attacked destroyer *Shaw* in a drydock. Hit by three bombs and set on fire, the ship was abandoned and later destroyed by a magazine explosion. Other Type 99s were reported to have attacked destroyers *Dale* and *Helm* while both were underway. Two seaplane tenders also came under attack. A damaged dive-bomber crashed on *Curtiss* and started a fire, and the ship's hangar was later hit by a single bomb that caused heavy casualties. Seaplane tender *Tangier* was attacked by as many as five dive-bombers but suffered no damage.

OPPOSITE Wrecked destroyers *Downes* and *Cassin* in Drydock Number 1 after being struck by dive-bombers in the second wave. Battleship *Pennsylvania* is behind the destroyers, and the torpedo-damaged cruiser *Helena* is beyond the drydock to the right. (Naval History and Heritage Command)

ABOVE This view was taken from the 1010 Pier toward the Navy Yard's drydocks. The fire at right is destroyer *Shaw* burning in drydock. In the foreground is the capsized minelayer *Oglala* with light cruiser *Helena* further down the pier. The large fire beyond *Helena* is from Drydock Number 1, which contained *Pennsylvania* and the burning destroyers *Cassin* and *Downes*. (Naval History and Heritage Command)

RIGHT The very poor performance of the second attack wave's dive-bombers can be explained by examining this photograph. Several important factors affecting the accuracy of the dive-bombers are immediately evident. First is the large volume of smoke over the target area. The intensity of American antiaircraft fire is also noteworthy. Most important are the low clouds over the harbor, which prevented reliable target selection and made the aircraft conduct dives from lower altitudes. (Naval History and Heritage Command)

The results of the dive-bomber attack were extremely disappointing for the Japanese. They claimed 49 hits, but the actual number was probably 15. American antiaircraft fire was fairly heavy during this point in the battle, which resulted in the loss of 14 dive-bombers. An accuracy rate of under 20 percent against stationary targets is hard to explain. There was considerable smoke in the harbor area, but the best explanation was the 70–90 percent low overcast over the harbor during the attack. In addition to their poor accuracy, the dive-bomber pilots were also guilty of poor target selection and grossly exaggerated battle-damage assessment reports.

In addition to pummeling the ships in the harbor, first- and second-wave aircraft hit the various airfields located around the island. Beginning at 0751 *Zuikaku*'s dive-bombers attacked Wheeler Field where some 120 fighters were parked in neat rows. Thirty-three PBY patrol aircraft were present at Kaneohe Naval Air Station. Between *Shokaku* and *Zuikaku* fighters in the first wave and 18 level bombers from *Shokaku* in the second, 27 of the PBYs were destroyed with the remaining six damaged. Ewa Mooring Mast Field was the home of Marine Air Group 21 with 49 aircraft. At the end of the raid, 33 of Ewa's aircraft were damaged or destroyed.

Ford Island Naval Air Station was home to two patrol squadrons and many other miscellaneous aircraft. After the work of *Shokaku* dive-bombers and level bombers, aided by *Kaga* fighters, 33 aircraft were lost including 19 PBY patrol planes. Hickam Field was a key target as it was the principal bomber base on the island. At the beginning of the attack, 12 B-17s, 32 B-18s, and 12 A-20s were lined up in rows. After the work of dive-bombers, fighters, and level bombers, five B-17s, seven B-18s, and two A-20s were destroyed and another 19 damaged.

Despite a persistent myth to the contrary, the Japanese never seriously considered launching a third wave. Nagumo was content to withdraw as soon as he recovered his aircraft. The first wave began to return at about 0950 hours and immediately began its recovery. By 1115, aircraft of the second wave began their recovery and one hour later the last aircraft was aboard. Heavy seas made the recovery challenging, and according to one Japanese source, as many as 20 aircraft were forced to ditch or were thrown overboard as a result of unrepairable battle damage or heavy landings. Following the recovery, the fleet headed northwest at 26 knots.

The Japanese raid on Pearl Harbor accounted for 18 American ships either sunk or damaged. Damage was concentrated on the eight battleships present. Of these, three returned to service in just weeks, one in 1943, and two in 1944 while two (*Arizona* and *Oklahoma*) never returned to service. Since slow battleships were not useful in the kind of war the Pacific Fleet now faced, Yamamoto had

This view of Battleship Row taken on December 10 shows the aftermath of the Japanese attack. Visible in the upper left is *California*, which has settled on the harbor floor. From left to right are *Maryland* (lightly damaged) with the capsized *Oklahoma* outboard, *Tennessee* (lightly damaged) with the sunken *West Virginia* outboard, and *Arizona* showing the effect of the explosion of her forward magazines. (Naval History and Heritage Command)

failed to deal the Americans a knockout blow. The strategic considerations of the attack are beyond the scope of this book, but since the attack galvanized American society and undermined any prospects of a negotiated peace, Pearl Harbor was a strategic disaster for the Japanese.

What was undeniable was the striking power displayed by the *Kido Butai*. In return for sinking or damaging 18 ships, destroying 97 USN and 77 US Army aircraft, and killing 2,335 American personnel and wounding another 1,143, Japanese losses were ridiculously small. Aircraft losses totaled 29, consisting of nine Zeros, 15 Type 99s, and five Type 97s. The cost to ravage the Pacific Fleet's battle line was only five torpedo planes. Only one dive-bomber and three Zeros were lost attacking the airfields. Another 17 dive-bombers, 11 Zeros, and at least 18 Type 97s were damaged, and some were forced to ditch when they returned to their carriers. Between the destroyed and damaged aircraft, about a third (55) of the 183 aircraft in the first wave were hit. The second wave suffered more heavily as the volume of antiaircraft fire increased. Of the 167 aircraft, 20 were lost (14 dive-bombers and six Zeros) and 16 Type 97, 41 dive-bombers, and eight Zeros were damaged for a total of 85 aircraft. These were heavy losses against a surprised enemy and would have made a third attack difficult had the Japanese seriously considered it.

AFTER PEARL HARBOR: THE *KIDO BUTAI* RUNS AMOK

Following the Pearl Harbor attack, the Japanese executed their plan to seize a list of objectives throughout the Pacific. It was at this point that Yamamoto began a pattern of dividing up the *Kido Butai* to support various operations concurrently. Had it been maintained as a single force, the *Kido Butai* would have possessed overwhelming strength against any possible combination of USN carriers. The division of the Combined Fleet's carrier force gave the USN opportunities to defeat it piecemeal and led directly to the disaster at Midway.

On December 11 the Japanese invasion of Wake was repulsed by the Marine garrison. To take the island before the Americans could mount a relief operation, on December 16 Yamamoto ordered the detachment of *Soryu* and *Hiryu* to support a second invasion attempt. From 350nm away, the carriers launched a strike of 29 dive-bombers and 18 Zeros on the morning of December 21. The strike encountered no opposition. The following day, 33 Type 97s escorted by six Zeros struck the island again. The last two Marine F4F Wildcats were shot down, but in return the Japanese lost two Type 97s and a third was forced to ditch. The next morning, Japanese troops landed on the island with the carriers flying five strikes to provide cover.

The *Kido Butai* was busy after the Pearl Harbor attack. This is a Zero taking off from *Zuikaku* on January 20, 1942, during the attack on Rabaul in the South Pacific. (Yamato Museum)

The same day, the rest of the *Kido Butai* reached Hashirajima Anchorage in the Inland Sea. After a short rest, it departed on January 8 for Truk in the Central Pacific with orders to support the occupation of Rabaul. In a case of using a hammer to smash an egg, on January 20, *Akagi*, *Kaga*, *Shokaku*, and *Zuikaku* arrived at a point some 200nm north of Rabaul and launched a strike of 111 aircraft (47 Type 97, 38 Type 99, and 26 Zeros). There were few targets to hit. Meager Royal Australian Air Force opposition was brushed aside, and only three Japanese aircraft were lost. The following day *Akagi* and *Kaga* hit targets at Kavieng, while *Shokaku* and *Zuikaku* moved into the Bismarck Sea to hit targets on New Guinea. Opposition was negligible and no aircraft were lost. On January 22, Rabaul was subjected to another attack by 18 Type 97s, 16 Type 99s, and only 12 Zeros and two dive-bombers were lost. Rabaul was occupied on January 23 against weak Australian opposition. The *Kido Butai* provided cover for the landings and then headed back to Truk.

While the bulk of the *Kido Butai* was in the South Pacific, *Hiryu* and *Soryu* were sent south to support operations in the Netherlands East Indies (NEI). They reached Palau on the 17th and on January 24 launched a strike of 54 aircraft against Ambon in the eastern NEI. No worthwhile targets were found and no aircraft were lost. Both carriers detached nine dive-bombers and nine fighters to operate from shore bases. Following the occupation of Rabaul, *Akagi* and *Kaga* joined *Hiryu* and *Soryu* at Palau on February 8, while *Shokaku* and *Zuikaku* remained in home waters to contend with any possible USN carrier raid.

The reformed *Kido Butai* now prepared to hit Darwin, which was the major Allied base in northwestern Australia feeding reinforcements to the NEI. The fleet departed Palau on the 15th and four days later was located some 220nm north of Darwin. A total of 188 aircraft were launched, making this the biggest air attack since Pearl Harbor. The strike consisted of 71 dive-bombers and 81 Type 97s escorted by 36 Zeros. Against ineffective opposition, the Japanese sank six large ships (including a USN destroyer) in the harbor and shot down 30 Allied aircraft. However, these bombing results were disappointing since another 20 ships survived. Accuracy from the Type 97s dropping from 10,000 feet was poor, and the dive-bombers that followed had problems with target selection and smoke from the preceding level bomber attack. In the afternoon two additional ships were attacked by dive-bombers north of Darwin and sunk. Total Japanese losses were two dive-bombers, one Type 97, and one Zero.

The *Kido Butai* returned to Staring Bay in the Celebes on February 21 and departed four days later for its next operation. With the invasion of Java scheduled for late February, the Japanese expected a large number of ships to flee the NEI as Allied defenses collapsed. Accordingly, the *Kido Butai* took up a position south of the Sunda Strait on March 1. Dive-bombers sank two USN ships (an oiler and a destroyer) the same day. On March 5 the *Kido Butai* sent a 149-aircraft strike to hit the port of Tjilatjap in southern Java, which was now the only port available for evacuation. Against no opposition, the Japanese sank a Dutch minelayer under construction and five merchant ships. Another nine ships were damaged and were later scuttled to prevent their capture. No Japanese aircraft were lost and the fleet returned to Staring Bay on March 11. On the 15th, *Kaga* was ordered to return to Japan since damage suffered on February 9 in a grounding incident at Palau had got worse and required permanent repair.

The next operation of the *Kido Butai* was one of its largest of the war and second only to the Pearl Harbor operation. *Shokaku* and *Zuikaku* arrived at Staring Bay on March 24. Two days later the fleet departed and headed for the Indian Ocean. This sortie was mounted to cover the movement of a large Japanese troop convoy to Rangoon in Burma, but its larger mission was to cripple British sea power in the region. For the only time in the war, the *Kido Butai* included all four Kongo-class battleships. Carrier *Ryujo* also participated with a group of cruisers to disrupt British shipping along the Indian coast.

On April 3 the *Kido Butai* entered the Indian Ocean and headed for Ceylon for a planned April 5 strike on Colombo. The following day the fleet was spotted by a British flying boat, but Nagumo decided to stick to the original plan. The Japanese knew that the Royal Navy had assembled a strong force in the region, but no information was available on its movements. On the morning of April 5, the Japanese began launching a strike of 38 dive-bombers, 53 Type 97s

This is the *Kido Butai* on March 26, 1942 departing Staring Bay in the NEI on its way to conduct the raid in the Indian Ocean. This impressive display of naval might was taken from *Akagi* and includes *Soryu*, *Hiryu*, the four Kongo-class battleships, *Zuikaku*, and *Shokaku*. (Yamato Museum)

with bombs, and 36 Zeros to hit Colombo. A force of dive-bombers and torpedo-armed Type 97s was held in reserve in case the British fleet was spotted. Despite having a day's warning, a considerable amount of British shipping was still in the harbor when the Japanese arrived. British opposition was heavy with 42 defending fighters and intense antiaircraft fire. Contending with this and thick cloud cover over the harbor, the dive-bombers only managed to sink an armed merchant cruiser and damage a submarine depot ship. The level bombers sank a destroyer and damaged a merchant ship. Thirty-three British aircraft were shot down by the Zeros, while Japanese losses were six dive-bombers and a Zero.

The limited bombing results prompted Fuchida to recommend a second attack to Nagumo. Having seen nothing of the British fleet, Nagumo ordered that the reserve Type 97s armed with torpedoes aboard *Shokaku* and *Zuikaku* be rearmed with bombs. Some of the dive-bombers aboard the other carriers were reloaded with bombs more suited for land attack. As this was occurring, a floatplane from cruiser *Tone* spotted two British cruisers only 150nm west of the *Kido Butai*. Doctrine called for a combined torpedo-dive-bomber attack against such heavily armored warships, so Nagumo ordered the rearming of the Type 97s reversed and the torpedoes remounted. A second report from a different floatplane identified the ships as destroyers. Nagumo ordered the reserve dive-bombers sent aloft to deal with this force. A third report from another floatplane identified the cruisers correctly as British Kent-class heavy cruisers, so the Type 97s continued to prepare for an attack.

The 53 dive-bombers already launched were under the command of Egusa. What followed was an almost perfect display of dive-bombing. The Type 99s approached from dead ahead and out of the sun, blinding the ships' antiaircraft gunners. One of the dive-bombers could not release its weapon, but the other 52 did with remarkably accurate results. Most of the pilots scored direct hits or near misses. *Dorsetshire* quickly sank after ten hits and many near misses and *Cornwall* followed her down after nine hits and six near misses.

After this success, the *Kido Butai* withdrew and prepared to strike Trincomalee on northeast Ceylon on April 9. Despite being spotted by British flying boats on the 8th, Nagumo pressed on and launched a strike of 91 Type 97s escorted by 38 Zeros as scheduled the next morning. All the fleet's dive-bombers were kept in reserve in case the British fleet was spotted. Most shipping had already cleared the harbor, but the level bombers sank one merchant ship and damaged monitor *Erebus*. The Zeros destroyed nine defending British fighters in the air, and another 14 British aircraft were destroyed on the ground.

While Trincomalee was under assault, Japanese floatplanes spotted warships that had earlier fled the harbor. This time the targets included carrier *Hermes* and

several other smaller ships. Nagumo quickly dispatched his reserve force of 85 dive-bombers and nine Zeros to deal with this threat. After some difficulty, *Hermes* was spotted and another display of dive-bombing excellence ensued. Of the 45 bombs dropped, the Japanese claimed 37 hits. This was confirmed by British reporting of the attack. In addition to *Hermes*, a nearby Australian destroyer, a corvette, two tankers, and a freighter were also sunk.

The first aircraft carrier sunk by carrier aircraft was the Royal Navy's *Hermes* in April 1942. Against the dive-bombers of the *Kido Butai*, the slow *Hermes*, with an inadequate antiaircraft battery and no fighter protection, stood no chance. (Naval History and Heritage Command)

British fighters arrived too late but managed to shoot down four Type 99s and damage another five.

For the first time in the war, the *Kido Butai* came under attack on April 9. The attack was mounted by Number 11 Squadron, Royal Air Force (RAF), with 11 Blenheim IV light bombers from Colombo. Two of the aircraft were forced to abort, leaving nine bombers to press on. The *Kido Butai* had no radar and on this occasion the lookouts totally failed to spot the British aircraft. The first sign of trouble was when bombs exploded around *Akagi* and cruiser *Tone*. None of these hit their targets, but the British had gained complete surprise, and the *Akagi* did not even fire a single shot in self-defense. The Zeros finally reacted and shot down five bombers in exchange for two of their own. Had the British bombers been more proficient in maritime attack, the Japanese could have suffered an embarrassing and serious blow.

AMERICAN CARRIER OPERATIONS AFTER PEARL HARBOR

The failed Japanese attempt to take Wake Island on December 11 gave Vice Admiral William S. Pye, acting Pacific Fleet Commander, the opportunity to mount a relief operation. After much delay, a relief force consisting of *Saratoga* with three heavy cruisers, nine destroyers, a seaplane tender, and an oiler was assembled and placed under the command of Rear Admiral Fletcher. *Lexington* and *Enterprise* were also deployed, but remained beyond support range of the relief force. On December 21 the relief operation gained urgency when reports came in of the island being subjected to carrier air attack. Had Pye concentrated his three carriers, he would have had a perfect opportunity to defeat part of the *Kido Butai*. When a Japanese landing on the island looked imminent, Pye called off the relief attack late on December 22. This was a wise choice; had *Saratoga* pressed on against *Hiryu* and *Soryu*, the result would probably have been disaster.

When Nimitz took over the Pacific Fleet on December 31, King directed him to consider carrier raids against the Japanese-held Gilbert and Marshall island groups. Nimitz needed no urging to act aggressively and by January 2 had orders in place for the first USN carrier raids of the war. The Pacific Fleet received an important reinforcement when King sent *Yorktown* to the Pacific. The carrier entered San Diego on December 30, bringing the Pacific Fleet's carrier strength to four. This did not last long. On January 11, *Saratoga* was hit by a single torpedo from Japanese submarine *I-6* some 400 miles southwest of Pearl Harbor. Repairs were estimated to take several months; in fact, the ship did not return to service until June.

The first American carrier raid of the war was to have been conducted by *Lexington* against Wake. However, when the task force's accompanying oiler was sunk by a Japanese submarine, the raid was called off. Other planned carrier raids included *Enterprise* attacking targets in the Marshalls-Gilberts with *Yorktown* concurrently attacking targets in the Gilberts. Many officers on Nimitz's staff considered the raids too risky since there seemed little prospect of gaining surprise. With the support of Halsey, Nimitz brushed aside such caution and planning continued.

The first raid by the *Enterprise* and *Yorktown* task groups was scheduled for February 1. Aircraft from *Enterprise* would hit targets on Wotje, Taroa, Roi, and Kwajalein Islands in the northern Marshalls. Surface ships would follow up with bombardments of Wotje, Maloelap, and Taroa. *Yorktown*, under Fletcher, was ordered to hit targets on Makin in the Gilberts, and Jaluit and Milli in the southern Marshalls. Japanese opposition was expected to be light. In fact, no major Combined Fleet units were present in the area, and the 24th Air Flotilla had only 33 fighters, nine Type 96 twin-engined attack aircraft, and nine flying boats available.

Both American task forces approached their targets undetected. The ensuing air strikes faced generally weak opposition. Epitomizing Halsey's offensive mindset, at one point *Enterprise* had all her aircraft in the air and was escorted by only a handful of destroyers. *Enterprise*'s strikes included 18 Devastators armed with bombs and 46 Dauntlesses. The American pilots claimed severe damage to ships anchored offshore and to infrastructure ashore. In fact, damage was light with a light cruiser, an old minelayer, and five auxiliary or transport ships being damaged. Only one small auxiliary gunboat was sunk. Four Japanese aircraft were shot down and some ten destroyed on the ground. Six American aircraft were lost. Heavy cruiser *Chester* suffered a hit from a small bomb and was lightly damaged. The most serious moment for Halsey was when five Type 96 medium bombers lined up for an attack on *Enterprise* in the early afternoon. The ship's radar picked up the approaching Japanese, but the fighter direction officer had difficulty determining if the contacts were enemy or friendly. The bombers survived a Wildcat interception and each released three bombs against the carrier. These were dodged by skillful maneuvering by the ship's captain, but one still landed just 30 feet away from the port side. One of the bombers, previously damaged by the Wildcats, headed for *Enterprise* with the intention of crashing on the ship. The bomber hit the flight deck and crashed over the side, causing little damage, but destroyed a Dauntless in the process. Later in the afternoon, two more Type 96s were able to approach the carrier for a second attack. The combat air patrol did not engage, so the ship's 5-inch guns opened up on the approaching Japanese. The bombers survived to drop their weapons some 125 yards from *Enterprise*, and Wildcats subsequently shot down one of the retreating aircraft. On her raid against Makin, Jaluit, and Milli, *Yorktown* launched a strike of 37 aircraft but they inflicted little damage. Four Devastators and two Dauntlesses failed to return.

Next up was the newly captured Japanese base at Rabaul. Vice Admiral Wilson Brown, commanding *Lexington* escorted by four heavy cruisers and ten destroyers, conceived the idea of the attack that was approved for February 21. The plan called for an air attack launched only 125nm away from Rabaul followed by a surface bombardment. Allied intelligence on Japanese forces at Rabaul was scanty, but the Japanese were much stronger than they had been in the Marshalls and Gilberts. The Japanese were expecting a carrier raid, and on the morning of February 20 their suspicions were confirmed when an H6K4 Type 97 flying boat spotted the American task force some 460nm east of Rabaul. Having lost the element of surprise, Brown canceled the raid. The Japanese sent 17 G4M medium bombers from Rabaul to destroy the retreating carrier. Each carried two 551lb bombs as no torpedoes were available. The aircraft were detected on radar 76nm from *Lexington*. The first group of nine bombers was ravaged by Wildcats. Only four survived to drop their bombs and these all missed. One bomber was hit by antiaircraft fire and tried to crash on *Lexington* but missed 75 yards astern. The second group of eight bombers was also intercepted, but only two Wildcats were available to mount an

The first American early war carrier raid was conducted by *Enterprise* against the Marshall Islands on February 1, 1942. The carrier was subjected to two air attacks; in this scene .50-caliber machine guns are in action against the Japanese. Note the Dauntless dive-bomber in the background. (Naval History and Heritage Command)

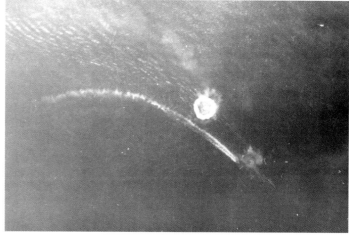

ABOVE A Douglas TBD-1 Devastator from *Enterprise* flies over Wake Island during the February 24, 1942 raid. Little damage was done to the Japanese on this occasion or on any of the early 1942 raids. (Naval History and Heritage Command)

RIGHT The most impactful early war American carrier raid was the March 10, 1942 attack at Lae-Salamaua. In this view, taken by a Devastator from *Yorktown*, seaplane tender *Kiyokawa Maru* is under attack. The ship was damaged and was forced to miss Operation MO. Most importantly, the raid stopped Japanese expansion in the South Pacific until protection could be provided against further American carrier raids. (Naval History and Heritage Command) immediate attack. Fortunately for the Americans, one of these was piloted by Lieutenant Edward "Butch" O'Hare, known as an expert marksman. He quickly flamed four bombers; the other four dropped their weapons with the closest hitting 100 feet astern of the carrier. All told, only two of the 17 G4Ms returned to base.

To keep the Japanese off balance and in the vain hope that further raids could slow Japanese advances in Southeast Asia, Nimitz planned additional operations. Halsey again led *Enterprise* with two heavy cruisers and six destroyers to hit Wake. The raid took place on February 24 with 36 strike aircraft escorted by six Wildcats. Only one aircraft was lost against ineffective opposition, but damage to the Japanese was meager. The air attack was followed by a brief surface bombardment. On March 4, Halsey hit Marcus Island with 37 aircraft, again losing only a single aircraft but also inflicting little damage. *Yorktown* was to have supported these raids with one against Eniwetok in the Carolines but was recalled to provide cover for crucial troop convoys in the South Pacific.

Yorktown joined *Lexington* in the South Pacific as Japanese pressure grew in the region. On March 8 the Japanese conducted landings on New Guinea at two points. Fletcher was in charge of the task force which featured two carriers in the same formation in combat for the first time. He took both carriers north to launch a 104-aircraft strike over the Owen Stanley Mountains against Japanese shipping off Lae and Salamaua on March 10. The Americans achieved complete surprise and proceeded to bomb against little opposition. Despite the aviators' claims of great success, actual Japanese losses consisted of an armed merchant cruiser, a transport, and a converted minesweeper sunk and several other ships damaged. However, this raid had strategic implications since it convinced the Japanese that further advances in the South Pacific could not be made until the Combined Fleet provided carrier cover.

While *Yorktown* and *Lexington* were busy in the South Pacific, the Pacific Fleet's other two carriers were preparing for the most audacious raid of all. On April 2 the newly arrived *Hornet* departed San Francisco with a deckload of 16 B-25 medium bombers. The bold plan was to use these to hit Tokyo and two other Japanese cities. *Hornet* rendezvoused with *Enterprise* on April 13 and headed west under Halsey's command. Early on April 18 the task force was spotted by a line of Japanese picket boats while still some 700nm from Japan. Halsey ordered the B-25s to take off even at this extended range. The Japanese, unaware that the Americans would launch medium bombers off carriers, did not expect an attack on the 18th. The bombers reached their targets in Tokyo, Nagoya, and Kobe and caught the Japanese totally by surprise. Only light damage was inflicted on the Japanese, though one bomber did hit light carrier *Ryuho* being converted at Yokosuka. The American task force withdrew at high speed and reached Pearl Harbor on April 25.

The most spectacular American early war carrier operation was the April 1942 raid on the Japanese Home Islands conducted by the B-25 medium bombers shown here on *Hornet*. The raid may have buoyed American morale, but it also prevented Nimitz from achieving overwhelming superiority against the Japanese invasion of Port Moresby. (Naval History and Heritage Command)

The raid on Tokyo has become legend. But the raid was no more than a stunt conducted at the behest of President Roosevelt to improve American morale. A myth associated with the raid is that it prompted the Japanese to attack Midway in a bid to lure the American carriers to their destruction. This is entirely false, as, on April 5, almost a full two weeks before the B-25s appeared over Tokyo, the Japanese had already decided to conduct the Midway operation. The biggest strategic impact of the raid was that it took two carriers out of circulation for almost the entire month of April. It was during this period that Nimitz decided to marshal all his available carriers to oppose the next Japanese move in the South Pacific, which intelligence indicated could happen in early May. This resulted in the first carrier battle of the war in the Coral Sea. *Lexington* and *Yorktown* were in position to check this Japanese advance, but Nimitz wanted all four carriers in the Coral Sea to create a numerical advantage against the two fleet carriers the Japanese were assessed to have committed to the operation. The Tokyo diversion meant that *Enterprise* and *Hornet* arrived in the Coral Sea a few days after the battle had concluded. Had all four American carriers been in the Coral Sea at the start of the battle, the outcome could have been even more disastrous for the Japanese.

The first six months of war were full of surprises for both sides. After Pearl Harbor the aircraft carrier became the paramount fleet unit. Most American and Japanese battleships were reduced to irrelevance since they lacked the speed to keep up with the carriers. The power of the *Kido Butai* was evident for all to see; the Japanese ability to mass naval air power had carried all before it. But even the *Kido Butai* did not have everything its own way. By May 1942 accumulated aircraft losses were enough to prevent any Japanese carrier from embarking a full complement of aircraft. During the Indian Ocean adventure of April 1942, issues came to light that were a portent of more problems to come. The Japanese recognized the necessity of improving their air search procedures and the need for better ship recognition training. To augment the slow Type 97s and floatplanes used for scouting, two pre-production Yokosuka D4Y1 Navy Carrier Bombers (hereafter referred to as D4Y) with a top speed of 343mph were modified as reconnaissance aircraft and embarked on *Soryu*. The Japanese took measures to address the speed and accuracy of reconnaissance reports, but the real problem was the lack of search depth. IJN doctrine called for a single-phase search, meaning that a scouting track was flown by a single aircraft, instead of a two-phase search in which a second aircraft would fly along the same scouting track after a specific time interval. In the era before radar and in poor visibility conditions, a two-phase search provided much better coverage. Air defense was shown to be a potential weakness as the sudden appearance of nine RAF Blenheims over the *Kido Butai* on April 9 dramatically demonstrated. No radar and no system for fighter direction was a recipe for disaster against an opponent trained for ship attack.

The series of American carrier raids gave the ships and their air groups invaluable operational experience even though they had little or no effect on Japanese naval capabilities. It is questionable if the raids were worth the risk. The risk was especially high for Halsey during the Marshalls raid, when he operated in the same area for several hours within range of three Japanese airfields. If any of the American carriers had suffered an unlucky hit which impaired its steaming capability, the likelihood of the ship being lost was high. The early raids showed the immaturity of American fighter direction efforts and shipboard antiaircraft defenses. The Lae-Salamaua raid in March showed the utility of two carriers operating in a single task force. The raids did restore the Pacific Fleet's morale after a string of defeats. American admirals were confident of the capabilities of their carriers going into the first of four carrier battles in 1942.

CHAPTER 3
CLASH OF CARRIERS IN THE CORAL SEA

JAPAN'S PATH TO THE CORAL SEA

The First Operational Stage outlined by the Japanese at the start of the war included the occupation of the Philippines, British Malaya, the NEI, Burma, and Rabaul. In the Second Operational Phase, Japan planned to increase its strategic depth by adding eastern New Guinea, New Britain, the Aleutians, Midway, the Fijis, Samoa, and "strategic points in the Australian area." Once Rabaul was captured, the Japanese thought it was necessary to seize additional points to the south to provide defensive depth. These included eastern New Guinea and Tulagi in the Solomons. Once these were occupied, the Japanese could create a network of air bases to defeat Allied attacks. Accordingly, the Naval General Staff approved the seizure of Lae, Salamaua, Tulagi, and Port Moresby in eastern New Guinea on January 29, 1942. Port Moresby was especially valuable, as its capture would eliminate the threat of American long-range bombing attacks on Rabaul while providing Japanese aircraft access to the Coral Sea and targets in northeastern Australia.

The first part of the Second Operational Phase unfolded when Lae and Salamaua were captured on March 8. However, the entire situation in the South

Pacific was altered on March 10 when aircraft from *Lexington* and *Yorktown* struck the Lae and Salamaua invasion force. This action deterred additional Japanese advances in the South Pacific until they were reinforced to deal with potential future intervention by American carriers.

The prospects for getting some of the Combined Fleet's carriers allocated to support further advances in the South Pacific looked uncertain in March. The Naval General Staff and the Navy Section of Imperial General Headquarters favored further expansion in the South Pacific and began to study operations to seize New Caledonia, the Fijis, and Samoa after the rescheduled Port Moresby operation. Yamamoto's priority was in the Central Pacific where he planned to force a decisive battle with what he considered the USN's center of gravity – its carriers. He preferred to delay any South Pacific advance until after what he believed would be a decisive clash at Midway. During the first week of April, Yamamoto got the Midway operation approved, but to placate the Naval General Staff it was agreed that the *Kido Butai*'s Carrier Division 5 would support the invasion of Port Moresby before it was allocated to the Midway operation.

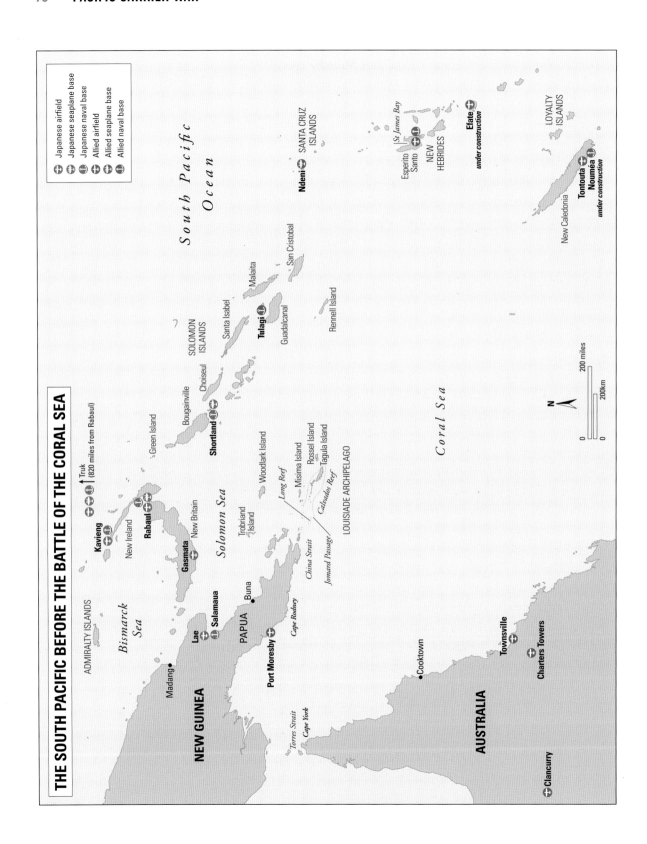

THE SOUTH PACIFIC BEFORE THE BATTLE OF THE CORAL SEA

Japanese airfield
Japanese seaplane base
Japanese naval base
Allied airfield
Allied seaplane base
Allied naval base

Truk
(820 miles from Rabaul)

ADMIRALTY ISLANDS

Madang

NEW GUINEA

Bismarck
Sea

Kavieng

New Ireland

Rabaul
New Britain

Gasmata

Salamaua
Lae

PAPUA
Buna

Port Moresby

Cape Rodney

Solomon Sea

Trobriand
Island

China Strait

Jomard Passage

Long Reef

Calvados Reef

LOUISIADE ARCHIPELAGO

Woodlark Island

Misima Island

Rossel Island

Tagula Island

Green Island

Bougainville

Choiseul

Shortland

SOLOMON
ISLANDS

Santa Isabel

Tulagi
Guadalcanal

Malaita

San Cristobal

Rennell Island

SANTA CRUZ
ISLANDS

Ndeni

St James Bay

Esperito
Santo

NEW
HEBRIDES

Efate
under construction

LOYALTY
ISLANDS

Tontouta
Nouméa
under construction

New Caledonia

South Pacific
Ocean

Coral Sea

Cape York
Torres Strait

Cooktown

Townsville

Charters Towers

AUSTRALIA

Clancurry

N

0   200 miles

0   200km

Operation MO (the IJN name for the Port Moresby operation) featured a force of some 60 ships assigned to Vice Admiral Inoue Shigeyoshi's South Seas Force. This included *Shokaku* and *Zuikaku*, light carrier *Shoho*, six heavy cruisers, three light cruisers, and 15 destroyers. Altogether, some 250 aircraft were assigned to the operation with some 140 aircraft aboard the three carriers. In the first phase of the operation, Tulagi in the southern Solomon Islands would be captured on May 3 to protect the left flank of the operation and extend the range of Japanese air searches. The occupation of Tulagi would be supported by the MO Main Force that included *Shoho* and four heavy cruisers.

The next phase of Operation MO focused on neutralizing Allied air and naval power. Inoue considered Allied land-based aircraft as the greatest threat to the Port Moresby invasion. The problem for the Japanese was that the principal Allied bases in northeastern Australia were beyond the range of Japanese land-based bombers at Rabaul. Local Japanese commanders believed that there were no American carriers in the South Pacific even though Fletcher's March 10 raid had provided clear evidence to the contrary. The supposed absence of American carriers made the primary mission of the MO Striking Force the neutralization of Allied air bases in Australia. To minimize the chances of early discovery, the two fleet carriers under Vice Admiral Takagi Takeo would pass between San Cristobal and Espiritu Santo and enter the Coral Sea from the east. Approaching from this direction, not from the north as the Allies would expect, would ostensibly permit the carriers to conduct surprise air raids on Townsville air base on May 7.

After the surprise attack on Townsville, the carriers would refuel and move to the center of the Coral Sea to intercept and attack reacting Allied naval forces. Additional air raids could be conducted on other Allied air bases as required. Following Operation MO, the carriers were scheduled to support the occupation of Ocean and Nauru Islands. Only after this would all three carriers assigned to Operation MO return to Japan to prepare for the invasion of Midway.

The MO Operation would culminate with a planned landing at Port Moresby on May 10. This required a slow transit by the invasion convoy over 1,000nm from Rabaul, scheduled to begin on May 4. Direct support for the convoy would be provided by the MO Main Force after it finished covering the Tulagi landing. The MO Covering Force was ordered to set up a seaplane base at Deboyne Island in the central Louisiades to provide reconnaissance support.

Japanese planning for Operation MO was a combination of wishful thinking and unsupported assumptions. It depended on the close coordination of widely separated forces; any delay had the potential to throw the entire operation into disarray. The complex MO Operation plan met resistance from the admirals expected to execute it. Rear Admiral Hara, commander of Carrier Division 5,

Rear Admiral Frank Fletcher was the commander of Allied naval forces at the battle of the Coral Sea. He was responsible for inflicting Japan's first strategic defeat of the Pacific War. (Naval History and Heritage Command)

advised against the planned air strikes against Australia primarily due to his belief that there was no hope of achieving surprise. This, and the growing suspicion that American carriers were still in the South Pacific, prompted Yamamoto to cancel the carrier strikes against bases in Australia. The primary mission of the MO Striking Force was now engaging American carriers.

How to provide air cover for the MO Invasion Force as it transited to Port Moresby presented a serious challenge. The 25th Air Flotilla based at Rabaul lacked the range to attack Allied air bases in Australia. This placed the burden of providing air defense for the invasion convoy on *Shoho* with her 12 fighters. With so few resources, defending the convoy against air attack for the last two days of its transit as it moved the final 350 miles to Port Moresby would have been problematic at best. The most damning part of the plan for Operation MO was its utter disregard for the actions of the enemy. By committing only a portion of the *Kido Butai* to the operation, Yamamoto not only jeopardized its success, but exposed the two carriers to defeat in detail. If lost or damaged, they would be unable to participate in Yamamoto's decisive Midway operation. The two carriers of Carrier Division 5 constituted the IJN's decisive edge over the USN's four-carrier force. Yamamoto had made his critical Midway operation hostage to the outcome of the subsidiary MO Operation.

AMERICAN PLANS FOR CORAL SEA

King's first orders to Nimitz after he took command of the Pacific Fleet were to hold Hawaii and Midway in the Central Pacific while protecting the sea lines of communication to Australia. The Japanese seizure of Rabaul on January 23 heightened fears that the Fijis or New Caledonia were next. In response, the Americans dispatched the *Lexington* task group to the South Pacific in January and the *Yorktown* task force followed in mid-February. Nimitz gained King's endorsement to send *Enterprise* and *Hornet* to the South Pacific after their return from the Tokyo raid, but this force could not arrive in the Coral Sea earlier than May 14–16. Nimitz's decision to move all of the Pacific Fleet's striking power into the South Pacific was bold as it left Pearl Harbor uncovered by carriers. The movement of all four carriers into the South Pacific almost resulted in an excellent opportunity to defeat the *Kido Butai* in detail.

In contrast to the elaborate Japanese plan, the American plan for the forthcoming battle was simple. The combined Allied force was under the command of Rear Admiral Fletcher. On April 22, Nimitz warned Fletcher about the impending Japanese offensive and gave him an idea of the size of the enemy force, which was assessed to include three or four carriers. Fletcher was charged with stopping the Japanese advance by causing attrition to enemy ships and aircraft. Nimitz did not tell Fletcher how to accomplish the mission – that was totally up to Fletcher. On April 29, Nimitz issued further instructions along with updated intelligence. The latest intelligence predicted strikes on Port Moresby and Tulagi. Four primary Japanese task forces were identified – an invasion force for Tulagi and Port Moresby, a support force, and the carrier force. The estimate of enemy carriers was refined to three, but the intelligence did not discern the approach of the Japanese carriers from the east.

Fletcher's combined force consisted of TF 17's original *Yorktown*, three cruisers, and four destroyers and TF 11's *Lexington*, two cruisers, and five destroyers. Fletcher's strategy was to stay beyond the range of air searches from Rabaul (about 700nm) and seek favorable opportunities to intercept Japanese forces moving into the Coral Sea or down the Solomons. After the two task forces combined on May 1, Fletcher decided to move his force 325nm south of Guadalcanal to be prepared to react to any Japanese movement. Fletcher's plan was simple and flexible. With half of the Pacific Fleet's operational carriers entrusted to him, he displayed a combination of prudence and opportunistic aggressiveness. His focus was on protecting Port Moresby. Fletcher was hamstrung by inadequate air reconnaissance and logistical resources, both beyond his control. If there was a fault with his planning, it was the focus on the Coral Sea and the approaches to Port Moresby. No air searches were focused on the area east of the Solomons where, unknown to Fletcher, the greatest danger lay. Fletcher's deployment of his oilers was also faulty, again due to his ignorance of the danger on his eastern flank.

THE BATTLE OPENS

The MO Operation began to unfold at the end of April. On April 28, five H6K4 Type 97 flying boats were staged to a base at Shortland Island in the Solomons. These aircraft possessed the range to cover much of the Coral Sea. The next day, the Tulagi Invasion Force departed Rabaul and the Main Body departed Truk. On May 1 the MO Striking Force left Truk.

The battle opened on the morning of May 3 when Special Naval Landing Force troops landed unopposed on the islands of Tulagi and Gavutu in the southern Solomons. The occupation was supported by aircraft from Rabaul and from *Shoho*, which had moved to a position 180nm west of Tulagi.

CORAL SEA ORDERS OF BATTLE
IMPERIAL JAPANESE NAVY

TASK FORCE "MO" (VICE ADMIRAL INOUE SHIGEYOSHI)

MO Carrier Striking Force (Vice Admiral Takagi Takeo)
Carrier Division 5 (Rear Admiral Hara Tadaichi)
Carrier: *Shokaku* (Captain Jojima Takaji)

Shokaku Air Group (Lt Cdr Takahashi Kakuichi)	1 Type 99
Shokaku Carrier Fighter Unit	18 Zero
Shokaku Carrier Bomber Unit	20 Type 99
Shokaku Carrier Attack Unit	19 Type 97

TOTAL: 58 (56 operational) Plus 3 Zero for Tainan Air Group in Rabaul

Carrier: *Zuikaku* (Captain Yokogawa Ichihei)

Zuikaku Air Group (Lt Cdr Shimazaki Shigekazu)	1 Type 97
Zuikaku Carrier Fighter Unit	20 Zero
Zuikaku Carrier Bomber Unit	22 Type 99
Zuikaku Carrier Attack Unit	20 Type 97

TOTAL: 63 (53 operational) Plus 5 Zero for Tainan Air Group in Rabaul
Strengths as of May 6, 1942

Cruiser Division 5: Heavy Cruisers *Myoko*, *Haguro*
Destroyer Division 7: Destroyers *Ushio*, *Akebono*
Destroyer Division 27: Destroyers *Ariake*, *Yugure*, *Shiratsuyu*, *Shigure*
Oiler *Toho Maru*

MO Main Force (Rear Admiral Goto Aritomo)
Light Carrier *Shoho* (Captain Izawa Ishinosuke)
Shoho Air Group (Lt Notomi Kenjiro)

Shoho Carrier Fighter Unit	8 Zero, 4 Type 96 A5M2 Carrier Fighters
Shoho Carrier Attack Unit	6 Type 97

TOTAL: 18 (18 operational)
Strength as of May 6, 1942

Cruiser Division 6: Heavy Cruisers *Aoba*, *Kako*, *Kinugasa*, *Furutaka*
Destroyer *Sazanami* (from Destroyer Division 7)

MO Invasion Force (Rear Admiral Kajioka Sadamichi)
Destroyer Flotilla 6
   Light Cruiser *Yubari*
   Destroyer Squadron 29: Destroyers *Oite*, *Asanagi*
   Destroyer Squadron 30: Destroyers *Mutsuki*, *Mochizuki*, *Yayoi*
   Destroyer Squadron 23: Destroyer *Uzuki*
Minelayer: *Tsugaru*
Fleet Minesweeper Number 20
Navy Transports: *Goyo Maru*, *Akihasan Maru*, *Shokai Maru*, *Chowa Maru*, *Mogamikawa Maru*,
Ocean tug *Oshima*; Army Transports: *Matsue Maru*, *Taifuku Maru*, *Mito Maru*, *China Maru*,
Nichibi Maru, *Asakasan Maru* carrying bulk of 3rd Kure Special Naval Landing Force,
10th Establishment Unit (construction troops), and 144th Infantry Regiment (South Seas Detachment)

Covering Force (Rear Admiral Marumo Kuninori)
Cruiser Division 18: Light cruisers *Tatsuta*, *Tenryu*
Seaplane carrier *Kamikawa Maru* (with air group from *Kiyokawa Maru*)
5th Gunboat Squadron: Auxiliary gunboats *Nikkai Maru*, *Keijo Maru*
Transport *Shoei Maru* carrying elements of 3rd Kure Special Naval Landing Force

14th Minesweeper Flotilla: *Hagoromo Maru*, *Noshiro Maru Number 2* (from Tulagi Invasion Force May 3)

Tulagi Invasion Force (Rear Admiral Shima Kiyohide)
Minelayer *Okinoshima*
23rd Destroyer Squadron: Destroyers *Kikuzuki*, *Yuzuki*
14th Minesweeper Flotilla: *Tama Maru*, *Hagoromo Maru*, *Noshiro Maru Number 2* (moved to MO Covering Force May 3)
Special Minesweeper Number 1, *Special Minesweeper Number 2*
56th Submarine Chaser Squadron: Patrol boats *Tama Maru Number 8*, *Toshi Maru Number 3*
Transports *Azumayama Maru* and *Koei Maru* carrying elements of 3rd Kure Special Naval Landing Force and
7th Establishment Unit (construction troops)
Supply Units: Oilers *Ishiro*, *Hoyo Maru*

Land-based Air Force
25th Air Flotilla (Rear Admiral Yamada Sadayoshi at Rabaul)
 28 Zero fighters (18 operational)
 11 Type 96 A5M2 fighters (6 operational)
 28 G4M land-based bombers (17 operational)
 26 G3M land-based bombers (25 operational)
 16 H6K4 flying boats (12 operational)
 Strength as of May 1, 1942

ALLIED FORCES

TASK FORCE 17 (REAR ADMIRAL FRANK FLETCHER)

Task Group 17.5 (Rear Admiral Aubrey Fitch)
Carrier: *Lexington* (Captain Frederick Sherman)

Lexington Air Group (Cdr William Ault)	1 SBD-3
Fighting Two	21 F4F-3
Bombing Two	18 SBD-2/3
Scouting Two	17 SBD-3
Torpedo Two	13 TBD-1
TOTAL: 70 (66 operational)	

Carrier: *Yorktown* (Captain Elliott Buckmaster)

Yorktown Air Group (Lt Cdr Oscar Pederson)	
Fighting Forty-two	17 F4F-3
Bombing Five	18 SBD-3
Scouting Five	17 SBD-3
Torpedo Five	12 TBD-1
TOTAL: 64 (62 operational)	

Strengths as of May 7, 1942
Destroyers: *Morris*, *Anderson*, *Hammann*, *Russell*

Task Group 17.2 (Rear Admiral Thomas Kinkaid)
Heavy cruisers: *Minneapolis*, *New Orleans*, *Astoria*, *Chester*, *Portland*
Destroyers: *Phelps*, *Dewey*, *Farragut* (attached to TG 17.3 May 7), *Alywin*, *Monaghan*
(TG 17.2 never operated as an independent entity)

Task Group 17.3 (Rear Admiral J.G. Grace, Royal Navy)
Cruisers: HMAS *Australia*, HMAS *Hobart*, *Chicago*
Destroyers: *Perkins*, *Walker*
(TG 17.3 was the renamed TF 44 from the Southwest Pacific Area)

Fueling Group Task Group 17.6 (Captain John Phillips)
Oilers: *Neosho*, *Tippecanoe*
Destroyers: *Sims*, *Worden*

Even at this early point the tightly synchronized MO plan ran into trouble. The Striking Force was given the seemingly simple mission of ferrying nine Zeros from Truk to Rabaul. This was scheduled for May 2, when the carriers would be closest to Rabaul on their way south. But when the nine fighters took off, they were forced to return due to bad weather. The operation was attempted again the following day, but it was also thwarted by weather. This time one of the fighters was lost. The Striking Force was now two days behind schedule, but the Japanese persisted since the delivery of the fighters was viewed as critical if the 25th Air Flotilla was to gain air superiority over Port Moresby. The entire episode demonstrated the fragility of a plan which left little room for emerging problems, as in this case something as small as the simple transfer of nine fighters.

As the Japanese carriers were tied up with their fruitless ferry mission, on the evening of May 3, Fletcher received reports of the invasion of Tulagi. This was the information Fletcher had been waiting for in order to strike the Japanese. Early on May 3, TF 17 was moving slowly westward into the central Coral Sea as *Lexington* and TF 11 completed refueling. Strict radio silence denied Fletcher knowledge of TF 11's exact location, so when he learned of the invasion of Tulagi he chose to react immediately with TF 17. Fletcher and TF 17 headed north by 2030 hours, increasing speed to 27 knots to be in position to attack Japanese forces off Tulagi at dawn on May 4.

YORKTOWN STRIKES

Following the occupation of Tulagi, the Japanese invasion force was without air cover. *Shoho* had departed to cover the Port Moresby invasion convoy, and the MO Striking Force was still in the area of Rabaul completing its frustratingly difficult ferry mission. When *Yorktown*'s aircraft appeared over Tulagi on the morning of May 4, Japanese shipping off the island was caught completely by surprise and was largely defenseless.

At 0630, *Yorktown* began launching what would be the first of four strikes. The first wave consisted of 28 Dauntlesses and 12 Devastators armed with torpedoes. No fighter escort was provided since no air opposition was expected. The strike arrived over Tulagi at 0820. The most valuable targets were the large minelayer *Okinoshima* and two destroyers. Destroyer *Kikuzuki* was hit, forced to beach, and became a constructive loss. The first strike was quickly rearmed and refueled, and just after noon 27 Dauntlesses and 11 Devastators were again over Tulagi. A third wave of 21 dive-bombers departed *Yorktown* at 1400. Four fighters were also launched to strafe the Type 97 flying boats observed in Tulagi harbor. The overall return for this intensive effort was unimpressive. The Americans claimed two destroyers, one freighter, and four patrol craft sunk and a light cruiser driven aground. In reality only *Kikuzuki*, three small minesweepers, and four landing barges had been sunk. The most important result was the destruction of the five flying boats at the hands of strafing Wildcats. Total Japanese casualties were 87 killed and 124 wounded.

THE CARRIER FORCES MOVE TO CONTACT

Following the strike against Tulagi, Fletcher headed south at high speed to escape any Japanese counterattack. On the morning of the next day, TF 17 rendezvoused with TF 11 approximately 325nm south of Guadalcanal. From there Fletcher moved southeast and began to refuel TF 17. Around 1100, a Wildcat from *Yorktown* shot down a Type 97 flying boat from Shortland Island. Though the aircraft did not have time to send a signal that it was under attack, its destruction gave the Japanese a rough idea of the location of an American carrier.

Throughout May 5, neither carrier force had any real idea where the other was. The American raid on Tulagi had found the MO Striking Force refueling north of the Solomons. In response to the American attack, Takagi rushed to the southeast expecting to find an American carrier east of Tulagi. Since *Yorktown* was already steaming south, Takagi found nothing. Thus, he returned to the original plan and after rounding San Cristobal Island in the southern Solomons on the evening of May 5 turned west. Takagi planned to refuel on May 6, 180nm west of Tulagi, before entering the Coral Sea.

Though Fletcher was completely unaware of the position of the MO Striking Force, he was receiving extensive reporting from MacArthur's land-based aircraft on the location and movement of Japanese ships in the Solomon Sea. These included reports of carriers. At around noon on May 4, an American bomber reported a carrier off Bougainville in the northern Solomons. This was eventually reported to Fletcher as *Kaga*. On May 5, another contact was reported of a Japanese carrier southwest of Bougainville. MacArthur's airmen had actually sighted *Shoho* headed north to cover the MO Invasion Force.

On May 6 Fletcher merged his entire force into TF 17. His total strength was now two carriers, eight cruisers (two Australian), and 11 destroyers. In worsening weather, Fletcher ordered his combined force to head southeast throughout the day while refueling. The morning searches from TF 17 found nothing, although one Dauntless ended its planned search track a mere 20 miles from the MO Striking Force. Just after noon MacArthur's airmen

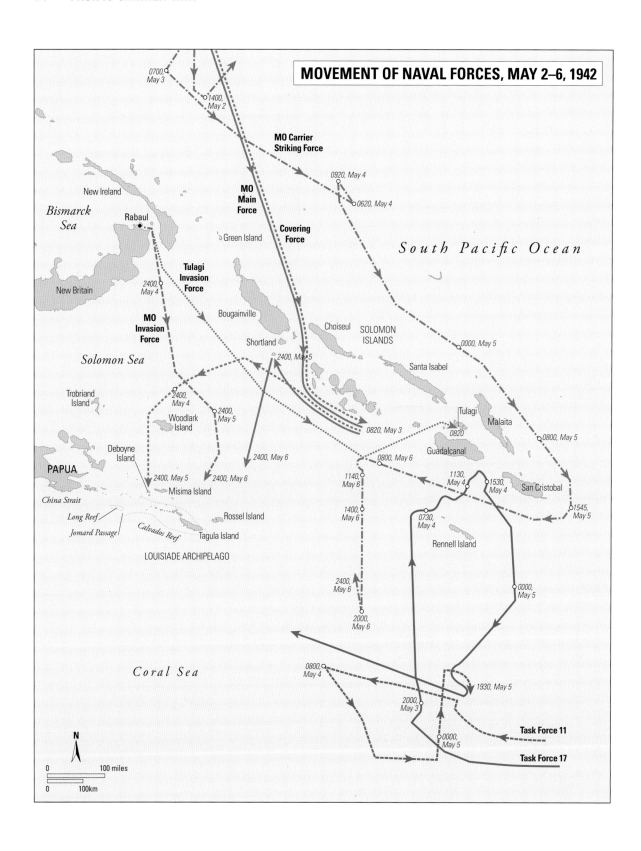

MOVEMENT OF NAVAL FORCES, MAY 2–6, 1942

0700, May 3

1400, May 2

MO Carrier Striking Force

0920, May 4

0620, May 4

New Ireland

Bismarck Sea

Rabaul

MO Main Force

Covering Force

South Pacific Ocean

Green Island

Tulagi Invasion Force

2400, May 4

MO Invasion Force

Bougainville

Choiseul

SOLOMON ISLANDS

0000, May 5

New Britain

Shortland

Santa Isabel

Solomon Sea

Trobriand Island

2400, May 5

2400, May 4

2400, May 5

Woodlark Island

Tulagi

Malaita

0820

0800, May 5

Deboyne Island

2400, May 6

0820, May 3

Guadalcanal

0800, May 6

PAPUA

2400, May 5

2400, May 6

Misima Island

1140, May 6

1130, May 4

1530, May 4

San Cristobal

China Strait

Long Reef

Rossel Island

1400, May 6

0730, May 4

1545, May 5

Jomard Passage

Calvados Reef

Tagula Island

Rennell Island

LOUISIADE ARCHIPELAGO

2400, May 6

0000, May 5

2000, May 6

Coral Sea

0800, May 4

1930, May 5

2000, May 3

N

2400, May 6

0000, May 5

Task Force 11

0   100 miles

Task Force 17

0   100km

reported a carrier and four other warships southwest of Bougainville. TF 17's afternoon search flew 275nm to the north and northwest but still found nothing. With the reconnaissance efforts of Allied land-based aircraft focused on the Solomon Sea and the Louisiades, Fletcher remained oblivious to the true location of Takagi's carriers, which were located to his northeast.

While Fletcher's searches came up empty, radar on TF 17 indicated the presence of a Japanese reconnaissance aircraft at 1015 hours. Although Wildcats on CAP were unable to find the snooper, Fletcher now had to assume that his force had been located. With no intelligence forthcoming from his own scout aircraft, Fletcher accepted that the numerous contact reports from Allied aircraft confirmed the signals intelligence he had been given by Nimitz that Japanese carriers were going to strike Port Moresby on May 7, and that the Japanese invasion convoy would transit the Louisiades by the Jomard Passage on May 7 or 8. Accordingly, on the evening of May 6, Fletcher brought TF 17 to the northwest, increasing speed so as to be 170nm southeast of Deboyne Island on the morning of May 7 in order to strike the Japanese forces reported off Misima Island in the central Louisiades.

The American radar contact near TF 17 on the morning of May 6 was, in fact, a Type 97 flying boat. It provided Takagi with his first solid information on the location of the American carriers. The report placed TF 17 420nm southwest of Tulagi. Unfortunately for the Japanese, the position was off by about 50nm and provided an incorrect course and speed. The report was received by Takagi at 1050 but caught the Japanese carriers in the middle of refueling. The American carriers were plotted to be 350nm south (but were actually 300nm south). Not until noon were *Shokaku* and *Zuikaku*, escorted by two destroyers, released to head south to close the contact. Hara's response to this priceless information was cautious. He decided not to launch a long-range strike or conduct his own searches so as not to reveal his presence.

Both sides had missed opportunities on May 6. American carrier search aircraft had come close to spotting the MO Striking Force in the morning. Hara's failure to aggressively react to the contact provided by the flying boat is hard to explain. At this point in the battle, the advantage in the ongoing game of potential ambushes seemed to be with the Japanese. Hara had a very good idea of the location of the American carriers, while Fletcher continued to believe that the Japanese carriers were operating to his northwest. There remained the real possibility that Hara could execute his ambush the following day. With both carrier forces in close proximity, a carrier clash on May 7 was seemingly inevitable.

THE FIRST CARRIER CLASH

On the morning of May 7, both sides found themselves out of position. TF 17 was approximately 150nm south of Rossel Island, roughly positioned between the two main Japanese forces. The MO Invasion Force was located north of the Jomard Passage supported by the Main Force located northwest of the convoy. The MO Striking Force was approximately 300nm southwest of Tulagi, which placed it approximately 200nm southeast of Fletcher. Fletcher's intention was to strike the Japanese force in the Solomon Sea, including the carriers he assumed were somewhere south of Bougainville. He still had no idea of the true location of Takagi's carriers. The Japanese still hoped to ambush the unsuspecting American carriers, but the Striking Force was behind schedule. Further, the American carrier force was now blocking the advance of the Invasion Force and was closer to the transports than were the Japanese carriers. Fletcher had the option of waiting and reacting to Japanese moves, but the Japanese would have to force a decision quickly if the operation was to stay on schedule.

The first side to receive solid information on the other's carriers would probably be the first to launch a strike and thus would gain a huge advantage. Events on May 7 were shaped by a series of errors and both sides lost opportunities for the all-important first strike. Allied land-based aircraft continued to focus on the area north of the Louisiades and the Solomon Sea. Fletcher augmented this with his morning search of ten Dauntlesses from *Yorktown* that were launched during the 0600 hour. These aircraft were assigned sectors to the northwest out to 250nm. Japanese reconnaissance efforts were very thorough, with aircraft from Rabaul, the Shortlands, Tulagi, and the newly created seaplane base on Deboyne Island being assigned search sectors south of the Louisiades. Hara decided to use 12 Type 97 carrier attack aircraft to search from 160 to 270 degrees out to a distance of 250nm. The search aircraft flew their routes in pairs with the southernmost sector covered by some of the most inexperienced Type 97 crews.

Fletcher decided to detach TG 17.3 under the command of British Rear Admiral Grace on the morning of May 7. Grace was given three cruisers (two Australian) and three destroyers. His mission was to prevent the MO Invasion Force from passing south of the Louisiades. This detachment was controversial, as it removed one-third of Fletcher's already weak carrier screen and placed a surface force with no air cover within range of Japanese land-based aircraft. Additionally, it was debatable whether Grace's weak force could even accomplish its assigned mission. If the carrier battle went badly for the Americans, the Japanese would have little difficulty sweeping aside Grace's force. On the other hand, if the carrier battle went well for the Americans, the Japanese would have to suspend the

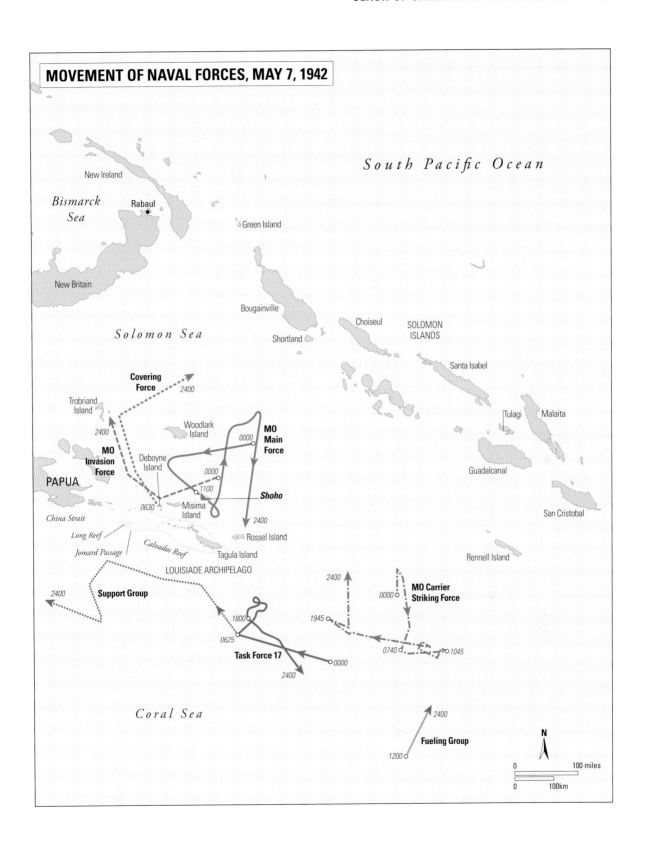

MOVEMENT OF NAVAL FORCES, MAY 7, 1942

South Pacific Ocean

New Ireland

Bismarck Sea

Rabaul

Green Island

New Britain

Bougainville

Choiseul

SOLOMON ISLANDS

Solomon Sea

Shortland

Santa Isabel

Tulagi   Malaita

Covering Force   *2400*

Trobriand Island

2400

Woodlark Island

MO Main Force   *0000*

Deboyne Island

MO Invasion Force

0000

Guadalcanal

PAPUA

1100

Shoho

0630   Misima Island

2400

San Cristobal

China Strait

Rossel Island

Long Reef

Calvados Reef

Jomard Passage   Tagula Island

LOUISIADE ARCHIPELAGO

2400

MO Carrier Striking Force   *0000*

Rennell Island

2400   **Support Group**

1945

1800

0625

0740   *1045*

Task Force 17

0000

2400

Coral Sea

2400

Fueling Group

1200

N

0   100 miles

0   100km

invasion anyway. Fletcher's rationale was that if the carrier battle neutralized both forces, as had often happened in prewar USN exercises, then Grace was positioned to contest the Japanese advance into the Coral Sea. Under the circumstances, this seemed a good insurance move by Fletcher.

With a relatively small battle area now filled with many ships and aircraft, contact reports began to filter up to the respective commanders. Hara was the first to receive a solid contact report and his subsequent actions will be dealt with first. The 12 Type 97s used as scouts departed at 0600 and headed south and southwest. These did not find TF 17 since the Americans had moved north. The most important event of the day happened at 0722, when the two southernmost *Shokaku* Type 97s reported an American force of one carrier, one cruiser, and three destroyers only 163nm south of Hara's force. This was followed by another report of an oiler and a cruiser some 25nm southeast of the carrier contact. This report fitted perfectly with Hara's estimate of where the Americans should be. He immediately sent another Type 97 to confirm the sighting and ordered a full strike. By 0815 a total of 68 aircraft (18 Zeros, 24 Type 97s with torpedoes, and 26 dive-bombers) under command of Lieutenant Commander Takahashi were on their way toward the reported position of the American carrier.

It did not take long for Hara's ambush to turn into potential disaster. Upon arriving in the area of the reported contact just after 0900, Takahashi quickly found the oiler and its escort at 0912. He ordered an enlarged search of the area but after two hours found nothing more. While this was occurring, a floatplane from cruiser *Kinugasa* searching south of the Louisiades reported American carriers southeast of Rossel Island. The American force consisted of a Saratoga-class carrier and a second carrier that were in the process of launching aircraft at 1008. Hara's frustration mounted when at 1051 the Type 97 that had made the original contact returned to *Shokaku* and revealed that it had only spotted an oiler and that the original report of a carrier was in error. Faced with this alarming turn of events, Hara recalled the strike at 1100.

Takahashi unleashed his dive-bombers on the only targets in view before heading back to his carriers. The torpedoes carried by the Type 97s were too valuable to waste on an oiler. Four dive-bombers selected destroyer *Sims* for attack and quickly hit her with three 550lb bombs. The destroyer sank by the stern with heavy loss of life – only 15 of 250 crewmen survived. Oiler *Neosho* was attacked by over 30 dive-bombers that straddled her 15 times and gained seven hits. More damage was inflicted when one of the pilots of a *Zuikaku* dive-bomber, doomed by antiaircraft fire, crashed his burning aircraft into the oiler. This was the only dive-bomber lost during the 18-minute attack. *Neosho* was left listing, aflame, and without power. The oiler refused to sink, so half the crew reboarded her and put

The Japanese attempt to ambush Fletcher's carriers miscarried on May 7 when oiler *Neosho* was misreported as a carrier by an inexperienced *Shokaku* air crew. This is *Neosho* refueling *Yorktown* on May 1, before the battle. (Naval History and Heritage Command)

out the fires. *Neosho* was finally scuttled and the remaining crew rescued on May 11 by destroyer *Henley*.

The erroneous carrier contact report meant the Japanese had squandered a golden opportunity to ambush Fletcher and win the battle. The last aircraft from the strike did not return to *Shokaku* and *Zuikaku* until 1515 hours, which made a daylight strike on the real American carriers all but impossible. The only positive for the Japanese was that the strike against *Neosho* had not revealed the position of the Striking Force, but Hara could not know this. *Sims* sent an aircraft contact report but it was not received by TF 17. *Neosho* could only manage a short report at 1021 that she was under attack by three aircraft. A report of only three aircraft could have meant these were long-range aircraft from Tulagi. The resulting confusion prevented Fletcher from knowing that Japanese carrier aircraft had destroyed his supporting oiler.

Ironically, events on the morning of May 7 developed in a very similar fashion for the Americans. Scouting reports began to reach Fletcher as early as 0735. The first was of two cruisers northwest of Rossel Island. This was followed at 0815 by a report of two carriers and four cruisers north of Misima Island. This report seemed valid to Fletcher, but it was 225nm northwest of TF 17, which meant it was beyond the range of the Wildcats and Devastators. Fletcher's staff judged an attack was possible since the Japanese force was reported moving south and TF 17 was headed north. After waiting over an hour, Fletcher ordered a full strike. Beginning at 0926 *Lexington* launched ten Wildcats, 28 Dauntlesses, and 12 Devastators. *Yorktown* followed at 0944 with the first of two deckloads with a total of eight Wildcats, 25 Dauntlesses, and ten Devastators.

As the strike aircraft headed north in two separate formations, things began to go awry for the Americans. American radar reported air contacts in the vicinity of TF 17 throughout the morning. Responding Wildcats were unable to locate the snoopers and forced Fletcher to correctly assume that his carriers had been located. At 1021 the report from *Neosho* that she was under attack arrived. Most unsettling was the return of the Dauntless that had reported the two carriers. The aircrew indicated that the actual report should have been of four light cruisers and two destroyers. Now Fletcher faced the same dilemma as Hara had earlier, but Fletcher declined to recall his strike. Allied land-based aircraft had reported heavy Japanese activity in the area of the planned strike. At 1022 a report was received from Port Moresby that two hours earlier a B-17 bomber had sighted a large force including a carrier, ten transports, and 16 other ships just south of the false carrier report. Fletcher decided to pass this new information to the strike groups in the expectation they would still find profitable targets. This decision placed the two strike groups over the MO Main Force and sealed the fate of *Shoho*. Weather in the target area was clear, which guaranteed the American strike groups would find the highest priority target, which was the light carrier. American air activity had already prompted the Japanese to turn the MO Invasion Force north to avoid air attack. The diversion of the invasion convoy placed the entire operation further behind. On top of the danger posed by the American carriers, another threat emerged when Grace's force was spotted south of the Jomard Passage and incorrectly reported as two battleships, a cruiser, and four destroyers.

THE DEATH OF *SHOHO*

Shoho was steaming with her escort of four heavy cruisers directly in the path of two American carrier air groups with 93 aircraft. The carrier was located in clear weather, had only a small CAP on station, and was therefore extremely vulnerable. *Shoho*'s first and last battle was destined to be very short. *Lexington*'s strike group was the first to spot the carrier at around 1040. *Shoho* had just recovered a CAP of four Zeros and was planning to launch a small strike on TF 17 with her six Type 97 aircraft. When *Lexington*'s aircraft were spotted at 1050, *Shoho*'s CAP consisted of only one Zero and two Type 96 fighters.

Lexington's air group then conducted one of the best-coordinated attacks by any USN carrier air group during the entire war. Commander William Ault, the air group commander, ordered the dive-bombers of his command element and VS-2 to attack *Shoho* immediately while the remainder of the air group set up a coordinated attack. The first aircraft to attack at 1110 were Ault's three dive-bombers, but their bombs all missed when *Shoho* conducted a sharp turn to

port. A sharp turn into a full circle was the standard Japanese evasion maneuver, and it made the ten following VS-2 dive-bombers also miss in turn. Japanese antiaircraft fire was ineffective, as were the attempts of the two Type 96 fighters to attack the diving Dauntlesses. The single Zero on CAP damaged a Dauntless during its dive and then shot down a dive-bomber that was pulling out of its dive. The next to dive on *Shoho* was VB-2 beginning at 1118. These aircraft placed two 1,000lb bombs on the forward part of *Shoho*'s flight deck. The two bombs penetrated the unarmored flight deck and exploded on the hangar deck. Massive fires took hold, fed by the fuel and ordnance from the Type 97s being readied for the strike against TF 17. While the Japanese focused on the dive-bombers, the Devastators of VT-2 descended to attack altitude, found a gap through the four escorting heavy cruisers, and began to drop their torpedoes at 1119. This proved one of the most deadly USN torpedo attacks of the war – five of the usually unreliable Mark 13 weapons hit *Shoho* and exploded. Devoid of armored protection, the light carrier soon experienced uncontrolled flooding.

When *Yorktown*'s strike group arrived in the area, it should have been obvious that the burning and listing *Shoho* was doomed. Because there was not a single strike commander to coordinate attacks, *Yorktown*'s squadrons decided to pummel the crippled *Shoho*. All but one of the 25 Dauntlesses from VB-5 and VS-5 dove on the carrier beginning at 1125. The American pilots claimed 15 hits on the non-maneuvering target; Japanese sources confirmed as many as 11 hits. This pounding brought *Shoho* to a stop. VT-2 Devastators attacked minutes later and claimed ten hits. Surviving Japanese crewmen recalled at least two hits, but the

ABOVE LEFT *Shoho* under attack from *Lexington*'s air group. The ship is already burning from two 1,000lb bomb hits, and this photo shows one of the five torpedo hits from *Lexington*'s Devastators. (Naval History and Heritage Command)

ABOVE Light carrier *Shoho* was attacked by a strike of 93 aircraft from carriers *Lexington* and *Yorktown* and destroyed by at least seven torpedoes and as many as 13 bombs. This is *Shoho* afire during the attack. (Naval History and Heritage Command)

actual total was probably higher. No carrier could survive such a beating. *Shoho* quickly sank; only 203 men survived from a crew of 834. American losses were only one Dauntless from *Yorktown* and two from *Lexington*.

Both American air groups recovered aboard their carriers by 1450. The aircraft were quickly respotted on deck and prepared for possible further strikes, but Fletcher decided against a second strike against Japanese forces located in the Solomon Sea or even to launch an afternoon search to look for the main Japanese carrier force. This was a defensible decision, since it would have been impossible to launch and recover a strike before dark and the weather around TF 17 was poor. Fletcher was encouraged by the events of the day. His aviators had definitely sunk the first Japanese carrier of the war and the invasion convoy had been observed turning north. Most importantly, TF 17 had evaded a retaliatory strike from the Japanese. Fletcher still had one huge problem though – he had no information on the location of the main Japanese carrier force.

The abortive attempts by both sides to ambush the other's main carrier force on May 7 was not the only air strike of the day. One of the lesser-known events of the battle was a large Japanese land-based air strike against Grace's TG 17.3 on the afternoon of May 7. Grace's cruisers steamed throughout the day to the southeast of the Jomard Passage, waiting for the Japanese to emerge headed toward Port Moresby. This placed Grace's command within easy range of land-based bombers from Rabaul, which was potentially disastrous since the small force was without friendly air cover. Grace's force was spotted in the morning, and during the 1400 hour, two groups of Type 96 G3M2 medium bombers arrived from Rabaul. The first wave consisted of 12 bombers carrying torpedoes. The Allied ships put up an impressive antiaircraft barrage which encouraged the Japanese to launch their weapons at excessive range. None of the torpedoes found a target and five Japanese bombers were shot down. Approximately 30 minutes later, 19 Type 96 bombers executed a high-altitude bombing attack, but again none of Grace's ships were hit. Japanese land-based bombers had been much more successful against maritime targets during the Malaya and NEI campaigns, but this action demonstrated that their skills had atrophied. Grace's skillful maneuvering and the ability of the Allied ships to generate a heavy barrage against the vulnerable low-flying torpedo bombers undoubtedly contributed to the lack of Japanese success. The Japanese pilots compounded their lack of skill with a wildly excessive claim of a California-class battleship and an Augusta-class heavy cruiser sunk, a Warspite-class battleship heavily damaged, and possible damage to a Canberra-class cruiser.

The apparent success of the land-based bombers from Rabaul was the only good news for the Japanese during May 7. The MO Operation was further in trouble. *Shoho*'s destruction forced a delay of the Port Moresby landings by two days since the invasion convoy had to be moved out of carrier air attack range. The MO Main Force was split up and two heavy cruisers sent to augment the screen of the MO Striking Force. The only chance to get Operation MO back on track was if the Striking Force could find and neutralize the American carriers. Given the number of aircraft involved in the attack on *Shoho*, it was apparent to Takagi and Hara that they were facing at least two American carriers. Now the increased urgency of finding and attacking the American carriers induced Hara to take risks. The most recent information available on the American carriers was a report from one of cruiser *Aoba*'s floatplanes from early in the 1400 hour. This report placed the American force out of range of the MO Striking Force but also indicated that the Americans were headed southeast. If they maintained this course, the Americans would be within range by 1830. Hara ordered a search launched at 1530 with eight Type 97s flying in pairs out to a range of 200nm. Since the Americans were believed to be some 360nm away, the purpose of this search was not clear except perhaps to provide an idea of the weather facing the strike Hara was contemplating launching next. The search aircraft returned, beginning at 1815 after finding nothing.

Needing to act quickly to attack the American carriers and based on the projected course of the American force from the last contact from the *Aoba* floatplane, Hara ordered a dusk strike with his most experienced aircrews. The strike was led again by Takahashi with orders to fly almost due west out to 280nm and then return for a night landing. Nine Type 97s and six dive-bomber crews were selected from *Zuikaku*, joined by six more Type 97s and six dive bombers from *Shokaku*. Some of the crews had just returned from the seven-hour strike earlier in the day and were now ordered to take off again in increasingly bad weather to conduct a strike against an unlocated enemy. The whole undertaking was a desperate venture.

Not surprisingly, the dusk attack was a fiasco. The strike group departed at 1615 and headed to the west. TF 17 was located only some 150nm to the west-northwest of the Japanese carriers but was hidden under heavy clouds. On its outbound leg, the Japanese strike passed some 30nm south of TF 17. The radar on both American carriers detected the Japanese aircraft at 1745 and Wildcats were vectored to intercept. They ran into the rear of the Japanese formation consisting of *Zuikaku* Type 97s at 1803. Five of the torpedo aircraft were quickly destroyed, joined by two more from *Shokaku*. Another *Shokaku* Type 97 was damaged but headed back to its carrier and was never seen again. The rest of the torpedo aircraft jettisoned their weapons and headed back to their carriers.

Takahashi took his dive-bombers out 280nm and found nothing. At 1820 he ordered the formation to return home after jettisoning their bombs. This was an extremely poor decision, since after some 30 minutes of flying east, the exhausted Japanese spotted two carriers in the process of landing aircraft. Led by Takahashi, the Japanese dive-bombers prepared to land. Both sides took a few minutes to understand what was happening, but at 1909 any confusion was removed when *Yorktown* extinguished her landing lights and opened fire at the strange aircraft overhead. One dive-bomber was shot down by antiaircraft fire, and the rest resumed their track to the east where Hara had ordered his carriers to be illuminated to guide his remaining aircraft to safety. By 2210 hours 18 of the original 27 aircraft were back onboard their carriers. The loss of nine aircraft was significant since eight of the aircraft were Type 97s – the lack of torpedo bombers was a critical factor in the events of the next day. After their return, the surviving Japanese aviators confirmed that TF 17 was less than 100nm to the west. Neither side had any doubt that the battle would be decided the following day.

PREPARING FOR BATTLE

Both sides maneuvered during the night to be in a better position for the climactic clash on May 8. TF 17 moved southeast until after midnight and then turned to the west. Destroyer *Monaghan* was detached to rescue survivors from *Neosho* and *Sims,* leaving TF 17 with only seven escorting destroyers. The Americans possessed a significant edge in aircraft on the morning of May 8. Operational aircraft totaled 117, including 31 Wildcats, 65 Dauntlesses, and 21 Devastators. Rear Admiral Aubrey Fitch devised an extensive search plan for the coming morning. Because he was uncertain about the movement of the Japanese carriers during the night, a full search was required, as it was possible the Japanese carriers could still be close. Fitch devoted a considerable percentage of his Dauntless force to search operations. The full 360-degree search he thought necessary required 18 Dauntlesses from *Lexington*'s VS-2 and VB-2. These were ordered to fly out 200nm to the north and 125nm to the south. After returning, the search aircraft would be assigned to buttress the CAP by flying anti-torpedo plane patrols. Both carriers allocated eight Wildcats for CAP, and *Yorktown* dedicated an additional eight Dauntlesses for anti-torpedo plane duty. Strike aircraft were spotted on the flight decks of *Lexington* and *Yorktown* so Fletcher could send them off immediately when the search aircraft reported back.

After recovering its aircraft, the MO Striking Force headed due north and was some 140nm northeast of Rossel Island at dawn on May 8. Since the failed night attack took so long to return, the Japanese carriers had to steam to the east to

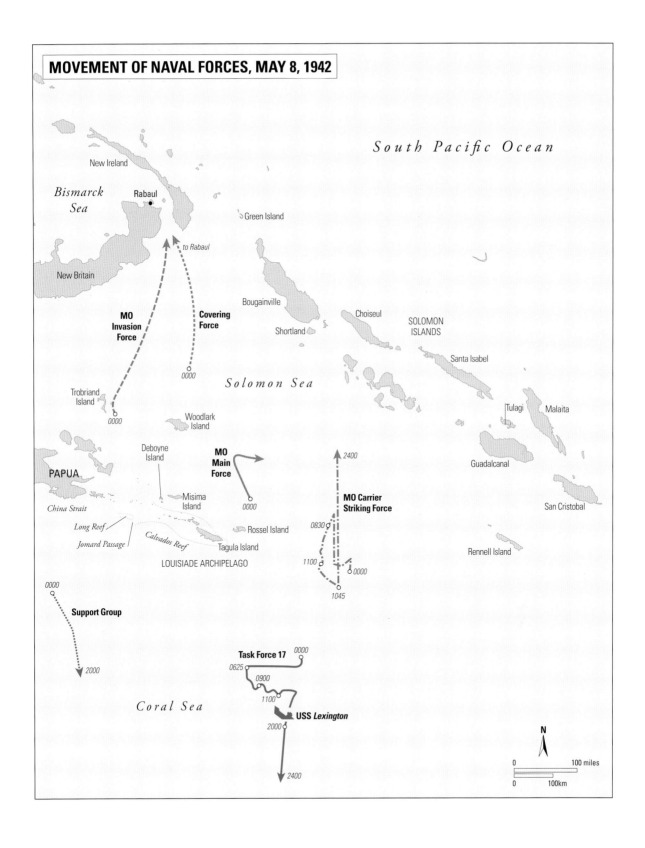

MOVEMENT OF NAVAL FORCES, MAY 8, 1942

South Pacific Ocean

New Ireland

Bismarck Sea

Rabaul

Green Island

to Rabaul

New Britain

MO Invasion Force

Covering Force

Bougainville

Choiseul

SOLOMON ISLANDS

Shortland

Santa Isabel

0000

Solomon Sea

Trobriand Island

0000

Woodlark Island

Tulagi

Malaita

Deboyne Island

MO Main Force

2400

Guadalcanal

PAPUA

Misima Island

0000

MO Carrier Striking Force

San Cristobal

China Strait

0830

Long Reef

Rossel Island

Calvados Reef

1100

0000

Rennell Island

Jomard Passage

Tagula Island

LOUISIADE ARCHIPELAGO

1045

0000

Support Group

0000

Task Force 17

2000

0625

0900

1100

Coral Sea

USS *Lexington*

2000

N

0   100 miles

0   100km

2400

recover aircraft until just after 2200. Hara wanted to keep heading east or to head south in order to hit the American carriers from their flank. Takagi rejected this advice but did concur with Hara's recommendation to move to a dawn position northeast of Rossel Island. Hara thought this position would allow him to conduct a more refined search to the south rather than an omni-directional search. This meant that fewer aircraft were required to conduct searches and more aircraft could be devoted to strike missions; preserving maximum offensive potential was always an IJN priority. This was important since the Japanese had fewer carrier aircraft available on the morning of May 8 than the Americans. *Shokaku* and *Zuikaku* possessed 96 operational aircraft – 38 Zeros, 33 dive-bombers, and 25 Type 97 carrier attack planes. However, TF 17 possessed a considerable edge in dive-bombers, with the two sides being equal in fighters and torpedo aircraft.

The Japanese search plan for May 8 was more austere than that of TF 17. According to IJN doctrine, cruiser floatplanes were preferred for search missions to save the carrier aircraft for strike missions. On the morning of May 8, rough seas prevented the Japanese heavy cruisers from operating their aircraft, which meant Hara was forced to allocate seven Type 97s to cover the southern search sectors out to a distance of 250nm. This time the aircraft were all flown by experienced crews.

As dawn broke on May 8, the MO Striking Force was located some 220nm northeast of TF 17 under heavy weather. Takagi was steering north to meet with cruisers *Kinugasa* and *Furutaka,* which had been detached from the MO Main Force to augment his screen. The MO Main Force, Invasion Force, and Covering Force were moving to a point 40nm east of Woodlark Island by the afternoon of May 8. After the MO Striking Force cleared the American carriers out of the way, the invasion convoy would proceed to Port Moresby to conduct the invasion now rescheduled for May 12.

Weather played an important role in the events of May 8 and definitely favored the Japanese. The edge of the weather front moved to the north and

For the only time in the four 1942 carrier battles, all American carriers present at Coral Sea operated in the same formation throughout the battle. This is *Lexington* viewed from *Yorktown* on May 8. (Naval History and Heritage Command)

northeast, which meant that TF 17 was now under an area of light haze that offered little protection from enemy reconnaissance. In contrast, the Japanese carriers were covered by thick clouds and squalls.

TF 17 STRIKES

The seven Japanese search aircraft were in the air by 0615 followed by the 18 TF 17 Dauntlesses at 0635. The Japanese scout aircraft were the first to find their target. At 0802 *Yorktown*'s radar reported a contact 18nm to the northeast, but the CAP was unable to find or intercept the snooper. The radar contact was a Type 97 that issued a contact report at 0822 that it had sighted two American carriers 235nm distant at a bearing of 205 degrees from the MO Striking Force. Radio intelligence units on both *Lexington* and *Yorktown* confirmed that the Japanese aircraft had spotted TF 17 and issued a report.

The first report received by Fletcher and Fitch was at 0820, when a VS-2 Dauntless spotted the Japanese carriers in bad weather. The contact was reported to be 175nm from TF 17 to the north-northeast and was headed away from the American carriers. At that distance the Japanese carriers were at the edge of the striking range of the Wildcats and Devastators; nevertheless, Fletcher approved the recommendation to launch an immediate full strike while steaming TF 17 toward the contact to reduce the distance the American strike aircraft had to fly to return to their carriers.

Fletcher's quick decision meant the Americans were the first to get a strike airborne. At 0900 *Yorktown* began launching 39 aircraft (six Wildcats, 24 Dauntlesses, and nine Devastators) followed at 0907 by 36 aircraft from *Lexington* (nine Wildcats, 15 Dauntlesses, and 12 Devastators). With the carrier battle being joined, Fletcher transferred tactical control of TF 17 to Fitch at 0908. By 0925 the two American air groups were headed toward the Japanese carriers after one *Lexington* Devastator aborted because of engine problems. The two air groups were widely separated and there was not a single strike commander. Additional reports from a VS-2 Dauntless at 0934 placed the Japanese carriers 191nm from TF 17, which was farther than the first report.

Yorktown's air group had no difficulty finding the MO Striking Force which was separated into two sections. *Zuikaku*, escorted by heavy cruisers *Myoko* and *Haguro* and three destroyers, was some 9,000 yards ahead of *Shokaku*, with heavy cruisers *Furutaka* and *Kinugasa* trailing far astern. As the Americans maneuvered into attack position, *Zuikaku* and her escorts disappeared into a squall. Only a single *Yorktown* fighter saw *Zuikaku* during the battle. Since only *Shokaku* was visible, she took the full brunt of *Yorktown*'s attack. The 24 Dauntlesses only

ABOVE This photo shows *Shokaku* under attack from *Yorktown* dive-bombers. The carrier is in the process of making a high-speed evasive turn. Note the almost total absence of antiaircraft fire and the lack of any escort ships. (Naval History and Heritage Command)

RIGHT *Shokaku* conducts radical maneuvers to avoid attack from *Yorktown*'s dive-bombers. A fire from the first bomb hit on the ship's forecastle can be seen, and the column of smoke signals that the second 1,000lb bomb has hit just aft of the island. The second hit caused large fires, but these were extinguished by the ship's damage control teams. (Naval History and Heritage Command)

gained two 1,000lb bomb hits; the effectiveness of the Dauntless's attacks was impeded by fogging of their canopies and persistent attacks by the Zeros on CAP. Only two dive-bombers were lost. The first bomb hit started a fire in the forecastle and the second hit near the island started fires on both the flight and hangar decks. The American pilots claimed six bomb hits and thought the carrier was mortally damaged. The attack of VT-5 was completely ineffective since all nine torpedoes were dropped against a single side of the carrier and from excessive distance; *Shokaku* had no problem evading them. The Japanese concentrated their antiaircraft fire on the torpedo bombers but none were shot down. *Yorktown*'s attack caused significant damage to *Shokaku* which prevented her from launching or recovering aircraft, but the ship was never in danger of sinking. During the attack, Japanese antiaircraft fire was largely ineffective, and the Zeros focused on the approaching Devastators. The escorting Wildcats did an excellent job defending the Devastators and managed to shoot down two Zeros.

Lexington's air group attacked some 30 minutes later. Unlike the well-coordinated *Yorktown* attack, the weather over the target area scattered *Lexington*'s air group, which made a coordinated attack impossible. Only four of the 15 Dauntlesses were able to locate *Shokaku*; one was able to score another 1,000lb bomb hit. The 11 VB-2 dive-bombers were forced to return after finding nothing to attack and then running low on fuel. The 11 Devastators found *Shokaku* and were attacked by seven Zeros on CAP, but four escorting Wildcats drew most of the Japanese fighters away from the vulnerable torpedo bombers. None of the Devastators were lost to Zeros, and all were able to launch their weapons. The well-handled carrier was again able to avoid all torpedoes aimed at her. A total of three Wildcats and one Dauntless were lost in the attack, and another fighter and two dive-bombers did not find their way back to *Lexington*. Of the 13 Zeros on CAP, two were shot down and one damaged by Wildcats.

The result of the strike by two carrier air groups was disappointing. *Zuikaku* was hidden by clouds throughout the battle and emerged unscathed. *Shokaku* was hit by three 1,000lb bombs, which created severe damage and fires. The fires were extinguished by noon, but the damage left her unable to operate aircraft. Personnel casualties were heavy with 109 dead and another 114 wounded. Unable to take further part in the battle, *Shokaku* was ordered back to Truk at 30 knots under escort of two destroyers.

THE JAPANESE STRIKE

The Japanese also had their strike ready to launch upon the receipt of a valid spotting report. The 0822 contact report provided Hara enough information to order the strike to launch, and, beginning at 0910 hours, 18 Zeros, 33 dive-bombers, and 18 Type 97s with torpedoes took off under the command of Takahashi who was making his third sortie in two days. The strike departed at 0930 and proceeded south in a single group. Takagi ordered the MO Striking Force to steam south at 30 knots to decrease the distance the strike would have to cover on its return. Had he maintained his position, the American Devastators probably would not have had the fuel to reach the Japanese carriers.

TF 17 with its two carriers, five cruisers, and seven destroyers prepared anxiously for the strike it knew was coming. This was the first test of the war of the ability of an American carrier force to protect itself from Japanese carrier air attack. Fitch mounted the strongest CAP possible. Eight Wildcats were already aloft supported by 18 Dauntlesses on anti-torpedo plane duty. At 1055 radars on *Lexington* and *Yorktown* detected a large group of aircraft 68nm to the north. This allowed the launch of nine more Wildcats and five additional Dauntlesses to augment the CAP. Despite the warning time and the large number of aircraft, the CAP was poorly directed and achieved little. The nine newly launched Wildcats were ordered to proceed down the radar line of bearing to intercept the Japanese as far as possible from TF 17. These fighters failed to intercept the Japanese dive-bombers until they had commenced their dives, while the Wildcats assigned to intercept the low-flying torpedo planes missed them in the clouds. Only one *Zuikaku* Type 97 was shot down before the attack began. The ineffective CAP interception allowed Takahashi to set up a well-coordinated attack. He took his 33 dive-bombers upwind from TF 17 while the 18 Type 97s were ordered to conduct an immediate attack. Fourteen of these approached *Lexington* from both bows, which left only four to attack *Yorktown* from her port beam.

The torpedo aircraft were the first to attack. Despite the efforts of the Wildcats and Dauntlesses on anti-torpedo plane patrol, 15 of the 18 Type 97s survived to launch their torpedoes. During their torpedo runs and subsequent withdrawal, two *Zuikaku* and five *Shokaku* torpedo planes were destroyed. The four allocated against *Yorktown* all missed with the loss of two aircraft. The attack against *Lexington* was a much different story, since the Japanese were able to conduct an anvil attack from both beams and because the huge carrier had limited maneuverability. Nine torpedoes were launched at the carrier. The first were launched from two groups attacking from each beam, but the carrier's skipper avoided them all. However, this exposed *Lexington* to the last group of four Type 97s. Two torpedoes ran deep under *Lexington*'s keel but the final two scored hits on the port side. The first hit at 1120 would eventually prove fatal. It struck forward and jammed the two elevators in the raised position. Not evident at that moment was the buckling of the port aviation fuel tank that opened small cracks, allowing gasoline vapors to spread. The second torpedo hit under the island near the boiler rooms. Three filled with water, forcing three boilers off line. Additionally, several fuel bunkers were opened to the sea which created a large oil slick. The damage caused a 6–7-degree list to port but this was corrected by counterflooding.

Takahashi ordered 19 dive-bombers from *Shokaku* to deal with *Lexington* with the 14 from *Zuikaku* dispatched to attack *Yorktown*. The poorly directed American

LEFT This photo was taken from one of the Japanese aircraft attacking *Lexington*. The carrier is on fire and the bomb splashes around the ship indicate the photo was taken during the dive-bombing attack from *Shokaku*'s Type 99s. (Naval History and Heritage Command)

BELOW This is *Lexington* under attack from Type 97 torpedo bombers. Note the Type 97 approaching the carrier off its port side. (Naval History and Heritage Command)

BOTTOM Of the 19 *Shokaku* Type 99 dive-bombers that attacked *Lexington*, only two scored direct hits. This is *Lexington* surrounded by a deluge of bombs. (Naval History and Heritage Command)

CAP and the work of the escorting Zeros protected the dive-bombers so almost all were able to attack their targets. *Lexington* was struck first since she was closer. The Japanese aviators pressed home their attacks against heavy antiaircraft fire, but their skill did not match their bravery. Two *Shokaku* Type 99s hit *Lexington* but caused only minor damage. The first bomb hit the flight deck, knocking out the forward port-side 5-inch guns. The second hit the port side of the massive stack, causing little damage but inflicting casualties on nearby antiaircraft gun crews. Five near misses were also recorded. American gunners destroyed two dive-bombers. The last group of three dive-bombers was attacked by the late-arriving CAP; the leader was shot down and the other two forced to switch targets to *Yorktown*.

Against *Yorktown* the Japanese had even less success, with the 14 *Zuikaku* dive-bombers scoring only a single hit. This was due to the efforts of two defending Wildcats, good ship handling by *Yorktown*'s captain, and a crosswind drop. The carrier was deluged by a dozen near misses, but only a single 550lb semi-armor-piercing bomb hit the center of the flight deck forward of the middle elevator. It penetrated four decks before exploding, where it wiped out a damage repair party and caused structural damage. The resulting fire produced dense smoke that emerged through the small hole left in the flight deck. Three boiler rooms were temporarily evacuated which reduced speed to 25 knots. One of the near misses exploded amidships on the port side and opened several fuel bunkers to the sea, creating a large slick. *Yorktown*'s crew quickly extinguished the fires and the boiler rooms were re-manned, bringing her speed up to 28 knots.

After the attack *Lexington* appeared battle-worthy and in no danger of sinking and both carriers could recover aircraft. However, the Japanese thought that both were finished as fighting units. Takahashi radioed back at 1125 that a Saratoga-class carrier had sunk as a result of nine torpedo and ten bomb hits. He also claimed a Yorktown-class carrier as damaged after two torpedo hits and as many as ten bomb hits.

In exchange for their success in damaging both carriers, the Japanese suffered enormous aircraft losses. The CAP of 17 Wildcats and 23 Dauntlesses, combined with the withering antiaircraft fire, accounted for an immediate total of five dive-bombers and eight Type 97s. Another seven aircraft were forced to ditch on their return leg because of damage and another 12 were pushed overboard due to battle damage after they landed

Both of the bomb hits on *Lexington* caused minor damage. The first bomb to hit exploded near the forward port-side 5-inch/25-caliber gun gallery, as shown here. (Naval History and Heritage Command)

on *Zuikaku*. Wildcats returning from the *Yorktown* strike accounted for two Japanese aircraft, and both were noteworthy. One was the Type 97 that spotted TF 17 and shadowed it skillfully for over an hour; when the pilot of this aircraft encountered the Japanese strike headed for TF 17, he decided to guide the strike to its target, knowing that this act meant he would not have enough fuel to return. The second notable loss was strike leader Takahashi who had commanded *Shokaku*'s air group since Pearl Harbor. The net effect of these heavy aircraft losses was to essentially neutralize the offensive potential of two Japanese fleet carriers. The total cost to the Americans was three Wildcats and five Dauntlesses.

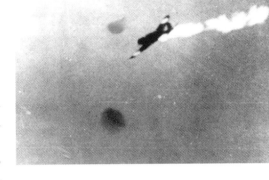

A Type 97 going down in flames on May 8. Overall losses for Japanese torpedo planes were catastrophic during the battle; only eight were operational on May 10 of the 39 that had been available on May 6. (Naval History and Heritage Command)

AFTER THE STRIKES

Both the Japanese and American air groups were shattered by the events of May 8, which made another strike in the afternoon impossible. *Yorktown*'s strike returned at 1300 hours with only 12 Dauntlesses and eight Devastators. Only seven torpedoes remained in *Yorktown*'s magazines. *Lexington*'s strike returned some 20 minutes later but was caught onboard after a huge explosion shook the carrier at 1247. Given *Lexington*'s uncertain condition, the heavy attrition to *Yorktown*'s air group (especially in fighters), and growing concern with TF 17's fuel status since the loss of *Neosho*, at 1315 Fletcher proposed that TF 17 retire to the south. Fitch concurred and effectively brought the battle to an end.

Though the battle was over, the cost for the Americans was about to rise dramatically. The torpedo that hit outboard of *Lexington*'s port-side aviation gasoline tanks created cracks allowing vapors to escape. These vapors reached the motor generators in the internal communications room by 1247 and initiated a large explosion and heavy fires in the forward part of the ship. Damage control parties could not control the fires, and further massive explosions occurred at 1442 and 1525. The ship's captain decided to abandon ship at 1707 before darkness made the rescue of the crew difficult. *Lexington* was later scuttled by destroyer torpedoes and finally sank at 1952.

The condition of the MO Striking Force was not much better. *Shokaku* had already departed the battle area, leaving *Zuikaku* to recover all returning aircraft. Between 1310 and 1410, *Zuikaku* recovered 44 aircraft. Of these, 12 (three Zeros, four dive-bombers, and five Type 97s) were pushed over the side. Some were not

In spite of having taken two bomb and two torpedo hits, *Lexington* remained operational after the Japanese attack. This view shows the carrier underway on the afternoon of May 8 after recovering her air group. The only sign of damage in this view is that the ship is clearly down by the bow from torpedo damage. (Naval History and Heritage Command)

even badly damaged, but the flight deck crew did not take the time to assess their condition since they were unsure how many aircraft *Zuikaku* would have to handle. When the Japanese had a chance to take stock later in the afternoon, 24 Zeros, nine dive-bombers, and six Type 97s were operational. In addition, another Zero, eight dive-bombers, and four Type 97s were considered repairable. After learning this, Takagi informed his superiors that a second strike was impossible, and the MO Striking Force headed north at 1500 to refuel as some destroyers were down to 20 percent of capacity.

As the carrier duel played out, Operation MO was on life support. Vice Admiral Inoue ordered all forces not involved in the carrier battle to move northeast on the morning of May 8. Meanwhile, search aircraft from Rabaul reported an Allied force of one battleship, two cruisers, and four destroyers between the Louisiades and Port Moresby. A plan to attack this force with bombers from Rabaul was scratched when heavy rains soaked their airfields. This placed an Allied force with heavy units on the path to Port Moresby and, in the afternoon, Inoue learned the results of the carrier battle. With *Shokaku* knocked out of the battle and only a relatively few aircraft left on *Zuikaku*, Inoue knew that an invasion of Port Moresby was now impossible. At 1545 he ordered all forces to head north; at 1620 he postponed the entire MO Operation.

When Combined Fleet headquarters learned of Inoue's postponement order, Yamamoto intervened. At 2200 he ordered Inoue to pursue the retreating American forces to complete their destruction. Inoue complied by shifting the two remaining heavy cruisers in the Main Body and several destroyers to reinforce the MO Striking Force. Thus reinforced, the MO Striking Force refueled on May 9 and then re-entered the Coral Sea the following day with the intent to restart the battle. *Zuikaku*'s operational aircraft had risen to 45: 24 Zeros, 13

dive-bombers, and eight Type 97s. Dawn on May 10 found Takagi some 340nm southwest of Tulagi. Searches found the derelict *Neosho* but no sign of TF 17. By the following day the futility of continuing the chase was obvious, and the MO Striking Force passed south of San Cristobal Island and headed north.

Takagi never had any real prospect of catching TF 17. Fletcher knew that the Japanese invasion convoy had retreated toward Rabaul, so he could safely assume the threat to Port Moresby was over. He could not risk losing another carrier, which would have turned the battle into a strategic disaster for the USN. On May 8 and 9, he moved quickly out of possible Japanese search and strike range. On May 15, TF 17 anchored at Tongatabu in the Tonga Islands and *Yorktown* proceeded to Pearl Harbor for repairs. That same day Halsey's TF 16 with *Enterprise* and *Hornet* was spotted by a Japanese flying boat approximately 450 miles east of Tulagi. These final moves in the battle of the Coral Sea were actually the prelude to the battle of Midway, now less than three weeks away.

ABOVE LEFT As a result of leaking fuel vapors, a series of massive explosions reduced *Lexington* to a burning hulk. Note *Yorktown* is just visible in the background. (Naval History and Heritage Command)

ABOVE After the first series of explosions, the crew of *Lexington* was ordered to abandon ship. The ship sank that evening, making her the first American carrier lost during the war. (Naval History and Heritage Command)

THE ACCOUNTING AND IMPACT OF CORAL SEA

The battle of the Coral Sea was Japan's first strategic defeat of the Pacific War. The overly ambitious MO Operation proved to be too fragile. After the IJN's interrupted run of successes of the previous five months, Victory Disease had infested the Naval General Staff and the Combined Fleet. Both counted on a passive enemy who would play his scripted role while an intricate Japanese operation unfolded. Unlike the first few months of the war when the Japanese were careful to conduct their operations under conditions of local air superiority, this was not achievable for Operation MO. Instead of facing only meager Dutch, British, or American land-based air forces, in May 1942 the Japanese had planned a major invasion in the face of an American carrier force backed by large land-based air forces.

In spite of the fragility of the Japanese plans, it did contain the seeds for success, if not against Port Moresby, then against TF 17. When the MO Striking Force rounded the Solomon Islands and moved into the Coral Sea, it was in position to ambush Fletcher's unsuspecting carriers. This opportunity was wasted by Takagi and Hara. For two days they did not conduct a search for the American carriers in order not to reveal their position. Though the coordination between Japanese land-based naval air forces and their carriers was far better than the coordination between Allied land-based aviation and TF 17, it was not good enough to allow Takagi to take such a passive role and rely solely on land-based air units to locate the American carriers. On May 6 and 7, the Japanese threw away solid chances to launch a devastating first blow against Fletcher's carriers. On May 7 in particular, the Americans were very fortunate that Japanese reconnaissance operations were so unbelievably haphazard. During the climactic carrier battle of May 8, Japanese aviators got the best of the exchange. Despite his heavy aircraft losses, Takagi should have realized that the true strategic prize was no longer Port Moresby but the American carriers. With this priority in mind, he should have relentlessly pursued the damaged *Yorktown* without Yamamoto having to order him to do so late on May 8. Coral Sea was a series of lost opportunities for the Japanese.

For the Americans, Nimitz accomplished his goals of stopping the Port Moresby invasion and inflicting significant attrition on the Japanese. When he saw an opportunity to engage a portion of the *Kido Butai*, Nimitz aggressively seized it. Fletcher fought a competent battle but became fixated on the Japanese forces approaching from his northwest which included, according to the intelligence he was provided by Nimitz, the Japanese carriers. Fletcher ignored his eastern flank which could have led to disaster on May 6 or 7. After taking the brunt of the exchange on May 8, Fletcher was unfortunate that a material defect caused the destruction of *Lexington*. His withdrawal on May 8 was undoubtedly the correct decision as was evidenced by *Yorktown*'s pivotal role at Midway a month later.

Overshadowed by the failure of the Port Moresby invasion were the severe losses inflicted to the Japanese carrier force. IJN losses were the most severe of any battle in the war to that point. Light carrier *Shoho* was sunk, making her the largest and most important Japanese ship lost thus far. In addition, a destroyer and several minor ships were lost in the American carrier raid on Tulagi. Most importantly, the severe bomb damage to *Shokaku* kept her in the shipyard until July 1942. Carrier aircraft losses were very severe. The total number of aircraft remaining (in all conditions) on *Zuikaku* on the evening of May 8 was 52. This meant that the fleet carriers had lost 69 aircraft since May 6. Combined with the loss of *Shoho*'s entire air group (18 aircraft), Japanese carrier aircraft losses totaled 87. The heavy aircraft losses crippled *Zuikaku*'s air group and kept the ship out of action for several months. Not only was Coral Sea a strategic disaster because of the failure to take Port Moresby, but the battle removed three of 11 carriers from the Combined Fleet's order of battle right before Yamamoto's decisive battle at Midway.

American losses were also severe, since *Lexington* constituted a quarter of the Pacific Fleet's operational carrier strength. *Yorktown* suffered minor damage but her survival allowed the Americans to rightfully claim a strategic victory. In addition to *Lexington*, an oiler and a destroyer were sunk. Total carrier aircraft losses were 81, including 35 when *Lexington* was scuttled.

For both the Americans and Japanese, the first carrier battle of the war was full of surprises and missed opportunities. With the Japanese advance in the South Pacific checked, both sides now prepared for the Japanese thrust against Midway in the Central Pacific. The most important carrier battle of the war was close at hand.

A burned-out Type 97 pictured on a South Pacific reef after the battle of the Coral Sea. The single white fuselage band indicates that the aircraft is from *Shokaku*. Japanese aircraft losses, particularly of strike aircraft, were very heavy during the battle. This was a pattern repeated throughout the 1942 carrier battles. (Naval History and Heritage Command)

Yorktown survived the battle and returned to Pearl Harbor on May 27 as shown in this view. After arriving, she immediately went into drydock for repairs. (Naval History and Heritage Command)

CHAPTER 4
AMBUSH AT MIDWAY

THE MYTHS OF MIDWAY AND THE IMPACT OF CORAL SEA

The clash of carriers at Midway Atoll in June 1942 has become the stuff of legend. It has become widely accepted that the battle was the most decisive of the Pacific War. Yamamoto assembled a seemingly invincible force to deliver a definitive blow against the Pacific Fleet. The Americans were grossly outnumbered and apparently without hope of success. Among the myths of Midway, the latter one is the most erroneous as will be examined later. Even though the IJN's carrier force was defeated at Midway, the battle was not decisive since the Japanese were able to quickly recover and fight two more carrier battles in 1942. One of these resulted in the most severe defeat to an American carrier force during the war. As will be seen later, the Guadalcanal campaign, which included two carrier battles, was the foremost event that destroyed Japanese carrier aviation as a force capable of achieving battle-winning results.

The results of Coral Sea played an important part in determining the outcome at Midway. Coral Sea is commonly accepted as an American strategic victory,

since the invasion of Port Moresby was stopped, but as a tactical defeat for the Americans since they lost *Lexington* in exchange for only a Japanese light carrier. This is a simplistic view since Coral Sea cannot be viewed in isolation. The battle should be properly seen as both a strategic and tactical defeat for the Japanese and a preface for the disaster at Midway.

The defeat of Operation MO had far-reaching implications. The principal objective of Yamamoto's Operation MI (the codename for the attack on Midway) was the destruction of the USN's Pacific Fleet. To conduct Operation MI successfully, Yamamoto's decisive victory plan depended on maintaining superiority in fleet carriers. Violating the principle of mass, Yamamoto only committed one-third of the *Kido Butai*'s carriers to Operation MO. Though neither was sunk in the operation, both were removed from his order of battle for Operation MI. Therefore, the results of the battle had strategic implications well beyond the Japanese failure to capture Port Moresby. Left with only four fleet carriers, Yamamoto had lost his decisive carrier edge that was necessary to guarantee success in a bid for decisive victory against the Pacific Fleet. The removal of Carrier Division 5 from the *Kido Butai* made Coral Sea both a strategic and tactical disaster for the Japanese.

ABOVE After her arrival at Pearl Harbor on May 27, *Yorktown* went into drydock. She was returned to battle-ready condition in only three days. The ship departed on May 30 for Midway. In contrast, the Japanese made no attempt to ready the undamaged *Zuikaku* for the upcoming Midway operation. (Naval History and Heritage Command)

Coral Sea held several important lessons that neither side had time to fully digest by the time Midway was fought just one month later. Both sides expected that enemy attacks would prove fatal for their own carriers, but this turned out not to be the case. The striking power of American carriers was restricted by the doctrine of mounting strikes by single air groups. Coordination issues present at Coral Sea were even worse at Midway. The performance of the Devastators at Coral Sea, during which they played a major role in sinking *Shoho*, served to camouflage their real vulnerability and ineffectiveness against more effective opposition. The primary striking power of American carrier air groups resided in their dive-bombers, which was amply demonstrated at Midway. Japanese carrier air groups demonstrated superior offensive potential at Coral Sea. This was primarily due to the combination of the Type 97 carrier attack aircraft with the reliable Type 91 aerial torpedo. This deadly combination was responsible for beginning the chain of events that sank all three American carriers lost in 1942 carrier engagements. At Coral Sea Japanese torpedo bombers were responsible for sinking *Lexington*; had they succeeded in putting just a single torpedo into *Yorktown*, the damage certainly would not have been repaired by the time of the Midway battle. The subtraction of *Yorktown* would have had incalculable consequences for the outcome of the battle. This makes the abortive night attack mounted by the Japanese at Coral Sea on May 7 such an important event since it meant the following day *Yorktown* faced only four attacking Type 97s. In contrast to the ship-killing power of the Type 97s, Japanese dive-bombers carried relatively small bombs that lacked the capability to severely damage large ships with well-trained damage control crews.

Coral Sea demonstrated that the defensive power of both carrier forces was inadequate. Both sides lacked sufficient fighters to mount an effective CAP while also providing an effective strike escort. Japanese CAP was particularly weak, especially against dive-bombers. Antiaircraft fire proved unable to protect American and Japanese carriers, but American antiaircraft fire was much more deadly and exacted a large toll on Japanese attackers. Though American defensive efforts were uneven at Coral Sea, they improved during each of the remaining 1942 carrier battles. The potential advantage of radar for fighter direction was unrealized at Coral Sea but became a major factor in future carrier battles.

YAMAMOTO PLANS HIS DECISIVE BATTLE

April 1942 witnessed tension between the Naval General Staff and the Combined Fleet when it came to the future course of Japanese naval strategy. While the Naval General Staff advocated for expansion in the South Pacific to cut the sea lines of

Midway Atoll is composed of two islands. Eastern Island in the foreground contains the airfield and Sand Island was home to a seaplane base. Yamamoto planned to use Midway as the lure to bring the Pacific Fleet to battle with the assembled might of the Combined Fleet. (Naval History and Heritage Command)

communication between the United States and Australia, Yamamoto had a different vision. He wanted an advance in the Central Pacific with the ultimate goal of seizing Hawaii. This had the added benefit of forcing the remnants of the Pacific Fleet into battle, thus providing Yamamoto with the decisive battle he desired.

This strategic debate between the Naval General Staff and the Combined Fleet ultimately resulted in a fatal compromise. Despite an agreement between the Imperial Army and Navy for further advances in the South Pacific, Yamamoto and the staff of the Combined Fleet clung to their view that Japan had to complete the destruction of American naval power to be victorious. To accomplish this Yamamoto needed a target that the Pacific Fleet would have to defend. The obvious choice was Hawaii, but its large garrison and land-based air force made it largely

Admiral Nagano Osami, chief of the Naval General Staff, differed on strategy with the Commander of the Combined Fleet, Admiral Yamamoto. Nagano was forced to acquiesce to Yamamoto's Midway plan, with disastrous results. (Naval History and Heritage Command)

impervious to attack and invasion. Yamamoto thought that Midway Atoll would achieve the same purpose. It was close enough to Hawaii that the Pacific Fleet would be forced to fight for it but far enough away that land-based air power from Hawaii could not play a direct role in the battle.

The debate between the Naval General Staff and the Combined Fleet came to a head during a series of meetings in Tokyo on April 2–5, 1942. The Naval General Staff pointed out the limited utility of Midway as a base to threaten Hawaii as well as the enormous difficulties in supplying a base so close to Pearl Harbor. Yamamoto did not compromise and, on April 5, emerged victorious by again using the implied threat of resignation as he had before Pearl Harbor. In exchange for his Midway operation, Yamamoto agreed to two demands of the Naval General Staff. Both of these directly compromised the success of the Midway operation, demonstrating the bankruptcy of Japanese naval planning. To get the advance in the South Pacific back on track, Yamamoto agreed to send part of the *Kido Butai* to protect the early May invasion of Port Moresby. Yamamoto also agreed to conduct operations to seize selected points in the Aleutians concurrent with the Midway operation, thereby reducing his strength for the decisive battle. Such a diversion is difficult to explain but probably stems from Yamamoto's confidence that the Combined Fleet was strong enough to conduct both operations at once.

The Midway operation was the largest IJN operation of the war. All eight of its operational carriers were committed as well as all 11 battleships. Of 18 heavy cruisers, 14 were assigned roles as were the bulk of the IJN's light cruisers and destroyers. This assemblage was under the command of 28 admirals. Operation MI consumed more fuel than an entire year of peacetime operations.

Operation MI was scheduled to open on the morning of June 3 with a trademark *Kido Butai* surprise attack against Midway. Nagumo's force consisted of four fleet carriers (*Akagi*, *Kaga*, *Soryu*, and *Hiryu*), escorted by two battleships, two heavy cruisers, one light cruiser, and 11 destroyers. Strategic and tactical surprise were assumed for the opening strike against Midway. Further air strikes were planned on June 4 preparatory to a landing. On June 5, the Seaplane Tender Group would land on Kure Island 60 miles west of Midway to set up a seaplane base.

The actual landing on Midway Atoll was scheduled for June 6. The Transport Group with 12 transports and three patrol boats (destroyers converted to land troops), escorted by one light cruiser and ten destroyers, carried 5,000 troops for the assault. The Second Combined Special Naval Landing Force of some 1,500 men was allocated against Sand Island and the Imperial Army's Ichiki Detachment (a 1,000-man reinforced battalion) targeted for Eastern Island. Both would attack from the southern side of their objectives where the coral reefs were less of an obstacle. In addition to the Invasion Force Main Body with two battleships, another four heavy cruisers, eight destroyers, and light carrier *Zuiho*, several other groups supported the invasion. These included the Close Support Group of four heavy cruisers, two destroyers, and a minesweeper group.

Following the planned quick capture of the island, two construction battalions would make the air base operational. To accomplish this before the expected clash with the American fleet, just one day was believed sufficient. The Japanese planned to protect their new base with 36 Zeros, six midget submarines, five motor torpedo boats, 94 cannon, and 40 machine guns.

The capture of Midway was the prelude to the most important part of Yamamoto's plan. One of the principal Japanese assumptions was that the attack would gain strategic surprise, and the Pacific Fleet would need three days to sortie from Pearl Harbor to Midway. Yamamoto was concerned that an overwhelming show of force could make the Americans think twice about giving battle. Yamamoto's dispersal of forces was probably a deception to prevent the Americans from gauging his true strength and to convince Nimitz that conditions were suitable for a major engagement. When the Pacific Fleet made its appearance, the dispersed Combined Fleet would converge to crush it.

To convince Nimitz to make an appearance, after Midway was captured Nagumo would take his carriers some 500nm to the northeast. The Invasion Force would remain near Midway as apparent bait. The other Japanese heavy forces would linger to the north out of range of American reconnaissance. The Main Body would be positioned some 300nm west of Nagumo's force, and the other battleship force, the Guard Force, would move to a position some 500nm north of the Main Body. The two carriers assigned to the Aleutians operation would move to a position some 300nm to the east of the Guard Force.

Once the Combined Fleet had assumed its positions, the Japanese assumed the Pacific Fleet would attack the Invasion Force as it patrolled near Midway. In another of a series of unfounded assumptions, the Japanese appear to have believed that the Pacific Fleet's response would include not only its remaining carriers but also its remaining battleships. This allowed the Combined Fleet to dust off its finely scripted prewar decisive battle plans. After Japanese submarines and aircraft caused great attrition, the final blow would be delivered by the Combined Fleet's massed battleships.

Other parts of the Japanese plan bear closer examination. Two picket lines of submarines were positioned on what the Japanese believed would be the route of the Pacific Fleet's advance from Pearl Harbor to Midway. Each line consisted of seven submarines with its own patrol box. Unbelievably, there was enough space between each patrol box for the Americans to move through undetected. Further, the submarines were older units with maintenance issues. Because of delays in leaving their bases, they could not even reach their stations until June 3, in some cases after the American carriers had passed through. Another submarine operation to gain intelligence on the location of Pacific Fleet units at Pearl Harbor was canceled when the Japanese discovered that the Americans had placed ships at the French Frigate Shoals located between Midway and Hawaii. This prevented the refueling of the flying boats from submarines, which meant Yamamoto received no advance warning of American fleet movements from his flying boats.

One of the most misunderstood aspects of the Midway operation was Operation AL, the Japanese plan to seize two islands in the Aleutian chain. It is commonly believed that the Aleutian operation was a diversion to draw American forces from Midway, but Japanese sources fail to suggest any diversionary aspect to the Aleutian landings. The notion that the Aleutians was a diversion does not pass the common-sense test when examined in the context of Yamamoto's desire to crush the Pacific Fleet at Midway instead of diverting it away from Midway. Operation AL included a carrier strike against the American base at Dutch Harbor on June 3, the same day as the originally scheduled strike on Midway. This was to be followed by landings on Kiska and Adak scheduled for June 6. The Adak landing was actually a raid to destroy the American facility thought to be there. An optional landing on Attu was planned for June 12.

The problem with Operation AL was that it diverted considerable forces from the decisive engagement off Midway. Among these forces were carriers *Junyo* and *Ryujo*. While not fleet carriers, they did embark 63 aircraft, which was equivalent to one of Nagumo's fleet carriers. Operation AL was a demonstration of Yamamoto's flawed objective prioritization and faulty force allocation. The Aleutians were clearly a secondary objective unworthy of the forces sent to take them. If Operation MI was the decisive battle, any diversion of forces violated the principle of mass and was unwise. If the Midway operation went well, the Aleutians could be seized at Yamamoto's leisure. If the Midway operation failed, any gains made in the Aleutians could not be held, as was proven by events in 1943. Any forces allocated to Operation AL were in no position to support Operation MI and were thus worthless in any clash with the Pacific Fleet.

Yamamoto's plan for Operation MI was riddled with flawed assumptions and a total disregard for the enemy's capabilities. This was driven by the complacency, arrogance, and overconfidence resulting from Victory Disease which was rampant in the Combined Fleet after many months of success. The operation was also overly complex. Though this was a hallmark of Japanese naval planning, Yamamoto took it to another level, with 12 different forces dispersed over a large swath of the Pacific Ocean. The plan violated the principle of concentration and made coordination among the far-flung groups difficult. Operation AL took 50 ships into a strategic dead end. Yamamoto's battleships were deployed so far to the rear that they were irrelevant to the outcome of the battle. A primary aspect of Yamamoto's plan was deception so as to lure the Pacific Fleet to its destruction. However, there was no way that such a large operation could be both deceptive and mutually supporting, and Yamamoto should have prioritized mutual support. The result of this flawed planning was that the Japanese were actually outnumbered at the point of contact. Nimitz's force of 26 ships faced the *Kido Butai* with its 20 ships. More importantly, the Americans mustered 348 aircraft (if Midway's aircraft are included) against Nagumo's 248.

NIMITZ PLANS HIS AMBUSH

Despite popular myth, Nimitz's decision to engage the Japanese at Midway was not a desperate gamble against impossible odds but a carefully calculated plan with great potential to cause serious damage to the enemy. Yamamoto was correct that Nimitz was prepared to fight for Midway, but it was not under the conditions Yamamoto assumed. Nimitz needed no prodding to aggressively engage the Japanese as soon as favorable conditions existed. These included committing his few precious carriers against a larger Japanese force if surprise could be gained. Nimitz had already demonstrated his aggressiveness at Coral Sea by sending two carriers to engage a larger Japanese force. He was prepared to do the same at Midway. After Coral Sea he only had two fully operational carriers in the Pacific – *Enterprise* and *Hornet*. *Saratoga* was still under repair and was not expected to return to service until late May. Nimitz's final carrier was the damaged *Yorktown*. Even without her, Nimitz was still determined to send *Enterprise* and *Hornet* to Midway to take on four Japanese fleet carriers – a daunting 1:2 inferiority. If *Yorktown* could be repaired in time, the odds would be much better for the Americans. Nimitz gave the shipyard at Pearl Harbor three days to make *Yorktown* serviceable. Compare this to the total lack of effort by the Japanese to give the undamaged *Zuikaku* a makeshift air group and include her in the operation.

Underpinning his aggressiveness was Nimitz's invaluable advantage of superior intelligence regarding his enemy's strength and intentions. This intelligence was far from omniscient, but it guaranteed that American naval strength was placed in the best position to do the most damage to the Japanese. The Americans had been making steady progress penetrating the main IJN communications code

In Halsey's absence, Rear Admiral Raymond Spruance was given command of TF 16 (this picture shows him as an admiral in April 1944). Though Fletcher was actually in command of the American carrier force at Midway, Spruance received the lion's share of the credit for the victory after he assumed overall command when Fletcher was forced to evacuate his flagship. (Naval History and Heritage Command)

since the start of the war. Real insights were made by April 1942 that allowed up to 85 percent of some messages to be read. From this, the Pacific Fleet's cryptologists assembled a close idea of Yamamoto's upcoming operation. The main target was correctly identified as Midway, where four to five large carriers, two to four fast battleships, seven to nine heavy cruisers (escorted by a commensurate number of destroyers), up to 24 submarines, and a landing force were expected. Additional forces, including carriers, were targeted against the Aleutians. The operation was scheduled for the first week of June but the precise timing remained unclear. Nimitz believed that June 5 was the scheduled day for simultaneous landings on Midway and in the Aleutians. The landing would be preceded by air attack from Japanese carriers on June 3 or 4 and by heavy bombardment by surface ships at night. Submarines were expected to be employed to track and attack American ships headed from Pearl Harbor to Midway, and flying boats refueled by submarines would repeat the March night bombing of Pearl Harbor. This was a fairly close approximation of Japanese plans but lacked some specifics. Nimitz had no knowledge of Yamamoto's decision to include his battleships in the operation, but since they were beyond support range of the *Kido Butai*, this ignorance proved unimportant. The high quality of the intelligence gave Nimitz the confidence to act. It should be noted that the intelligence provided to Fletcher at Coral Sea was faulty with respect to the deployment of the Japanese carriers. But the intelligence provided about Japanese intentions at Midway was largely correct and provided the basis for the only ambush in any of the carrier battles of the Pacific War.

Nimitz used his insights into Yamamoto's plan to carefully deploy his forces. Despite constant suggestions from King that the Pacific Fleet's seven battleships be aggressively employed, Nimitz decided that they should remain out of harm's way based in San Francisco. He lacked the assets to provide his battle line adequate air cover or screening and most importantly did not want his carriers to be hamstrung in any way by the slower battleships. Nimitz's two operational carriers, *Enterprise* and *Hornet*, were assigned to Rear Admiral Spruance (replacing the ill Halsey) as TF 16 and ordered to assume a position northeast of Midway by June 1. *Yorktown*, still designated TF 17, was repaired in only three days and ordered to join TF 16 off Midway by June 2. Rear Admiral Fletcher on *Yorktown* would assume overall command of the two carrier groups.

Intelligence indicated that the Japanese would conduct air strikes on Midway from the northwest. Nimitz placed his carriers 325nm northeast of the island on the *Kido Butai*'s flank to minimize any risk to them while still being in a position to spring an ambush as the Japanese carriers attacked Midway. The key to any potential ambush was scouting support from Midway, which was conducting searches out to 700nm to minimize the prospects for a surprise air raid on the island. The last intelligence provided by Nimitz to Fletcher and Spruance gave an almost precise assessment of Nagumo's force – four carriers, two battleships, two heavy cruisers, and 12 destroyers. Nimitz believed that the Japanese carriers would be in two separate groups each with two carriers. One group would attack Midway with the other providing cover. Nimitz hoped that his carriers could ambush the Japanese carriers attacking Midway, followed by a second phase where three American carriers faced just two Japanese carriers.

Nimitz also possessed the major advantage of fighting within range of friendly land-based aircraft. Midway was stuffed with 115 aircraft, including a large number of long-range reconnaissance aircraft, fighters to defend the base from air attack, and a mixed strike force of Marine, Navy, and Army Air Force aircraft.

Nimitz never saw the battle as a death-struggle for control of Midway. His orders to Fletcher and Spruance made this clear and provided the guidance that they were to "be governed by the principle of calculated risk which you shall interpret to mean the avoidance of exposure of your forces to attack by superior enemy forces without good prospect of inflicting, as a result of such exposure, greater damage to the enemy." In addition to this written order, Nimitz personally instructed Spruance not to lose the carriers no matter what. It must be assumed that Nimitz provided the same instruction to Fletcher. If necessary, Nimitz was prepared to let the Japanese attempt a landing on Midway. He assessed that even if Midway was lost, it could be recaptured later.

Tactically, Nimitz planned that TF 16 would constitute the main strike force. When the Japanese carriers were detected, TF 16 would launch an all-out strike. TF 17 would serve as a search and reserve force to be used at Fletcher's discretion.

Each American carrier air group had a different approach for the upcoming battle and each had a real impact on the battle. *Hornet*'s air group was the least experienced. The ship's commanding officer, Captain Marc Mitscher, decided to allocate only ten Wildcats to strike escort. Since this was not enough to cover both the dive-bombers and torpedo squadrons which were at very different altitudes, he ordered the fighters to stay with the dive-bombers to maintain a height advantage. The commander of *Hornet*'s torpedo squadron was justifiably concerned with the lack of direct fighter protection. *Hornet*'s air group would launch in two deckloads and proceed to the target in two separate groups. The dive-bombers would fly at 20,000 feet and were ordered to keep the torpedo bombers, flying at 1,500 feet, in sight so that a coordinated strike could be executed.

MIDWAY ORDERS OF BATTLE (AS OF JUNE 4, 1942)

IMPERIAL JAPANESE NAVY

FIRST CARRIER STRIKING FORCE (VICE ADMIRAL NAGUMO)
Carrier Division 1 (Vice Admiral Nagumo)
Carrier: *Akagi* (Captain Aoki Taijiro)
  Akagi Air Group (Cdr Fuchida Mitsuo)

Akagi Carrier Fighter Unit	18 Zero
Akagi Carrier Bomber Unit	18 Type 99
Akagi Carrier Attack Unit	18 Type 97

  TOTAL: 54
  6 Zero from 6th Air Group (the Midway garrison unit)
Carrier: *Kaga* (Captain Okada Jisaku)
  Kaga Air Group (Lt Cdr Kusumi Tadashi)

Kaga Carrier Fighter Unit	18 Zero
Kaga Carrier Bomber Unit	18 Type 99
Kaga Carrier Attack Unit	27 Type 97

  TOTAL: 63
  9 Zero from 6th Air Group

Carrier Division 2 (Rear Admiral Yamaguchi)
Carrier: *Hiryu* (Captain Kaku Tomeo)
  Hiryu Air Group (Lt Cdr Tomonaga Joichi)

Hiryu Carrier Fighter Unit	18 Zero
Hiryu Carrier Bomber Unit	18 Type 99
Hiryu Carrier Attack Unit	18 Type 97

  TOTAL: 54
  3 Zero from 6th Air Group
Carrier: *Soryu* (Captain Yanagimoto Ryusaku)
  Soryu Air Group (Lt Cdr Egasa)

Soryu Carrier Fighter Unit	18 Zero
Soryu Carrier Bomber Unit	16 Type 99
	1–2 D4Y1
Soryu Carrier Attack Unit	18 Type 97

  TOTAL: 53–54
  3 Zero from 6th Air Group

Battleship Division 3, Section 2: Battleships *Haruna*, *Kirishima*
Cruiser Division 8: Heavy Cruisers *Tone*, *Chikuma* (each with five search planes)
Destroyer Squadron 10: Light Cruiser *Nagara*
  Destroyer Division 4: Destroyers *Nowaki*, *Arashi*, *Hagikaze*, *Maikaze*
  Destroyer Division 10: Destroyers *Kazagumo*, *Yugumo*, *Makigumo*
  Destroyer Division 17: Destroyers *Urakaze*, *Isokaze*, *Tanikaze*, *Hamakaze*
Supply Group: 5 Oilers, Destroyer *Akigumo*

MAIN FORCE (ADMIRAL YAMAMOTO)
Battleship Division 1: Battleships *Yamato*, *Nagato*, *Mutsu*
Carrier *Hosho* (8 B4Y1 Carrier Attack Aircraft)
Seaplane Tenders: *Chiyoda*, *Nisshin* (both carrying midget submarines for Midway)
Destroyer Squadron 3: Light Cruiser *Sendai*
  Destroyer Division 11: Destroyers *Fubuki*, *Shirayuki*, *Murakumo*, *Hatsuyuki*
  Destroyer Division 19: Destroyers *Isonami*, *Uranami*, *Shikinami*, *Ayanami*
1st Supply Unit: 2 Oilers

GUARD FORCE (VICE ADMIRAL TAKASU SHIRO)
Battleship Division 2: Battleships *Ise, Hyuga, Fuso, Yamashiro*
Cruiser Division 9: Light Cruisers *Oi, Kitakami*
Destroyer Division 20: Destroyers *Asagiri, Yugiri, Shirakumo, Amagiri*
Destroyer Division 24: Destroyers *Umikaze, Yamakaze, Kawakaze, Suzukaze*
Destroyer Division 27: Destroyers *Ariake, Yugure, Shigure, Shiratsuyu*
2nd Supply Unit: 2 Oilers

MIDWAY INVASION FORCE (VICE ADMIRAL KONDO NOBUTAKE)
Light carrier: *Zuiho*
   Zuiho Air Group

Zuiho Carrier Fighter Unit	8 Zero, 6 Type 96 A5M4
Zuiho Carrier Attack Unit	12 Type 97
TOTAL: 26	

Plane Guard Destroyer: *Mikazuki*
Battleship Division 3 (Section 1): Battleships *Kongo, Hiei*
Cruiser Division 4 (Section 1): Heavy Cruisers *Atago, Chokai*
Cruiser Division 5: Heavy Cruisers *Myoko, Haguro*
Destroyer Squadron 4: Light Cruiser *Yura*
   Destroyer Division 3: Destroyers *Murasame, Samidare, Harusame, Yudachi*
   Destroyer Division 9: Destroyers *Asagumo, Minegumo, Natsugumo*
Supply Group: 4 Oilers, Repair Ship *Akashi*

CLOSE SUPPORT GROUP (VICE ADMIRAL KURITA TAKEO)
Cruiser Division 7: Heavy Cruisers *Kumano, Suzuya, Mogami, Mikuma*
Destroyer Division 8: Destroyers *Arashio, Asashio*
1 Oiler

Transport Group (Rear Admiral Tanaka Raizo)
Destroyer Squadron 2: Light Cruiser *Jinstu*
   Destroyer Squadron 15: Destroyers *Kuroshio, Oyashio*
   Destroyer Squadron 16: Destroyers *Yukikaze, Amatsukaze, Tokitsukaze, Hatsukaze*
   Destroyer Squadron 18: Destroyers *Shiranuhi, Kasumi, Kagero, Arare*
Transports: 12 and *Patrol Boats #1, #2, #34*
Oiler: *Akebono Maru*

Seaplane Tender Group (Rear Admiral Fujita Ryutaro)
Seaplane Tenders: *Chitose* (20 aircraft) and *Kamikawa Maru* (12 aircraft)
Destroyer: *Hayashio*
Patrol Boat #35

Minesweeper Group
4 Converted Minesweepers
3 Submarine Chasers
3 Supply/Cargo Ships

Advance Force (Vice Admiral Komatsu Teruhishi)
Submarine Squadron 3: Submarines *I-168, I-169, I-171, I-174, I-175*
Submarine Squadron 5
   Submarine Division 19: Submarines *I-156, I-157, I-158, I-159*
   Submarine Division 30: Submarines *I-162, I-165, I-166*
   Submarine Division 13: Submarines *I-121, I-122, I-123*

ALEUTIANS FORCE
Second Carrier Striking Force (Rear Admiral Kakuta Kakuji)
Carrier Division 4
Light Carrier *Ryujo*
   Ryujo Air Group

Ryujo Carrier Fighter Unit	12 Zero
Ryujo Carrier Attack Unit	18 Type 97
TOTAL: 30	

Light Carrier *Junyo*
   Junyo Air Group

Junyo Carrier Fighter Unit	18 Zero
Junyo Carrier Bomber Unit	15 Type 99
TOTAL: 33	

Cruiser Division 4 (Section 2): Heavy Cruisers *Maya, Takao*
Destroyer Division 7: Destroyers *Akebono, Ushio, Sazanami*
1 Oiler

Main Body (Vice Admiral Hosogaya Moshiro)
Heavy Cruiser: *Nachi*
Destroyers: *Ikazuchi, Inazuma*
2 Oilers
3 Cargo Ships

Attu-Adak Invasion Force (Rear Admiral Omori Sentaro)
Light Cruiser: *Abukuma*
Destroyer Division 21: Destroyers *Wakaba, Nenohi, Hatsushimo, Hatsuhara*
1 Minelayer
1 Troop Transport

Kiska Invasion Force (Captain Ono Takeji)
Cruiser Division 21: Light Cruisers *Kiso, Tama*, 2 Auxiliary Cruisers
Destroyer Division 6: Destroyers *Hibiki, Akatsuki, Hokaze*
2 Troop Transports
3 Converted Minesweepers

Seaplane Tender Force (Captain Ujuku Keiichi)
Seaplane Tender: *Kimikawa Maru* (8 Aircraft)
Destroyer: *Shiokaze*

Submarine Detachment (Rear Admiral Yamazaki Shigeaki)
Submarine Squadron 1: Submarine *I-9*
   Submarine Division 2: Submarines *I-15, I-17, I-19*
   Submarine Division 4: Submarines *I-25, I-26*

AMERICAN FORCES

TASK FORCE 17 (REAR ADMIRAL FLETCHER)
Carrier Group Task Group 17.5
Carrier: *Yorktown* (Captain Elliott Buckmaster)
   Yorktown Air Group (Lt Cdr Oscar Perderson)

Fighting Three (Lt Cdr John Thatch)	25 F4F-4

Bombing Three (Lt Cdr Maxwell Leslie)	18 SBD-3
Scouting Five (Lt Wallace Short)	19 SBD-3
Torpedo Five (Lt Cdr Lance Massey)	13 TBD-1
TOTAL: 75	

Cruiser Group Task Group 17.2: Heavy Cruisers *Astoria*, *Portland*
Destroyer Screen Task Group 17.4: Destroyers *Morris*, *Anderson*, *Hammann*, *Russell*, *Hughes*, *Gwin*

TASK FORCE 16 (REAR ADMIRAL SPRUANCE)
Carrier Group Task Group 16.5
Carrier: *Enterprise* (Captain George Murray)

Enterprise Air Group (Lt Cdr Clarence McClusky)

Fighting Six (Lt James Gray)	27 F4F-4
Bombing Six (Lt Richard Best)	19 SBD-2/3
Scouting Six (Lt Wilmer Gallaher)	19 SBD-2/3
Torpedo Six (Lt Cdr Eugene Lindsey)	14 TBD-1
TOTAL: 79	

Carrier: *Hornet* (Captain Marc Mitscher)

Hornet Air Group (Cdr Stanhope Ring)

Fighting Eight (Lt Cdr Samuel Mitchell)	27 F4F-4
Bombing Eight (Lt Cdr Robert Johnson)	19 SBD-2/3
Scouting Eight (Lt Cdr Walter Rodee)	18 SBD-1/2/3
Torpedo Eight (Lt Cdr John Waldron)	15 TBD-1
TOTAL: 79	

Cruiser Group Task Group 16.2
Heavy Cruisers: *Minneapolis*, *New Orleans*, *Vincennes*, *Northampton*, *Pensacola*; Light Cruiser *Atlanta*
Destroyer Screen Task Group 16.4: Destroyers *Phelps*, *Alywin*, *Monaghan*, *Worden*, *Balch*, *Conyngham*, *Benham*, *Ellet*, *Maury*
Oiler Group: Oilers *Cimarron*, *Platte*; Destroyers *Dewey*, *Monssen*

Submarine Force (Rear Admiral Robert English)
Task Group 7.1 Midway Patrol Group: Submarines *Cachalot*, *Flying Fish*, *Tambor*, *Trout*, *Grayling*, *Nautilus*, *Grouper*, *Dolphin*, *Gato*, *Cuttlefish*, *Gudgeon*, *Grenadier*
Task Force 7.2 "Roving Short-stops": Submarines *Narwhal*, *Plunger*, *Trigger*
Task Force 7.3 (North of Oahu): Submarines *Tarpon*, *Pike*, *Finback*, *Growler*

HAWAIIAN SEA FRONTIER
Deployed at French Frigate Shoals: Destroyer *Clark*; Seaplane Tenders *Ballard*, *Thornton*
Deployed at Pearl and Hermes Reef: Oiler *Kaloli*; Minesweeper/Tug *Vireo*; Converted Yacht *Crystal*
Deployed at Lisianski, Gardner Pinnacles, Laysan and Necker: 4 Patrol Boats
Midway Relief Fueling Unit: Oiler *Guadalupe*; Destroyers *Blue*, *Ralph Talbot*
Midway Atoll Garrison (Captain Cyril Simard)
Midway Naval Air Station (Captain Simard)
Marine Aircraft Group 22 (Lt Col Ira Kimes)

VMF-211	21 F2A-3 Buffalo (20 operational June 4)
7 F4F-3	(6 operational)
VMSB-241	19 SBD-2 (18 operational)
	21 SB2U-3 Vindicator (14 operational)
VT-8 (Detachment)	6 TBF-1 Avenger (6 operational)
Patrol Squadron (VP) 24	6 PBY-5A (6 operational)
VP-44	8 PBY-5A (7 operational)
VP-51	3 PBY-5A (3 operational)
Sand Island Seaplane Base	
VP-23	14 PBY-5 (13 operational)

MIDWAY ORDERS OF BATTLE (AS OF JUNE 4, 1942) (CONT.)

UNITED STATES ARMY AIR CORPS VII ARMY AIR FORCE DETACHMENT

22nd and 69th Bombardment Squadrons (Medium)

31st, 42nd, 72nd, 431st Bombardment Squadrons (Heavy)
and 7th Air Force Headquarters:

349th Bombardment Squadron (Heavy)

4 B-26 Marauder (4 operational)

16 B-17E Flying Fortress (14 operational)
1 B-17D (1 operational)

Midway Local Defenses

6th Marine Defense Battalion (reinforced with elements of the Third Marine Defense Battalion and two companies from 2nd Raider Battalion)

Total strength of garrison: 3,652 personnel

Motor Torpedo Boat Squadron 1: 10 PT Boats, 4 Patrol Craft

ALEUTIANS FORCES

Task Group 8 (Rear Admiral Robert Theobald)

Heavy Cruisers: *Indianapolis, Louisville*; Light Cruisers *Nashville, St. Louis, Honolulu*

Destroyer Division 11: Destroyers *Gridley, McCall, Gilmer, Humphreys*

Destroyer Striking Group (Cdr Wyatt Craig): Destroyers *Case, Reid, Brooks, Sands, Kane, Dent, Talbot, King, Waters*

Submarine Group (Cdr Burton Lake): Submarines *S-18, S-23, S-27, S-28, S-35*

Tanker Group (Captain Houston Maples): Tankers *Sabine, Brazos*; Transport *Comet*

The inexperience of *Hornet*'s air group was demonstrated by the decision to launch the escort fighters in the first deckload. This made them wait for the entire strike to be launched and formed up before departing for the target. The failure to preserve the fuel of the short-legged Wildcats would prove disastrous.

Enterprise's more experienced air group opted to launch its strike in two deckloads with the escort fighters part of the second deckload. All squadrons were to fly within sight of one another so that a coordinated strike could be executed. The commander of the fighter squadron decided to provide direct support to the dive-bombers, but promised the acting commander of the torpedo squadron that he would bring his fighters to support the Devastators if conditions required. *Yorktown*'s air group decided to send all eight of its escort fighters with the more vulnerable torpedo bombers. Before the battle the size of a fighter squadron was increased to 27 aircraft, which was made possible by the introduction of the F4F-4 model with folding wings. Most of these were allocated to fleet air defense.

OPENING MOVES

The *Kido Butai* departed Hashirajima Anchorage on May 27, which was one day later than scheduled. Because the landing day on Midway Atoll was fixed due to tidal conditions, Yamamoto did not modify the timing for Operation MI.

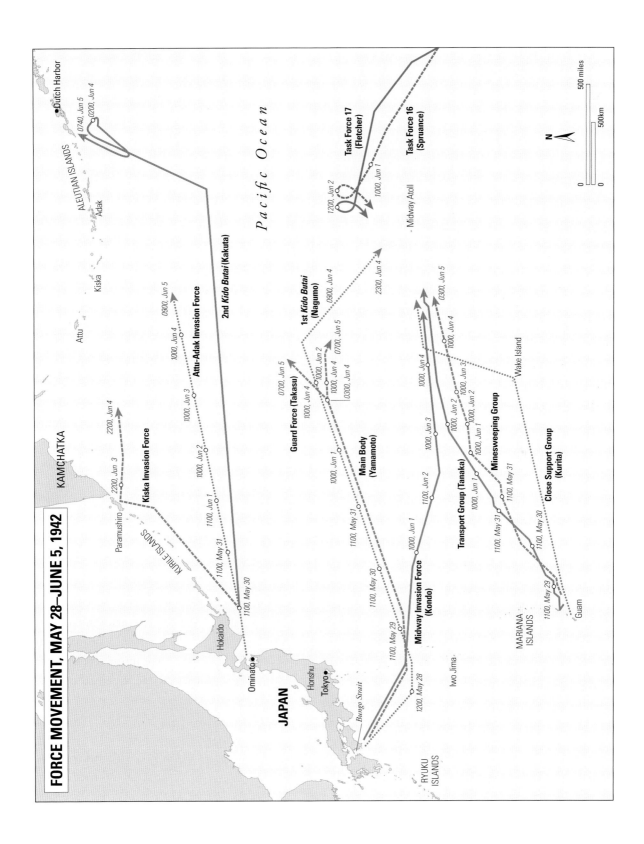

FORCE MOVEMENT, MAY 28–JUNE 5, 1942

Dutch Harbor

0740, Jun 5
0200, Jun 4

ALEUTIAN ISLANDS

Adak

Attu

Kiska

KAMCHATKA

2200, Jun 4

2200, Jun 3

Paramushiro

Kiska Invasion Force

KURILE ISLANDS

1100, May 31

1100, Jun 1

1100, Jun 2

1000, Jun 3

1000, Jun 4

0900, Jun 5

Attu-Adak Invasion Force

2nd *Kido Butai* (Kakuta)

1100, May 30

Hokaido

Ominato

Honshu

Tokyo

JAPAN

Bungo Strait

1200, May 28

RYUKU ISLANDS

Iwo Jima

MARIANA ISLANDS

Guam

1100, May 29

Close Support Group (Kurita)

1100, May 30

Transport Group (Tanaka)

1100, May 31

1000, Jun 1

Minesweeping Group

1000, Jun 2

1000, Jun 3

1000, Jun 4

0300, Jun 5

Wake Island

1100, May 29

1100, May 30

1100, May 31

1100, Jun 2

1000, Jun 1

Midway Invasion Force (Kondo)

1000, Jun 1

1000, Jun 2

1000, Jun 3

1000, Jun 4

Main Body (Yamamoto)

1100, May 31

1000, Jun 1

Guard Force (Takasu)

1000, Jun 4

0700, Jun 5

1000, Jun 2

1000, Jun 4

0300, Jun 4

0700, Jun 5

0900, Jun 4

2300, Jun 4

1st *Kido Butai* (Nagumo)

Pacific Ocean

Midway Atoll

1000, Jun 1

1200, Jun 2

Task Force 17 (Fletcher)

Task Force 16 (Spruance)

N

500 miles

500km

It simply meant that there was one day less to neutralize American defenses on Midway before the scheduled landing; this provided another indication of Japanese overconfidence.

Other parts of Operation MI were also behind schedule. The submarines failed to meet their planned June 1 arrival on the picket line between Hawaii and Midway. Some submarines arrived on station as late as June 3, which was well after TF 16 and TF 17 passed through the area. Incredibly, the responsible commander did not think it important to inform Yamamoto of his submarines' late arrival. The flying boat reconnaissance of Pearl Harbor (Operation K) was canceled on May 31 when submarine *I-121* approached the French Frigate Shoals and found American warships present.

Despite the failure of the submarines to provide any early warning of the movements of the Pacific Fleet, there were other signs that indicated heightened American readiness. Submarine *I-168* conducted a reconnaissance of Midway on June 2 and reported heavy air activity during the day and work continuing at night. Analysis of USN radio traffic noted an increase in American naval radio traffic with many messages marked "urgent." This led to a new Japanese intelligence assessment that the Pacific Fleet was not sitting idly in Pearl Harbor. This was ignored since it did not conform with the presumption that Operation MI was guaranteed tactical and strategic surprise.

The Pacific Fleet was far from idle. TF 16 arrived at Pearl Harbor on May 26 following its brief South Pacific deployment. The damaged *Yorktown* arrived at Pearl Harbor the next day and went into drydock the following morning for essential repairs. Spruance led TF 16 out of the harbor on May 28 and headed to its position

A US Army Air Force B-17 heavy bomber takes off from Midway during the battle. Despite extensive claims of success by B-17 pilots during the battle, not a single B-17 bomb hit its target. (Naval History and Heritage Command)

northeast of Midway. *Yorktown* completed her hurried repairs on May 29 and departed the next morning to join TF 16 off Midway. The two task forces rendezvoused on June 2 and Fletcher assumed command of the combined force.

Not knowing that the *Kido Butai* was one day behind schedule, the Americans expected the opening Japanese air strikes on Midway to begin on June 3. Fletcher ordered *Yorktown* to launch 20 Dauntlesses to conduct searches and then moved his carriers to a new position some 175nm further west in anticipation of the Japanese attack. No contact was made with the Japanese since the *Kido Butai* was both behind schedule and shielded from detection by very bad weather north of Midway.

THE BATTLE OPENS

Yamamoto's refusal to alter his plan after the delayed departure of Nagumo's carriers meant that the battle did not open with the surprise air raid on Midway. The other Japanese forces continued their approach to Midway as planned, and by June 3 were within range of Midway's air searches. At 0843 hours on June 3, a PBY spotted the Minesweeper Group. Less than an hour later, another PBY spotted the Transport Group some 700nm west of Midway. The contact was incorrectly reported as the Japanese "Main Body." This prompted the first attack of the battle, which was delivered by nine B-17s from the 431st Bombardment Squadron. The strike departed Midway after noon; bombing from their standard altitude, the bombers hit nothing. Though unsuccessful, the attack shattered the Japanese illusion that strategic surprise was guaranteed. The Americans followed up with a night attack against the Transport Group mounted by four radar-equipped PBYs rigged to carry torpedoes. One of the lumbering flying boats aborted because of weather but the other three arrived over the target at about 0130 hours on June 4. The first two PBYs launched their torpedoes with no success but the third hit tanker *Akebono Maru*, killing 23 crewmen. The tanker was able to continue in formation, but the Americans had drawn first blood.

The *Kido Butai* made its presence felt later on the morning of June 4. Beginning at 0430 hours from a position 210nm to the northwest of Midway, Nagumo launched a large strike of 108 aircraft to cripple American defenses on the island. The attack consisted of 18 dive-bombers from *Akagi* and *Kaga* and 18 Type 97s carrying bombs from *Soryu* and *Hiryu*. One of *Hiryu*'s aircraft was forced to abort after experiencing engine problems. The strike was given a strong fighter escort of nine Zeros from each carrier. Fuchida normally would have led such an important attack but he was laid up after an appendectomy, so the responsibility fell to Lieutenant Tomonaga Joichi from *Hiryu*. The Japanese expected to catch Midway's aircraft on the ground where they could be easily destroyed. To guard against this,

ABOVE The Japanese raid on Midway inflicted heavy damage on the island's fixed facilities as shown in this view of a destroyed hangar. More importantly, the Japanese suffered heavily with 11 aircraft lost and another 14 severely damaged. (Naval History and Heritage Command)

RIGHT Lt Tomonaga Joichi, commander of *Hiryu*'s air group, played an important part in the battle. As the commander of the Japanese strike on Midway on the morning of June 4, he called for a second strike on the island, which started a chain of events leading to the calamitous American air strike on the *Kido Butai*. Later in the day, he led the second strike on *Yorktown* which ultimately led to her sinking. (Naval History and Heritage Command)

the American commander on Midway had already taken measures to avoid being caught flat-footed. He launched a dawn CAP at 0350 hours, which was followed by the launch of 22 PBYs for search operations at 0415 hours. All 15 B-17s were launched next for another attack on the Transport Group, but they departed with orders to head north if the Japanese carriers were detected. The rest of Midway's strike aircraft were readied for immediate launch once the Japanese carriers were located.

The Japanese Midway strike headed south at 0445 hours and at 0615 their target was in sight. All available fighters from Marine Fighter Squadron VMF-211 were scrambled and made a radar-directed interception of the Japanese some 30 miles from the island at 0620 hours. Against the 36 Zeros, the Marines could muster six Wildcats and 18 F-2A Buffalos. The Japanese fighters were caught out of position, so the Marines were able to get a firing pass against the bombers. Two *Hiryu* Type 97s were shot down and several damaged, including Tomonaga's. The Zeros quickly gained the upper hand and all but massacred the Marines; two Wildcats and 13 Buffalos were shot down for only two Zeros damaged. Only two of the remaining nine Marine fighters returned to Midway undamaged.

With the Marine fighters routed, the Type 97s opened the attack with their 1,760lb bombs against facilities on Eastern and Sand Islands. American antiaircraft fire was very heavy and it accounted for another *Hiryu* Type 97 bomber. Next came the dive-bombers at 0640 hours. *Akagi*'s aircraft struck targets on Eastern Island while *Kaga*'s dive-bombers hit facilities on Sand Island. One *Kaga* Type 99 was destroyed by antiaircraft fire and another four were damaged. The Zeros followed with strafing attacks; two were shot down. The Japanese attack met terrific resistance and one strike was clearly insufficient to neutralize the islands' defenses, so Tomonaga signaled to Nagumo "there is need for a second attack wave." Not only had the attack failed to neutralize Midway but it had suffered much in the process. American fighters and antiaircraft fire accounted for 11 Japanese aircraft shot down or ditched – eight Type 97s, two Zeros, and one dive-bomber. In addition, many aircraft – as many as 43 – were damaged. Fourteen were so heavily damaged that they were not operational. Of particular importance for events later in the day, *Hiryu*'s carrier attack plane squadron was down to just eight fully operational aircraft.

THE CARRIER BATTLE BEGINS

Just as at Coral Sea, weather played a factor at Midway. There were heavy clouds to the north, northeast, and east of Midway that favored the Americans. Throughout June 4 there was a calm breeze from the southeast that forced carriers from both sides to turn into the wind at high speeds to get sufficient wind over the deck to launch aircraft. This meant that the American carriers were steaming to the southeast during flight operations, which was actually away from the Japanese. This was an important factor as it increased the distance their short-range strike aircraft had to cover to reach their targets. The Japanese carriers possessed the advantage of generally steaming toward their targets during launches.

As always, reconnaissance was key, and here the Americans had a huge advantage as they could rely on the PBYs from Midway to find the Japanese carriers. At 0430 hours, Fletcher's carriers were some 200nm north-northeast of Midway. To cover his northern flank, Fletcher launched ten *Yorktown* Dauntlesses to search to the north out to 100nm. After the scout aircraft were launched, Fletcher turned back to the northeast.

One of the key aspects of the battle was the *Kido Butai*'s lack of emphasis on search operations. On the morning of June 4, Fletcher's carriers were located some 215nm east of the *Kido Butai*, which placed it well within range of Japanese reconnaissance aircraft. Had Nagumo insisted on a robust search plan, the huge American intelligence advantage would have amounted to little. Better reconnaissance might have given the Japanese a chance to turn the tables on the Americans and deliver a shattering blow against Fletcher's force. After the events off Ceylon two months earlier, Yamamoto gave orders that half of the *Kido Butai*'s air strength be held in reserve in case the American fleet made an unexpected appearance. This powerful force included 43 Type 97s aboard *Akagi* and *Kaga* armed with torpedoes, and the dive-bomber squadrons aboard *Hiryu* and *Soryu* with a total of 34 Type 99s; 24 Zeros were allocated for escort. Yamamoto's concern with a possible early appearance by the Pacific Fleet was not shared by Nagumo or his staff.

Nagumo's staff developed a reconnaissance plan that included only seven aircraft. Five of these were floatplanes from the battleships and cruisers and were augmented by a mere two Type 97s. Six were ordered to fly out to 300nm and the last out to 150nm in a widely spaced pattern. This effort was half-hearted at best, but was closer to being negligent. Even Genda admitted after the war, "the planning of the air searching was slipshod." The seven aircraft left large gaps in coverage even in good weather, and the weather was far from good especially in the areas where the American carriers were waiting in ambush. On top of this, several search aircraft were not launched as planned at 0430 hours. The two aircraft from heavy cruiser *Tone* were launched 12 and 30 minutes late, and the delays were not even reported to Nagumo.

The American reconnaissance efforts paid off first. At 0530 hours, Fletcher received a report of "Enemy Carriers" from a Midway PBY. Next was a report at 0552 hours from another PBY of "Many planes headed Midway, bearing 310 distance 150." The PBY that issued the vague report of enemy carriers later clarified its sighting, but this report was not received aboard TF 16 or TF 17. Fletcher did copy the Midway rebroadcast of the report at 0603 hours, which was sent to the B-17s already airborne – "Two carriers and battleships, bearing 320 degrees, distance 180, course 135, speed 25." This was the report Fletcher had been waiting for, and the report of two carriers corresponded with the intelligence provided by Nimitz. Fletcher's staff calculated that the Japanese were 180nm from TF 16 which put them within striking range. However, the report was inaccurate, and the *Kido Butai* was actually 200nm from TF 16 and thus just beyond range.

Fletcher seized the opportunity to attack first and ordered Spruance to take TF 16 to the south and launch a full strike. There was an element of risk in his action since only two Japanese carriers had been reported – intelligence suggested the other two could be operating separately and these were unlocated. Fletcher decided to hold *Yorktown*'s aircraft in reserve until the missing carriers were located. Around 0630 hours *Yorktown* recovered her ten scout Dauntlesses and headed southwest at high speed to follow Spruance.

Spruance and his staff planned a launch for 0700 hours, when it was calculated that the Japanese carriers would be some 155nm away, which would make it easier for the short-ranged Wildcats and Devastators. On *Hornet*, Mitscher and his air group commander opted to send their strike on a course of 265 degrees, which was well to the north of the reported position of the Japanese carriers. The reason for this miscalculation has never been explained, but its consequences were huge.

TF 16's strike began to launch at 0700 hours as planned. The launch took considerable time since two deckloads were required. It was not until 0755 hours that *Hornet*'s strike group headed toward the Japanese. *Enterprise*'s performance was worse, since by 0745 hours its second deckload was still not airborne. At this point Spruance ordered Commander Wade McClusky and the dive-bombers to proceed independently to the target. *Enterprise*'s fighters were the last to be launched and, once airborne, sighted *Hornet*'s torpedo-bomber squadron and decided to escort them. Instead of two air groups headed to their targets with their squadrons in loose company in order to launch a coordinated attack, Spruance's big blow was actually dispersed into three groups. The largest was the *Hornet* air group with *Enterprise*'s fighters trailing behind. *Enterprise*'s delayed launch put her dive-bombers and torpedo aircraft in two separate groups. There was little chance that these groups could mount a coordinated strike since each was taking a separate course to the target. Nevertheless, the Americans had succeeded in putting 116 aircraft – 20 fighters, 67 dive-bombers, and 29 torpedo planes – into the air and they were headed for the unsuspecting Japanese.

MIDWAY ATTACKS THE JAPANESE CARRIERS

The first American aircraft to attack Nagumo's carriers were Midway's strike groups. When the PBY contact reports were received, the strike aircraft were launched at once to avoid being caught on the ground. All the Midway fighters were allocated to defend the airfield, so the 51 Navy, Marine, and Army Air Force aircraft proceeded without escort.

The first aircraft spotted Nagumo's force just after 0700 hours. There was no attempt to mount a coordinated attack, so the ensuing action developed into a series of uncoordinated small-scale attacks. The Japanese were ready and had 29 Zeros on CAP.

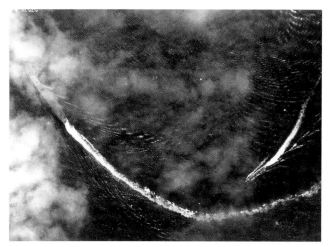

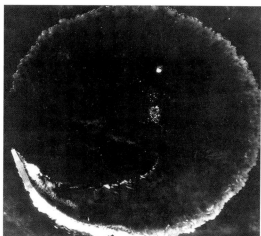

ABOVE *Akagi* pictured under attack by B-17s during the 0800 hour on June 4. The ship behind *Akagi* is destroyer *Nowaki* assigned as *Akagi*'s plane guard. Note the absence of any aircraft on *Akagi*'s flight deck and the large Rising Sun painted forward. (Naval History and Heritage Command)

ABOVE RIGHT This is *Soryu* under attack from B-17s during the 0800 hour. The ship is using the preferred Japanese evasion maneuver of steering in a tight circle. There is a single aircraft spotted aft; *Soryu* also carries a large Rising Sun forward. (Naval History and Heritage Command)

RIGHT *Hiryu* was also targeted for attack by B-17s between 0800 and 0830 hours as indicated by the string of bombs off her starboard quarter. A *shotai* of three Zeros is visible on the flight deck near the bridge; Japanese records indicate that these fighters took off at 0825 hours, so the picture was taken before then. As on the *Kido Butai*'s other carriers, a large Rising Sun has been painted on the forward section of the flight deck. (Naval History and Heritage Command)

The first attack was conducted at 0710 hours by six TBF Avenger torpedo planes and four Army Air Force B-26 Marauder medium bombers operating as torpedo bombers. The Avenger was making its combat debut. The Zeros swarmed over the unescorted American aircraft, shooting down all but one Avenger and two B-26s. Two TBFs were able to launch torpedoes at *Hiryu* and a single B-26 launched its weapon against *Akagi*, but all were easily avoided. Two Zeros were lost.

Next to arrive over the *Kido Butai* shortly after 0800 hours were 16 Marine Dauntless dive-bombers. The squadron's commander, Major Lofton Henderson (for which the airfield on Guadalcanal was later named), did not believe his

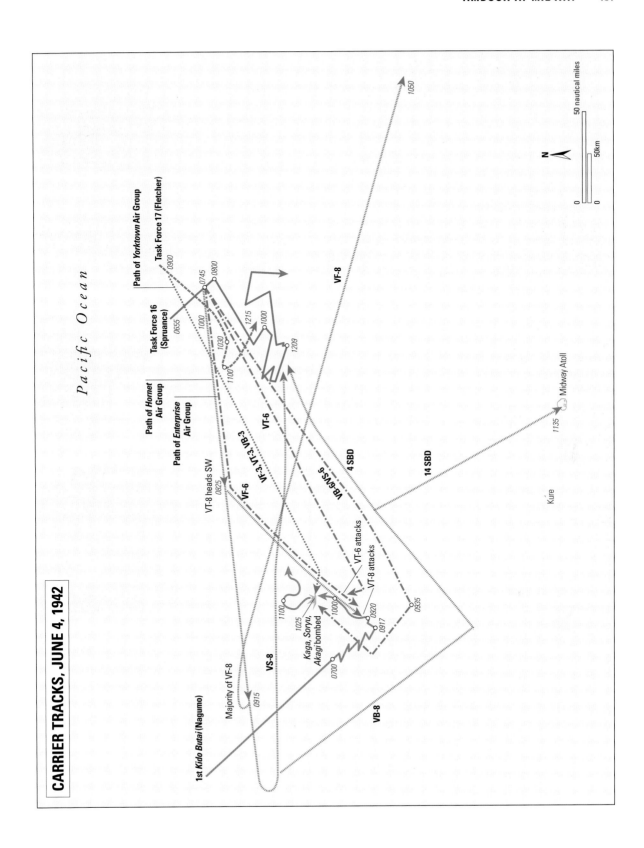

CARRIER TRACKS, JUNE 4, 1942

Pacific Ocean

Path of *Yorktown* Air Group

Task Force 17 (Fletcher)

0900

0745
0800

Task Force 16
(Spruance)

0655
1000

1000

1215

1030

1100

1209

VF-8

Path of *Hornet*
Air Group

Path of *Enterprise*
Air Group

VF-6

VT-8 heads SW

VF-3 · VT-3 · VB-3

0825

VF-6

VB-6·VS-6

4 SBD

14 SBD

Midway Atoll

1135

Kure

VT-6 attacks

VT-8 attacks

0935

0920
0917

1000

1100

1025

*Kaga, Soryu,
Akagi* bombed

VS-8

Majority of VF-8

0915

0700

VB-8

1st *Kido Butai* (Nagumo)

N

50 nautical miles

50km

0

0

1050

inexperienced pilots could execute a full dive-bomb attack, so he ordered a less demanding glide-bomb attack on the nearest carrier. This target was *Hiryu* and she was heavily defended by 13 Zeros on CAP with another six on the way. The Zeros shot down eight Marine aircraft (including Henderson's) and damaged another four beyond repair, but the Marines pressed their attack home. None of their bombs hit *Hiryu* but there were several near misses. One *Hiryu* fighter was lost.

Midway's aircraft continued their attacks unabated. Next to arrive were 14 B-17s that delivered a high-altitude attack against *Soryu*, *Hiryu*, and *Akagi* from an altitude of over 20,000 feet. From this altitude there was virtually no chance of a hit on the maneuvering carriers; in fact, the B-17s failed to score a single hit during the entire battle. The B-17s departed by 0820 hours with no success. Nine *Soryu* Zeros and three from *Kaga* engaged the heavy bombers, but no aircraft were lost on either side. Midway's final attack was conducted by 11 Marine SB2U-3 Vindicator dive-bombers. This was the sole combat appearance of these obsolescent aircraft during the war. Their commander wisely decided not to attempt to reach the carriers against the swarming Zeros, so the Vindicators conducted a glide-bomb attack on battleship *Haruna*. None of their bombs struck the battleships but seven of the obsolescent aircraft returned to Midway.

NAGUMO UNDER PRESSURE

Midway was a complex battle with an interwoven chain of events. Each commander had to assess his best course of action under severe time constraints and with inaccurate or incomplete information. Fletcher had already made his decision to launch his knockout blow based on solid intelligence, but Nagumo's situation soon spiraled out of his control. These decisions shaped the outcome of the battle. Per Yamamoto's orders, Nagumo held a large reserve force armed for attacks on American ships. This force constituted the most powerful strike elements available to Nagumo – the carrier attack squadrons aboard *Akagi* and *Kaga* with 43 Type 97s and the dive-bomber squadrons on *Hiryu* and *Soryu* with 34 Type 99s.

Events began to unravel for Nagumo with Tomonaga's 0700 hours recommendation that a second Midway strike was required. Air attacks by the aircraft from Midway began to unfold minutes later, and the massive strike from Spruance's carriers was just being launched. This was also the time that Japanese scout aircraft would reach the end of their outward search leg. Since there were no reports from his scouts of any American ships in the area, Nagumo decided to disobey Yamamoto's orders at 0715 hours and directed that the reserve aircraft be armed for a strike on Midway. This would take time. Replacing the torpedoes on the Type 97s with 1,760lb bombs could take as much as two hours under normal conditions. In comparison, the switch from semi-armor-piercing bombs used to attack ships to land-attack high-explosive bombs on the dive-bombers was much easier and quicker.

As the rearming process was beginning, Nagumo received a vague but alarming report at 0740 hours. The report came from cruiser *Tone*'s search plane Number 4: "Sight what appears to be ten enemy surface ships, in position bearing 010 degrees distance 250 miles from Midway. Course 150 degrees, speed over 20 knots." The report was from the *Tone* aircraft that had been 30 minutes late in launching. Perhaps to make up for this, the Aichi E13A Navy Type 0 Reconnaissance Seaplane (hereafter referred to as an E13A floatplane) only flew out 250nm instead of the planned 300nm before turning north for its dog leg prior to returning home. This was actually a huge stroke of luck for the Japanese since this change of course placed the floatplane near TF 17. Earlier, search plane Number 1 from cruiser *Chikuma* missed TF 17 even though its planned route put it within 20nm of the American carriers at about 0630 hours. Whether off-course due to poor navigation or because of cloud cover, the aircraft sighted nothing.

The *Tone* floatplane report was more than just alarming. It was actually incorrect by some 50nm and frustratingly vague. It was still enough for Nagumo to order the suspension of the rearming effort at 0745 hours. He ordered the search aircraft at 0747 hours: "Ascertain ship types and maintain contact." This took until 0830 hours, when *Tone* Number 4 radioed, "the enemy is accompanied by what appears to be a carrier." Nagumo ordered the immediate launch of the prototype D4Y1 reconnaissance aircraft on *Soryu* to track this new contact.

This was the pivotal moment of the battle. Nagumo still had the means to deal with this unexpected threat. Most of the 43 Type 97s still retained torpedoes, and the 34 dive-bombers had the proper ordnance for attacking ships. Since most of the Zeros allocated as strike escorts had been launched to reinforce the CAP, only six were immediately available. Having just seen the unescorted aircraft from Midway massacred by his CAP, Nagumo was reluctant to send his strike off without sufficient escort. He had to make a quick decision since the Midway strike was due back at 0815 hours and many of these aircraft were damaged or low on fuel. Nagumo had two choices – launch an immediate strike with whatever was available or wait to launch a massive strike after his Midway strike had landed and the new strike could be properly armed and escorted. Rear Admiral Yamaguchi on *Hiryu*, known for his aggressiveness, advised Nagumo to launch an immediate strike. Genda advised that a coordinated strike would be best. Nagumo ignored Yamaguchi's counsel and decided to launch an attack which was properly armed and escorted.

The problem with this course of action was that Nagumo needed time to execute it. With most of the Midway aircraft still to attack and over 100 of Spruance's aircraft headed for the *Kido Butai*, the Japanese did not have the luxury of time. In hindsight, it should have been obvious what the original *Tone* contact report meant even if it was frustratingly vague. What were ten ships doing on Nagumo's flank heading into the wind? Had Nagumo launched his strike force immediately, almost all of the Type 97s would still have had their torpedoes and the strike could have been launched before the Midway strike had to land. Enough fighters could have been mustered from the CAP to provide an adequate escort. This window for action quickly closed at 0753 hours when more American aircraft were spotted. For the next 40 minutes, the *Kido Butai* was attacked by three groups of American aircraft. This kept the carrier decks busy recovering and launching CAP aircraft, which meant there was no chance to bring any aircraft up from the hangar decks and spot them for launch.

Nagumo was not the only admiral under pressure. At 0815 hours, *Enterprise*'s radar detected an unidentified aircraft 30nm to the south. Wildcats were sent to intercept the intruder but could not make contact. The intruder was *Tone* search plane Number 4 and the Americans had intercepted its contact reports. Fletcher now knew his force had been spotted. Since he believed that two Japanese carriers had not yet been spotted, this development was extremely worrisome. Not wanting to be caught with fueled and armed planes on deck, Fletcher decided to launch most of the *Yorktown* strike that he had kept in reserve. This began at 0830 hours and took 30 minutes to complete. Now another 17 Dauntlesses, 12 Devastators, and six Wildcats were heading toward the *Kido Butai*. Only 17 dive-bombers and six fighters remained uncommitted.

THE BATTLE IS DECIDED

Nagumo needed until 1030 hours to prepare his grand strike consisting of 34 dive-bombers, 43 Type 97s carrying torpedoes, and 12 Zeros for escort. Until that time the CAP could deal with the brave but ineffective American attacks. At 0837 hours, the *Kido Butai* turned into the wind to recover the Midway strike. After this was completed by 0918 hours, Nagumo changed course to the northeast and increased speed to 30 knots to close the carrier contact.

As Nagumo tried to buy time, aircraft from three American carriers were about to arrive over the *Kido Butai* and begin the series of attacks that would decide the battle. During the span of time from 0915 to 1040 hours, the *Kido Butai* would go from a seemingly invincible to a defeated force. Despite the lack of coordination in the American attacks, the fortunes of war placed the USN's

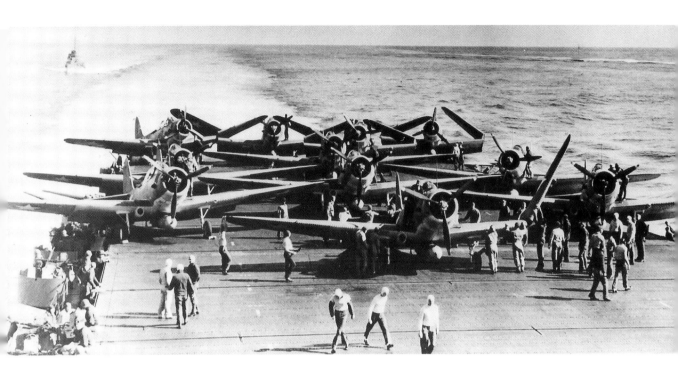

most accurate and powerful weapons over three undefended Japanese carriers at the exact moment when they were most vulnerable.

The first American aircraft to find the *Kido Butai* were *Hornet*'s torpedo squadron under Lieutenant Commander John Waldron. He led his squadron away from the *Hornet* air group formation at 0825 hours and headed to the southwest where he was sure the enemy was located. His certainty was rewarded when he spotted the Japanese carrier force headed directly toward him at 0915 hours. Waldron ordered an immediate attack on the nearest carrier, which happened to be *Soryu*. Since the Devastators were unescorted, they were virtually defenseless against the 18 Zeros on CAP. All 15 of the slow Devastators were methodically and mercilessly destroyed between 0920 and 0937 hours. Only a single Devastator got close enough to launch a torpedo at *Soryu*, but the weapon was readily avoided by the nimble carrier.

Immediately after the last *Hornet* Devastator was shot down, *Enterprise*'s torpedo squadron under Lieutenant Commander Eugene Lindsey began its attack. He had lost sight of the *Enterprise* dive-bombers but at 0930 hours noted smoke 30nm to the northwest. Lindsey took his 14 Devastators to investigate and soon sighted the *Kido Butai* headed northeast at high speed. The nearest Japanese carrier was *Kaga*, which Lindsey attempted to hit with an anvil attack. By this time there were 27 Zeros on CAP, which were guided to the approaching Americans when *Tone* opened fire at the Devastators with her main battery at

Torpedo Squadron Six spotted on *Enterprise*'s flight deck on the morning of June 4. Only four of these aircraft returned to *Enterprise*. (Naval History and Heritage Command)

0940 hours. The Zeros had another field day, shooting down nine more Devastators. Remarkably, five got close enough to launch their torpedoes against *Kaga*, but since the weapons were released at extreme range and with bad target angles, none hit. The five Devastators flew through the *Kido Butai* and exited to the east. Only four recovered on *Enterprise*. While Waldron's squadron was being manhandled by the Zeros, the ten Wildcats from *Enterprise* assigned to escort them were circling overhead the *Kido Butai* at 22,000 feet. The Wildcats were not spotted by the Japanese for some 30 minutes, indicating that their attention was fixated on the Devastators at low altitude. The fighters made no attempt to intervene since they never heard Lindsey's cries for assistance. After making a contact report at 0956 hours, the Wildcats headed back to *Enterprise*.

A key part of Spruance's strike was the 34 Dauntlesses from *Hornet*. None of these aircraft sighted a Japanese ship on June 4, making their operations one of the most controversial aspects of the battle. As mentioned above, *Hornet*'s air group under Commander Stanhope Ring was ordered to fly a course of 265 degrees to the target. Since the PBY contact report placed the Japanese carriers on a course of 240 degrees from TF 16, Ring's heading would take his air group to the north of the *Kido Butai*. Waldron sensed that Ring was headed to nowhere, so he took his torpedo squadron to the southwest where he quickly found the Japanese, with fateful consequences. Ring's Dauntlesses, escorted by ten Wildcats, passed well north of the *Kido Butai*. When the formation was some 150–160nm from *Hornet*, the Wildcats turned back due to fuel concerns. They never found *Hornet* and all ten were forced to ditch; fortunately, all but two of the pilots were later rescued. At 225nm out, the formation disintegrated. Ring and 14 other Dauntlesses headed back to *Hornet* and again passed north of the *Kido Butai*. The other 18 dive-bombers headed south in an attempt to locate the Japanese. When they were finally forced to turn east to return to *Hornet*, they passed south of the *Kido Butai*. Eventually, four of the aircraft recovered aboard *Hornet* with the rest forced to land on Midway.

The total failure of *Hornet*'s dive-bombers left *Enterprise*'s dive-bombers as the most powerful remaining American air element now headed toward the *Kido Butai*. Lieutenant Commander Wade McClusky launched with 33 Dauntlesses (reduced to 32 after one abort) and departed on a course of 231 degrees. After reaching a point about 140nm out where he expected to find the Japanese, McClusky saw nothing. He assessed that the Japanese were to his northwest, so he changed course in that direction at 0935 hours. Almost at the end of his planned northwesterly track, he spotted a Japanese destroyer steaming north-northeasterly at high speed at 0955 hours. With battle-winning logic, he assessed the destroyer was headed to rejoin the main Japanese force, so he took his dive-bombers in the

LEFT *Enterprise* steaming at high speed with an escorting cruiser in the background. Midway marked the finest moment of the war for the USN's most decorated ship. The ship's air group was responsible for the destruction of *Akagi* and *Kaga* and jointly sank *Soryu* with aircraft from *Yorktown*. (Naval History and Heritage Command)

BELOW LEFT *Yorktown* pictured on the morning of June 4, with her strike group spotted on deck. Fletcher kept these aircraft as his reserve, but ordered their launch at about 0900 hours. *Yorktown's* air group was responsible for the destruction of *Soryu*. (Naval History and Heritage Command)

same direction. Within minutes, McClusky was rewarded when the *Kido Butai* came into view some 35nm to the northeast at 1002 hours.

In contrast to the air groups from *Hornet* and *Enterprise*, the *Yorktown* air group had no problem finding the Japanese and even launched a coordinated attack. By pure chance, *Yorktown*'s attack developed at the same time McClusky's dive-bombers arrived in the target area. The Americans faced 41 Zeros on CAP but these were out of position. Fourteen Zeros were near the carriers, 11 were chasing *Enterprise*'s torpedo bombers, and ten were off to the southeast. Three each from *Hiryu* and *Soryu* were preparing to launch. The Zeros were at low altitudes, which meant the approaching Dauntlesses could do their work undisturbed.

Chikuma spotted *Yorktown*'s Devastators at 1010 hours still 14 miles from the nearest Japanese carrier. The cruiser fired her 8-inch main battery guns in the direction of the oncoming aircraft to alert the Zeros on CAP. *Yorktown*'s Devastators enjoyed an escort of six Wildcats; two provided close support and four were at higher altitude on overwatch. Not only did the Wildcats successfully defend the Devastators, but they drew the attention of most of the Zeros on CAP. Up to 20 Zeros launched continual attacks on the overwatch Wildcats and shot down one. The other three went into a defensive formation known as the Thach Weave to ward off the Japanese fighters and succeeded in shooting down three Zeros. Meanwhile, the two Wildcats on close escort kept the Zeros away from the Devastators and shot down two more Zeros in the process. The efforts of the Wildcats meant that only one Devastator was shot down before they commenced their attack run. Nagumo ordered his ships to present their sterns to the torpedo bombers to create as small a target as possible. The torpedo squadron commander, Lieutenant Commander Lance Massey, declined an attack with such a poor angle so he headed north to strike *Hiryu*.

As *Yorktown*'s torpedo bombers continued to be the focus of Japanese attention and the Zeros were drawn down to low altitude to duel with the Wildcats, McClusky's and *Yorktown*'s dive-bombers appeared over the *Kido Butai* unnoticed by the Japanese. McClusky's 32 dive-bombers were from two different squadrons; McClusky ordered the leading squadron, VS-6, to hit the nearest carrier, *Kaga*, and for VB-6 to hit the more distant *Akagi*. This was contrary to doctrine and the resulting confusion found both squadrons preparing to attack *Kaga*. At 1022 hours, McClusky and his two wingmen, VS-6, and most of VB-6 commenced their dives on *Kaga*. The dive-bombers were unmolested by fighters or even antiaircraft fire since surprise was complete. Four 1,000lb bombs hit the ship and turned her into an instant inferno.

In one of the most important moments of the battle, Lieutenant Richard Best, commanding officer of VB-6, realized that both *Enterprise* dive-bomber squadrons were attacking *Kaga* and that *Akagi* might go untouched. To prevent this, Best and two other VB-6 aircraft aborted their dives and proceeded north to attack *Akagi*. Again the Japanese failed to notice this attack, and the three dive-bombers did not face antiaircraft fire as they dove on Nagumo's flagship. One Dauntless gained a near miss alongside *Akagi*'s stern, but Best placed his 1,000lb bomb on the ship's middle elevator. The bomb penetrated to the upper hangar deck where it exploded among the armed and fueled aircraft. The cost for crippling *Kaga* and *Akagi* was two Dauntlesses, both of which were shot down as they withdrew.

Yorktown's 17 dive-bombers selected *Soryu* as their target. Only 13 still carried their bombs after a faulty electrical arming switch resulted in the loss of the 1,000lb bombs aboard the squadron commander's aircraft and three others. Once again the dive-bombers gained almost complete surprise; beginning at 1025 hours against light antiaircraft fire and no CAP, three hits were placed on *Soryu*, which was set ablaze. None of the Dauntlesses were lost.

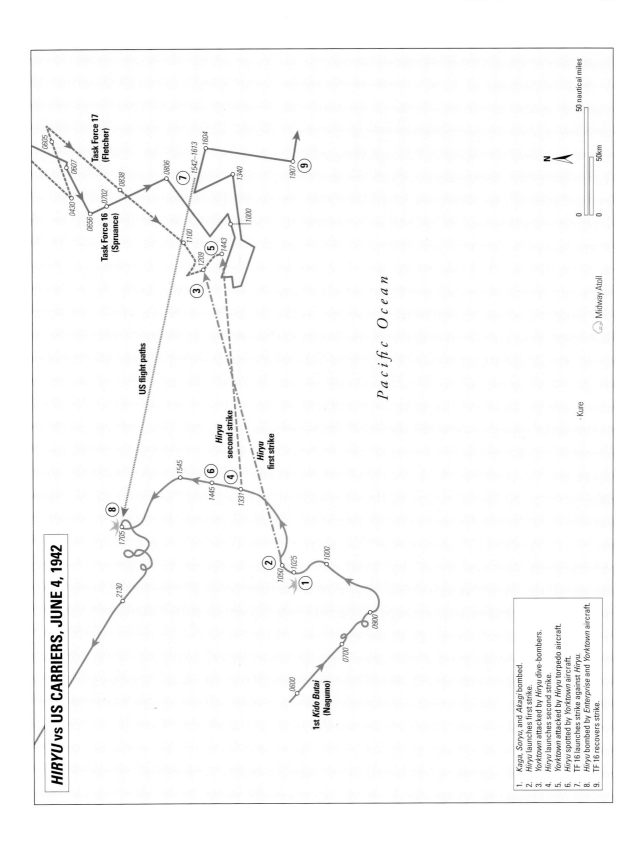

HIRYU vs US CARRIERS, JUNE 4, 1942

Task Force 17
(Fletcher)

Task Force 16
(Spruance)

US flight paths

Hiryu
second strike

Hiryu
first strike

Pacific Ocean

1st Kido Butai
(Nagumo)

Kure

Midway Atoll

N

50 nautical miles

50km

1. *Kaga, Soryu,* and *Akagi* bombed.
2. *Hiryu* launches first strike.
3. *Yorktown* attacked by *Hiryu* dive-bombers.
4. *Hiryu* launches second strike.
5. *Yorktown* attacked by *Hiryu* torpedo aircraft.
6. *Hiryu* spotted by *Yorktown* aircraft.
7. TF 16 launches strike against *Hiryu.*
8. *Hiryu* bombed by *Enterprise* and *Yorktown* aircraft.
9. TF 16 recovers strike.

Massey's Devastators were the last to attack. His decision to head north to attack *Hiryu* gave the Zeros additional opportunities to hack away at the torpedo bombers as they maneuvered to execute an anvil attack. The Devastators' attack runs took place between 1035 and 1040 hours. Ten of the 12 Devastators were shot down, but five survived long enough to launch their torpedoes 600–800 yards away from *Hiryu*'s starboard side. None of the torpedoes found their target.

In the span of a few minutes, Dauntlesses placed eight bombs on three Japanese carriers. This decided the battle since all three ships were put out of action and would later sink. The cost to the Americans had been high, with 35 of 41 Devastators lost. Only two Dauntlesses were shot down in the target area, but *Enterprise*'s and *Hornet*'s aircraft had a difficult time finding TF 16 because the carriers were not in the location they had been briefed. This was due to sloppy work by Spruance's staff. *Hornet*'s air group suffered heavy losses without even spotting the Japanese. All ten Wildcats were lost when they ran out of fuel. Most of VB-8 headed to Midway; three ditched en route and three more were damaged by friendly antiaircraft fire during their approach to the atoll. While inflicting no damage to the Japanese, *Hornet*'s air group lost 15 Devastators, ten Wildcats, and only 20 of 34 Dauntlesses recovered aboard the carrier. *Enterprise*'s air group also took heavy losses, with only four of 14 Devastators and 15 of 33 Dauntlesses returning. *Yorktown*'s 15 Dauntlesses all returned, but for reasons described below were ordered to land on *Enterprise*. As the strike groups were returning, Fletcher launched ten of *Yorktown*'s 17 remaining Dauntlesses on a search to the northwest out to 200nm to find any undetected Japanese carriers.

THE JAPANESE SITUATION

The *Kido Butai*'s air defense system suffered a catastrophic failure on the morning of June 4. The CAP responsible for defending the carriers not only failed in its mission but also lost 11 Zeros with another three damaged and forced to ditch. There was no warning of the approach of the American dive-bombers which struck three carriers when they were most vulnerable. None of the three carriers had their strike aircraft spotted on the flight deck when they were attacked, but their hangar decks were full of armed and fueled aircraft. There were also large amounts of ordnance on the hangar decks as a result of the chaotic rearming process. This perilous state helped fires spread on all three carriers after the explosions from 1,000lb bombs.

The bomb damage and subsequent fires proved mortal to all three carriers. On *Soryu* the three hits at approximately 1025 hours set off huge fires that spread to the second hangar deck and later engulfed the entire ship. The ship went dead in the water by 1040 hours. With no hope of extinguishing the flames, the order was given to abandon ship. *Soryu* sank at 1913 hours with the loss of 711 officers and men, including her captain who refused to leave his ship. The same story unfolded on *Kaga* where fires took hold on the upper hangar deck. The captain and damage control officer were killed on the bridge when it was hit by a bomb. This forced command of the struggle against the raging flames to pass to the ship's senior aviators who were inexperienced in damage control. The fire could not be controlled and soon power was lost. In the middle of the struggle against the fire, submarine *Nautilus*, which had been playing a cat-and-mouse game all morning with various escorts of the *Kido Butai*, selected *Kaga* for attack and launched a spread of torpedoes at the burning carrier. One torpedo hit but failed to explode. Fire-fighting efforts having proved futile, surviving crewmen were ordered to abandon ship. At 1925 hours *Kaga* was scuttled by destroyer torpedoes. Personnel casualties were heavy, totaling 811 officers and men. Only a single bomb hit *Akagi*, but it ignited the fueled and armed aircraft on the hangar deck. These flames spread, and at 1042 hours the ship's steering failed probably due to the near miss astern. After the ship lost power at 1350 hours, there was little the crew could do to control the inferno. At about 1700 hours the crew was taken off with the exception of the 263 who had perished. Yamamoto personally ordered the ship scuttled the next morning.

Yamaguchi was already preparing an immediate retaliatory strike on the American carriers from the sole remaining Japanese carrier. *Hiryu* was down to 36 operational aircraft – ten Zeros, 18 dive-bombers, and eight Type 97s. Yamaguchi decided to commit *Hiryu*'s intact dive-bomber squadron first and then follow up with a strike by *Hiryu*'s remaining torpedo bombers. Six Zeros were allocated for escort for each strike. The first strike was led by Lieutenant Kobayashi Michio. After a brief by *Hiryu*'s captain and a personal farewell from Yamaguchi, the 24 aircraft were launched at 1050 hours and flew toward the American carriers now located less than 100nm away.

The Japanese were looking at long odds, with *Hiryu* facing three intact American carriers but this was still unknown to the Japanese. Two E13A floatplanes were snooping around TF 16, and after 1100 hours the D4Y1 reconnaissance aircraft was able to confirm that there were actually three American carriers present. This critical information did not reach Yamaguchi until the D4Y1 returned at about 1300 hours because of a faulty radio. Corroboration was provided when the commander of Destroyer Division 4 reported the results of the interrogation of a captured *Yorktown* Devastator pilot. He confirmed the identity of the three American carriers and stated that *Yorktown* was operating separately. The American pilot was subsequently murdered by the crew of destroyer *Arashi*.

HIRYU ATTACKS

Kobayashi had no difficulty finding the American carriers. En route to the target, his Zero escort spotted a group of six *Enterprise* Dauntlesses and impulsively left the formation to engage them. One Zero was damaged in the ensuing fight and another expended all its ammunition, so both were forced to return to the ship. The remaining four struggled to catch up with Kobayashi's formation. This left the Japanese dive-bombers vulnerable to the American CAP.

At 1151 hours, *Yorktown*'s radar gained contact on a group of aircraft 32nm to the southwest. The arrival of Kobayashi's attack group caught *Yorktown*'s CAP at a bad time. Twelve Wildcats had just taken off at 1150 hours and were not yet at their proper altitude. Kobayashi sighted TF 17 at 1155 hours some 25nm away. He ordered his dive-bombers to climb to 10,000 feet to gain proper attack altitude. His escort was still far behind.

When the Wildcats reached 10,000 feet, the 18 Type 99s were in two groups of nine with one stacked slightly above the other. Five Wildcats mounted an immediate slashing attack on one group and then hit the other with a head-on attack. This shattered the Japanese formation; seven Type 99s were shot down, three by a single Wildcat pilot, and another two or three were forced to jettison their bombs. Among those forced to shed his weapon was Kobayashi who now assumed the role of observer. Ten dive-bombers survived the initial interception but two of these were without bombs. Those with bombs split into two groups, with one group of three headed directly toward *Yorktown* while the second group of five circled to the southwest to approach the target from out of the sun. The group of five had two more encounters with Wildcats but only lost a single dive-bomber. At 1209 hours, *Yorktown* sighted the Japanese aircraft closing from her starboard quarter. TF 17, with the two cruisers and five destroyers arranged in a circle 1,500–2000 yards from the carrier, changed course to the southeast to head away from the Japanese aircraft.

Of the seven Type 99s which dove on *Yorktown*, three scored direct hits and two scored damaging near misses. This was an impressive achievement by any measure and confirmed the elite status of *Hiryu*'s dive-bombing squadron. Most of the attacking aircraft held their dives to under 1,000 feet to ensure hits. The attack began at 1211 hours. The first dive-bomber was shot down by one of *Yorktown*'s aft 1.1-inch quad mounts, but not before the Type 99's 533lb high-explosive bomb hit near the amidships elevator where it penetrated to the hangar deck and started a fire. The second dive-bomber was also shot down by antiaircraft fire. Its bomb was a near miss astern but started fires on the fantail. The fifth dive-bomber scored the most damaging hit at 1214 hours. Its 550lb semi-armor-piercing bomb landed just

ABOVE Taken from one of her escorts, this remarkable photo shows *Yorktown* under dive-bombing attack. One of *Hiryu*'s Type 99 carrier bombers is about to splash, minus its tail, forward of *Yorktown*. Another dive-bomber is visible above *Yorktown* after completing its dive, but its bomb missed aft. (Naval History and Heritage Command)

LEFT *Yorktown* was left dead in the water and burning after the attack by *Hiryu*'s dive-bombers. Her condition looked serious, but in a short period of time damage control teams extinguished the fires and restored power. (Naval History and Heritage Command)

inboard of the island. The explosion in the air uptakes for the stack caused several boilers to shut down that caused the ship to slow to six knots. The next dive-bomber conducted a shallow glide-bomb attack from the carrier's bow. Its semi-armor-piercing bomb hit the forward elevator and exploded deep in the hull. The final Type 99 scored a near miss to starboard. As the few surviving dive-bombers headed back to *Hiryu*, *Yorktown* was left dead in the water and was issuing thick black smoke from the bomb hole amidships. At 1245 hours, one of *Hiryu*'s returning dive-bombers radioed that they had left one American carrier burning. The cost for damaging *Yorktown* was very high; 13 of *Hiryu*'s 18 dive-bombers were destroyed along with three of the escorting Zeros.

Yamaguchi had only one card left – *Hiryu*'s torpedo-bomber squadron. By now he knew that he was facing three American carriers. His dive-bombers had just disabled one, but he still faced two operational American carriers with very few strike aircraft remaining. *Hiryu*'s torpedo squadron was in bad shape. It had begun the day with 18 aircraft, but after the Midway strike only eight remained fully serviceable. At 1130 hours an *Akagi* Type 97 assigned to morning search duties recovered on *Hiryu*. Yamaguchi's second strike was led by Tomonaga. Only 16 could be mustered – nine *Hiryu* and one *Akagi* Type 97 escorted by six Zeros, four from *Hiryu* and two from *Kaga*. One of the torpedo bombers was Tomonaga's aircraft, which was damaged on the left wing during the Midway strike. The holes in the wing had been patched but there was not enough time to repair the leaking fuel tanks. Other pilots offered to exchange their aircraft for Tomonaga's, but he refused, virtually ensuring he would not be able to return.

The remnants of *Hiryu*'s first strike returned at 1315 hours. One of the surviving dive-bombers was assessed to be damaged beyond repair. Tomonaga's strike was spotted on the flight deck with orders from Yamaguchi to hit one of the undamaged American carriers. At 1331 hours the 16 aircraft headed east toward TF 17, now only 83nm miles distant. One hour later Tomonaga sighted an American carrier task force some 35nm away with one seemingly intact carrier, five cruisers, and 12 destroyers. The carrier was *Yorktown*, whose crew had put out the fires and restored steam so that the carrier could increase speed to 25 knots. Tomonaga immediately ordered an attack.

TOP In a photo taken from heavy cruiser *Pensacola*, Tomonaga's group of four Type 97 torpedo bombers races toward *Yorktown*. Note the heavy antiaircraft fire as the aircraft approach the carrier. (Naval History and Heritage Command)

ABOVE This photo shows the second group of Type 97s attacking *Yorktown*. Two Type 97s are visible, one above and one astern of *Yorktown*, and both have already dropped their Type 91 torpedoes. Of the five aircraft in this group, two scored hits. (Naval History and Heritage Command)

LEFT A Type 97 turns away from *Yorktown* after launching its torpedo. The aircraft is being viewed from one of *Yorktown*'s 20mm gun positions. A thin plume of smoke can be seen trailing from the plane's port wing root. (Naval History and Heritage Command)

The Americans' first indication of the next attack was when cruiser *Pensacola* gained radar contact on Tomonaga's attack force 45nm to the northwest at 1427 hours. At 1429 hours four of the six Wildcats on CAP were ordered to intercept the oncoming Japanese; two minutes later the other two fighters were also sent to the northwest. *Yorktown*'s fighter direction officer (FDO) requested reinforcements from TF 16; eight of the 15 fighters aloft were sent to *Yorktown*'s aid.

Tomonaga ordered his heavily laden torpedo aircraft into a gentle dive to gain air speed. He split his force into two groups of five so that they could conduct an anvil attack.

Unlike during the dive-bomber attack, American CAP was ineffective and the escorting Zeros performed their mission well. The first four Wildcats sent out missed the low-flying torpedo planes in the clouds. The other two Wildcats did spot the approaching Japanese and caught a section of Type 97s by surprise. One was shot down before the escorting Zero fighters intervened and flamed both Wildcats. At 1440 hours the ten Wildcats on *Yorktown*'s flight deck were hurriedly launched.

This remarkable photograph shows the moment of impact of the first torpedo to hit *Yorktown*. Another Type 91 hit the carrier seconds later. These set up a chain of events leading to *Yorktown*'s loss. (Naval History and Heritage Command)

Four Type 97s led by Tomonaga penetrated the screen aft of cruiser *Pensacola*. *Yorktown*'s skipper turned hard to starboard away from Tomonaga's aircraft. Tomonaga ordered his aircraft to split up in response. The first Wildcat off *Yorktown*'s deck, piloted by Lieutenant Commander Thach (originator of the Thach Weave), headed for the nearest torpedo plane, engaged it, and set it afire. This was Tomonaga's aircraft; he was able to hold his burning aircraft level and drop his torpedo but it missed. Tomonaga's wingman also missed with his weapon and was shot down exiting the area by TF 16 fighters coming up from the south. The other two aircraft of Tomonaga's group approached from *Yorktown*'s port side. One launched its torpedo and missed, and the other was forced to jettison its weapon. Both were shot down.

The attack of Tomonaga's four aircraft set up a successful attack by the second group of Type 97s. *Yorktown* started a starboard turn to present her stern to these attackers but could not turn fast enough. One of the scrambled Wildcats headed for the Type 97s but was engaged by two Zeros. Two other Wildcats intervened and shot down both Japanese fighters. This drew the attention of the *Kaga* Zeros. The fighter duel covered the approach of the five Type 97s. Four launched their torpedoes successfully, but the release system of the *Akagi* aircraft failed to operate. Two of these hit *Yorktown*'s port side with devastating effect. Three boiler rooms and the forward generator room were flooded, causing a 23-degree list. All the boilers were knocked offline which brought *Yorktown* to a stop. All five Type 97s from the second group and four of the Zeros survived the attack and returned to *Hiryu* at 1545 hours.

THE DEATH OF *HIRYU*

Fletcher's decision earlier in the morning to launch a search with ten *Yorktown* Dauntlesses now paid off. At 1445 hours one of these aircraft spotted *Hiryu* after the pilot expanded his search area. This also highlighted Nagumo's poor decision to head toward the American carriers instead of using his advantage in aircraft range to steam away from the Americans and still remain within striking range. The contact report placed *Hiryu* some 160nm northwest of TF 16. Spruance ordered an immediate strike with the 25 Dauntlesses aboard *Enterprise* (14 of which were from *Yorktown*). These were launched without escort at 1530 hours. In another inexcusable display of sloppy staff work, Spruance's staff did not include *Hornet* in the pre-launch planning and did not signal *Hornet* until the launch began. Thirty minutes after *Enterprise*'s strike departed, *Hornet* sent 16 dive-bombers aloft. Another 15 were left on deck after Mitscher ordered a premature course change, bringing the ship out of the wind and concluding the launch.

On the morning of June 5, a Type 96 carrier attack aircraft from *Hosho* was sent to locate *Hiryu*. The resulting photographs became iconic images of the Pacific War. Clearly shown is the devastation caused by the four 1,000lb bombs which hit the forward part of the flight deck. The forward elevator was blown out of its well and was thrown against the island. Fires continue to burn aft, and the ship is dead in the water. (Naval History and Heritage Command)

As the American dive-bombers were already on their way to attack *Hiryu*, Yamaguchi was contemplating how to neutralize the third American carrier. When the returning Type 97 pilots were debriefed, they claimed three torpedo hits on a Yorktown-class carrier. With two American carriers now damaged or sunk, *Hiryu* faced only a single operational American carrier. To strike this target Yamaguchi planned a third strike for 1800 hours. Japanese fortunes were now tied to the four dive-bombers, five Type 97s, and nine escort fighters left on *Hiryu*. Yamaguchi hoped that this small strike could reach its target under the cover of dusk. One hour before the planned strike, the D4Y1 reconnaissance aircraft would launch to guide the strike aircraft to the target. But before he could launch his dusk strike, Yamaguchi learned that both *Enterprise* and *Hornet* were operational when they were spotted by a *Tone* floatplane at 1550 hours; the American carriers were only 120nm northwest of *Hiryu*.

Yamaguchi's scheme to salvage the battle for the Imperial Navy was about to play out. *Enterprise*'s strike group, now reduced to 24 Dauntlesses after one aborted, had no problem finding its target. The strike leader, VS-6's Lieutenant

Wilmer Gallaher, sighted the Japanese 30nm away. He took his aircraft to the southwest to launch his attack out of the afternoon sun. It was not until 1701 hours that the Japanese spotted the American aircraft overhead. Incredibly, for the fourth time on June 4, American dive-bombers gained complete surprise against a Japanese carrier. A total of 13 Zeros from *Akagi*, *Kaga*, and *Soryu* were airborne on CAP but once again were not deployed to deal with a dive-bombing attack. *Hiryu* was preparing to launch the pre-strike D4Y1 reconnaissance aircraft. The Dauntlesses began their attack at 1705 hours, with the Zeros desperately clawing to gain altitude; once the dive-bombers commenced their attack there was little chance of stopping them. *Hiryu*'s skipper executed a sharp turn to port to bring his bow into the attacking aircraft. This maneuver made the first few bombs miss, but four 1,000lb bombs landed on the forward part of *Hiryu*'s flight deck clustered around the large Rising Sun which the American pilots used as an aim point. Three Dauntlesses were lost, all to Zeros. The four hits on *Hiryu* set the ship aflame. Part of the forward elevator was thrown against the bridge. Fire took hold on the hangar deck where the 1800 hours strike was being prepared for launch. For the fourth time that day, Japanese damage control crews were unable to control the fires on their carrier. At 2123 hours *Hiryu* went dead in the water. The crew was ordered off by 0430 hours the next morning, but *Hiryu*'s captain and Yamaguchi chose to remain aboard. At 0510 hours a Japanese destroyer fired a Type 93 torpedo into the hulk to scuttle it and then departed the area. This was clearly unsuccessful since an aircraft from *Hosho* found and photographed the still-burning carrier at 0630 hours. Since survivors were observed still aboard, another destroyer was sent to rescue them. Before the destroyer arrived, *Hiryu* sank early in the 0900 hour. *Hiryu*'s casualties totaled 383 men. Another 35 were rescued by the Americans.

YAMAMOTO'S REACTION

The demise of *Hiryu* essentially brought the battle to an end. Yamamoto's first indication that Operation MI had gone awry was a 1050 hours message that *Akagi*, *Kaga*, and *Soryu* were afire and that only *Hiryu* remained operational. In response, Yamamoto issued a flood of orders in an attempt to rectify the catastrophic situation. He ordered the Main Body south to assist Nagumo, the Transport Group was moved to the northwest to await developments, and Vice Admiral Kondo's Invasion Force was ordered to join Nagumo. The carriers in the Aleutians were ordered to move south but they still had to recover aircraft and refuel. At 1310 hours, he ordered Kondo to "shell and destroy" the airfield on Midway. Even after he learned of *Hiryu*'s destruction, Yamamoto failed to accept that his decisive battle had ended in disaster. He still envisioned capturing Midway and finishing off the American fleet in a surface engagement. Kondo was put in command of the large force for the coming night battle. By 2330 hours Kondo's advancing forces were unable to find any American forces and it was obvious that no surface engagement was forthcoming. A further advance to the east would only place his forces in a position vulnerable to American air attack in the morning. Recognizing this, Yamamoto issued orders to Kondo to head west early on June 5. At 0255 hours on June 5, Yamamoto succumbed to the inevitable by canceling Operation MI.

THE DEATH OF *YORKTOWN*

The only major question left for the Americans was the fate of *Yorktown*. Captain Buckmaster ordered the carrier abandoned at 1455 hours on June 4. He feared that the ship could capsize as a result of the two torpedo hits and the entire crew might be lost. After the entire crew was taken off the ship, Fletcher ordered TF 17 to join TF 16, leaving *Yorktown* temporarily unattended. A destroyer was later ordered to guard the listing carrier. Fletcher planned to return early on June 5 to assess whether the ship could be salvaged.

Not until 1800 hours on June 5 did Buckmaster assemble a salvage party of 170 men and return to *Yorktown*. By counterflooding and jettisoning anything that was loose topside, the salvage party had made obvious progress by June 6. Fleet tug *Vireo* arrived in the early afternoon to take the carrier in tow for Pearl Harbor. But Yamamoto was not about to let the carrier escape. The Japanese were aware of the ship's position and condition since two different search planes reported it during the afternoon of June 4. Yamamoto ordered *I-168* to depart its station near Midway to finish off *Yorktown*. Approaching the carrier undetected, *I-168* fired a full salvo at *Yorktown* at 1336 hours. Two torpedoes struck the carrier and a third hit a destroyer ranged alongside and broke her in half. The salvage crew left the carrier at 1555 hours. After taking a beating far in excess of what she was designed to sustain, *Yorktown* slipped under the waves at 0501 hours on June 7.

After a fearful pounding, *Yorktown* sank on the morning of June 7. Note the large torpedo hole in the hull. In 1998 the ship was discovered by explorer Robert Ballard in an almost upright position some 17,000 feet below. (Naval History and Heritage Command)

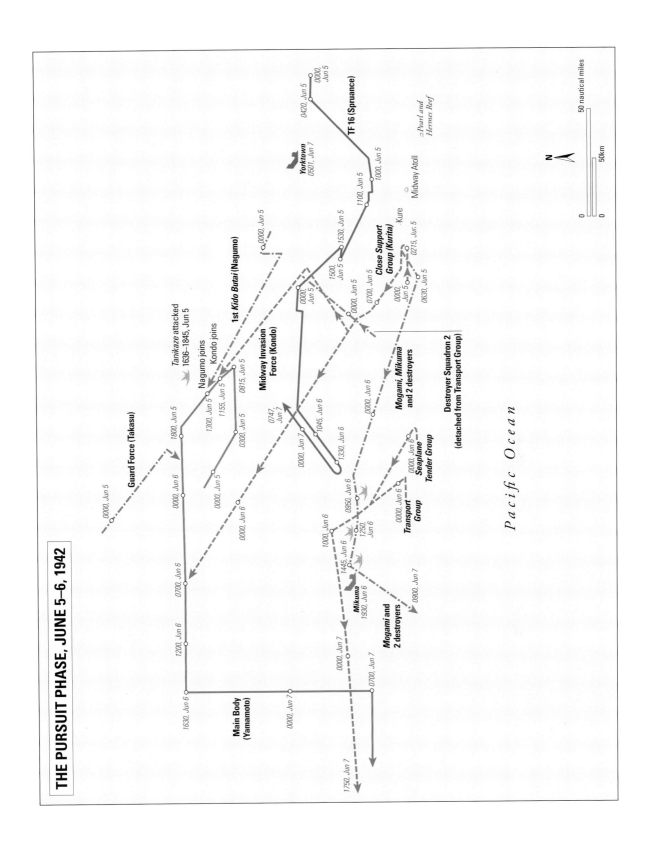

THE PURSUIT PHASE, JUNE 5–6, 1942

0000, Jun 5

0420, Jun 5

TF 16 (Spruance)

Yorktown
0501, Jun 7

1000, Jun 5

1000, Jun 5

1100, Jun 5

Midway Atoll

⊐*Pearl and
Hermes Reef*

50 nautical miles

N

50km

1530, Jun 5

1500,
Jun 5

0215, Jun 5

Kure

**Close Support
Group (Kurita)**

0630, Jun 5

0000, Jun 5

0700, Jun 5

0000,
Jun 5

0000, Jun 5

1st *Kido Butai* (Nagumo)

0000, Jun 5

Tanikaze attacked
1636–1845, Jun 5

Nagumo joins
Kondo joins

**Midway Invasion
Force (Kondo)**

0815, Jun 5

1155, Jun 5

1300, Jun 5

0300, Jun 5

0000, Jun 6

0000, Jun 6

Mogami, Mikuma
and 2 destroyers

**Destroyer Squadron 2
(detached from Transport Group)**

0747,
Jun 7

1045, Jun 6

1330, Jun 6

0000, Jun 7

0950, Jun 6

1250,
Jun 6

0000, Jun 6

**Seaplane
Tender Group**

**Transport
Group**

1000, Jun 6

1445, Jun 6

0900, Jun 7

Mikuma
1930, Jun 6

***Mogami* and
2 destroyers**

Guard Force (Takasu)

1800, Jun 5

0000, Jun 5

0000, Jun 6

0000, Jun 6

0700, Jun 6

1200, Jun 6

Pacific Ocean

**Main Body
(Yamamoto)**

1630, Jun 6

0000, Jun 7

0700, Jun 7

0000, Jun 7

1750, Jun 7

THE BATTLE COMES TO AN END

Fletcher handed over tactical command to Spruance on the evening of June 4. Spruance's primary concern from that point was not to be lured into a surface engagement with superior Japanese forces while using his remaining air power to strike targets of opportunity. Spruance possessed a calculating mind and tended to act cautiously, which made him the perfect commander for this phase of the battle. At 1915 hours he ordered TF 16 to head east; this easily put him beyond the reach of Kondo's forces seeking a night engagement. On June 5 Spruance chose to wait for the results of Midway's morning scouting missions before deciding what to do. By 1100 hours Spruance was confident that no immediate threat existed against Midway, so he took TF 16 to the northwest to investigate PBY reports of a phantom fifth Japanese carrier. This prompted the launch of 26 *Hornet* dive-bombers during the 1500 hour against a target 240nm away. The only target encountered was destroyer *Tanikaze,* which had been dispatched to ensure that *Hiryu* had sunk. Twelve *Hornet* Dauntlesses failed to hit the destroyer, as did 32 Dauntlesses from *Enterprise* later in the day and 18 B-17s from Midway as well.

The only Japanese force still within range was the Close Support Group with its four heavy cruisers and two destroyers. Yamamoto had ordered them to shell the airfield on Midway. They had advanced to within 50nm of the island when Yamamoto canceled Operation MI, which left them in a very exposed position. This exposure increased early on the morning of June 5, when heavy cruiser *Mogami* smashed into her sister ship *Mikuma. Mikuma* suffered light damage, but *Mogami*'s bow was crushed and she could only make 12 knots. The other two cruisers were ordered to retire to the west, leaving *Mikuma* to escort the crippled *Mogami.* It took the Americans two days to deal with the crippled ships. On June 5, 12 Midway dive-bombers and eight B-17s attacked the cruisers without success. The following day TF 16 took a crack at the tough cruisers. *Hornet* launched a strike of 26 dive-bombers in the morning. The first hits of the entire battle by a *Hornet* aircraft were recorded when *Mogami* was hit twice. *Enterprise* launched a strike of 31 dive-bombers and three torpedo planes later in the morning. The Dauntlesses concentrated on *Mikuma,* which had incorrectly been identified as a battleship. The cruiser took five direct hits and two near misses that set the ship afire and brought her to a stop. The fires spread to the torpedo room and several of the huge Type 93 torpedoes exploded, wrecking the cruiser's aft portion. As *Mikuma*'s crew was abandoning ship, *Hornet*'s second strike of the day appeared with 24 dive-bombers. In the final attack of the day, the Dauntlesses hit *Mogami* and a destroyer each with a single bomb, but both ships escaped. *Mikuma* sank later in the day with 700 of her

crew. Following this, just after 1900 hours, Spruance ordered TF 16 to the northeast to refuel.

THE ACCOUNTING

The *Kido Butai* fought unsupported, suffered from more than its share of bad luck, and was smashed. All four of its carriers were sunk and all 248 aircraft on those ships lost. Losses in aircrew were heavy but were not catastrophic as is commonly believed. A total of 110 aircrew were killed with the heaviest losses being from *Hiryu*'s air group as a result of its three strikes on June 4. Japanese dead totaled 3,057 men, most from the crews of the four carriers. In addition to the aircrew losses, 721 skilled aircraft technicians were killed aboard the four carriers. Heavy cruiser *Mikuma* was sunk and *Mogami* so badly damaged she would not return to service until April 1943.

American losses were small in comparison. *Yorktown* and a destroyer were sunk, 144 aircraft lost, and 362 sailors, Marines, and airmen killed. Midway was a strategic victory as it halted the tide of Japanese expansion, but it was not a decisive victory. The focus of naval combat was now to shift to the South Pacific. The Japanese quickly rebuilt their carrier force and two more carrier battles were still to be fought in 1942.

Another iconic image of the battle came from two reconnaissance Dauntlesses from *Enterprise* dispatched on June 6 to record the condition of *Mikuma*. In this view, *Mikuma* is afire and the total devastation of her amidships superstructure area is evident. The guns of her Number 3 8-inch gun turret are askew as the result of the first bomb to hit the ship. (Naval History and Heritage Command)

CHAPTER 5
THE BATTLE OF THE EASTERN SOLOMONS

THE ROAD TO THE SOLOMONS

Midway stopped the Japanese advance in the Central Pacific and put plans by the Naval General Staff to resume the advance in the South Pacific on life support. While the Japanese were figuring out what to do next, Admiral King moved to take the initiative from the Japanese. King had been focused on the South Pacific since the beginning of the war. With the Japanese threat to Hawaii gone, he was free to look for ways to initiate offensive operations in the South Pacific. King was not content with a defensive strategy of guarding the sea line of communications between the United States and Australia. As early as March 1942 King envisioned an offensive north through the Solomon Islands to recapture Rabaul.

Events in the South Pacific created heightened concern, not just for King but for all Allied commanders in the Pacific. As part of Operation MO, the Japanese had seized Tulagi in the southern Solomons on May 3. On June 13, the Japanese decided to build an airfield on Guadalcanal, a large island only some 20nm away from Tulagi. On July 6, a 12-ship Japanese convoy arrived on Guadalcanal with two construction units to begin work on the airfield. Even before this alarming

development, King was working with Nimitz to retake "Tulagi and adjacent positions." Planning proceeded at a breakneck pace to meet the original attack date of August 1. Guadalcanal was added as an objective after American intelligence assessed that Japanese construction troops were on the island. The invasion force was rapidly assembled and planning accelerated, but problems in Wellington, New Zealand loading the First Marine Division forced the landings to be delayed until August 7. To oversee the invasion, Vice Admiral Robert Ghormley assumed the position as Commander, South Pacific Area on June 19. With Halsey still sick, Fletcher retained command of the carrier force.

The first American counteroffensive of the war began on August 7 and achieved complete surprise. There was brief intense combat on Tulagi and neighboring Gavutu-Tanambogo Islands but these were very quickly captured. The main landing on Guadalcanal met little resistance, and by the end of the second day the Marines had seized the incomplete airfield. The Japanese mounted an immediate air and naval response to the landings. Air attacks with G4M medium bombers from Rabaul targeted shipping off Guadalcanal on August 7 and 8 but suffered heavy losses in exchange for a single American transport and a destroyer sunk.

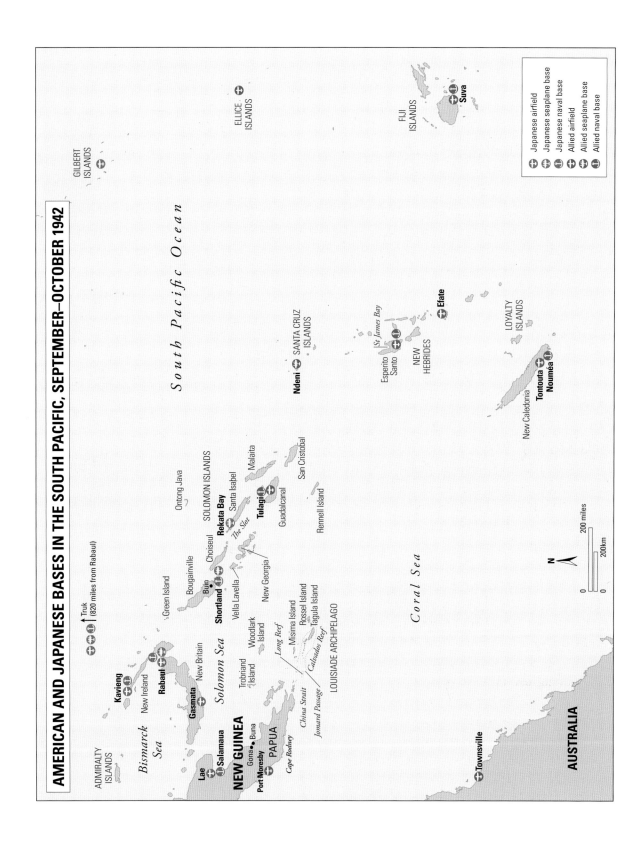

AMERICAN AND JAPANESE BASES IN THE SOUTH PACIFIC, SEPTEMBER–OCTOBER 1942

ADMIRALTY
ISLANDS

GILBERT
ISLANDS

ELLICE
ISLANDS

Bismarck Sea

Kavieng

New Ireland

Rabaul

Gasmata

New Britain

Green Island

Truk
(820 miles from Rabaul)

Bougainville

Choiseul

Buin

Shortland

Vella Lavella

New Georgia

The Slot

Rekata Bay

Santa Isabel

Ontong Java

SOLOMON ISLANDS

Tulagi

Guadalcanal

Malaita

San Cristobal

Rennell Island

Solomon Sea

NEW GUINEA

Lae

Salamaua

Gona

Buna

Port Moresby

PAPUA

Cape Rodney

China Strait

Jomard Passage

Calvados Reef

Long Reef

Trobriand
Island

Woodlark
Island

Misima Island

Rossel Island

Tagula Island

LOUISIADE ARCHIPELAGO

Coral Sea

South Pacific Ocean

SANTA CRUZ
ISLANDS

Ndeni

Esperito
Santo

St James Bay

NEW
HEBRIDES

Efate

LOYALTY
ISLANDS

New Caledonia

Tontouta

Nouméa

FIJI
ISLANDS

Suva

N

0   200 miles

0   200km

AUSTRALIA

Townsville

✈	Japanese airfield
✈	Japanese seaplane base
⚓	Japanese naval base
✈	Allied airfield
✈	Allied seaplane base
⚓	Allied naval base

Japanese surface forces from Rabaul mounted a much deadlier response. By the evening of August 7, Japanese naval commanders at Rabaul had formulated a plan, assembled a counterattack force, and departed to attack the Allied invasion force off Guadalcanal. Despite being spotted by Allied reconnaissance aircraft, the Japanese surface force gained complete tactical surprise against the Allied covering force on the morning of August 9. Using superior night combat tactics and training, the Japanese inflicted a humiliating defeat on the Americans by sinking four Allied heavy cruisers for no loss to themselves.

On August 20 the first Marine aircraft arrived at the just-completed airfield named Henderson Field after Major Lofton Henderson who was lost at Midway. The presence of American aircraft on Guadalcanal greatly increased the difficulty the Japanese would have retaking the island. The following day the first Japanese attempt to capture the airfield with a ground attack failed. The Japanese initially believed the American landing was nothing more than a raid, but by the end of August Yamamoto had assembled sufficient forces for a major operation to recapture the island. Covered by the rebuilt carrier force, the operation aimed to move reinforcements to the island and destroy the American fleet providing support to the Marines.

ABOVE Admiral Ernest King was the principal force in determining American naval strategy across all theaters. In the aftermath of Midway, he demanded offensive action in the South Pacific, which resulted in the invasion of Tulagi and Guadalcanal in August 1942. (Naval History and Heritage Command)

ABOVE Vice Admiral Robert Ghormley was given command of the South Pacific Ocean Area, making him the commander of the American offensive into the Solomons. He never believed in the operation and became pessimistic about its chances for success. Nimitz took the extraordinary step of relieving him of command in October just before a major Japanese offensive. (Naval History and Heritage Command)

Henderson Field on Guadalcanal pictured in late August 1942 by an aircraft from *Saratoga*. Note the bomb craters marking the many Japanese air raids against the airfield. Possession of Henderson Field gave the Americans control of the waters around Guadalcanal during the day and eventually decided the entire campaign in their favor. (Naval History and Heritage Command)

THE USN'S CARRIER FORCE AT THE BEGINNING OF THE GUADALCANAL CAMPAIGN

The destruction of four Japanese fleet carriers at Midway for the loss of only *Yorktown* altered the carrier balance in the Pacific. Of the seven fleet carriers the USN had begun the war with, five were still afloat in August 1942. One of these was *Ranger*, which was assessed to lack the survivability required against the Japanese. This left four carriers for potential deployment in the Pacific. The last prewar-built carrier to move into the Pacific was *Wasp*. After ferrying British fighters to Malta in the Mediterranean in April and May 1942, *Wasp* arrived in the Pacific in June 1942. She immediately joined *Enterprise* and *Saratoga* in the South Pacific under Fletcher's command. *Hornet* was kept in the Central Pacific to protect Hawaii.

One of the primary lessons from Midway was that more fighters were needed in an American carrier air group. Accordingly, the complement of a fighter squadron was increased from 27 to 36 Wildcats. The carrier air groups kept their four-squadron structure, with each of the dive-bomber squadrons and the torpedo squadron having a nominal strength of 18 aircraft. Heavy losses at Midway and the prudent policy of rotating veterans back to training commands required that the carrier air groups be rebuilt by August 1942. The heavy losses experienced during the first two carrier battles forced the USN to scrap its prewar policy of assigning an air group to a specific ship on a permanent basis. *Saratoga*'s air group

included a fresh fighter squadron with no combat experience but with a number of experienced pilots. The dive-bombing squadrons included *Yorktown*'s VB-3 that had fought at Coral Sea and Midway, and a sister squadron that had no combat experience. The torpedo squadron was *Hornet*'s former VT-8, which was rebuilt after its annihilation at Midway. *Enterprise*'s air group suffered heavy losses at Midway and had to be rebuilt. The original fighter squadron was retained but lost almost all its combat veterans. The dive-bomber squadrons came from *Enterprise* and *Yorktown*. The torpedo squadron was *Yorktown*'s that had also suffered near total destruction at Midway. *Hornet*'s air group remained unchanged since its unsuccessful combat debut at Midway.

There was one major change in the aircraft aboard American carriers – the Grumman TBF-1 Avenger torpedo bomber replaced the Douglas TBD-1 Devastator. The Avenger offered significantly better range and was faster. Also, it possessed a much better defensive armament and a greater ability to absorb battle damage. However, the standard American air-launched torpedo was still the Mark XIII that was infamous for its unreliability. Given this, the Avenger was often armed with bombs for maritime strike missions. The continuing torpedo problems meant the Douglas SBD-3 Dauntless dive-bomber remained the principal striking platform of American carrier air groups during the Guadalcanal campaign. The standard American carrier fighter during the campaign was the Grumman F4F-4 Wildcat. At Coral Sea and Midway, the Wildcat more than held its own against the Japanese Zero as long as pilots used appropriate tactics.

American admirals were still struggling with carrier tactics. In spite of the massive coordination problems at Midway, the standard offensive tool remained the single air group strike with the constituent squadrons proceeding loosely to the target in hopes of being able to conduct a coordinated strike. A more contentious issue was whether carriers should be concentrated or not. The minority

Hornet joined the Pacific Fleet in April 1942. This picture from May shows the ship in her distinctive Measure 12 (modified) camouflage scheme. After missing the Eastern Solomons because she was held in the Central Pacific to guard Hawaii, *Hornet* was sent to the South Pacific in September and was sunk at Santa Cruz the following month. (Naval History and Heritage Command)

American antiaircraft gunnery became an important part of the 1942 carrier battles as it took an increasing toll of attacking Japanese aircraft. The 20mm Oerlikon gun, shown here on *Yorktown*, was the most effective antiaircraft weapon in terms of the number of Japanese aircraft shot down. The gun's short effective range though meant that most Japanese aircraft had already dropped their weapons before being shot down. (Naval History and Heritage Command)

view, which included Fletcher, was that carriers were more effective when deployed in the same formation since this increased mutual support and protection. Most importantly, it facilitated the massing of fighters and escorts to increase the defensive power of the task force. This was the tactic Fletcher used at Coral Sea. In comparison, at Midway, Fletcher's single carrier fought by itself beyond the range of continual support from TF 16 and was sunk. Most other carrier commanders, including most of the aviators and the authoritative King, supported more dispersion with the carriers operating 15–20nm apart. They believed this decreased the likelihood that a single Japanese search aircraft could find more than one carrier which meant that not all carriers would be attacked. Another reason for single-carrier formations, according to the aviators, was that flight operations by two carriers in the same formation were too unwieldy. During the Guadalcanal campaign, dispersal was used with mixed results. At Eastern Solomons *Enterprise* and *Saratoga* operated in separate task forces and *Saratoga* escaped attack. The aviator admirals attributed this to the distance between them, but Fletcher more accurately believed that it was because of the effective CAP. At Santa Cruz *Enterprise* and *Hornet* operated separately but only 10nm apart. This offered neither concentration nor true separation since it was too far away to allow concentration of CAP or escorts and was too close to confuse the Japanese.

At Coral Sea and Midway, American air defenses were able to inflict significant attrition on attacking Japanese air groups, but were unable to prevent the Japanese from striking hard at their main targets. This trend continued into the second half of 1942 with Japanese losses increasing. The Americans enjoyed the significant advantage of air search radar but this had not translated into consistently effective CAP coverage. Detection of Japanese aircraft up to 70nm away was sufficient to launch Wildcats and even get them to altitude, but the lack of a height finder radar precluded truly efficient fighter control. Fighter direction was still an evolving art that depended on the experience of the FDO and a number of tactical factors that were often beyond his control. American shipboard defenses were continually upgraded in 1942 as new, more powerful, ships entered the fleet and existing ships received additional antiaircraft guns. The doctrine of maneuvering carrier task groups as a single entity to successfully mass firepower over the carrier had proved successful thus far. During this period the 20mm gun was the most effective weapon against Japanese aircraft despite the weapon's short range. Every ship from destroyers up to the carriers received an impressive number of these guns, which could be fitted anywhere with a clear arc of fire. The excellent 5-inch/38 dual-purpose gun was deployed in greater numbers aboard the new Atlanta-class light cruisers and the North Carolina and South Dakota-class battleships which were integrated into carrier task forces.

REBUILDING THE *KIDO BUTAI*

The debacle at Midway necessitated a wholesale reorganization of the IJN's carrier force. In spite of his reputation as an aviation-minded reformer, Yamamoto retained the battleship as the most important element of the Combined Fleet as illustrated by his plan for Operation MI. The July 14 reorganization of the Combined Fleet finally recognized the aircraft carrier as the centerpiece of the fleet. The First Air Fleet was renamed the Third Fleet and became the Combined Fleet's primary offensive force. Yamamoto left Nagumo in charge of the carrier force probably because he was the IJN's most experienced carrier commander. The Second Fleet, traditionally the IJN's scouting force of heavy cruisers and destroyers, took on a modified role as the advanced screen for the Third Fleet. This force was deployed between 100 and 150nm in advance of the carriers where it could finish off any American ships crippled by air attack. The Advance Force was also expected to draw off some of the American air attacks intended for the Japanese carriers.

As noted previously, Midway eliminated the Japanese advantage in fleet carriers. After Midway the IJN only had two fleet carriers plus three light or converted carriers and another scheduled to join the fleet soon. Compared with the six carriers of all types the Japanese could operate, the Pacific Fleet only had four; however, the four American carriers had a greater aircraft capacity than the six Japanese carriers. The new Third Fleet comprised two carrier divisions. Carrier Division 1 (directly under Nagumo's command) included *Shokaku* and sister ship *Zuikaku*. The converted light carrier *Zuiho* joined the two big carriers. The idea behind the inclusion of the light carrier was that it would focus on air defense and search operations, leaving the fleet carriers free for offensive operations. Carrier Division 2 was under the command of Rear Admiral Kakuta, who had commanded the carriers in the Aleutians operation. It comprised converted carriers *Junyo* and *Hiyo* (completed in July) and the light carrier *Ryujo*. The Third Fleet was also allocated a larger number of escorts which addressed one of the lessons learned at Midway.

The bitter lessons of Midway also drove change in the composition of Japanese carrier air groups. On the two big fleet carriers, the fighter squadrons were increased to 27 aircraft, as were the dive-bomber squadrons. Torpedo bombers were assessed as more vulnerable and the number of Type 97s was reduced to 18. The two Hiyo-class converted carriers reflected a similar structure, with 48 aircraft broken down into 21 Zeros, 18 dive-bombers, and nine Type 97s. The aircraft complement of the two light carriers reflected their focus on air defense. *Ryujo* carried 24 Zeros and nine Type 97s while *Zuiho* carried 21 and six, respectively.

When the Americans landed on Guadalcanal on August 7, the reorganization of the IJN's carrier force was still underway. Yamamoto scrambled to respond to the American move, but by the middle of the month only Carrier Division 1 was ready. To do this the Japanese had to strip Carrier Division 2 of its fighters and dive-bombers. As a result, Carrier Division 2 was not combat ready until September. Because most IJN aviators survived Midway, all fighter squadrons contained a large number of veterans, and the dive-bomber and torpedo squadrons were at least led by combat-experienced aviators.

Japanese carrier doctrine and tactics were also modified after Midway. The biggest and most obvious lesson was the importance of reconnaissance. For the next three carrier battles of the war, Japanese reconnaissance was equal to or better than American scouting efforts. The Japanese also took measures to reduce the vulnerability of their carriers. Strike aircraft were not kept fueled and armed; if they could not be launched, the aircraft were defueled and their ordnance removed. Offensively, the Japanese still demonstrated a superior ability to orchestrate air attacks by multiple carriers. Japanese carriers did not operate as single units but rather as part of a carrier division. The aircraft of the carrier division were wielded as a single tactical unit. This translated into greater flexibility, quicker launches, and larger strikes than the Americans. Another lesson from Midway was the vulnerability of torpedo bombers. Prevailing Japanese doctrine against heavily defended naval targets was to attack simultaneously with dive- and-torpedo bombers to overwhelm the target's defenses and minimize losses to the more vulnerable torpedo bombers. For the first carrier battle of the Guadalcanal campaign, the Japanese chose to hold their torpedo bombers in reserve until the American carriers were first crippled by dive-bombers. The dive-bombers proved unable to cripple a carrier by themselves so this tactic failed at the Eastern Solomons. By the second carrier battle in October, the Japanese had returned to their traditional combined-arms approach with simultaneous dive- and torpedo-bomber attacks.

Though the Japanese were proficient at massing and coordinating carrier air power, they were far less capable of providing air defense of their carriers. Their air defense failed totally at Midway through a lack of radar, poor CAP doctrine, and weak antiaircraft gun capabilities. Combined with poor damage control procedures, the result was disaster. No changes were made in CAP doctrine by the start of the Guadalcanal campaign. Early warning was improved by the deployment of the Advance Force as an air defense picket and by the first employment of radar on a Japanese carrier. In August, *Shokaku* received a Number 21 radar with an effective range of approximately 60nm against a high-flying group of aircraft. At the Eastern Solomons the Japanese were still learning to use radar so it played no effective role in the battle. However, the improvements in early warning, combined with much better reconnaissance, greatly diminished the likelihood that Japanese carriers would be totally surprised as they had been at Midway.

THE BATTLE OF THE EASTERN SOLOMONS

As outlined by Ghormley on August 11, Fletcher and his carriers were tasked with several missions. These included: destruction of the Japanese carrier force if possible, protection of the Espiritu Santo–Noumea line of communications, support of the Marines on Guadalcanal and Tulagi, and protection of supply and reinforcement convoys to Guadalcanal. This mission set required that Fletcher maintain his carriers close to Guadalcanal so they could intercept a major Japanese operation against the island. At the same time Fletcher did not want to be so close that the carriers were within range of Japanese reconnaissance and strike aircraft operating from Rabaul. For warning of an impending major Japanese naval operation, Fletcher was reliant on long-range PBY Catalina flying boats. He also expected strategic warning of major Japanese operations from intelligence. However, American commanders did not enjoy the same insights into Japanese intentions during the Guadalcanal campaign as they did before Coral Sea and Midway. Before the first carrier battle of the campaign, Fletcher did not possess solid knowledge of Japanese intentions or their order of battle. The lack of intelligence was exacerbated on August 18 when the IJN changed its radio call signs, making analysis of Japanese radio traffic temporarily impossible. As late as August 21, Fletcher was being told that the Japanese carriers were still in Japan. Fletcher was so unclear about Japanese intentions that he detached one of his three carriers for refueling just before the battle.

To balance between avoiding exposure to Japanese attack and readiness to respond to any major Japanese thrust, Fletcher operated his carriers between San Cristobal and Espiritu Santo. This was beyond Japanese air search range and was 12 hours from being within striking range of Guadalcanal. In the days before the battle of the Eastern Solomons, Fletcher was given adequate time from air searches and intelligence to move his carriers north to intervene against Yamamoto's first offensive to push the Americans off Guadalcanal.

Though the Japanese were caught completely by surprise when the Americans landed on Guadalcanal, Yamamoto responded quickly and within two weeks had the bulk of the Combined Fleet at Truk in preparation for a major offensive. Yamamoto's plan had two objectives. The primary one was the destruction of the American fleet supporting the Marines on Guadalcanal. The secondary objective was to move reinforcements to the island. To accomplish this, the operation included a reinforcement convoy of three ships with 1,500 troops. However, the convoy could not approach the island unless Henderson Field was neutralized. The airfield was to be neutralized by daily air raids from Rabaul and nightly shelling from cruisers offshore. If these failed, responsibility for knocking out Henderson Field would fall on Nagumo's carrier force. This caused problems, as Yamamoto did not want to use Nagumo's carriers for this mission as it would disclose their presence to the Americans. The compromise solution was to use the carriers to strike Henderson Field on August 24, if necessary, but only if they had not been spotted by August 23. The primary mission of Nagumo's carrier force, in conjunction with the Vanguard Force and the Support Force, was the destruction of the American carriers. If the American fleet was destroyed, the Marines on the island would be forced into surrender.

The mission of Nagumo's carriers was muddled in the days before the battle when the Japanese failed to eliminate the air threat from Henderson Field. To suppress the airfield by August 24, when the convoy was scheduled to land, Yamamoto ordered a carrier strike against the airfield. Light carrier *Ryujo*, escorted by heavy cruiser *Tone* and two destroyers, was detached from Nagumo's force to carry this out. This was not a diversion or lure to draw the attention of the American carriers as is almost always portrayed in accounts of the battle.

The plan hatched by Yamamoto and his staff had significant flaws. With only two fleet and one light carriers, the IJN's carrier force had at best parity in fleet carriers with the Americans. Any assumption that it could decisively defeat the American fleet and drive it from the waters around Guadalcanal was therefore wishful thinking. The secondary objective of landing the 1,500 reinforcements on Guadalcanal was meaningless since the Marine garrison on Guadalcanal was over 10,000 men strong with thousands more on Tulagi. Why Yamamoto would mount a major fleet operation to land only 1,500 troops can only be explained by the Japanese assumption that the American invasion of Guadalcanal was no more than a raid. If the Japanese had been paying attention, this assumption was proved disastrously wrong when the first Japanese ground offensive by some 900 troops was annihilated on August 21. Further, the use of a single light carrier to suppress

The standard American long-range search plane of 1942 was the PBY Catalina. During the two carrier battles of the Guadalcanal campaign, PBYs, operating from Espiritu Santo and tenders in the Santa Cruz Islands, rendered outstanding support to the USN's carrier forces. Unfortunately for the Americans, the potential advantage from PBY contact reports was wasted because of communication problems. (Naval History and Heritage Command)

Henderson Field was doomed to failure. It was folly for the Japanese to believe that the air group of a light carrier could succeed in doing in a single raid what scores of aircraft flying from Rabaul had failed to do over the past two weeks.

American intelligence and air reconnaissance provided many indications of an imminent Japanese offensive. On August 23, PBYs spotted the Japanese transport force. In response, Nagumo turned his carriers north to avoid being detected and consequently remained unlocated during the day. When Fletcher received the PBY report at 0950 that the Japanese transports were approximately 250nm north of Guadalcanal, he ordered *Saratoga* to launch a strike of 31 Dauntlesses and six Avengers. However, after being spotted by the PBY, the transport convoy changed course to the north and found the cover of bad weather. This prevented *Saratoga's* raid from locating the convoy, so it headed for Guadalcanal and landed there after dark. The American air units on Guadalcanal (known as the Cactus Air Force) also launched a strike of nine Dauntlesses, one Avenger, and 12 Wildcats at the convoy, but they also failed to find their target. The convoy's diversion to the north forced the Japanese to reschedule its arrival at Guadalcanal until August 25.

Nagumo knew American carriers were operating off Guadalcanal, and this made him very cautious. Conversely, Fletcher did not possess knowledge that Japanese carriers were in the area. The intelligence report he received on August 23 indicated *Shokaku* and *Zuikaku* were en route to Truk from Japan. Based on this faulty intelligence and lack of any contradictory information from American reconnaissance aircraft, Fletcher made one of the most important decisions of the battle. He sent the *Wasp* task force south to refuel. The two carriers still available would be more than adequate to prevent the small reinforcement convoy from reaching Guadalcanal.

EASTERN SOLOMONS ORDERS OF BATTLE

All strengths as of 0500 hours on August 24: ( ) denotes operational aircraft

IMPERIAL JAPANESE NAVY

Third Fleet (Main Body) (Vice Admiral Nagumo aboard *Shokaku*)

Carrier Division 1 (Nagumo)
Carrier: *Shokaku* (Captain Arima Masafumi)

Shokaku Air Group Commander (Lt Cdr Seki Mamoru)	
Shokaku Carrier Fighter Unit	27 (26) Zero
Shokaku Carrier Bomber Unit	27 (27) Type 99
Shokaku Carrier Attack Unit	18 (18) Type 97
TOTAL: 72	

Carrier: *Zuikaku* (Captain Notomo Tameteru)

Zuikaku Air Group Commander (Lt Cdr Takahashi Sadamu)	
Zuikaku Carrier Fighter Unit	27 (25) Zero
Zuikaku Carrier Bomber Unit	27 (27) Type 99
Zuikaku Carrier Attack Unit	18 (18) Type 97
TOTAL: 72	

Destroyer Divisions 10 and 16: *Kazegumo, Yugumo, Makigumo, Akigumo, Hatsukaze, Akizuki*

Vanguard Force (Rear Admiral Abe Hiroaki in *Hiei*)

Battleship Division 11
Battleships: *Hiei, Kirishima*
Cruiser Division 7: Heavy Cruisers *Kumano, Suzuya*
Cruiser Division 8: Heavy Cruiser *Chikuma*
Destroyer Squadron 10: Light Cruiser *Nagara*
    Destroyer Divisions 4 and 17: *Nowaki, Maikaze, Tanikaze*

Detached Carrier Strike Force (Rear Admiral Hara in *Tone*)

Light Carrier: *Ryujo* (Captain Kato Tadao)

Ryujo Air Group Commander (Lt Notomi Kenjiro)	
Ryujo Carrier Fighter Unit	24 (23) Zero
Ryujo Carrier Attack Unit	9 (9) Type 97
TOTAL: 33	

Heavy Cruiser: *Tone*
Part of Destroyer Division 16: *Amatsukaze, Tokitsukaze*

Advance Force (Vice Admiral Kondo Nobutake in *Atago*)

Cruiser Division 4: Heavy Cruisers *Atago, Maya, Takao*
Cruiser Division 5: Heavy Cruisers *Haguro, Myoko*
Destroyer Squadron 4: Light Cruiser *Yura*
    Destroyer Divisions 9 and 15: *Kuroshio, Oyashio, Hayashio, Minegumo, Natsugumo, Asagumo*
Seaplane Carrier: *Chitose* with 22 aircraft

UNITED STATES NAVY

Task Force 61 (Vice Admiral Fletcher)

Task Force 11 (Fletcher)

Carrier: *Saratoga* (Captain Dewitt C. Ramsey)

Saratoga Air Group (Cdr Harry D. Felt)	1 (1) SBD-3
Fighting Five	27 (27) F4F-4
Bombing Three	17 (17) SBD-3
Scouting Three	15 (15) SBD-3
Torpedo Eight	13 (13) TBF-1
Utility Unit	1 (1) F4F-7
TOTAL: 74	

Heavy Cruisers: *Minneapolis, New Orleans,* HMAS *Australia*
Light Cruiser: HMAS *Hobart*

Destroyer Squadron 1: *Phelps, Farragut, Worden, Macdonough, Dewey, Patterson, Bagley*

Task Force 16 (Rear Admiral Thomas C. Kinkaid)

Carrier: *Enterprise* (Captain Arthur C. Davis)

Enterprise Air Group (Lt Cdr Maxwell F. Leslie)	
Fighting Six	29 (28) F4F-4
Bombing Six	17 (17) SBD-3
Scouting Five	18 (16) SBD-3
Torpedo Three	15 (15) TBF-1
Utility Unit	1 (1) F4F-7
TOTAL: 80	

Battleship: *North Carolina*
Heavy Cruiser: *Portland*
Light Cruiser: *Atlanta*

The next day, August 24, witnessed the third carrier battle of the war. Nagumo detached *Ryujo*, heavy cruiser *Tone*, and two destroyers at 0400 to carry out a strike against Henderson Field. *Ryujo* was ordered to be 200nm north of the airfield at noon to launch the raid, assuming the American carriers remained unlocated. At 0600 hours the Combined Fleet changed course to the southeast. The Vanguard Force, with two battleships, three heavy and a light cruiser, and three destroyers, was deployed some 6nm ahead of the carriers. Kondo's Advance Force was deployed some 120nm to the east of Nagumo's carriers, reflecting concern that the American carriers were operating in that direction.

Reflecting his new emphasis on reconnaissance, Nagumo allocated considerable assets to scouting. From *Shokaku* and *Zuikaku*, 19 Type 97s were launched at 0615 to search to the east. Kondo's Advance Force contributed seven floatplanes. The primary strike of 54 dive-bombers escorted by 24 Zeros was readied on the two fleet carriers. If conditions were appropriate, a follow-up strike of 36 Type 97s armed with torpedoes with 12 Zeros as an escort was planned.

Fletcher also planned a comprehensive search for August 24. Twenty Dauntlesses from *Enterprise* took off just before 0600 to cover the area north of TF 61. Fletcher could also count on support from six PBYs flying from a tender anchored at Ndeni, the largest of the Santa Cruz Islands. The PBYs flew 650nm to the northwest and proved to be the most effective scout aircraft on either side during the battle. This was proven when *Enterprise*'s aircraft reported nothing, but contact reports from the PBYs began to arrive at 0935. The first PBY report confirmed the presence of *Ryujo* and her escorts some 280nm northeast of TF 61. This placed *Ryujo* out of strike range. The PBYs also detected elements of both the Advance and Vanguard Forces, but Nagumo's carriers were not detected. With the lessons of Coral Sea no doubt in mind, Fletcher opted not to launch a strike on a single small carrier in the absence of any locating information on the main Japanese carrier force. To clarify the situation, at 1239 another 23 scout aircraft were launched from *Enterprise* to conduct searches to the northwest and northeast.

As he waited for his scout aircraft to report, other events forced Fletcher's hand. *Saratoga*'s strike group returned from Guadalcanal by 1100. Since *Enterprise* had used most of her dive-bombers for scouting missions, this was Fletcher's primary strike force. At about noon, and again at 1300, two Japanese search aircraft were destroyed in close proximity to the American carriers. Fletcher was forced to assume that he had been spotted, but, in fact, neither Japanese aircraft was able to send a contact report. Just after noon, *Ryujo* launched her strike of six Type 97 carrier attack planes, each carrying six 132lb bombs, and 15 Zeros to neutralize Henderson Field. At about 1430, the Type 97s unloaded their bombs over the airfield, causing little damage. In the ensuing dogfight with 16 defending

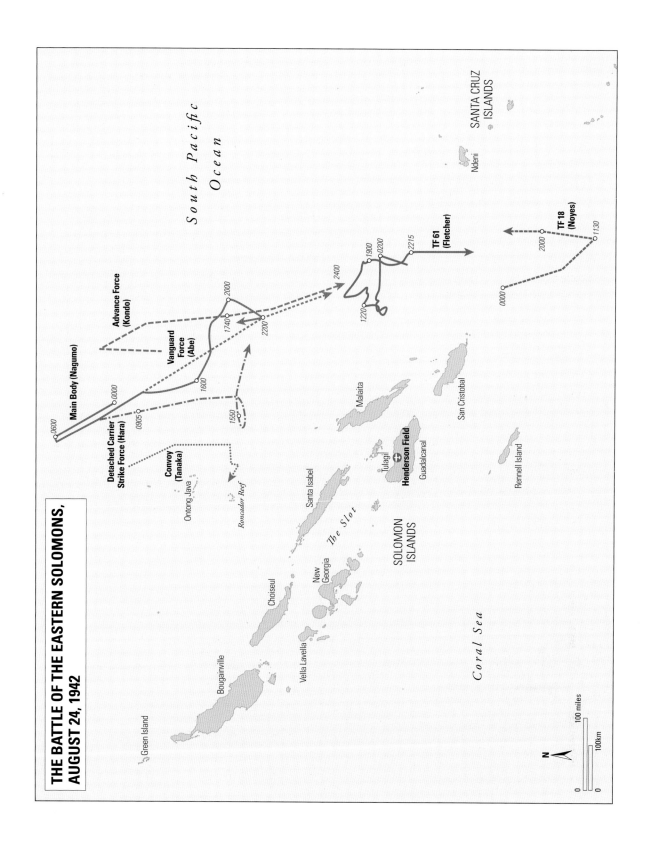

THE BATTLE OF THE EASTERN SOLOMONS, AUGUST 24, 1942

South Pacific Ocean

SANTA CRUZ ISLANDS

Ndeni

TF 18 (Noyes)

TF 61 (Fletcher)

Advance Force (Kondo)

Vanguard Force (Abe)

Main Body (Nagumo)

Detached Carrier Strike Force (Hara)

Convoy (Tanaka)

Roncador Reef

Ontong Java

Malaita

San Cristobal

Henderson Field

Tulagi

Guadalcanal

Rennell Island

Santa Isabel

The Slot

SOLOMON ISLANDS

New Georgia

Choiseul

Vella Lavella

Bougainville

Green Island

Coral Sea

N

100 miles

100km

Wildcats and two P-400s, the Japanese lost three Zeros and four Type 97s for three Wildcats shot down. Predictably, the Japanese carrier air strike on Henderson Field failed to accomplish its mission.

The first major development in the carrier battle occurred at 1400 when a *Chikuma* floatplane spotted Fletcher's carriers. This was the news Nagumo had been waiting for. The first strike of 18 dive-bombers and four fighters from *Shokaku* and nine dive-bombers and six Zeros from *Zuikaku* was quickly launched and headed south just before 1500. At 1600 another wave of 18 dive-bombers and six Zeros from *Zuikaku* and another nine dive-bombers and three fighters from *Shokaku* was launched and headed toward the American carriers. The first two waves totaled 73 aircraft; per the new Japanese doctrine, no torpedo bombers were committed to the strike.

Fletcher refused to commit his strike assets even as numerous reports were received of *Ryujo*'s movements. Aircraft available for offensive missions included 11 dive-bombers, seven Avengers, and 15 Wildcats on *Enterprise* and *Saratoga*'s air group that had returned from Guadalcanal in the late morning. With no information available on Nagumo's main carrier force and not wanting to get caught with his strike aircraft on deck, at about 1340 Fletcher decided to launch his primary strike from *Saratoga*, consisting of 30 Dauntlesses and eight Avengers, against *Ryujo*. After the abort of an Avenger and a Dauntless, the strike group headed north to *Ryujo*'s last reported position. Following the strike's departure, information began to come in from the *Enterprise*'s afternoon search. At 1410 *Ryujo* was located by two Avengers; these aircraft attacked the carrier from high altitude at 1428 without success. Two different Avengers found *Ryujo* again, but one Avenger was shot down by Zeros. At 1440 Dauntlesses spotted the Advance Force and bombed heavy cruiser *Maya*. At 1500 *Saratoga* received a post-attack report by two *Enterprise* dive-bombers which had spotted *Shokaku* and *Zuikaku* and unsuccessfully attacked *Shokaku*.

This is the flight deck of *Zuikaku* on May 5, 1942 on which are spotted 12 Zero fighters and 17 Type 99 dive-bombers. The scene on *Zuikaku*'s flight deck must have been nearly identical on August 24 when the carrier prepared to launch her Zeros and dive-bombers at the American carriers. (Yamato Museum)

This development put Fletcher in a tactically precarious position. His main strike was en route to strike a secondary target, and now he had information on the location of the main Japanese carrier force. After having some difficulty finding *Ryujo*, the attack by *Saratoga*'s air group began at 1550. After going into a tight turn to starboard to evade the Dauntlesses, *Ryujo* dodged the first ten bombs. Eventually at least three Dauntlesses did score a hit, and an anvil attack by the Avengers resulted in one confirmed torpedo hit. The carrier sank at 2000 with the loss of 121 crewmen. All of her aircraft were lost, though the aircrew from the surviving Henderson Field strike aircraft and the Zeros on CAP were rescued.

As *Ryujo* met her end, the Japanese strike on Fletcher's carriers was getting underway. *Enterprise*'s radar gained first contact on a large group of aircraft 88nm to the northwest at 1602. Given more than adequate warning, the CAP protecting TF 61 was increased to 53 Wildcats. The Japanese strike commander split his 27 dive-bombers into two groups and approached from the north at 16,000 feet. The defending fighters were not deployed high enough, which resulted in almost all the Wildcats being placed at a serious tactical disadvantage. Added to this initial problem was the bigger issue of the narrow-frequency fighter direction circuit being overloaded with unnecessary transmissions that made effective fighter control impossible. Of the 53 Wildcats, between five and seven were able to attack the Type 99s before they began their attack dives, and another ten Wildcats chased the Japanese dive-bombers into their dives. The Japanese strike leader ordered *Zuikaku*'s 18 dive-bombers to hit *Enterprise* and the nine Type 99s from *Shokaku* to target *Saratoga*, but in the aftermath of the Wildcat interception that caused heavy losses, all surviving dive-bombers attacked *Enterprise*.

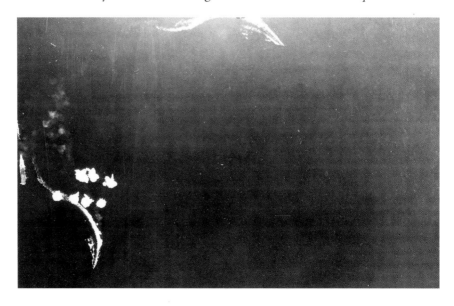

B-17s from Espiritu Santo conducted several raids on Japanese shipping during the battle of the Eastern Solomons. On one of these occasions, three of the heavy bombers attacked the crippled *Ryujo* (shown dead in the water in the left side of the picture) just after 1800. No hits were scored as is evident in this photo. (Naval History and Heritage Command)

TOP LEFT Both sides were tentative at the battle of the Eastern Solomons as shown by the fact that only *Enterprise* came under Japanese attack, and that this attack was only mounted by dive-bombers. Of the 15 *Shokaku* and three *Zuikaku* dive-bombers which attacked *Enterprise*, only three scored hits and these inflicted only moderate damage. This photo shows one of the many near misses on the carrier. (Naval History and Heritage Command)

LEFT The view from heavy cruiser *Portland* shows one of the three Japanese bomb hits on *Enterprise*. (Naval History and Heritage Command)

ABOVE This well-known but still spectacular photograph shows the third bomb to hit *Enterprise*. The explosion was from a 532lb high-explosive bomb that probably rendered only a low-order detonation. The Type 99 that delivered this weapon did not survive the attack. (Naval History and Heritage Command)

The Japanese airmen bombed with their usual accuracy, hitting *Enterprise* three times. The first bomb hit at 1644 hours near the aft elevator and penetrated several decks before exploding in a messroom, killing 35 men. A second bomb struck seconds later in the same location and killed another 33 men. The third and final bomb struck the flight deck near the amidships elevator but resulted in a low-order detonation. Seven dive-bombers attacked *North Carolina*, trailing 2,500 yards astern *Enterprise*. A couple of near misses caused only superficial damage. At the conclusion of the attack, *Enterprise* was damaged but was in no danger of sinking. The flight deck was quickly repaired which allowed flight operations to resume at 1746. Though damage was fairly light, personnel casualties were heavy with 75 dead and 95 wounded. The attack cost the Japanese 17

TOP RIGHT In this photograph one of the Type 99s which attacked *Enterprise* is shown in flames directly over the carrier presumably at the conclusion of its dive. Once again, Japanese aircraft losses were heavy. Only eight of the 27 dive-bombers that attacked TF 16 returned to their carriers. (Naval History and Heritage Command)

RIGHT None of the three bombs that hit *Enterprise* rendered critical damage. The effect of one of the hits is shown in this photograph. A 532lb high-explosive bomb hit near the starboard quarter 5-inch/38-gun battery, and the resulting flames engulfed the gun position killing all 38 men of the battery and setting off the ready 5-inch ammunition lockers. (Naval History and Heritage Command)

Type 99s and three Zeros; another dive-bomber and three Zeros were forced to ditch returning to their carriers. The Americans lost eight defending Wildcats.

Enterprise suffered a steering casualty at 1821 that caused her to reduce speed and circle helplessly. Steering was not repaired until 1858. During this time the second wave of Japanese dive-bombers approached the American formation and appeared to be postured to cripple the struggling *Enterprise*. In an extremely favorable turn of events for the Americans, the strike commander (Lieutenant Takahashi of Coral Sea fame) could not find his target after an updated position report was copied incorrectly by his radio operator. Radar on *Enterprise* watched the Japanese aircraft pass 50nm south before turning northwest and then departing the area. The Japanese had wasted a golden opportunity to possibly finish off *Enterprise*. It proved the last chance to strike either American carrier since Nagumo declined to launch another strike and instead ordered his carriers north to refuel.

Japanese problems getting their strikes on target were more than matched by the Americans. Just before the arrival of the first wave of Japanese dive-bombers, Fletcher ordered all ready Dauntlesses and Avengers to launch and seek out the Japanese carriers. From *Enterprise*, 11 dive-bombers and seven Avengers departed with orders to attack *Ryujo*. *Saratoga* contributed just two Dauntlesses and five Avengers; these were ordered to join with the *Enterprise* group. The rendezvous never occurred and none of the *Enterprise* aircraft found a target. The small *Saratoga* strike did succeed in finding the Advance Force at 1735 and attacked the largest ship present, the seaplane carrier *Chitose*. All the aircraft were carrying bombs; two near misses caused flooding and a list, but *Chitose* survived and in 1943 was converted into a light carrier.

With the tentative carrier battle over, the only issue left to decide was the fate of the Japanese reinforcement convoy. Yamamoto ordered it to turn south toward Guadalcanal very late on August 24, even though Henderson Field had not been neutralized and the American carriers remained a threat. The next day the convoy was hit by Cactus Air Force dive-bombers, which damaged a light cruiser and one of the three transports. B-17s from Espiritu Santo sank a destroyer alongside the damaged transport later in the morning. This finally prompted Yamamoto to cancel the transport operation.

The battle of Eastern Solomons ended indecisively, but the results of the half-hearted engagement favored the Americans. Yamamoto failed to achieve either of his objectives – the American fleet was obviously not destroyed or even significantly reduced and the operation to land reinforcements on Guadalcanal was a complete failure. Japanese losses were significant with *Ryujo*, a destroyer, and a transport sunk and 75 aircraft lost. Heavy losses in aircrew were also a concern and continued the steady attrition of the prewar highly trained aviators.

In return, the Americans had thwarted the first major Japanese operation to retake Guadalcanal, for a small cost. A total of 25 aircraft were lost and *Enterprise* was damaged enough to force her to return to Pearl Harbor for repairs. In spite of the favorable outcome of the battle, the Americans could not be satisfied with their performance. No major attack on the main Japanese carrier force was mounted due to continuing difficulties in getting information from air searches to the right command authority in a timely manner and because of continuing problems mounting coordinated strikes. Fighter direction continued to be a problem, with only a third of the fighters on CAP making an interception. The Americans were fortunate that a communications failure resulted in the failure of the second wave of Japanese dive-bombers to locate the wounded *Enterprise*.

CARRIER OPERATIONS AFTER EASTERN SOLOMONS

Both sides were coming to the realization that Guadalcanal was emerging as the decisive battle of the war to date. The Japanese were wrestling with how to move a large ground force to the island to capture the airfield. As long as the airfield was operational, the only way to move troops to the island was by destroyer, a lengthy and inefficient process. Yamamoto readied another major operation to sweep American naval forces from the waters around the island. The Americans were forced to maintain their carrier force near Guadalcanal to counter any major Japanese effort.

After Eastern Solomons *Enterprise* returned to Pearl Harbor on September 10 and immediately went into drydock for repairs. This left *Saratoga* and *Wasp* to counter any Japanese offensive. On August 29, *Hornet* rendezvoused with TF 61 as a replacement for *Enterprise*. Fletcher continued his pattern of steaming north during the night to be within strike range of Guadalcanal in the morning and then heading south during the day to stay out of range of Japanese search aircraft. Since this was occurring in waters frequented by Japanese submarines, it was not hard to predict eventual trouble. The inevitable happened early on August 31 when submarine *I-26* hit *Saratoga* with a single torpedo. The damage brought her to a temporary halt and resulted in flooding. *Saratoga* was out of the war again for several months of repairs, but most of her aircraft ended up on Guadalcanal, which constituted an important reinforcement for the Cactus Air Force. The damaged carrier arrived at Pearl Harbor on September 21 with Fletcher aboard. His performance during the Guadalcanal campaign was marked by a clear lack of aggression that translated into a loss of confidence from King and Nimitz. Fletcher was relieved of duty for some much-needed rest and never returned to carrier duty. Rear Admiral Leigh Noyes took over command of TF 61.

Yamamoto's next operation to recapture the island took place in mid-September and was linked to the second Japanese ground offensive. On September 9, *Shokaku*, *Zuikaku*, and *Zuiho* departed Truk as part of a force ordered to eliminate the American carriers after Henderson Field had been captured. This operation derailed when the ground offensive was repulsed on the night of September 13 with heavy Japanese losses. To protect the Marine garrison from naval attack, *Wasp* and *Hornet* assumed a position northeast of the Santa Cruz Islands but were unable to locate the Japanese carriers that were also at sea. Japanese search aircraft located TF 61, but Noyes moved to the southeast before the Japanese could attack. The following day, PBYs located the Japanese Advance Force and Noyes launched strikes from both his carriers. The strikes found nothing since Yamamoto had ordered the Advance Force north to refuel. Had the American strikes struck the Advance Force, Nagumo would have headed south in support and a carrier battle would have been fought on September 15.

The outcome of a carrier battle probably could not have been worse for the Americans than actual events on September 15. TF 61 blundered into a scouting line of Japanese submarines; one of these, *I-19*, was able to fire a full salvo of six torpedoes at *Wasp*. Two torpedoes struck the carrier, which created huge fires; subsequent gasoline vapor explosions doomed the ship. *Wasp* was abandoned at about 1420 and sank later that evening. Adding to the disaster, the remaining torpedoes from *I-19*'s salvo continued to the northeast toward TF 17 some 7nm away. Another torpedo hit *North Carolina*, creating a large hole in her port bow forcing her to head to Pearl Harbor for repairs. Yet another torpedo hit destroyer *O'Brien* and the ship sank on her way to Pearl Harbor. The Americans now possessed a single operational carrier in the Pacific and another Japanese attempt to recapture Guadalcanal was expected. For their part, the Japanese had five operational carriers for the next carrier battle off Guadalcanal.

The IJN's submarine force is usually criticized for its lack of success in the war, but it did have a significant impact on the carrier battles of 1942. Aside from sinking *Yorktown* at Midway, and keeping *Saratoga* in the yards for most of 1942, on September 15 *I-19* torpedoed *Wasp* south of San Cristobal Island. With *Wasp*'s sinking, the USN was reduced to a single operational carrier in the South Pacific. (Naval History and Heritage Command)

CHAPTER 6
SHOWDOWN AT SANTA CRUZ

THE JAPANESE SITUATION

After two failed attempts to dislodge the Marines from Guadalcanal in August and September, Yamamoto changed his operational approach from destroying the American fleet to mounting and supporting a larger land offensive to seize Henderson Field. This required that the airfield be neutralized to permit the movement of sufficient ground forces to the island. The decisive ground attack to take Henderson Field was planned for the night of October 22. However, the Japanese failed to take into account the dense jungle terrain with which the attack force would have to contend to reach its pre-attack assembly areas, so a delay in the start of the attack was inevitable. For this attack the Japanese assembled a full division. Combined with the continued underestimation of the number of Americans on the island, this led Yamamoto to assess that the capture of the airfield was assured. Once the Imperial Army signaled that the airfield had been captured, Yamamoto would order the Combined Fleet south to destroy American naval forces supporting the Marines.

Yamamoto committed the bulk of the Combined Fleet to support the October offensive. Most units were allocated to the Support Force under Vice Admiral

Kondo, which consisted of the Advance Force under his direct command and Nagumo's Main Body. The Advance Force would operate 100–120nm in advance of the carrier force. Carrier Division 2 was now operational and was assigned to the Advance Force. If all went according to plan, the Advance Force would reach a final position southeast of Guadalcanal to cut the American garrison off from resupply and reinforcement. Nagumo's Main Body was tasked to destroy the American carriers. It was built around Carrier Division 1 with fleet carriers *Shokaku* and *Zuikaku* and light carrier *Zuiho* and allocated a screen of one heavy cruiser and eight destroyers. The rest of Nagumo's force was formed into the Vanguard Force with two battleships, three heavy cruisers, a light cruiser, and seven destroyers. The Vanguard Force was charged to cover Nagumo's left flank.

The Japanese plan began to unfold on October 11. Yamamoto planned to move a large reinforcement convoy to Guadalcanal with six fast transports escorted by eight destroyers. To cover the convoy's movement, two battleships bombarded Henderson Field during the early hours of October 14 with 918 14-inch rounds, destroying 40 aircraft and placing the airfield temporarily out of commission. The Japanese convoy arrived offshore at Guadalcanal on the night of

October 14–15 preceded by two heavy cruisers that shelled the airfield. Zeros from *Junyo* and *Hiyo* flew CAP over the convoy, but American aircraft from Henderson Field still sank three of the six transports. Overall, the convoy operation was successful since 4,500 men got ashore with most of their supplies and equipment.

In the initial stages of the Japanese offensive, the only operational American carrier was *Hornet*. On October 16, *Hornet* closed to within 95nm of Guadalcanal and launched four strikes against the three beached Japanese transports. The next day Yamamoto ordered Carrier Division 2 to attack shipping in the Lunga anchorage off Guadalcanal. The strike by 18 Type 97s armed with bombs, escorted by 18 Zeros, was a complete failure. No American ships were hit and only eight bombers returned to their carriers. More troubles for Carrier Division 2 followed. On October 21 an engine room fire broke out on *Hiyo*. Though repairs restored her top speed to 16 knots, this was insufficient for fleet operations. *Hiyo* transferred three Zeros, one dive-bomber, and five Type 97s to *Junyo* before heading to Truk. *Hiyo*'s departure took 16 Zeros and 17 dive-bombers out of the impending carrier battle.

THE AMERICAN SITUATION

The Japanese October offensive found the Americans at a low ebb. Nimitz found the situation so alarming that he took the extraordinary step of relieving Ghormley. The energetic and aggressive Halsey was given command on October 18 with the responsibility of holding the island against the expected onslaught. Halsey immediately decided to go on the offensive, and within days devised a bold plan to do so. Not surprisingly, Halsey intended to use his carriers aggressively. TF 61 was reinforced on October 24 when *Enterprise* joined *Hornet* northeast of the New Hebrides. The carriers were under the command of non-aviator Rear Admiral Thomas C. Kinkaid. Halsey ordered him to take the carriers north of the Santa Cruz Islands and search aggressively for Japanese forces; if nothing was encountered, TF 61 would continue toward San Cristobal Island. At this point, if TF 61's searches indicated the lack of a major Japanese move against Guadalcanal, Halsey intended to mount a spoiling attack against Japanese shipping in the Shortland Islands anchorage that was the principal Japanese staging base for ferrying reinforcements to Guadalcanal.

This plan was extremely aggressive and could even be portrayed as foolhardy. Halsey was committing the only two operational carriers in the entire Pacific to an operation for which support from land-based air was limited. After the battle Halsey told Nimitz that he had only intended for TF 61 to proceed past Santa Cruz if no Japanese forces were present. If true, Kinkaid did not understand this

critical aspect of his orders. Halsey's bold operation risked much. If both carriers were lost or severely damaged, his ability to provide naval support to the Marines on Guadalcanal would have been crippled. Prudence would have dictated that the carriers be retained in a position south or southeast of Guadalcanal where they could rely on searches by long-range PBYs and B-17s to provide warning of a major Japanese move against Guadalcanal. However, this conservative approach was incompatible with Halsey's character.

As he was contemplating plans for TF 61, Halsey had only a vague notion of the location of the Japanese carrier force. The Office of Naval Intelligence headquarters in Washington, DC provided a weekly assessment of the dispositions and intentions of Japanese naval units, but in the weeks before Santa Cruz these assessments were consistently inaccurate. Nimitz had warned Halsey of an impending Japanese operation against Guadalcanal as early as October 17, but the estimates on Japanese force dispositions were off the mark. Of the six Japanese carriers, Nimitz's senior intelligence officer assessed that only *Shokaku* and *Zuikaku* were in the South Pacific. Carrier Division 2 was still assessed to be in Japanese home waters (it actually arrived at Truk on October 9). Light carrier *Zuiho* was unlocated. This faulty intelligence provided the basis for Halsey's risky plan of sending his two carriers to fight a much larger Japanese carrier force.

ABOVE LEFT Rear Admiral Thomas Kinkaid is shown here on *Enterprise* in July 1942. As the senior admiral between the two USN carrier task forces at Santa Cruz, he was in overall command during the battle. His performance was less than stellar, but he went on to establish a fine war record in non-carrier commands. (Naval History and Heritage Command)

ABOVE George Murray, pictured here on the left as a captain during an awards ceremony on *Enterprise* in May 1942, was commander of TF 17 at Santa Cruz. He was one of the pioneers of American naval aviation and commanded *Enterprise* from the start of the war up until June 30, 1942. (Naval History and Heritage Command)

SANTA CRUZ ORDERS OF BATTLE

All strengths as of 0500 hours October 26, 1942: ( ) denotes operational aircraft

IMPERIAL JAPANESE NAVY

SUPPORT FORCE (VICE ADMIRAL KONDO NOBUTAKE IN *ATAGO*)
Advance Force (Kondo)
Carrier Division 2 (Rear Admiral Kakuta in *Junyo*)
Carrier: *Junyo* (Captain Okada Tametsugu)
   Junyo Air Group Commander (Lt Shiga Yoshio)

Junyo Carrier Fighter Unit	20 (20) Zero
Junyo Carrier Bomber Unit	18 (17) Type 99
Junyo Carrier Attack Unit	7 (7) Type 97
TOTAL: 38	

Carrier *Hiyo* and destroyers *Isonami* and *Inazuma* had been detached October 22 for Truk
following the engine room fire on *Hiyo*
Battleship Division 3: Battleships *Kongo*, *Haruna*
Cruiser Division 4: Heavy Cruisers *Atago*, *Takao*
Cruiser Division 5: Heavy Cruisers *Maya*, *Myoko*
Destroyer Squadron 4: Light Cruiser *Isuzu*
   Destroyers from Destroyer Divisions 15, 24, and 31: *Kuroshio*, *Oyashio*, *Hayashio*,
   Kawakaze, *Suzukaze*, *Umikaze*, *Naganami*, *Takanami*, *Makinami*

Third Fleet (Main Body) (Vice Admiral Nagumo aboard carrier *Shokaku*)
Carrier Division 1 (Nagumo)
Carrier: *Shokaku* (Captain Arima Masafumi)
   Shokaku Air Group Commander (Lt Cdr Seki Mamoru)

Shokaku Carrier Fighter Unit	22 (18) Zero
Shokaku Carrier Bomber Unit	21 (21) Type 99
Shokaku Carrier Attack Unit	24 (24) Type 97
Reconnaissance Aircraft	1 (1) D4Y1
TOTAL: 68	

Carrier: *Zuikaku* (Captain Notomo Tameteru)
   Zuikaku Air Group Commander (Lt Cdr Takahashi Sadamu)

Zuikaku Carrier Fighter Unit	21 (20) Zero
Zuikaku Carrier Bomber Unit	24 (22) Type 99
Zuikaku Carrier Attack Unit	20 (20) Type 97
TOTAL: 65	

Light Carrier: *Zuiho* (Captain Obayashi Sueo)
   Zuiho Air Group Commander (Lt Sato Masao)

Zuiho Carrier Fighter Unit	19 (18) Zero
Zuiho Carrier Attack Unit	6 (6) Type 97
TOTAL: 25	

Heavy Cruiser: *Kumano*
Destroyers from Destroyer Divisions 4 and 16: *Amatsukaze*, *Hatsukaze*, *Tokitsukaze*,
Yukikaze, *Arashi*, *Maikaze*, *Teruzuki*, *Hamakaze*

Vanguard Force (Rear Admiral Abe Hiroaki in *Hiei*)
Battleship Division 11: Battleships *Hiei*, *Kirishima*
Cruiser Division 7: Heavy Cruiser *Suzuya*
Cruiser Division 8: Heavy Cruisers *Chikuma*, *Tone*
Destroyer Squadron 10: Light Cruiser *Nagara*

Destroyers from Destroyer Divisions 10 and 17: *Akigumo, Makigumo, Yugumo, Kazegumo, Isokaze, Tanikaze, Urakaze*

UNITED STATES NAVY

TASK FORCE 61 (REAR ADMIRAL KINKAID)
Task Force 16 (Kinkaid)
Carrier: *Enterprise* (Captain Osborne B. Hardison)

Carrier Air Group 10 (Cdr Richard K. Gaines)	1 (1) TBF-1
Fighting Ten	34 (31) F4F-4
Bombing Ten	14 (10) SBD-3
Scouting Ten	20 (13) SBD-3
Torpedo Ten	9 (9) TBF-1
TOTAL: 78 (64)	

Battleship: *South Dakota*
Heavy Cruiser: *Portland*
Light Cruiser: *San Juan*
Destroyer Squadron 5: Destroyers *Porter, Mahan, Cushing, Preston, Smith, Maury, Conyngham, Shaw*

Task Force 17 (Rear Admiral George D. Murray)
Carrier: *Hornet* (Captain Charles P. Mason)

Hornet Air Group (Cdr Walter F. Rodee)	1 (1) TBF-1
Fighting Seventy Two	38 (33) F4F-4
Bombing Eight	15 (14) SBD-3
Scouting Eight	16 (10) SBD-3
Torpedo Six	15 (15) TBF-1
TOTAL: 85 (73)	

Heavy Cruisers: *Northampton, Pensacola*
Light Cruisers: *San Diego, Juneau*
Destroyer Squadron 2: Destroyers *Morris, Anderson, Hughes, Mustin, Russell, Barton*

Task Force 64 (Rear Admiral Willis A. Lee)
Battleship: *Washington*
Heavy Cruiser: *San Francisco*
Light Cruisers: *Helena, Atlanta*
Destroyers: *Aaron Ward, Benham, Fletcher, Lansdowne, Lardner, McCalla*

MOVEMENT TO CONTACT

After the ground attack was pushed back one day to October 23, Yamamoto ordered Kondo to move north until noon on the 22nd before turning south toward Guadalcanal. By the morning of October 23, after the expected capture of Henderson Field, the Advance Force would be 200nm northeast of Henderson Field with Nagumo's carriers another 100nm behind. As Nagumo maneuvered cautiously north of Guadalcanal, PBYs spotted the Vanguard Force and one of his carriers on October 23. This confirmed that strong Japanese forces were in the area, but Halsey did not change his plan to send his carriers north of the Santa Cruz Islands.

The Imperial Army's march through the jungle to a point south of Henderson Field was much more arduous than expected. This forced another attack delay until the night of October 24. This latest delay prompted the Support Force to head north again. Yamamoto suspected the American carriers were southeast of the Support Force and ordered Kondo and Nagumo to search in that direction. Nagumo's post-Midway caution was exacerbated by events on October 24. PBYs delivered an unsuccessful attack on the Vanguard Force during the early morning hours. Keeping in mind that his carriers had been discovered the day before, Nagumo decided to continue steaming north longer than Yamamoto had ordered. The carriers continued northwest until the afternoon of October 24, and Nagumo failed to inform Kondo and Yamamoto of this until that afternoon. Kondo had already turned south according to the overall plan but had to reverse course when he learned of Nagumo's alteration. At 2147 Yamamoto ordered Nagumo and Kondo to get back on schedule. Accordingly, at 2300 on October 24, Nagumo reversed course to the south and increased speed.

When the Japanese ground attack finally kicked off on the night of October 24, it turned into an immediate debacle. The poor terrain allowed the Marines to defeat the attack piecemeal. With confusion rampant, at 0130 hours on October 25 the Imperial Army signaled the capture of the airfield. In reality it remained in American hands. This fact was quickly made apparent later during October 25 when American fighters contested the first of a series of Japanese air raids. Among these was a strike by 12 Zeros and 12 dive-bombers from *Junyo* at about 1600.

When Yamamoto learned during the morning that the report of capturing Henderson Field was false, he ordered Kondo and Nagumo to again turn north. Both Japanese commanders spent a harrowing day on October 25, due to the excellent work of the PBYs and B-17s flying from Espiritu Santo and the PBYs staging from seaplane tender *Ballard* deployed to the Santa Cruz Islands. A B-17 spotted the Advance Force at 0930 and just minutes later a PBY sighted the Vanguard Force. Another PBY spotted and began to shadow Nagumo's Main Body at 1000. By 1103 it had visual contact on all three of Nagumo's carriers.

First reports of the PBY contacts did not reach Kinkaid until 1025 and indicated the presence of battleships and their escorts but no carriers. The Japanese were plotted 375nm northwest of TF 61, which was well beyond striking range. A subsequent PBY report received on *Enterprise* placed two Japanese carriers 355nm west of TF 61. Though still out of strike range, Kinkaid and his staff pondered how to take advantage of this priceless information. The same report reached Halsey and he curtly ordered Kinkaid, "Strike, Repeat, Strike." Whatever Halsey's orders, mounting a strike on such a distant target was going to be difficult. Kinkaid did not receive the report until 1150 and, with the wind coming from the southeast, TF 61 would have to turn away from the contact to launch a strike. The best Kinkaid could do was increase speed to 27 knots to reduce the distance to the target and hope the Japanese maintained their course to the east. With luck, an afternoon strike would be possible if the opposing carriers continued to close.

Kinkaid had assigned *Enterprise* as the duty carrier for October 25 so her air group handled searches and CAP duties. A full strike was armed and spotted on *Hornet*'s flight deck. Later in the day, Kinkaid inexplicably designated *Enterprise*'s inexperienced air group for the afternoon strike instead of *Hornet*'s more experienced air group that was already on alert. At 1330 hours Kinkaid launched an afternoon search of 12 Dauntlesses to scout to the northwest out to 200nm. *Enterprise* began to launch a strike at 1400 to fly 150nm to the northwest to await information from the search aircraft. The search and strike mission by 16 Wildcats, 12 Dauntlesses, and seven Avengers turned into a shambolic mess. When the strike departed at 1425, it had only eight Wildcats, five Dauntlesses, and six Avengers. Then at 1510 Kinkaid learned that a group of B-17s had just bombed the Vanguard Force which was headed north at 25 knots. The assumption that the strike could find a target was based on the Japanese continuing to head for TF 61. With the latest report showing the Japanese were actually heading north, the strike had no chance of hitting anything. Things got worse when the strike commander ignored his orders to proceed only 150nm before returning; instead, he led his group out to 200nm and then made an 80nm dog leg to the north. This delay in returning meant a night recovery for the inexperienced pilots. One Wildcat, four Dauntlesses, and three Avengers were lost or damaged beyond repair.

Japanese movements late on October 25 made a carrier clash inevitable the following day. Kondo's Advance Force headed south at 1900, followed an hour later by Nagumo's force. The Vanguard Force assumed station 60nm ahead of the carriers. The Support Force had been at sea since October 11 and fuel was becoming an issue. But by this point Yamamoto was tired of the many delays. At 2218 his chief of staff sent a message to Kondo and Nagumo directing them to make greater efforts to bring the Americans to battle the next day. On the morning of October 26, Nagumo's three carriers were ready with search, CAP, and strike aircraft spotted on deck. A second strike was fueled and armed on the hangar decks (Japanese fleet carriers had two hangar decks). Including the aircraft on *Junyo* in the Advance Force, the Japanese possessed 194 operational aircraft on four carriers.

Together, *Enterprise* and *Hornet* possessed 137 operational aircraft. Neither Halsey nor Kinkaid understood that in the war's fourth carrier battle the Japanese would outnumber the Americans in every important category. After a major flight deck crash and the abortive strike of October 25, *Enterprise*'s air group was reduced to 31 Wildcats, 23 Dauntlesses, and ten Avengers. Kinkaid designated *Enterprise* as the duty carrier for October 26, which made *Hornet*'s air group the designated strike group.

THE BATTLE BEGINS

With both commanders under orders to attack, there was no doubt that October 26 would witness another carrier clash. The action began in the early hours as PBYs continued to probe Japanese dispositions. The first PBY report was issued at 0022, noting a Japanese force some 300nm northwest of TF 61. This aircraft followed with a torpedo attack on what it identified as a heavy cruiser. The attack, which was unsuccessful, was actually against a destroyer of the Vanguard Force. Another PBY spotted *Zuikaku* and executed a glide-bombing attack at 0250. The four 500lb bombs missed the carrier by some 300 yards to starboard. These attacks by the lumbering PBYs were enough to bring out Nagumo's cautious side.

Nagumo's force had now been located, and this increased his fear of an ambush by American carriers he assessed were operating to his east. At 0330 he ordered his carriers to head north and that all aircraft in the hangar bays be de-fueled and de-armed. At first light he mounted a robust search with 14 Type 97s to cover the sectors to the east and south out to a distance of 300nm. *Shokaku* and *Zuikaku*

Zuiho photographed conducting flight operations on an unknown date in October 1942 just before the battle of Santa Cruz. The aircraft that has just taken off is a B5N. However, most of the aircraft carried aboard *Zuiho* at this time were Zero fighters, and these played an important role in the battle. (Yamato Museum)

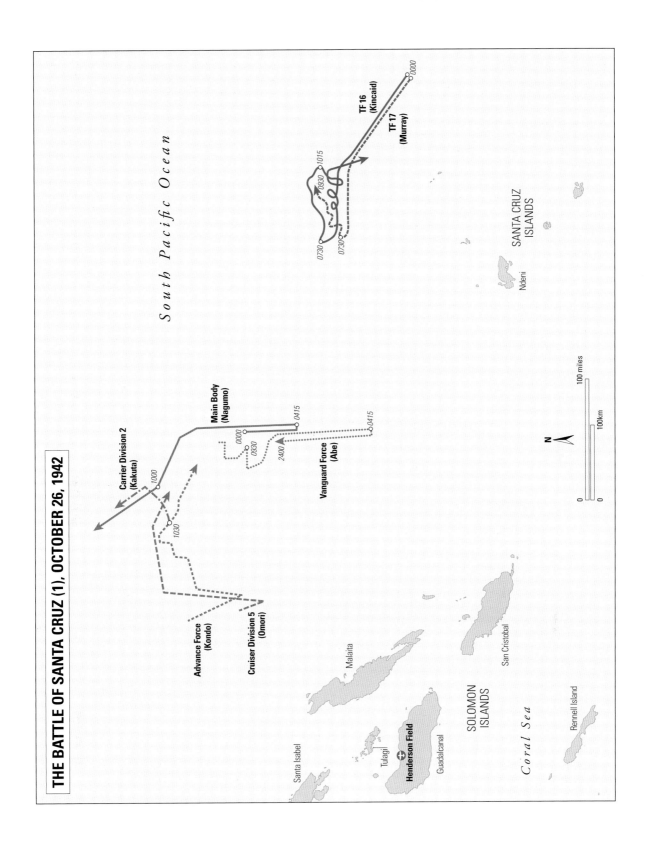

THE BATTLE OF SANTA CRUZ (1), OCTOBER 26, 1942

TF 16 (Kincaid)

TF 17 (Murray)

0000

1015

0930

0730

0730

South Pacific Ocean

SANTA CRUZ ISLANDS

Ndeni

Carrier Division 2 (Kakuta)

1000

1030

Main Body (Nagumo)

0000

0930

0415

2400

Vanguard Force (Abe)

0415

Advance Force (Kondo)

Cruiser Division 5 (Omori)

N

100 miles

100km

0

0

Malaita

San Cristobal

SOLOMON ISLANDS

Santa Isabel

Tulagi

Henderson Field

Guadalcanal

Coral Sea

Rennell Island

each contributed four Type 97s and *Zuiho* six. Following the 0445 launch of the search aircraft, *Zuiho* launched the first CAP mission at 0520. The first strike remained on deck ready for immediate launch.

The flight decks of *Enterprise* and *Hornet* were also busy with early morning activity. *Enterprise* launched seven Wildcats for CAP and 16 Dauntlesses to search in pairs out 200nm to the west. At sunrise *Hornet* added another seven fighters to the CAP. Dedicating 16 Dauntlesses to search missions would have been unnecessary if the PBY contact reports had reached Kinkaid earlier. He did not learn of the PBY attack on *Zuikaku* until 0512. Other ships in TF 61 copied the message an hour earlier but did not pass it to Kinkaid's flagship. Persistent communication problems had cost the Americans a chance to catch Nagumo's carriers with their planes on deck. When Kinkaid's staff finally learned that PBYs had spotted Nagumo's carriers, they urged that *Hornet*'s ready strike be launched for a search and strike mission. Kinkaid declined, probably because the previous day's debacle by *Enterprise*'s air group was still on his mind.

The Americans retained the initiative as reports from *Enterprise*'s scouts came in. Two Dauntlesses spotted the Vanguard Force only 170nm to the west of TF 61 at 0617. Heavy cruiser *Tone* was attacked by two Dauntlesses at 0645. Both aircraft missed with their 500lb bombs and one Dauntless was lost to antiaircraft fire. About the same time another pair of Dauntlesses spotted one of Nagumo's carriers and by 0700 had sighted all three. The Japanese remained oblivious to the Dauntlesses overhead for several minutes. When the Americans were finally spotted, the CAP was reinforced by 17 Zeros from *Shokaku* and *Zuikaku*.

The Dauntless contact of the Japanese carriers put them 185–200nm to the northwest of TF 61. This was barely within strike range, but Kinkaid ordered an immediate attack by both carriers. To close the range, Kinkaid steered toward the contacts and increased speed to 27 knots. The targets would be at maximum strike range since the Japanese were headed north at high speed, and the prevailing winds meant that Kinkaid would have to head to the southeast to launch his aircraft. *Hornet* had her strike already spotted on her flight deck so she was the first to launch. By 0743 eight Wildcats, 15 Dauntlesses, and six Avengers with torpedoes were in the air. A second wave of seven Wildcats, nine Dauntlesses, and ten Avengers (armed with 500lb bombs instead of torpedoes) quickly followed. The two groups proceeded to the target separately. Kinkaid's order to launch caught *Enterprise* unprepared. She was only able to assemble a strike of eight Avengers and three Dauntlesses escorted by eight Wildcats. Accompanying the strike was the air group commander flying an unarmed Avenger. *Enterprise*'s strike was ordered to proceed independently, so three different American strike groups were headed to attack Nagumo with no coordination among them.

Enterprise's strike operations were disjointed on October 26. This photograph shows an Avenger ready for takeoff. The signs in the background highlight the confusion. The one on the left states "JAP CV SPEED 25 AT 0830" but fails to give an updated target location. The sign on the right reads "PROCEED WITHOUT HORNET" confirming the inability of TF 61 to mount coordinated attacks. (Naval History and Heritage Command)

This photograph shows a strike preparing to take off from either Shokaku or Zuikaku. Zero fighters are spotted forward since they needed less space to take off and the heavier Type 99 dive-bombers are spotted behind them. This flight deck scene is believed to have been taken during the battle of Santa Cruz. (Naval History and Heritage Command)

Unknown to Kinkaid, he had already lost his chance to ambush the Japanese. One of *Shokaku*'s scouts spotted an American carrier at 0612 only 210nm away. Nagumo did not receive the report until 0658, but his reaction was immediate. The D4Y1 reconnaissance aircraft on *Shokaku* was dispatched to confirm the sighting and by 0710 hours the launch of the first strike was underway. The attack force totaled 22 Type 97s (20 from *Shokaku* armed with torpedoes and one each from *Zuikaku* and *Zuiho* as unarmed tracker aircraft) and 21 dive-bombers from *Zuikaku*. A heavy escort of 21 Zeros (four from *Shokaku*, eight from *Zuikaku*, and nine from *Zuiho*) was provided. The strike was under the command of Lieutenant Commander Murata, the same man who had laid waste to Battleship Row on December 7, 1941.

As soon as the first wave had launched, aircraft handlers aboard *Shokaku* and *Zuikaku* began moving the second wave from the hangar decks to the flight deck. During this vulnerable period two Dauntlesses arrived over Nagumo's force. The dive-bombers were not detected by *Shokaku*'s radar or by the 21 Zeros on CAP. The two American pilots commenced a dive on what they thought was a Shokaku-class carrier at 0740. Both claimed their 500lb bombs hit the carrier and both escaped after being pursued 45nm by Zeros. The Dauntlesses actually attacked *Zuiho*, and one of their bombs hit the carrier aft. The ship's damage control teams succeeded in extinguishing the fires, but the carrier's arresting gear was wrecked. With *Zuiho* unable to recover aircraft, she was out of the battle and was ordered to retire to Truk.

Nagumo was very fortunate that the surprise Dauntless attack was not directed at one of his two large carriers. They were at their most vulnerable, being in the process of arming and fueling the aircraft of the second attack wave. Very mindful of the events of Midway, the flight deck crews on both carriers worked feverishly to launch the aircraft as quickly as possible. This desire to get the aircraft off as soon as possible resulted in a fragmented launch. The dive-bombers on *Shokaku* needed less time to prepare than the Type 97s on *Zuikaku* that were still being loaded with Type 91 torpedoes. To decrease his vulnerability, at 0810 Nagumo ordered the immediate launch of the aircraft from *Shokaku*. The launch proceeded efficiently, and by 0818 five Zero fighters and 20 dive-bombers (one later aborted) were headed toward the American carriers. *Zuikaku*'s launch of 17 Type 97s (including one unarmed tracker) and four Zeros followed. Each strike group proceeded independently.

Since the Japanese possessed a considerable advantage in surface firepower, Kondo maneuvered his force for a surface engagement. The Advance Force increased speed and moved to join with Nagumo's Advance Force. This had the effect of bringing *Junyo* into strike range. The Vanguard Force increased speed to 26 knots and headed toward TF 61 in two groups. One group consisted of heavy cruisers *Tone* and *Chikuma* and two destroyers with the balance of the Vanguard Force in the other group.

THE AMERICANS STRIKE

Since the American and Japanese strike groups were on roughly reciprocal courses there was bound to be some interaction between them. At about 0835 the escort of the first Japanese attack group spotted the *Enterprise* group. The leader of the nine Zeros from *Zuiho* decided to attack the unsuspecting Americans. Diving down from 14,000 feet out of the sun, the Japanese gained complete surprise. The ensuing melee was costly for both sides. The Americans lost three Wildcats and two Avengers; another two Avengers and a Wildcat were forced to return to *Enterprise*. Four Zeros spun into the water below and another was heavily damaged. *Enterprise*'s already small strike was reduced to just five Avengers (including the unarmed air group commander's aircraft), three Dauntlesses, and four escorting Wildcats. The impact on the Japanese was worse. All five surviving *Zuiho* fighters were forced to return to their ship. The removal of all nine *Zuiho* fighters from the strike was to prove critical.

Hornet's first wave was the first to reach the target area. The Japanese were as ready for them as they could be. *Shokaku*'s radar gave adequate early warning when it detected the American aircraft 78nm away at 0840. Twenty-three Zeros were aloft on CAP. Twenty of these were arrayed over the carriers at various altitudes to defend against both dive-bombing and torpedo attack, while the final three fighters were placed over the Vanguard Force. *Hornet*'s strike spotted *Tone* and *Chikuma* at 0850 hours, and the flight leader continued to the northwest where he spotted the rest of the Vanguard Force at about 0910. At this point the three *Zuiho* Zeros on CAP attacked the American formation. After two passes, the Zeros stripped the fighter cover from *Hornet*'s strike and separated the 15 Dauntlesses from the six Avengers. In response to the Zero attack, the leader of the *Hornet* dive-bombers, Lieutenant Commander William Widhelm, took his aircraft into some clouds. Minutes later he spotted ships 25nm ahead. Among them were a large carrier and a smaller one issuing black smoke. Widhelm had spotted *Shokaku* and the damaged *Zuiho*. *Zuikaku* was under cloud cover and was not visible to Widhelm.

The alert Japanese CAP reacted immediately and went after the approaching Dauntlesses. Widhelm's Dauntless and another dive-bomber were shot down before the surviving Dauntlesses began their attack dives on *Shokaku* at 0927. The Americans attacked from astern, but the first three or four 1,000lb bombs missed the wildly maneuvering carrier. In the heaviest American blow of the

Very few of the attacks by American aircraft on October 26 were directed at a Japanese carrier. *Chikuma* came under several attacks by aircraft unable to find the Japanese carriers. In this view, the heavy cruiser is steaming at high speed with all her forward 8-inch gun turrets trained to port. Note the aerial recognition mark is on the second turret and that both catapults have been swung out. The ship was hit by a 1,000lb bomb on its forward superstructure where smoke is evident in this view. *Chikuma* survived the battle despite heavy damage. This photograph was taken from the Avenger of *Hornet*'s air group commander, Commander Rodee. (Naval History and Heritage Command)

battle, the remaining Dauntlesses scored at least four and possibly as many as six bomb hits. In his raft nearby, Widhelm counted six hits. The damage caused by this barrage of 1,000lb explosive projectiles was extensive. One hit near the island and the others around the center and aft elevators. Though the flight deck was destroyed aft, the ship was in no danger of sinking. A large fire was ignited but, as there were no aircraft in the hangar bays and the fuel lines had been secured, the fire was brought under control after five hours of struggle by *Shokaku*'s well-trained damage control teams. The damage did not affect the ship's machinery, so *Shokaku* was able to maintain full speed. Unable to conduct flight operations and with some 130 of her crew dead, *Shokaku* was also out of the fight.

The last *Hornet* Dauntless attacked destroyer *Teruzuki* without success. *Hornet*'s six Avengers missed Widhelm's turn north and did not receive his radio messages with the location of the Japanese carriers. Since he never saw Nagumo's carriers, the commander of the six Avengers decided to attack elements of the Vanguard Force. The only targets in sight were *Tone* and *Chikuma*. The six torpedo-armed Avengers lined up on *Tone*; the Americans claimed three torpedo hits; in fact, none of the five torpedoes dropped hit the cruiser.

Hornet's second wave also failed to spot the Japanese carriers. The nine Dauntlesses and ten Avengers (all armed with bombs) flew over *Tone* and *Chikuma* at about 0920. This group also missed Widhelm's messages with the locations of the Japanese carriers. Having no other option, the leader of the dive-bombers decided to attack *Chikuma*. The cruiser was struck by a 1,000lb bomb on the bridge and another on the forward superstructure.

The Avengers also decided to go after the cruisers but were subjected to an attack by two Zeros on their approach. The surviving nine Avengers, all armed with four 500lb bombs, selected *Chikuma* as their target. The Americans approached the cruiser from astern for a glide-bomb attack, but the well-handled cruiser evaded all but one of the bombs. That bomb struck the starboard aft torpedo mount, starting a fire and destroying a reconnaissance floatplane on the starboard catapult. Damage to *Chikuma* was extensive, but she was able to maintain speed and was in no danger of sinking. From her crew of about 900, 192 were killed and 95 wounded.

The last American aircraft to attack were *Enterprise*'s small strike of three Dauntlesses and five Avengers escorted by four Wildcats. The *Enterprise* group heard Widhelm's messages about attacking a Japanese carrier, but the group commander failed to realize that Widhelm had turned north instead of continuing to proceed to the northwest. *Enterprise*'s strike maintained course to the northwest and spotted *Tone* and *Chikuma* followed by the main body of the Vanguard Group. After a further search with no results, the flight commander turned back to attack the Vanguard Group. The Avengers attacked the nearest large ship, heavy cruiser *Suzuya*, at 0930. Only three Avengers were able to launch their torpedoes and all missed. The three Dauntlesses were separated from the Avengers during the target search and ended up attacking the damaged *Chikuma* at 0939. The cruiser took two near misses to starboard that caused flooding and reduced her speed.

Despite their massive coordination problems, American aircraft damaged two carriers and inflicted heavy damage to *Chikuma*. The 16 *Enterprise* Dauntlesses assigned to the morning scout mission performed excellently by providing critical location data on the Japanese fleet, keeping Nagumo off balance, and knocking *Zuiho* out of the battle. Kinkaid's main strike of 75 aircraft had not done as well. Only ten aircraft actually attacked a Japanese carrier and did so almost by accident after Widhelm's impromptu decision to head north to avoid Zero attack. The American attacks displayed their familiar lack of cohesion and verged on haphazard. Direct combat losses totaled four Wildcats, two Dauntlesses, and two Avengers; many others were forced to ditch, returning to TF 61. The Japanese tactic of deploying the Advance Force in front of the carriers and the much-improved performance by Japanese CAP further reduced the effectiveness of the American strikes. For the first time, Japanese radar provided advance warning and the CAP was well positioned at different altitudes. Five Zeros were lost on CAP; one was later forced to ditch. In addition, four of *Zuiho*'s fighters that had mauled the *Enterprise* strike group were lost. *Shokaku* remained afloat in spite of the beating she had taken.

This view, taken by one of *Hornet*'s returning aircraft, shows TF 17 maneuvering as it prepares for a Japanese air attack. *Hornet* is visible to the left with her escorts close by. (Naval History and Heritage Command)

THE JAPANESE STRIKE

In comparison to the disjointed American strikes, the Japanese strike groups were about to give a virtuoso performance. The Americans had plenty of warning that the Japanese were on their way. *Hornet*'s outgoing strike warned of Japanese aircraft inbound at 0830 hours. In response TF 16's CAP was reinforced to 22 fighters. *Hornet* added another seven Wildcats to her CAP for a total of 15. The key to a successful fighter defense was getting the CAP to intercept the Japanese as far from the carriers as possible and placing the Wildcats at the correct altitude. What ensued was further proof that fighter direction was still an evolving art form. The first problem was that TF 16 and TF 17 were operating 10nm apart with *Hornet* to the southwest. This distance was far enough to make mutual support impossible. TF 61's FDO placed seven Wildcats at 10,000 feet over TF 16 and four between TF 16 and TF 17. Eight Wildcats were placed over *Hornet* at 10,000 feet. The altitude decision proved disastrous. Thinking that radar would give him plenty of warning to move the fighters higher if required, the FDO positioned the Wildcats at 10,000 feet to conserve fuel and oxygen.

Strike leader Murata spotted *Hornet* and TF 17 at 0853; clouds covered TF 16. An immediate attack was ordered. The strike was arranged in two groups – the 21 *Zuikaku* dive-bombers at 17,000 feet with eight escorting Zeros above them at

21,000 feet in a trail position, and the second group of 20 *Shokaku* Type 97s at 14,000 feet with an escort of four Zeros. The Japanese were not detected by radar until 0855 35nm west-southwest of *Hornet*. In response the FDO moved eight Wildcats to the west and the pilots decided to climb above 10,000 feet. *Hornet*'s fighters spotted the Japanese at 0859, but it was too late for an interception away from the ship. Murata deployed his Type 97s in two groups for an anvil attack. He led 11 Type 97s with the four Zeros to the south diving to gain speed; the remaining nine torpedo planes would attack from the north. The dive-bombers spotted *Hornet* at 0858 hours and rushed to attack. The Japanese had achieved a fully coordinated attack.

The dive-bombers split into three groups to disperse *Hornet*'s antiaircraft fire. Eight *Hornet* Wildcats gained enough altitude to conduct a head-on attack that accounted for at least three dive-bombers. Three more were severely damaged before the Zeros intervened and shot down three Wildcats and forced the others to retreat. A second group of *Hornet* fighters was able to shoot down one more Type 99. At 0910 the surviving Japanese dive-bombers began their dives on *Hornet*. TF 17 had increased speed to 28 knots; four cruisers and six destroyers were deployed 2,000 yards in a circular formation around the carrier. *Hornet* spotted the first seven dive-bombers approaching from the west at 0905 and opened up with her 5-inch antiaircraft battery at 10,500 yards.

One of Murata's Type 97 torpedo planes on its attack run against *Hornet*. The aircraft still carries its torpedo. Heavy cruiser *Northampton* is in the background. (Naval History and Heritage Command)

PREVIOUS PAGES This remarkable view taken from heavy cruiser *Pensacola* shows the fully coordinated Japanese attack against *Hornet* in progress. Above the carrier is a *Zuikaku* Type 99 dive-bomber which is about to crash onto the ship. A *Shokaku* Type 97 torpedo bomber is also visible in the background after launching its weapon at *Hornet*. (Naval History and Heritage Command)

The first seven dive-bombers emerged astern of *Hornet* through a cloud. The first dropped its bomb and missed to starboard. The second placed a 550lb semi-armor-piercing bomb in the center of the flight deck that penetrated three decks before exploding. The third Type 99 was destroyed by antiaircraft fire before it could release its bomb and crashed in the water a mere 30 feet from *Hornet*'s starboard bow. The fourth dive-bomber put its high-explosive bomb on the after flight deck before being hit by 20mm gunfire. As the aircraft crashed, the rear gunner bailed out by parachute and survived to be picked up by a Japanese destroyer the next day. The fifth attacker circled ahead and approached *Hornet* from her port bow. This aircraft skillfully placed another semi-armor-piercing bomb aft that passed through four decks before exploding and causing a heavy loss of life. The sixth aircraft also came in from the bow but missed. The final dive-bomber was attacked by Wildcats and failed to make an attack. Three of the six dive-bombers to dive on *Hornet* scored hits and four of the six survived.

In the middle of the dive-bombing assault, Murata's torpedo planes began their final attack runs. The escorting Zeros successfully defended their charges against the CAP, shooting down two Wildcats for the loss of a single Zero. Murata's plan to execute an anvil attack was disrupted when *Hornet* changed course to the northeast; *Hornet*'s captain was attempting to keep his stern to the attackers to present as small a target as possible. This maneuver forced Murata into a difficult stern attack. In response, the 11 Type 97s increased speed to set up for a more advantageous beam launch against the carrier. The first to attack were the three planes led by Murata. They approached *Hornet* from her starboard quarter at an altitude of 300 feet. The first Type 97 dropped its torpedo from 1,500 yards and was shot down. The next two closed to within 1,000 yards before dropping their weapons. Murata did not survive the attack; after banking away his aircraft was hit by antiaircraft fire and crashed off *Hornet*'s starboard beam.

The next photograph in the sequence from *Pensacola* shows the explosion from the Type 99 that has just struck *Hornet*'s signal bridge. Note the withdrawing Type 97 torpedo bomber at right. (Naval History and Heritage Command)

This photograph shows *Hornet*'s signal bridge after the crash of *Shokaku*'s Type 99 dive-bomber. The aircraft's bomb failed to explode, which greatly minimized damage. However, burning fuel from the aircraft killed seven men on the signal bridge, and the fuselage of the aircraft penetrated the flight deck and almost reached a ready room in the level below. (Naval History and Heritage Command)

This skillful torpedo attack was devastating and played a major role in deciding the entire battle. The first torpedo struck *Hornet* amidships at 0915. The second hit only seconds later in the engineering spaces. The forward engine room and two boiler rooms flooded; *Hornet* lost power and soon went dead in the water. A 10-degree starboard list also developed.

Eight more Type 97s were still boring in on *Hornet*. The next group of three had no success; the first aircraft jettisoned its torpedo and was shot down, and the next two launched their weapons but missed. The final five aircraft were faced with a worsening target angle as *Hornet* continued her turn to the northwest. The next group of three suffered the same fate as the previous group, with one aircraft jettisoning its torpedo and being shot down while exiting the formation; the other two launched their torpedoes and missed but both survived. The final

The first Japanese strike on *Hornet* by *Shokaku*'s torpedo planes and *Zuikaku*'s dive-bombers crippled the carrier as is evident in this view. The carrier is already listing to starboard because of two torpedo hits, and a fire is burning aft as a result of one of the bomb hits. (Naval History and Heritage Command)

two Type 97s changed their target to *Pensacola*. One launched its torpedo at the cruiser and missed, and the second attempted to crash into the cruiser after being struck by antiaircraft fire. The aircraft missed *Pensacola*'s bow by only a few feet. Of the 11 Type 97s from Murata's group, eight launched torpedoes at *Hornet* of which two struck. Six Type 97s survived the intense action.

The second group of *Zuikaku* dive-bombers attacked *Hornet* just as Murata's torpedo bombers were doing their deadly work. The six dive-bombers ran into *Enterprise* fighters dispatched to assist *Hornet*. Only one of the dive-bombers was shot down, leaving five to dive on *Hornet*. Approaching from the carrier's port beam, all dropped their bombs and missed. The last aircraft was already in flames when it appeared over *Hornet* at 0914. Assuming the pilot was still alive, he decided to crash on the carrier. The aircraft's starboard wing hit the edge of the stack and the fuselage penetrated the flight deck. The crash caused fires that burned for two hours. The final group of dive-bombers enjoyed no success. *Hornet* Wildcats shot down three and at 0914 *Enterprise* fighters accounted for another. Only three survived to attack *Hornet* and these all missed. Two more were subsequently shot down by Wildcats leaving the area of TF 17.

The final attack on *Hornet* was conducted by *Shokaku*'s nine Type 97s that Murata had ordered to attack from the north. Since these were unescorted, they proved easy targets for Wildcats, which splashed three of the low-flying torpedo bombers. Another attempted to crash into cruiser *Juneau* but was shot down short of its target. As the last five approached the screen, one was shot down by destroyer *Morris*. The final four closed to within 300–800 yards of *Hornet*'s bow before releasing their torpedoes, but all missed.

Two Japanese aircraft previously crippled by Wildcats concluded the assault on *Hornet*. The first, a dive-bomber, appeared at 0917 off *Hornet*'s stern. The smoking Type 99 dropped its bomb after a shallow dive, but it missed the ship by 50 yards. The Japanese pilot pulled up from his dive, reversed course, and headed back to *Hornet* with the intent of crashing into the ship. The aircraft hit the carrier's forward port beam and the wreckage landed in the forward elevator pit, starting a fire. One minute later a Type 97 from the northern group, which had jettisoned its torpedo, approached *Hornet* from dead ahead. The crippled aircraft crashed into the ocean before reaching the ship.

As the few surviving Japanese aircraft retreated, *Hornet* was afire and dead in the water. She had been hit by two torpedoes, three bombs, and two crashed aircraft. Counter flooding reduced the list to only two degrees, but without power her prospects of survival were low. The cost to the Japanese for crippling *Hornet* had been very high. Of 21 dive-bombers, only four returned to their carriers; of the 20 attacking Type 97s, again only four survived. The escorting Zeros had performed well, but only seven of 12 returned. Six Wildcats on CAP were lost, but two pilots were rescued.

With *Hornet* crippled by the first attack wave, the second Japanese attack had the opportunity to cripple *Enterprise* and turn the battle into a decisive victory. Japanese monitoring of American radio circuits, in particular the FDO circuit, confirmed there were at least two carriers present. *Enterprise* was sighted by aircraft

LEFT This is *Hornet* dead in the water and listing to starboard after the initial Japanese attack. A destroyer is off her port side and *Northampton* is standing by. (Naval History and Heritage Command)

BELOW TF 16 maneuvering under Japanese air attack. *Enterprise* is in the center-left part of the photograph with *South Dakota* positioned close by to her right. The large ship on the left side of the view is heavy cruiser *Portland*. (Naval History and Heritage Command)

from the first attack wave and the tracking Type 97 from *Zuikaku* radioed *Enterprise*'s updated location at 0937. With *Enterprise* as their target, the second Japanese wave approached in two separate groups. The lead group consisted of the 19 dive-bombers from *Shokaku* escorted by five Zeros. The second group of 17 Type 97s from *Zuikaku* escorted by four Zeros was 45 minutes behind. Initial detection of the second wave was gained by radar on *Northampton* at about 0930 at a distance of 76nm. TF 16 did not gain contact until 15 minutes later when *South Dakota* reported a group of aircraft 55nm out. *Enterprise*'s radar did not detect the Japanese until they were only 45nm distant. As the Japanese approached, Kinkaid turned TF 16 to the southeast and headed into some rain squalls at 27 knots.

Strike leader Lieutenant Commander Seki Mamoru led the second wave's dive-bombers. Approaching the battle area, he spotted *Hornet* but quickly discerned she was heavily damaged. Leading his dive-bombers further east, he soon spotted TF 16. Seki ordered an immediate attack at 1008. He divided his 19 Type 99s into three groups to disperse antiaircraft fire and deployed them to attack out of the sun. At this critical moment, *Enterprise*'s CAP was poorly deployed, with only eight Wildcats at 10,000 feet and another 13 at lower altitudes. Orders from TF 61's FDO kept most of the fighters at lower levels; as a result only two Wildcats engaged the dive-bombers before they began their dives and only one Type 99 was shot down. Because of the poor CAP deployment, almost all of Seki's dive-bombers reached their pushover point unmolested by Wildcats.

When the attack began at 1015, *Enterprise* was vulnerable since a strike of ten Dauntlesses was in various stages of being fueled and armed on the flight and hangar decks. The failure of the CAP meant antiaircraft batteries on *Enterprise* and *South Dakota*, trailing astern by 2,500 yards, would have to carry the main weight of defending the carrier. The first seven Type 99s approached *Enterprise* from her starboard bow, and each was subjected in succession to a barrage of accurate antiaircraft fire. Seki and three other dive-bombers were shot down and none of the aircraft scored a hit on *Enterprise*. Only two minutes later the second group of seven dive-bombers attacked from astern. The lead aircraft survived heavy antiaircraft fire to place its high-explosive bomb on the forward part of the flight deck at 1017. This hit was so far forward that the bomb penetrated the flight deck and forecastle to explode in midair off the port bow. The second hit one minute later by a 550lb semi-armor-piercing bomb landed just aft of the forward elevator. It penetrated to the hangar deck where it created a fire; six Dauntlesses were rolled over the side to avoid feeding the conflagration. The bomb continued to the second deck where it exploded, killing members of a repair party, and started another fire in the forward elevator well. Another dive-bomber placed a bomb very close aboard of the starboard quarter at 1020. The near miss caused minor flooding and resulted in a Wildcat and a Dauntless

ABOVE The Japanese dive-bombing attack continues; *Enterprise* is executing a sharp turn to port and is heeling to starboard. A Type 99 has been hit and is in flames above *Enterprise*. Ten of *Shokaku*'s 19 dive-bombers were shot down over TF 16. (Samuel Morison Collection courtesy of Naval History and Heritage Command)

LEFT This photograph shows the beginning of the dive-bombing attack by *Shokaku*'s 19 Type 99s. *Enterprise* is in the center of the scene and has already been subjected to several near misses. One dive-bomber can be seen forward of *Enterprise* after dropping its weapon and another is above the carrier to the left. Note the tremendous volume of antiaircraft fire; most was provided by *South Dakota*, which is just out of this scene some 2,500 yards astern of *Enterprise*. (Samuel Morison Collection courtesy of Naval History and Heritage Command)

being thrown overboard. The third group of Type 99s could only achieve one near miss at 1020 hours that opened underwater seams on the carrier's starboard side.

Once again, a Japanese attack on an American carrier had proven very costly, with ten of Seki's 19 dive-bombers being destroyed. One of the surviving pilots radioed that the carrier had been hit six times and was burning and listing to starboard. Actual damage to *Enterprise* was much less serious. The ship suffered no reduction in speed and remained capable of conducting flight operations. The attack had killed 44 crewmen and destroyed one Wildcat and nine Dauntlesses.

LEFT This photograph shows the height of the dive-bombing attack from *Shokaku*'s aircraft against *Enterprise*. *Enterprise* is at left and *South Dakota* is at right. At least two of the Type 99s are visible over *Enterprise*. (Naval History and Heritage Command)

ABOVE One of the last *Shokaku* Type 99s placed its bomb only 10 feet off *Enterprise*'s starboard quarter. The near miss opened hull plates, and the shock of the explosion left a Dauntless precariously balanced on the starboard 20mm gun gallery. Deck crews tried to push the aircraft over the side, which was finally accomplished when the ship's captain put the ship into a hard turn to port. (Naval History and Heritage Command)

The Japanese dive-bombers had done a poor job of softening *Enterprise*'s defenses for the Type 97 attack to follow. The first indication the Americans received of the approach of *Zuikaku*'s torpedo plane squadron with its escort of four Zeros was a radar contact by *Enterprise* at 1035. This time the FDO did a better job positioning the Wildcats against the Japanese formation approaching at about 13,000 feet. The Japanese flight leader spotted *Hornet* at 1035 but only minutes later made visual contact on TF 16 to the southwest. He chose the apparently undamaged *Enterprise* for attack and formed two eight-plane groups to attack the carrier from each bow. The first group headed south while the second, with all four Zeros, continued to the southeast.

The first group, led by the flight commander, attacked first. Wildcats shot down a single Type 97 before the surviving aircraft commenced their attack runs. Four aircraft approached *Enterprise*'s

In this remarkable view taken from the port side of *Enterprise*'s island, a *Zuikaku* Type 97 torpedo bomber heads away after dropping its torpedo. The ship in the photograph is *South Dakota*, which is firing her antiaircraft battery as can be seen by the smoke. (Naval History and Heritage Command)

starboard beam and were able to drop their torpedoes, but the ship's captain ordered a sharp turn to starboard that made all the torpedoes miss. Another Type 97 approached from dead ahead and dropped its weapon. The torpedo was not sighted until it was only 800 yards away, but another sharp turn made it miss by 100 yards off the starboard beam. The quadruple 1.1-inch antiaircraft mount on the ship's bow shot this aircraft down. The last two Type 97s were unable to get a good angle on *Enterprise* so went after *South Dakota* instead. Both successfully released their weapons but neither hit; both aircraft were destroyed by antiaircraft fire.

Despite the second group of Type 97s having a Zero escort, they were mauled by the American CAP. The Zeros failed to stay with their charges, and two Wildcats caught the Type 97s in their descent. One was shot down, another heavily damaged, one was forced to abort, and several others were damaged. The six remaining aircraft emerged from the clouds astern of TF 16. While flying over the screen, the pilot of one Type 97, which was already on fire, decided he could not reach *Enterprise* and instead chose to dive on the nearest ship. This was destroyer *Smith*; the aircraft struck the ship forward of the bridge, and soon the forward part of the ship was on fire fed by the aircraft's fuel and then by the explosion of the torpedo. The remaining five Type 97s approached *Enterprise* from astern with the ship's captain attempting to keep his stern to the approaching Japanese. One of the five Type 97s launched its torpedo from dead astern and was shot down by antiaircraft fire – the torpedo missed. The last four launched their weapons off the carrier's port quarter, but only one torpedo came close to the carrier. The attack was over by 1052 with *Enterprise* unscathed. This was a crucial missed opportunity for the Japanese. A single Type 91 torpedo hit could have meant disaster. In the three previous carrier battles, every time a Japanese air-launched torpedo hit a carrier it started a chain of events leading to the loss of the ship. The same fate awaited *Hornet*. Sixteen Type 97s had attacked *Enterprise*, nine launched their weapons, and none hit. *Enterprise* was saved by good ship handling and by her CAP, which savaged one of the two groups of torpedo planes and disrupted the coordination between the two groups.

Junyo's air group entered the battle next. At 0905 *Junyo* began launching her initial strike comprising 12 Zeros and 17 dive-bombers. At that point TF 61 was some 280nm distant. After the strike was away, Kondo detached *Junyo* and two destroyers to operate with Nagumo. The rest of the Advance Force steamed to the southeast in hopes of engaging the Americans in a surface battle.

The aviators of Carrier Division 2 were not as experienced as the aircrews from *Shokaku* and *Zuikaku* and that relative lack of experience showed. As *Junyo*'s strike approached TF 16, radar on *Enterprise*, which had been troublesome all day, ceased working. *South Dakota*'s radar detected the Japanese, but word was not passed to TF 61's FDO. By the time *Enterprise*'s radar returned to service, the Japanese were only 20nm away. This gave no time for the CAP to react, and in any event the FDO issued only vague directions. As a result *Junyo*'s dive-bombers were not intercepted by Wildcats. The Japanese strike leader spotted TF 16 through a break in the clouds at 1120 and ordered an immediate attack. The low ceiling helped the Japanese avoid the American CAP but also impeded the dive-bombers from getting into the best attack position. The Type 99s were forced to use shallow 45-degree dives that reduced accuracy and increased their vulnerability to antiaircraft fire. A group of eight dive-bombers was the first to attack after selecting

Destroyer *Smith* was crashed by a *Shokaku* Type 97 and is afire as seen in this photograph taken from *South Dakota*. (Naval History and Heritage Command)

Junyo's dive-bomber squadron delivered an ineffective attack on Enterprise. None of the eight Junyo Type 99s which attacked Enterprise gained a direct hit; one of the misses is shown in the view. (Naval History and Heritage Command)

Enterprise as their target. Only one of the dive-bombers enjoyed any measure of success by scoring a damaging near miss.

The second group of nine dive-bombers lost sight of *Enterprise* in the low clouds and ended up making disjointed attacks against other ships in TF 16. Four sighted *South Dakota* and dove on the battleship. Their first three bombs missed, but the last hit the heavy armor on the roof of the forward 16-inch turret. This caused no damage to the turret, but shrapnel wounded several crewmen including the ship's captain. The last five dive-bombers selected light cruiser *San Juan* for attack. The first three Type 99s missed but the fourth scored a near miss on the port beam. The final dive-bomber slammed its semi-armor-piercing bomb into the cruiser's stern, which passed through the thinly armored ship before exploding under the hull. Damage was moderate in the form of several flooded compartments and temporary loss of rudder control. During the attack none of the dive-bombers were hit by antiaircraft fire, but four were destroyed by Wildcats or Dauntlesses as they exited the battle area. The 12 escorting Zeros suffered no losses and probably accounted for two Wildcats and an Avenger.

AFTER THE INITIAL STRIKES

The morning witnessed a full exchange of strikes from six carriers. Losses were heavy on both sides. The Americans were down to a single operational flight deck and the Japanese two. Aircraft losses were also heavy, particularly for the Japanese. Nagumo's aircraft losses were so heavy they compromised his ability to exploit his

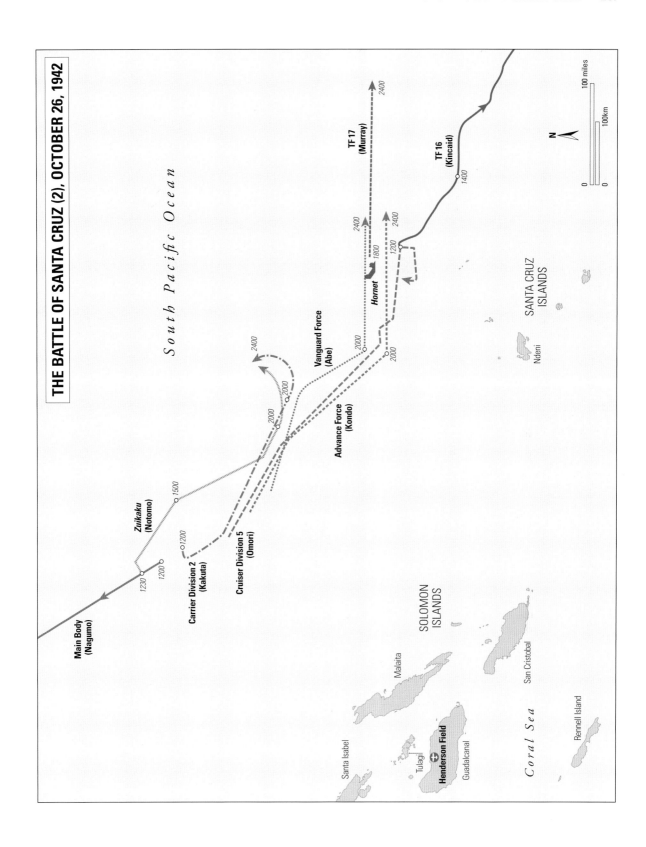

THE BATTLE OF SANTA CRUZ (2), OCTOBER 26, 1942

South Pacific Ocean

2400

TF 17
(Murray)

TF 16
(Kincaid)
1400

2400

2400

1200

1800

Hornet

2000

2000

Vanguard Force
(Abe)

Advance Force
(Kondo)

2400

2000

2000

Zuikaku
(Notomo)

1500

1200

Carrier Division 2
(Kakuta)

Cruiser Division 5
(Omori)

1230

1200

Main Body
(Nagumo)

SANTA CRUZ
ISLANDS

Ndeni

N

0   100 miles

0   100km

SOLOMON
ISLANDS

Malaita

Santa Isabel

Tulagi

Henderson Field

Guadalcanal

San Cristobal

Rennell Island

Coral Sea

Heavy cruiser *Northampton* attempted to tow *Hornet* out of the battle area. The crippled carrier was without air cover; after a third torpedo, the towing operation was abandoned. (Naval History and Heritage Command)

early success. When the surviving aircraft from the first wave started to recover at 1140, only ten Zeros, eight Type 97s, and one dive-bomber landed on *Zuikaku* and two Zeros, four dive-bombers, and one Type 97 on *Junyo*. Thirteen aircraft from the first wave were forced to ditch on the return flight to their carriers. After all aircraft had recovered, Nagumo detached *Zuikaku* and five destroyers to operate with *Junyo*. The rest of Nagumo's ships were ordered to head toward the Support Force that was steaming toward the last known position of the Americans in the hopes of initiating a surface action.

Even after the morning's action, Nagumo and his staff remained unsure as to how many American carriers were present. After analyzing aircrew debriefs and the radio intelligence mentioned earlier, the Japanese decided that they were facing three American carriers. One was the carrier dead in the water sighted numerous times during the morning, and the other two were operating to the north and northwest of the crippled carrier. This was an erroneous assessment not just of the numbers of carriers present but of their location. The effect of this misjudgment was that the Japanese afternoon strikes were sent to the wrong areas and never found *Enterprise*.

Wanting to exploit success, Yamamoto issued orders to Kondo to pursue and destroy the retreating Americans. Flight deck crews on *Junyo* and *Zuikaku* prepared to launch additional strikes. The first follow-up strike was sent from *Junyo* at 1313 and consisted of eight Zeros (from three different carriers) and seven Type 97s (six of which carried torpedoes). *Zuikaku*'s third strike of the day included five Zeros (from two different carriers), two dive-bombers, and seven

Type 97s (six carrying 1,760lb bombs and the last being an unarmed tracker aircraft). The strike was commanded by a lieutenant; the junior status of the flight commander and the small numbers of aircraft reflect the heavy losses suffered in the initial attacks.

The situation facing Kinkaid after the initial round of strikes was much more difficult. *Hornet* was still dead in the water, and attempts by heavy cruiser *Northampton* to tow the carrier had not been successful. *Enterprise* was unable to provide CAP for the stricken carrier. *Enterprise*'s damage did not preclude flight operations, so all surviving strike and CAP aircraft recovered on Kinkaid's only surviving flight deck which was operating without a functional forward elevator. Kinkaid's staff was sure that one or two Japanese carriers remained operational. To continue the battle only risked the loss of *Enterprise*, which would have been calamitous. Surveying his situation, Kinkaid made the decision to withdraw. He informed Halsey of his decision at 1135.

Once the decision to withdraw had been made, *Enterprise* moved out of Japanese strike range. The only issue remaining was whether *Hornet* could be saved. *Northampton* rigged a towing line by 1330 hours and attained a speed of three knots. Speed was later increased to six knots, providing a glimmer of hope the ship might be saved. But the Japanese had no intention of letting *Hornet* escape. Japanese aircraft monitored the progress of American attempts to salvage the carrier throughout the morning. At 1345 *Northampton*'s radar picked up the *Junyo* strike just over 100nm to the northwest. At 1400 the cruiser's radar detected *Zuikaku*'s strike 110nm to the northwest. Both groups of aircraft were looking for the undamaged American carrier assessed by Nagumo's staff to be operating north of *Hornet*. *Junyo*'s strike abandoned this fruitless search and at 1513 the strike leader spotted the damaged *Hornet*. With no other targets in sight, he decided to attack *Hornet*. *Northampton* was forced to cast off her tow line as the six Type 97s approached *Hornet*'s starboard beam. The strike leader skillfully placed his torpedo just aft of the two previous torpedo hits. The hit increased *Hornet*'s list to some 14 degrees and made any successful salvage operation unlikely. Inexplicably, the other five torpedo plane pilots failed to hit the huge target that was all but dead in the water. The strike leader and another Type 97 were shot down by antiaircraft fire. At 1541 the first of *Zuikaku*'s strike aircraft arrived overhead. The two dive-bombers attacked first but could only obtain a near miss.

With the ship's list increasing to 20 degrees, *Hornet*'s captain ordered his crew to abandon ship. As this process was beginning, the six *Zuikaku* Type 97s armed with bombs appeared overhead at 8,000 feet at 1555. Only one of the bombs hit; it struck the flight deck aft and caused little damage. *Junyo*'s and *Zuikaku*'s strikes returned between 1320 and 1400. Many of the aircraft were damaged and the

Hornet was abandoned after taking a terrific pounding from Japanese air attacks. Some of the ship's crew are visible in life rafts on the right. (Naval History and Heritage Command)

aircrews were physically and emotionally drained after flying two missions against fantastically heavy opposition from which most of their comrades had failed to return. *Zuikaku*'s captain decided that he could not mount a fourth strike. The more aggressive Kakuta on *Junyo* pushed his men harder and ordered another strike before dusk with any aircraft that could be readied. This final strike consisted of six Zeros and four Type 99s and was launched at 1535, finding *Hornet* just over an hour later. Only one of the four dive-bombers hit the stationary carrier; the bomb penetrated the flight deck and exploded on the hangar deck causing a fire. Abandoned and aflame, *Hornet*'s fate was clear.

After the final Japanese air attack, destroyer *Mustin* was ordered to sink *Hornet* while the rest of TF 17 steamed away to the east at 27 knots. *Mustin* fired eight torpedoes and four were seen to explode. These did not have the desired effect, so destroyer *Anderson* fired more torpedoes into the hulk. Six of her eight torpedoes were seen to explode, but even after this heavy punishment *Hornet* did not go down. Next, the two destroyers slammed 430 5-inch shells into the ship. This onslaught created a fire covering the length of the ship, but she remained afloat. Not wanting to be caught by the approaching Japanese, the two destroyers departed the area at 2030. Only some 30 minutes later, destroyers *Makigumo* and *Akigumo* arrived to find *Hornet* listing 45 degrees and consumed by fires. With salvage clearly impossible, the two Japanese destroyers fired two torpedoes each at the flaming wreck. *Hornet* finally sank at 0135 the next morning, making her the last American fleet carrier lost during the war.

THE ACCOUNTING

The Japanese were prepared to resume the battle on October 27, but their air searches found nothing and, on October 30, the Combined Fleet returned to Truk. For the first and last time in the war, the Japanese were the clear victors of a carrier battle. The Japanese believed they had scored a decisive victory and claimed three carriers, one battleship, one cruiser, one destroyer, and one unidentified large warship sunk. While their claims were more exaggerated than usual, the real toll on the Pacific Fleet was high enough. *Hornet* and destroyer *Porter* were sunk; *Enterprise* was damaged, along with *South Dakota*, *San Juan*, and destroyers *Smith* and *Mahan*. Eighty American aircraft were lost to all causes.

After Santa Cruz the Japanese made a major effort to neutralize Henderson Field and reinforce their garrison on Guadalcanal. The attempt was decisively defeated in part by aircraft from *Enterprise*. Shown here is one of the transports, *Kinugawa Maru*, lost in the attempt. (Naval History and Heritage Command)

In comparison, no Japanese ships were lost but three were damaged. *Zuiho* returned to service in December, *Chikuma* in February 1943, but *Zuikaku's* repairs were more extensive. She missed the rest of the Guadalcanal campaign and did not return to the fleet until March 1943. More importantly, Japanese aircraft losses were significant and aircrew losses were crippling. Of the 203 aircraft available at the start of the battle, only half survived. Strike aircraft took the brunt of the losses; 41 of 63 dive-bombers and 30 of 57 Type 97 carrier attack planes were destroyed. For the first time, American CAP and antiaircraft fire were responsible in equal parts for Japanese losses. Santa Cruz was a significant step in the destruction of the IJN's prewar aircrew cadre. In a single day the Japanese lost 145 aircrew including 68 pilots and 77 observers. Of these, 23 were section, squadron, or air group leaders.

The Guadalcanal campaign was not decided until November when Halsey used all means at his disposal to destroy a large Japanese troop convoy headed to the island. During this climactic battle, *Enterprise* played a key role along with Marine and Navy aircraft from Henderson Field. Yamamoto was so confident that he had destroyed the American carrier force at Santa Cruz that *Zuikaku* was sent back to Japan until January 1943. *Hiyo* and *Junyo* remained at Truk but were not able to provide air protection for the large convoy, nor were they able to neutralize Henderson Field. Yamamoto was unable to exploit his victory at Santa Cruz, and the losses suffered during the Solomons campaign were so crippling that the Japanese carrier force was not ready for a major engagement until mid-1944. When that battle finally occurred, it would be fought on much different terms than the four carrier battles of 1942.

CHAPTER 7
PREPARING FOR THE ULTIMATE CARRIER BATTLE

THE NEW AMERICAN CARRIER FORCE

Beginning in 1943, a flood of new ships reached what became known as the Fast Carrier Task Force. The new construction units included Essex-class fleet carriers, Independence-class light carriers, fast battleships, three new classes of cruisers, and scores of destroyers. By the end of 1943 enough new carriers and escorts were available to form four task groups each with one or two fleet carriers and one or two light carriers. Each task group was given an escort of three or four light or heavy cruisers and eight to 13 destroyers. The fast battleships were formed into a separate task group whenever a major encounter with the Japanese fleet appeared likely. Otherwise, the battleships were allocated to the screens of the carrier task groups. For example, at the battle of the Philippine Sea, the battle line consisted of seven battleships, four heavy cruisers, and 13 destroyers.

The Essex-class ships were the best carriers of the war. These 36,000-ton full load ships represented a fine mix of speed (33 knots maximum), range (15,000nm at 15 knots), survivability (none were lost during the war), and firepower. Each Essex-class ship carried an air group of 90–100 aircraft broken down into three squadrons. In

mid-1944 this included a 36-aircraft fighter squadron, a 36-aircraft dive-bomber squadron, and a torpedo-bomber squadron of 18 aircraft. Each ship also flew a detachment of four radar-equipped night fighters. Six Essex-class ships were available at the battle of the Philippine Sea and were joined by the veteran *Enterprise*.

Augmenting the fleet carriers were nine Independence-class light carriers, eight of which saw action at Philippine Sea. These were jammed down the throat of the Navy by President Roosevelt who insisted on a fairly austere conversion from Cleveland-class light cruisers. Grafted onto a cruiser hull, the conversions were fast and well protected. Each ship embarked an air group of 25 fighters and nine torpedo planes. The Independence-class conversions were much superior to the IJN's assortment of light carrier conversions.

The new ships were packed with new aircraft. Replacing the Wildcat was the Grumman F6F Hellcat that made its combat debut in September 1943. The Hellcat was fast (380mph top speed), well protected and rugged, well armed (six .50-caliber machine guns), and was easy to maintain. It was superior in all respects to the Japanese Zero except for low-speed maneuverability. The Dauntless had proved itself to be a reliable bombing platform during the first part of the war,

ABOVE *Yorktown* is shown underway during the invasion of the Marianas in June 1944. Note the profusion of antiaircraft guns and radar as well as the large number of aircraft spotted aft. (Naval History and Heritage Command)

MIDDLE RIGHT Of the USN's seven prewar carriers, *Enterprise* was the only one active at the battle of the Philippine Sea. Though unable to carry as many aircraft as an Essex-class carrier, she operated with the Fast Carrier Task Force for the remainder of the war. This is *Enterprise* underway on November 24, 1943 while supporting the invasion of the Gilbert Islands. (Naval History and Heritage Command)

RIGHT The Independence class comprised nine light carrier conversions from Cleveland-class light cruisers. These ships provided an insurance policy until the bulk of the Essex class entered service. Eight of the ships in this class fought at Philippine Sea. Independence-class carriers displaced 15,100 tons full load, carried a typical air group of 33 aircraft, were armed with 26 40mm and 40 20mm guns, and could steam at a top speed of 33 knots. This is *Belleau Wood* underway in December 1943. (Naval History and Heritage Command)

but it possessed a mediocre top speed and was restricted to a 1,000lb bomb load. The Curtiss SB2C Helldiver promised to be a major improvement over the Dauntless, but it had a long and painful development history. The SB2C-3 variant was not approved for fleet service until early 1943, and it took until the following year to iron out all the aircraft's problems. Many dive-bomber pilots preferred the easier-to-fly Dauntless, but the Helldiver proved deadly to Japanese shipping for the last 18 months of the war. The aircraft had a payload of 2,000 pounds and a top speed just under 300mph. The Avenger rounded out the carrier air groups and by 1944 was a proven ship killer after the Americans finally fixed the previously problematic Mark XIII torpedo. In 1944 this weapon was so reliable that the Avenger could drop it from 800 feet at speeds up to 270mph.

As noted previously, strike cohesion was a real problem for American carrier air groups in 1942. In 1944 strikes were still conducted separately by individual carriers, but rigorous pre-deployment air group training meant squadrons were better able to stick together on the way to their targets. Even in 1944 the principal weakness of USN carrier air groups was the short strike range of their aircraft. Depending on tactical circumstances, maximum strike range was limited to about 200nm. The typical search range of USN carrier aircraft was about 325nm, which was much less than their Japanese counterparts.

The Grumman F6F Hellcat was far superior to the Zero in armament, pilot protection, higher-speed maneuverability, and performance at altitude. This is an F6F-3 undergoing maintenance on *Essex* on July 30, 1944. The aircraft belongs to Commander David McCampbell who played an important role in the battle of the Philippine Sea. (Naval History and Heritage Command)

After a long gestation period, the SB2C-3 Helldiver proved reliable and tough in service and was responsible for the destruction of more Japanese shipping than any other USN aircraft. Approximately 175 were present at Philippine Sea; only two squadrons still operated the reliable SBD Dauntless. (Naval History and Heritage Command)

The USN had made great progress improving fleet air defense. In 1942 effective CAP proved the most powerful weapon in defeating Japanese air attack. The new Hellcat fighter had the potential to make CAP more effective, but the real key remained effective fighter direction. Throughout 1942 American efforts in this area met with mixed success. Early USN fighter direction efforts improved by trial and error, but by mid-1944 a solid doctrine was in place to maximize the chances of intercept. In the climactic carrier battle of 1944, the Fast Carrier Task Force (designated TF 58 in January 1944) was able to operate a centralized fighter direction scheme under the control of TF 58's FDO. Working with the FDOs in the other task groups and on each carrier, it was possible to shift available fighters from the control of one task group to the other while keeping a central reserve to handle future raids. During the battle of the Philippine Sea, fighter direction was well handled, with some Japanese raids intercepted by fighters as far as 60nm from the carriers, with the defending Hellcats positioned with an altitude advantage. As successful as these efforts generally were, it was impossible to defeat a large Japanese raid with CAP alone. Antiaircraft fire remained an important element of fleet air defense. The proliferation of 40mm guns in twin and quad mounts aboard ships from destroyers up through carriers, and the provision of proximity-fuzed shells for the ubiquitous 5-inch/38 gun, made American antiaircraft fire even more effective than it had been in 1942 when it was able to decimate attacking Japanese aircraft formations.

For Operation *Forager*, as the Marianas invasion was known, the USN assembled a highly capable command team. Nimitz retained his post as Commander-in-Chief, United States Pacific Fleet. Nimitz's theater was divided into three commands, Northern, Central, and Southern Pacific Ocean Areas. The Central Pacific Ocean Area included the Marianas. This command was assumed by Admiral Spruance in August 1943. When the Fifth Fleet was created in April 1944, Spruance was also given this command. This made him the principal command figure for the upcoming carrier battle off the Marianas. He possessed many traits of a great commander. Spruance was blessed with a sharp mind and was able to coolly think through all courses of action before making a decision. He delegated significant authority to his staff since he approached problems from a strategic perspective. If he had a shortcoming, it was an abundance of caution. This had served him well during the final stages of the battle of Midway but would turn out not to be a virtue in June 1944.

The Fifth Fleet's carrier task force (TF 58) was commanded by Vice Admiral Marc Mitscher. He, like Spruance, was unassuming and did not seek personal glory. Mitscher had been one of the pioneers of American naval aviation and had considerable experience as a carrier commander and a carrier task force commander. By mid-1944 Mitscher was at the peak of his game, but he suffered occasionally from Spruance's tendency to micromanage his direct subordinates, thereby reducing Mitscher's role. If Mitscher had a flaw, it was that he was not always attentive to details. Mitscher's carrier task group commanders were all aviators – Rear Admiral James "Jocko" Clark (TG 58.1), Rear Admiral Alfred E. Montgomery (TG 58.2), Rear Admiral John W. Reeves (TG 58.3), and Rear Admiral William K. Harrill. Clark was especially aggressive and went on to command carriers through the Korean War. Harrill was just the opposite and handled his task group poorly both before and during the upcoming battle.

BELOW RIGHT The principal American naval commanders at Philippine Sea are present in this photograph on heavy cruiser *Indianapolis* in February 1945. From left to right are Admiral Raymond A. Spruance, Vice Admiral Marc A. Mitscher, Fleet Admiral Chester W. Nimitz, and Vice Admiral Willis A. Lee. Nimitz set the overall objectives for Spruance and his Fifth Fleet, Mitscher was in tactical command of the Fast Carrier Task Force, and Lee was the USN's premier gunnery expert and assumed command of TF 58's battle line. (Naval History and Heritage Command)

BELOW Vice Admiral Marc A. Mitscher was the commander of Task Force 58 at Philippine Sea. This picture was actually taken in February 1945 and shows Mitscher, right, with his chief of staff Commodore Arleigh A. Burke aboard *Bunker Hill*. The two formed a good command team. (Naval History and Heritage Command)

FAST CARRIER TASK FORCE ON THE RAMPAGE

When the Pacific Fleet received its first Essex-class and Independence-class aircraft carriers, the Fast Carrier Task Force embarked on a series of raids to test its new ships and aircraft. In August 1943 aircraft from *Essex*, *Yorktown*, and *Independence* attacked Marcus Island. The next month aircraft from *Lexington*, *Princeton*, and *Belleau Wood* struck Tarawa Atoll in the Gilberts. Six carriers conducted a return raid on Wake Island in October. *Essex*, *Bunker Hill*, and *Independence* moved to the South Pacific to strike Rabaul in November and defeated a major Japanese air attack. In November, for the first time, the Fast Carrier Task Force had enough carriers to form four separate task groups during the invasion of the Gilberts. The weakened Japanese carrier fleet was overmatched by the six fleet carriers and five light carriers that the USN deployed to support the invasion, so the Japanese did not leave Truk to challenge the American onslaught. The only damage to the Fast Carrier Task Force during the Gilberts campaign was an air-dropped torpedo hit on *Independence* in a dusk attack. In December, six carriers raided Kwajalein Atoll during which *Lexington* was hit by an air-launched torpedo in another night air attack.

In 1944 the Fast Carrier Task Force increased the pace of its operations. Mitscher assumed command of the newly formed TF 58 in January. That same month, TF 58 covered the invasion of the Marshall Islands with *Enterprise*, *Saratoga*, four Essex-class carriers, and six Independence-class carriers deployed in four task groups. The Japanese fleet again declined to contest the landings. Beginning on the morning of February 17, TF 58 dramatically demonstrated its increased capabilities. A force of nine carriers (*Enterprise*, four Essex class, and four Independence class) launched a surprise attack against the powerful Japanese bastion at Truk. The Japanese guessed that a raid was imminent, so the Combined Fleet departed before the arrival of TF 58. Flying over 1,250 offensive sorties over two days, American aircraft devastated the base, destroying 250 aircraft and accounting for almost all of the 39 warships and merchant ships sunk by TF 58. Japanese air attacks succeeded in damaging carrier *Intrepid* with a torpedo from a Type 97 torpedo bomber.

The first attacks on the Marianas were conducted by two task groups from TF 58 on February 22. Palau Island was the next target on March 30 and April 1. Again the Japanese surmised that a raid was imminent, so the Combined Fleet got out in time. Plenty of targets remained; 36 merchant ships and auxiliaries were sunk totaling 130,000 tons. On April 21–22 the fast carriers hit Hollandia on New Guinea to support a landing by MacArthur's forces. TF 58 returned to Truk on April 29–30. This time the carriers flew 2,200 sorties that claimed almost 100 Japanese aircraft and neutralized Truk as a fleet base. After smaller strikes on

Marcus and Wake Islands, TF 58 returned to the anchorage at Majuro in the Marshall Islands for a short break before the invasion of the Marianas.

OPERATION *FORAGER*

The USN had long seen the Central Pacific as the best and quickest way to Japan. After the isolation of Rabaul, the USN wanted to get the Central Pacific advance on track as quickly as possible. The Quebec Conference held in Canada in August 1943 affirmed the importance of an offensive through the Central Pacific, and Admiral King ensured that the Mariana Islands were included as an objective. A primary reason for this was that the Army Air Force's new B-29 bomber possessed the range to hit targets in Japan from the Marianas. With this in mind, General Henry H. Arnold, commander of the Army Air Forces, supported the capture of the Marianas. The failure of basing B-29s in China to strike Japan drove Arnold to the realization that bases in the Marianas were required if the Army Air Forces wanted to strike Japan. The date for the invasion of the Marianas was not agreed until a planning conference in Washington, DC in February and March 1944. The participants accepted the schedule presented by Nimitz that called for Truk to be bypassed and the principal Japanese stronghold in the Marianas located on Saipan Island to be invaded by June 15.

Nimitz's plans for Operation *Forager* were issued on April 23, 1944. The actual landing on Saipan was confirmed for June 15. Building on Nimitz's campaign plan, Spruance's Fifth Fleet was given its orders on May 12. Before the landings, TF 58 was tasked to neutralize Japanese land-based air power within range of the landings. This put air bases and other targets on Saipan, Tinian, Guam, and the smaller islands of Rota and Pagan on the target list. TF 58 was expected to gain air superiority over the Marianas by June 14. On D-Day, TG 58.2 and 58.3 were tasked to maintain air control over the Marianas while TG 58.1 and 58.4 prepared to strike Iwo Jima and Chichi Jima (used by the Japanese to stage aircraft to the Marianas) on June 16 and 17. Following the initial landings, TF 58 would continue operations to maintain air control while moving to a position west of the Marianas to respond to any counterattack by the Japanese fleet.

The Americans expected that the invasion of Saipan would prompt a major response from the IJN. The USN's intelligence organizations produced excellent assessments of the First Mobile Fleet's order of battle and understood its tactics of attacking from unexpected directions and executing flank attacks. These insights were gained from the best source possible – the commander of the Combined Fleet himself. Admiral Koga, who had assumed command after the death of Yamamoto in April 1943, and his staff were moving by flying boat from Palau to

Davao in the southern Philippines when their three aircraft ran into a storm. Koga's aircraft disappeared, and a second with the staff officers aboard crashed with the survivors falling into the hands of Filipino guerrillas. With the officers was a copy of Combined Fleet Secret Order No. 73, better known as the "Z" Plan, that outlined how the Japanese would fight a decisive battle in the Central Pacific. The plan was transferred by an American submarine to Australia, quickly translated, and sent to major Allied commands.

THE IJN'S CARRIER FORCE

The Japanese carrier force took a terrible beating in the four carrier battles of 1942. Six carriers (four fleet and two light) were sunk in these engagements. More importantly, losses to the highly trained prewar aircrew cadre were extremely high. Of the 765 aircrew who participated in the Pearl Harbor attack, an estimated 409 were lost in 1942. When the Japanese evacuated Guadalcanal in January/February 1943, the attrition of Japanese carrier aircrew continued. To protect their bastion at Rabaul, the Japanese bitterly contested the American advance up the Solomons. Land-based Japanese air power proved unable to stop the Americans, so the Combined Fleet commander was under continual pressure to commit the air groups of the carriers based at Truk to assist the land-based air forces at Rabaul. On three occasions the Japanese moved their carrier air groups south to Rabaul. The first was Yamamoto's ill-conceived Operation *I-Go* in April. In March more than 100 aircraft from the air groups of *Zuikaku*, *Zuiho*, *Hiyo*, and *Junyo* were dispatched to Rabaul for a series of attacks on targets in New Guinea and Guadalcanal. From April 1 to 14, the Japanese conducted five raids to impede the Allied build-up in the region. Despite a large force of 350 aircraft, results of the operation were meager and some 50 Japanese aircraft were lost. However, Yamamoto believed the greatly exaggerated claims from his aircrews, and on April 16 he declared the operation a success and suspended further attacks. About 15 percent of the carrier air groups were lost.

After Yamamoto was killed in April, Admiral Koga assumed command of the Combined Fleet. Japanese commanders at Rabaul pressed Koga for aircraft reinforcements throughout the summer as the American advance continued up the Solomons. The only source of significant air reinforcement was still the air groups of the carriers at Truk. Koga knew that if he committed these aircraft to the Solomons campaign, they would not be available when the Combined Fleet was needed to contest the American drive in the Central Pacific. During the battle of New Georgia (a large island in the central Solomons), Koga sent the air group from *Junyo* to Buin air base on Bougainville Island on July 2 to respond to the

American invasion of Rendova Island (also in the central Solomons) on June 30. In two weeks one-third of the air group's aircraft were lost; the remainder returned to Truk having achieved nothing. In late September Koga led the Combined Fleet to ambush the American carrier force off Eniwetok Atoll in the Marshall Islands. Japanese naval intelligence was incorrect regarding this American operation, so the Combined Fleet returned to Truk without engaging the Americans.

In October Koga relented and sent a major portion of the Combined Fleet's carrier aircraft to Rabaul for ten days in expectation of an American invasion of Bougainville Island in the northern Solomons. This was given the name Operation RO and involved 173 aircraft (82 Zeros, 45 dive-bombers, 40 Type 97s, and six reconnaissance aircraft) from Carrier Division 1. The aircraft arrived at Rabaul on November 1 and immediately went into action. The following day some 100 aircraft attacked an American force of four light cruisers and eight destroyers. The ships had no air cover during the opening part of the battle, but all were new and equipped with the USN's best antiaircraft weapons and latest fire-control equipment. The American task force was well handled, and the Japanese dive-bombers showed little of their former skills and determination. Only two bombs hit the stern of light cruiser *Montpelier*, which caused minimal damage. The Americans claimed 17 aircraft shot down. On November 11 the Japanese launched a full strike against an American carrier force which had raided Rabaul that morning. The task force consisted of fleet carriers *Essex* and *Bunker Hill*, light carrier *Independence*, and a weak screen of nine destroyers. The Japanese attack force comprised 67 Zeros escorting 27 dive-bombers and 14 Type 97s armed with torpedoes. The American CAP intervened too late against the Japanese dive-bombers, so most were able to attack the carriers, with *Bunker Hill* being the main target. None of the three carriers were hit, but all suffered near misses. Of the 20 attacking dive-bombers, only three survived. The Type 97s followed, but all 14 were shot down without any torpedoes finding their marks.

This little-known engagement was the first major Japanese air attack on an American carrier group since Santa Cruz. It highlighted the diminished power of Japanese carrier air groups and the improvements made by the Americans in fleet air defense. In their short time at Rabaul, the aviators of Carrier Division 1 suffered crippling losses – 50 percent of fighters, 85 percent of dive-bombers, and 50 percent of torpedo aircraft. The virtual destruction of the best air groups in the Imperial Navy meant that, when the Americans landed in the Gilbert Islands in November, the Japanese carrier force was in no condition to give battle. The rebuilding of the IJN's carrier air groups was a slow process and was not complete by the time of the next carrier battle.

THE CONDITION OF THE JAPANESE CARRIER FORCE IN JUNE 1944

The Japanese struggled to match the growing capabilities of the Fast Carrier Task Force. In terms of the numbers and quality of ships, aircraft, and aircrew, the Japanese only fell further behind. The IJN's carrier force was vital to the decisive battle the Japanese were expecting and preparing for in 1944. Though Japanese efforts to rebuild the carrier force appeared to produce results by June 1944, the result was actually a hollow force with little prospect of success against TF 58.

On March 1, 1944 the IJN formally recognized the paramount position of the carrier in fleet operations. On this date the First Mobile Fleet was formed from the former First and Second Fleets that controlled the bulk of the IJN's battleships and heavy cruisers, and the Third Fleet that was the carrier force. Command of the Combined Fleet and the Mobile Fleet fell to a group of new officers by mid-1944. Following the death of Koga in an air crash, Admiral Toyoda Soemu took over command of the Combined Fleet in May 1944. Toyoda was regarded as a man of considerable experience and capability but was also viewed as hard-nosed and difficult to work with. The First Mobile Fleet was commanded by the very capable Vice Admiral Ozawa Jisaburo who was also in direct command of Carrier Division 1. He had an aviation background and had led the Third Fleet since November 1942. Ozawa's task force commanders had seen extensive combat action during the war. Vice Admiral Kurita Takeo commanded the Van Force

Commissioned in March 1944, *Taiho* was the best Japanese carrier design of the war, but her complexity made it impossible to mass produce and only a single ship was completed. At almost 37,000 tons full load, *Taiho* was large enough to carry 3.75 inches of armor on the flight deck and a large air group. This May 1944 photograph shows her enclosed hurricane bow and large island with a canted stack. *Shokaku* or *Zuikaku* is visible at right. (Yamato Museum)

Hiyo, photographed with sister ship *Junyo* on May 13: both were converted from large passenger liners and displaced 27,500 tons full load. Aside from the addition of minimal armor around the machinery and magazine spaces, the ships were unprotected and possessed a marginal top speed of 25.5 knots. Since they could embark an air group of over 50 aircraft, they were useful additions to the Combined Fleet. (Yamato Museum)

comprising the bulk of the First Mobile Fleet's battleships. Kurita had taken part in the invasion of the NEI, Midway, and Guadalcanal. Part of Kurita's Van Force was Carrier Division 3 commanded by Rear Admiral Obayashi Sueo. He was a noted aviation advocate who had held a succession of aviation billets since 1936

TOP RIGHT *Chitose* was converted into a light carrier from a seaplane carrier; this is the ship in August 1943 after the conversion was completed. As a light carrier, *Chitose* was capable of 29 knots and could embark 30 aircraft. The ship survived *A-Go* without damage but was sunk in October 1944 at Leyte Gulf. (Yamato Museum)

MIDDLE RIGHT *Chiyoda* was also converted from a seaplane carrier and possessed the same characteristics as *Chitose*. This December 1943 photograph shows the austere nature of the conversion. *Chiyoda* was damaged at Philippine Sea, but was repaired in time to participate in the battle of Leyte Gulf in which she was sunk. (Yamato Museum)

BELOW *Ryuho* was converted into a light carrier from a submarine tender in November 1942. She was the least successful of the IJN's light carrier conversions and Philippine Sea was her only combat operation. *Ryuho* survived the war in a damaged condition and is seen here in October 1945. (Naval History and Heritage Command)

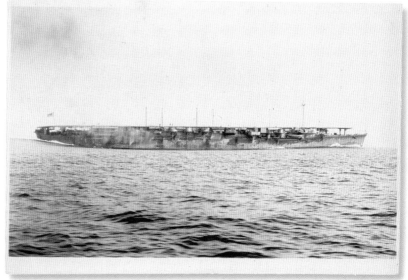

including command of *Zuiho* at Midway and Santa Cruz. Obayashi was particularly aggressive and later became one of the driving forces behind the IJN's adoption of kamikaze tactics. Rear Admiral Joshima Takaji commanded Carrier Division 2. He began the war as captain of *Shokaku*.

The Japanese shipbuilding industry had proved completely unable to replace war losses or to grow the size of the fleet. This is amply demonstrated by the fact that, for the decisive carrier battle of 1944, the First Mobile Fleet had only three purpose-built carriers and six carrier conversions of various types. The formidable *Shokaku* and *Zuikaku* formed the heart of the carrier force. Unfortunately for the Japanese, only one more fleet carrier was added by mid-1944. The new carrier *Taiho* was laid down in 1941. Although she was an excellent design incorporating a flight deck covered by 75mm–80mm of armor designed to withstand 1,000lb bombs, she was unsuited for mass production and thus was not the right design for the IJN. *Taiho* was fitted with radar, the excellent Type 98 3.9-inch antiaircraft gun, and carried a large air group of 75 aircraft. She joined the two Shokaku-class ships to form Carrier Division 1.

Complementing the three excellent fleet carriers was a collection of conversions. *Hiyo* and *Junyo* were useful ships since both could embark about

The Japanese were unable to deliver a new carrier fighter to their carrier fleet during the entire war. By June 1944 the standard IJN carrier fighter was the A6M5, which was a minor upgrade of the early war A6M2 Zero. The A6M5 featured an improved engine configuration that produced a slightly higher maximum speed. This slight improvement compared poorly to the F6F Hellcat, meaning that the Zero was totally outclassed as a fighter. The aircraft in this photograph was captured on Saipan and later tested by the Americans. The A6M2 version of the Zero was employed at Philippine Sea as a fighter-bomber and equipped to carry a 550lb bomb. (Naval History and Heritage Command)

The replacement for the Type 97 was the Nakajima Navy Carrier Attack Bomber B6N2 Model 12. It entered service after serious production delays. The only real improvement over the Type 97 was a more powerful engine that increased top speed to 299mph. This B6N, still carrying its torpedo, was photographed from light carrier *Monterey* probably during the April 30, 1944 raid on Truk. (Naval History and Heritage Command)

50 aircraft, but each had limited speed and protection. The balance of the carrier force comprised light carriers. *Zuiho* was still in service and was considered a lucky ship by her crew. *Ryuho* was another of the IJN's prewar shadow carrier fleet. The ship entered service in 1934 as a submarine tender. Conversion to a light carrier began in December 1941 and was completed in November 1942. *Ryuho* was the least successful light carrier conversion given her top speed of only 26 knots, small flight deck, lack of protection, and small air group. The last carriers to join the fleet were the two ships of the Chitose class. Both were originally built as seaplane carriers and saw service earlier in the war in this capacity. The Midway disaster prompted the Japanese to convert both into carriers, which was completed by early 1944. As carriers, they were comparable to the Shoho class. Carrier Division 2 was allocated *Junyo*, *Hiyo*, and *Ryuho*; the smaller *Chitose*, *Chiyoda*, and *Zuiho* comprised Carrier Division 3.

As difficult as it was for the Japanese to build carriers, training new carrier air groups proved even more difficult. Japanese planners estimated in March 1944 that the carrier force would be marginally ready for the upcoming decisive battle. Carrier Division 1 would be fully capable of daytime operations by the end of March with a planned 81 Zeros, 81 dive-bombers, 54 torpedo bombers, and nine reconnaissance aircraft from the 601st Air Group. Carrier Division 2 embarked the 652nd Air Group with a planned 81 Zeros, 36 dive-bombers, and 18 torpedo bombers. These aviators possessed a lower level of training than those on the fleet carriers. The aviators of Carrier Division 3's 653rd Air Group had significant training limitations; 63 fighters were unqualified for carrier operations and could only operate from land bases, and the 27 attack aircraft were not trained in strike operations. Between March and June, training opportunities were very limited with the result that the overall training level of First Mobile Fleet air groups did not improve significantly. In mid-1944 the air groups of Carrier Division 1 had an average of only six months' training, and the pilots of Carrier Division 3 had only three months. The average training for pilots in Carrier Division 2 was a pathetic 100 hours.

In 1944 Japanese carrier air groups looked like their 1942 cousins. Fleet carriers embarked three squadrons – a 27-aircraft fighter squadron, a dive-bomber squadron with 24 aircraft, and a torpedo squadron with 18 aircraft. A small number of reconnaissance aircraft were also embarked. The two Hiyo-class carriers carried a smaller air group consisting of a fighter squadron with 27 aircraft, a dive-bomber squadron of 18 aircraft, and a small torpedo squadron with six aircraft. Light carriers embarked 21 fighters and nine torpedo planes. *Ryuho*'s air group was modified to include 27 fighters and six torpedo planes. To increase striking power, some of the fighters on each carrier were designated as fighter-bombers and were fitted to carry 551lb bombs.

Under the pressures of war, the Japanese aeronautical industry was unable to design and build more capable carrier aircraft in a timely manner. As a result, some of the same types of aircraft present at Pearl Harbor were still on the decks of Japanese carriers in June 1944. The standard carrier fighter remained the Zero. The 1944 version was the A6M5 that had augmented thrust and a slightly higher speed than earlier versions. However, it was not in the same league as the Hellcat, being inferior in terms of armament, protection, high-altitude performance, and high-speed maneuverability. The Japanese also struggled to bring a new dive-bomber into carrier service. In late 1942 an improved version of the Type 99 was introduced that had a slightly higher top speed, but this did not change the aircraft's vulnerability to interception. Type 99s were still in service in mid-1944. The replacement for the Type 99 was the Yokosuka D4Y. This aircraft was introduced in 1942 (and initially used as a high-speed reconnaissance aircraft) and was a more survivable aircraft because of its top speed of 357mph while carrying a slightly greater bomb load. The Type 97 was

The main architect of the *A-Go* plan was Admiral Toyoda Soemu, Commander-in-Chief of the Combined Fleet. He is shown here in about September 1944 aboard his flagship, light cruiser *Oyodo*. After guiding the Combined Fleet to a decisive defeat at the battle of the Philippine Sea, he was also responsible for producing an even more unrealistic and disastrous plan to defend the Philippines only a few months later. (Naval History and Heritage Command)

still in service in 1944 although it was clearly obsolescent. The Type 97's replacement was the Nakajima B6N2 Navy Carrier Based Attack Bomber, Model 12 (hereafter referred to as the B6N2). This aircraft experienced a troubled development and its introduction was delayed, requiring small numbers of Type 97s to remain in front-line service. When it finally entered service, the B6N2 did not offer a significant improvement over the Type 97s other than its slightly higher top speed.

Japanese 1944 carrier air groups possessed a considerable range advantage over their American counterparts attributable to the lighter construction of Japanese aircraft that in most cases carried little armor and lacked self-sealing fuel tanks. The range advantage was especially evident in the search range (560nm) of Japanese carrier aircraft. Ozawa was well aware of this range difference and made it a central aspect of his battle plan. Unlike 1942, when Japanese carrier aircraft were as good or better than their American counterparts, by 1944 the Japanese operated a fleet of inferior aircraft.

Another major disadvantage facing the Japanese was the lack of at-sea support. The First Mobile Force could only receive fuel while underway and even this basic necessity was a problem by 1944. Japanese tanker losses to American submarine attacks were so heavy that accumulation of fuel stockpiles in the forward areas was impossible. The lack of refined oil products was so severe that the First Mobile Fleet lacked the range to engage the Americans in the Mariana Islands if this turned out to be the location of the decisive battle. This problem was solved only by lifting the requirement that all fuel used aboard ships had to be processed. This solution was possible when the First Mobile Fleet moved to the anchorage at Tawi-Tawi that was only 180nm from Tarakan Island off Borneo. The island had one of the five largest petroleum processing centers in the NEI with an oil refinery and four petroleum loading piers. The Tarakan oil fields produced a light crude oil that could be burned in ships' boilers without refining. However, the Tarakan crude had a high sulfur content that could damage boiler tubes and posed a serious risk in combat due to its highly volatile fumes. The First Mobile Fleet was operating on a logistical shoestring for the upcoming decisive battle with only six oilers organized into two supply groups. In the unlikely event the Japanese had achieved some level of success in a decisive battle in mid-1944, they did not have the capability to follow up that success. It would have taken weeks to collect enough fuel for another major fleet sortie, find replacement aircraft, and repair and re-provision ships. By this point of the war, the Imperial Navy essentially had been reduced to a raiding force and was not able to project power on a sustained basis.

PHILIPPINE SEA ORDERS OF BATTLE

UNITED STATES NAVY

FIFTH FLEET (ADMIRAL SPRUANCE IN HEAVY CRUISER *INDIANAPOLIS*)
Task Force 58 (Vice Admiral Mitscher in carrier *Lexington*)
Task Group 58.1 (Rear Admiral Clark in carrier *Hornet*)

Carrier: *Hornet*

Air Group 2	1 TBM-1C
VB-2	33 SB2C-1C
VF-2	36 F6F-3
VT-2	18 TBM/TBF-1C
VF(N)-76	(Night Fighter Detachment) 4 F6F-3N
TOTAL: 92	

Carrier: *Yorktown*

Air Group 1	1 F6F-3
VB-1	40 SB2C-1C
	4 SBD-5
VF-1	41 F6F-3
VT-1	17 TBM/TBF-1C
VF(N)-77 (Detachment)	4 F6F-3N
TOTAL:107	

Carrier: *Belleau Wood*

Air Group 24	
VF-24	26 F6F-3
VT-24	9 TBM/TBF-1C
TOTAL: 35	

Carrier: *Bataan*

Air Group 50	
VF-50	24 F6F-3
VT-50	9 TBM-1C
TOTAL: 33	

Heavy Cruisers: *Baltimore, Boston, Canberra*
Light Cruisers: *San Juan, Oakland*
Destroyers: *Izard, Charrette, Conner, Bell, Burns, Boyd, Bradford, Brown, Cowell, Maury, Craven, Gridley, Helm, McCall*

Task Group 58.2 (Rear Admiral Montgomery in carrier *Bunker Hill*)

Carrier: *Bunker Hill*

Air Group 8	1 F6F-3
VB-8	33 SB2C-1C
VF-8	37 F6F-3
VT-8	18 TBM/TBF-1C
VF(N)-76 (Detachment)	4 F6F-3N
TOTAL: 93	

Carrier: *Wasp*

Air Group 14	1 F6F-3
VB-14	32 SB2C-1C
VF-14	34 F6F-3
VT-14	18 TBM/TBF-1C
VF(N)-76 (Detachment)	4 F6F-3N
TOTAL: 89	

Carrier: *Monterey*

Air Group 28	
VF-28	21 F6F-3
VT-28	8 TBM-1C
TOTAL: 29	

Carrier: *Cabot*

Air Group 31	
VF-31	24 F6F-3
VT-31	9 TBF/TBM-1C
TOTAL: 33	

Light Cruisers: *Santa Fe, Mobile, Biloxi*
Destroyers: *Owen, Miller, The Sullivans, Stephen Potter, Tingey, Hickox, Hunt, Lewis Hancock, Marshall, Macdonough, Dewey, Hull*

Task Group 58.3 (Rear Admiral Reeves in carrier *Enterprise*)

Carrier: *Enterprise*

Air Group 10	
VB-10	21 SBD-5
VF-10	31 F6F-3
VT-10	14 TBM/TBF-1C
VF(N)-101 (Detachment)	3 F4U-2
TOTAL: 69	

Carrier: *Lexington*

Air Group 16	1 F6F-3
VB-16	34 SBD-5
VF-16	37 F6F-3
VT-16	17 TBF-1C
VF(N)-76 (Detachment)	4 F6F-3N
TOTAL: 93	

Carrier: *San Jacinto*

Air Group 51	
VF-51	24 F6F-3
VT-51	8 TBF/TBM-1C
TOTAL: 32	

Carrier: *Princeton*
Air Group 27

VF-27	24 F6F-3
VT-27	9 TBM-1C
TOTAL: 33	

Heavy Cruiser: *Indianapolis*
Light Cruisers: *Cleveland, Montpelier, Birmingham, Reno*
Destroyers: *Clarence K. Bronson, Cotton, Dortch, Gatling, Healy, Caperton, Cogswell, Ingersoll, Knapp, Anthony, Wadsworth, Terry, Braine*

Task Group 58.4 (Rear Admiral Harrill in carrier *Essex*)

Carrier: *Essex*
Air Group 15

	1 F6F-3
VB-15	36 SB2C-1C
VF-15	38 F6F-3
VT-15	15 TBF-1C
VF(N)-77 (Detachment)	4 F6F-3N
TOTAL: 94	

Carrier: *Langley*
Air Group 32

VF-32	23 F6F-3
VT-32	9 TBF/TBM-1C
TOTAL: 32	

Carrier: *Cowpens*
Air Group 25

VF-25	23 F6F-3
VT-25	9 TBM-1C
TOTAL: 32	

Light Cruisers: *Vincennes, Houston, Miami, San Diego*
Destroyers: *Lansdowne, Lardner, McCalla, Case, Lang, Sterrett, Wilson, Ellet, Charles Ausburne, Stanly, Dyson, Converse, Spence, Thatcher*

Task Group 58.7 (Vice Admiral Lee in battleship *Washington*)

Battleships: *Washington, North Carolina, South Dakota, Indiana, Alabama, Iowa, New Jersey*
Heavy Cruisers: *New Orleans, Minneapolis, San Francisco, Wichita*
Destroyers: *Mugford, Patterson, Bagley, Conyngham, Selfridge, Halford, Guest, Bennett, Fullam, Hudson, Twining, Monssen, Yarnall, Stockham*

Task Force 17 (Vice Admiral Lockwood)

Deployed near Bonin Islands: *Plunger, Gar, Archerfish, Plaice, Swordfish*
Deployed near Formosa: *Pintado, Pilotfish, Tunny*
Deployed west of Marianas: *Albacore, Seawolf, Bang, Finback, Stingray*
Deployed near Philippines and Ulithi: *Flying Fish, Muskallunge, Seahorse, Pipefish, Cavalla, Growler*

Seventh Fleet Submarines (Rear Admiral R.W. Christie)

Deployed southeast of Mindanao: *Hake, Bashaw, Paddle*
Deployed near Tawi-Tawi: *Harder, Haddo, Redfin, Bluefish*
Deployed near Luzon: *Jack, Flier*

Long-Range Aircraft

Seaplane Tender *Ballard* with 5 PBM-5 Mariner from Patrol Squadron 16

IMPERIAL JAPANESE NAVY

First Mobile Fleet (Vice Admiral Ozawa on carrier *Taiho*)
Force A (Vice Admiral Ozawa)

Carrier Division 1 embarking Air Group 601
Carrier: *Taiho*

Fighter Unit	20 Zero
Bomber Unit	27 D4Y1
	1 Type 99
Attack Unit	13 B6N1
Scout Detachment	3 D4Y1-C
TOTAL: 64	

Carrier: *Shokaku*

Fighter Unit	34 Zero
Bomber Unit	18 D4Y1
	3 Type 99
Attack Unit	9 B6N2
Scout Unit	9 D4Y1C
	3 B6N2 (radar-equipped)
TOTAL: 76	

Carrier: *Zuikaku*

Fighter Unit	24 Zero
Fighter-bomber Unit	11 Zero
Bomber Unit	18 D4Y1
	3 Type 99
Attack Unit	15 B6N1
Scout Detachment	2 D4Y1C
	2 B6N2 (radar-equipped)
TOTAL: 75	

Heavy Cruisers: *Myoko, Haguro*
Light Cruiser: *Yahagi*
Destroyers: *Asagumo, Urakaze, Isokaze, Hatsuyuki, Wakatsuki, Akizuki, Shimotsuki*

Force B (Rear Admiral Joshima)
Carrier Division 2 embarking Air Group 652
Carrier: *Junyo*

Fighter Unit	18 Zero
Fighter-bomber Unit	9 Zero
Bomber Unit	11 D4Y1
	9 Type 99
Attack Unit	5 B6N1
TOTAL: 52	

Carrier: *Hiyo*

Fighter Unit	17 Zero
Fighter-bomber Unit	9 Zero
Bomber Unit	19 Type 99
Attack Unit	5 B6N1
TOTAL: 50	

Carrier: *Ryuho*

Fighter Unit	18 Zero
Fighter-bomber Unit	9 Zero
Attack Unit	5 B6N1
TOTAL: 32	

Battleship: *Nagato*
Aircraft Cruiser: *Mogami*
Destroyers: *Michishio, Nowaki, Yamagumo, Shigure, Hamakaze, Hayashimo, Akishimo*

Force C (Vice Admiral Kurita in heavy cruiser *Atago*)
Carrier Division 3 embarking Air Group 653
Carrier: *Chitose*

Fighter Unit	6 Zero
Fighter-bomber Unit	15 Zero
Attack Unit	3 B6N1 (Pathfinder)
	6 Type 97 (Search)
TOTAL: 30	

Carrier: *Chiyoda*

Fighter Unit	6 Zero
Fighter-bomber Unit	15 Zero
Attack Unit	3 B6N1 (Pathfinder)
	6 B5N2 (Search)
TOTAL: 30	

Carrier: *Zuiho*

Fighter Unit	7 Zero
Fighter-bomber Unit	15 Zero
Attack Unit	3 B6N1 (Pathfinder)
	5 B5N2 (Search)
TOTAL: 30	

Battleships: *Yamato, Musashi, Kongo, Haruna*
Heavy Cruisers: *Atago, Takao, Maya, Chokai, Kumano, Suzuya, Tone, Chikuma*
Light Cruiser: *Noshiro*
Destroyers: *Shimakaze, Asashimo, Kishinami, Okinami, Tamanami, Fujinami, Hamanami*

1st Supply Force
Oilers: *Hayasui, Nichiei Maru, Kokuyo Maru, Seiyo Maru*
Light Cruiser: *Natori*
Destroyers: *Hibiki, Hatsushimo, Yunagi, Tsuga*

2nd Supply Force
Oilers: *Genyo Maru, Azusa Maru*
Destroyers: *Yukikaze, Uzuki*

Sixth (Submarine) Fleet (Vice Admiral Takagi on Saipan)
I-5, I-10, I-26, I-38, I-41, I-53, I-184, I-185
RO-36, RO-41, RO-42, RO-43, RO-44, RO-47, RO-68, RO-104, RO-105, RO-106, RO-108, RO-109, RO-112, RO-113, RO-114, RO-115, RO-116, RO-117

THE MYTH OF THE DECISIVE BATTLE

Even by 1944 the IJN still adhered to the decisive battle concept. The Japanese had already fought several "decisive" battles against the USN, but none of these had the desired outcome. Yet the notion that a single battle could decide the war, or in 1944 change the fortunes of war, was re-emphasized by the Combined Fleet in 1943. Planning for this latest decisive battle began in August 1943 as part of Koga's "Third Phase Operations of the War." The result was the "Z" Plan produced by Koga and his staff. Under this scheme, the Combined Fleet, operating from Truk, would sortie to defend strategic areas designated by Imperial General

Vice Admiral Ozawa Jisaburo was responsible for executing *A-Go*. He carried out Toyoda's battle plan as well as could be expected, but he was wielding a blunt instrument and experienced a shattering defeat. (Naval History and Heritage Command)

Headquarters. The Combined Fleet foresaw the most likely area for the decisive battle as the Central Pacific, but it also had contingency plans for any eventuality, from an attack on the Kurile Islands in the northern Pacific to an Allied attack as far south as western New Guinea. Once the main Allied attack had been identified, the Combined Fleet would sortie and seek a set-piece battle. Some of the components of the prewar decisive battle plans were identifiable in the 1943–44 iteration. The Japanese planned to detect the approaching American invasion force with aircraft, submarines, and smaller surface combatants. Submarines and land-based aircraft would inflict attrition on the American fleet, creating more favorable conditions for the decisive engagement. The climactic point of the decisive battle was the intervention of the First Mobile Fleet. The Z Plan had four tactical sub-plans designated A through D; two of these envisioned surface attacks only, one was a combined air and surface attack, and the fourth featured air attacks by carrier and land-based aircraft. The First Mobile Fleet's carriers would operate beyond the range of enemy reconnaissance aircraft and "maneuver to strike the enemy in the flank."

Responsibility for planning the decisive battle fell to Toyoda after Koga's death. Toyoda kept the Z Plan in its general form but made some adjustments. The re-worked plan was named "*A-Go*" and, after the American landings in the Gilberts and the Marshalls, it was focused on the Marianas. In April 1944 the Marianas were designated as an area of national importance that had to be defended at all costs. This included commitment of the First Mobile Fleet, all available land-based air units, and all submarines. The IJN's actual battle plan took much from the Z Plan. Advance warning of any major USN operation would be provided by land-based aircraft that were responsible for conducting reconnaissance of major USN anchorages and bases. In addition to their critical reconnaissance responsibilities, land-based air units were tasked to neutralize at least one-third of the American carriers before the decisive battle phase. Following strikes from Japanese land-based aircraft, the First Mobile Fleet would deliver the decisive blow. It was planned that the Japanese carriers would strike while operating beyond the attack range of TF 58. It is important to note that the Base Air Force and the First Mobile Fleet were targeted against the American carrier force, not the invasion force. Following the destruction of TF 58, the invasion force could be attacked and destroyed.

Operation *A-Go* was rehearsed in a series of tabletop maneuvers and war games. The first was held on Ozawa's flagship *Taiho* on April 27. On May 2, the Naval General Staff oversaw a war game and a staff study on the Combined Fleet's flagship, light cruiser *Oyodo* anchored in Tokyo Bay, on *Taiho*, and on the flagships of subordinate units. The results were critiqued the same day with Emperor

Hirohito in attendance. Additional tabletop maneuvers were conducted on *Taiho* on May 6. Following these high-level reviews, the final version of *A-Go* was issued on May 3. The plan, contained in Imperial General Headquarters Order Number 373 ("The Immediate Operational Policy to be Adhered by the Combined Fleet") emphasized air operations and surprise. The Base Air Force and the First Mobile Fleet would cooperate to destroy the enemy in a "single blow." Toyoda's parallel Order Number 76 to the Combined Fleet envisioned a decisive battle in the western Caroline Islands. If the Americans failed to cooperate and attacked the Marianas instead, they would be attacked by the Base Air Force and then lured toward Palau, which would become the scene of the decisive daylight battle. Success was predicated on sustained attrition by continuous air, surface, and submarine attacks to reduce the American carrier force, giving the First Mobile Fleet a real chance of victory.

CHAPTER 8
THE BATTLE OF THE PHILIPPINE SEA

Midway is arguably the best-known carrier battle of the Pacific War. Coral Sea has its unique position as the first carrier battle. Yet, in comparison, the largest carrier battle of the war, the battle of the Philippine Sea fought in June 1944, has been somewhat ignored. The fifth carrier battle of the Pacific War was indisputably the largest with 15 fleet and light carriers on the American side and nine on the Japanese side. In light of the evolution of naval warfare and weapons systems, it is inconceivable that a carrier battle of this size will ever be fought again. The carrier battle prompted by the American invasion of the Marianas was the central aspect of the second largest naval engagement of World War II. The size of the invading force was immense: The Americans used some 535 ships to carry and protect a ground force of over 127,500 troops. The invasion fleet included some 165 combatants and almost 900 aircraft from TF 58 complemented by another 170 aircraft on seven escort carriers. The Japanese brought over 50 combatants, just over 400 carrier-based aircraft, and more than 300 land-based aircraft to the battle. Forces of this size had not been seen previously in a Pacific War naval engagement. However, only a few months later both sides would muster even larger fleets to fight the battle of Leyte Gulf, another reason Philippine Sea has been overshadowed.

ABOVE The first American carrier raid on the Marianas was mounted on February 23, 1944. In this view, Japanese planes burn on a Saipan airfield; both Zero fighters and G4M medium bombers can be identified. Before the invasion of the Marianas in June, TF 58 mounted a successful campaign to weaken Japanese land-based air power. (Naval History and Heritage Command)

Strength Comparison, June 19, 1944		FIRST MOBILE FORCE	TASK FORCE 58
Air Power	Fleet carriers	5	7
	Light carriers	4	8
	Fighters/Fighter-bombers	206	475
	Dive-bombers	109	232
	Torpedo bombers	78	184
	Reconnaissance aircraft	14	
	Total carrier aircraft	416	906
Surface Combatants	Battleships	5	7
	Heavy cruisers	11	8
	Light cruisers	3	13
	Destroyers	27	56
	Total combatants	46	84

Another reason that Philippine Sea has been overlooked is the outcome. As detailed in the "Strength Comparisons" table, the USN entered the battle with an overwhelming advantage in most categories. However, the numbers fail to convey the American qualitative edge. The outcome was therefore not in doubt, and the battle itself lacked the dramatic turns evident in preceding carrier clashes.

There was a predetermined character to the battle. Spruance fought a cautious battle that left no room for the Japanese to exploit any American missteps. Despite intense efforts by the Japanese to prepare for and to plan what they intended to be a decisive battle, the capabilities of their carrier force were so meager that a Japanese victory was extremely unlikely. Of course, this assessment is derived with the benefit of hindsight. The Japanese certainly believed that they could achieve victory and attempted to set conditions to achieve it. The problem for the IJN was that the tactics and forces from 1942 carrier battles no longer stood a chance against the American carrier fleet of 1944. The result was the most decisive of any carrier battle of the war but not as envisioned by the Japanese. The battle was decisive – the Americans seized the Mariana Islands, enabling the long-range aerial bombardment of Japan, and in the process destroyed the Japanese carrier fleet as a viable force for the remainder of the war. While most of the Japanese carriers survived the battle, their aircraft and aircrews did not. By the time the Americans invaded the Philippines in October 1944, the Japanese had been unable to rebuild their carrier force. The desperate and ill-conceived Japanese plan at the battle of Leyte Gulf resulted in the virtual destruction of the Imperial Navy, completing the death spiral begun at the battle of the Philippine Sea.

DESTROYING JAPANESE LAND-BASED AIR POWER

Operation *Forager* was an enormous undertaking with forces moving from three main areas to the ultimate target at Saipan. It was the largest American operation of the war to date in the Pacific. The operation began to unfold in late May when the bulk of the invasion fleet departed Hawaii en route for the primary assembly area in the Marshall Islands. Spruance held a final planning conference with his key commanders at Eniwetok Atoll on June 7. As this was occurring, TF 58 was already underway. After a short respite at the new fleet anchorage at Majuro in the Marshalls, TF 58 departed on June 6 and refueled two days later. The Japanese had no specific information on the forthcoming operation, and their air reconnaissance efforts were unable to fill in the intelligence gaps. A Japanese flight over Majuro on June 5 confirmed the presence of TF 58. The next mission over Majuro on June 9 disclosed the departure of the carriers. Incredibly, TF 58 remained unlocated until the morning of June 11 when it appeared off the Marianas. Operation *A-Go* was off to a bad start.

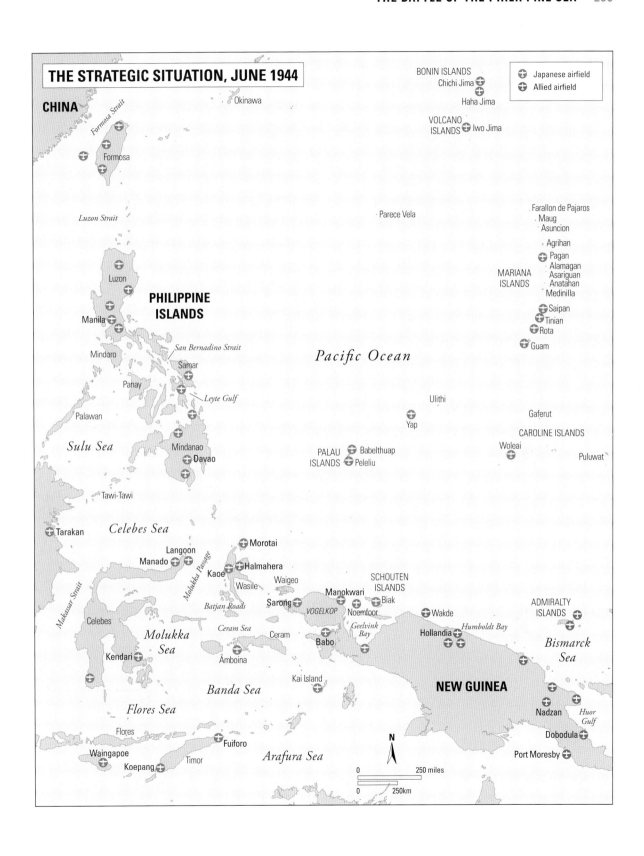

THE STRATEGIC SITUATION, JUNE 1944

⊕ Japanese airfield
⊕ Allied airfield

CHINA

BONIN ISLANDS
Chichi Jima
Haha Jima

Okinawa

VOLCANO
ISLANDS   Iwo Jima

Formosa Strait

Formosa

Luzon Strait

Parece Vela

Farallon de Pajaros
· Maug
· Asuncion

· Agrihan
⊕ Pagan
· Alamagan
· Asariguan
· Anatahan
· Medinilla

MARIANA
ISLANDS

Luzon

PHILIPPINE
ISLANDS

⊕ Saipan
⊕ Tinian
⊕ Rota

Manila

⊕ Guam

Mindoro

San Bernadino Strait

Pacific Ocean

Samar

Panay

Leyte Gulf

Ulithi

Gaferut

Palawan

Yap

CAROLINE ISLANDS

Sulu Sea

Mindanao
⊕ Davao

PALAU   ⊕ Babelthuap
ISLANDS ⊕ Peleliu

Woleai

Puluwat

Tawi-Tawi

⊕ Tarakan

Celebes Sea

Morotai

Langoon
Manado   Kaoe   ⊕ Halmahera
         Wasile

Waigeo

SCHOUTEN
ISLANDS

ADMIRALTY
ISLANDS

Molukka Passage

Manokwari   Biak

Makassar Strait

Batjan Roads

Sarong
VOGELKOP   Noemfoor

⊕ Wakde

Hollandia   Humboldt Bay

Bismarck
Sea

Celebes

Ceram Sea   Ceram

Geelvink
Bay

Babo

Molukka
Sea

Amboina

Kendari

Kai Island

NEW GUINEA

Banda Sea

Nadzan   Huor
              Gulf

Flores Sea

Flores

Dobodula

Waingapoe
Koepang   Timor

Fuiforo

Arafura Sea

Port Moresby

N

0   250 miles

0   250km

ABOVE On June 11, TF 58 began the process of annihilating Japanese land-based air power in the Marianas. This view is from an SBD Dauntless dive-bomber which has just taken off from *Lexington* on June 13. (Naval History and Heritage Command)

RIGHT One of the pillars of *A-Go* was that Japanese land-based air forces would exact heavy attrition on TF 58. This assumption was shown to be totally erroneous. In this view, a burning Japanese aircraft, probably a G4M from Truk, crashes astern *Lexington* on the evening of June 15. (Naval History and Heritage Command)

In order to take advantage of apparent surprise, the Americans decided to move up the opening air strikes against Japanese airfields in the Marianas by one day. Instead of the planned June 12 opening strikes, the attacks commenced on June 11. The morning of June 11 was clear, providing no concealment for TF 58 on its final run toward the Marianas. Several Japanese aircraft were shot down by CAP in the vicinity of TF 58, but it was clear from radio intercepts that the Americans had been sighted. By 1300, TF 58 reached a position some 200nm east of Guam. From the decks of 15 carriers, 208 Hellcats and eight Avengers were launched to pound targets on Guam, Saipan, and Tinian. Intense air opposition was encountered over Saipan and Tinian. The Hellcats claimed 86 Japanese aircraft destroyed in the air and another 33 on the ground for the loss of 11 Hellcats. Japanese records indicate that actual losses were much less – perhaps as few as 36 aircraft.

Initial Japanese reaction to this onslaught was muted. During the early hours of June 12, TF 58 was attacked by some ten G4M torpedo bombers from Truk. The bombers used flares to identify targets in the darkness, but no American ships were struck by torpedoes. The main event of the day occurred when TG 58.4 located and attacked a large Japanese convoy about 160nm northwest of Saipan. Several air strikes accounted for one Japanese torpedo boat, three subchasers, and ten cargo ships sunk.

Mitscher's efforts to neutralize Japanese air power in the Marianas were unrelenting. Three of TF 58's carrier groups continued raids on airfields and other installations on Saipan and Tinian on June 12–13. Activity on June 12 totaled 1,472 combat sorties with 31 American aircraft lost to all causes and another 76 damaged. TG 58.1 focused on attacking Guam during this period. By the end of June 13, the Americans assessed that Japanese land-based air power in the Marianas had been neutralized. The intensity of attacks decreased on June 14–15 as two carrier groups moved north to strike Chichi Jima and Iwo Jima, and the other two took the opportunity to refuel. On the evening of June 15, the Japanese mounted a small-scale air attack on TF 58 from Guam at dusk. Hellcats from TG 58.3 claimed seven Japanese aircraft destroyed with the remainder electing not to press their attack. A larger group from Yap Island in the Carolines attacked TG 58.3 after sunset. The attack was disrupted by two Hellcat night fighters; only about a dozen Japanese torpedo bombers mounted an attack, but no torpedoes found their marks.

Even as it became apparent that the Japanese fleet was headed to the Marianas, Spruance and Mitscher did not change plans to strike Chichi Jima and Iwo Jima. TGs 58.1 and 58.4 refueled on June 14 and headed north with the aggressive Clark leading the reluctant Harrill. Strikes on Japanese airfields began on the afternoon of June 15. The Japanese put up a robust defense with approximately

100 aircraft on Iwo Jima. Thirty-seven Zeros were already aloft when the American strike arrived, but 28 were shot down by Hellcats. Another seven Japanese aircraft were destroyed on the ground for the loss of only two American aircraft. Bad weather prevented morning strikes on June 16, but when the weather cleared enough to allow flight operations, Clark sent 54 aircraft to return to Iwo Jima in the afternoon. The attack achieved surprise and caught Japanese aircraft lined up on the runway; Clark's aviators claimed 63 destroyed. In return, only two American aircraft were lost to all causes. The excursion to strike staging bases at Chichi Jima and Iwo Jima was a success as some 100 Japanese aircraft were destroyed and thus were unavailable for the upcoming battle. Following the last strike on Iwo Jima, the two task groups steamed south to be in position off Saipan by June 18.

As TF 58 was finishing off Japanese land-based air power, the landing on Saipan proceeded on June 15 with two Marine divisions landing on four miles of beaches in the face of heavy Japanese resistance. By the end of the first day it was clear that the Americans had gained a solid beachhead. Mitscher's efforts against Japanese airfields shifted to Tinian and particularly Guam. Though the airfields on both those islands remained operational, the Japanese were unable to launch strikes from them against American shipping. The Japanese did launch strikes from airfields on Truk and Yap. On June 17 a small strike of five torpedo bombers and one J1N1-S night fighter departed Truk to attack a transport group east of Saipan. The convoy of small landing ships was struck at 1750; one torpedo hit the landing craft *LCI-468* that later sank. The Base Air Force's first major attack was mounted on June 18 from Yap. The attack consisted of 31 Zeros, 17 D4Y dive-bombers, and two P1Y twin-engine bombers. TG 58.2 gained radar contact on a large group of Japanese aircraft, but they were too distant for an intercept. The Japanese proceeded toward Saipan where they attacked shipping offshore. A tank landing ship was set afire but was later salvaged. A group of escort carriers was also attacked at dusk. Two of the carriers suffered near misses, and *Fanshaw Bay* was hit by a bomb that exploded on her hangar deck. The resulting fire was handled by the ship's damage control teams, but the carrier was forced to Eniwetok for repairs. Japanese aviators claimed that three or four carriers from TF 58 had been hit in this attack, which made it appear that the Base Air Force (the IJN's term for their land-based air units) had made a substantial contribution to the success of the upcoming battle. In reality, an important component of Operation *A-Go* had proven totally ineffective. From June 11 to 18, Japanese land-based air power within reach of the Marianas had been virtually wiped out for little cost to the Americans. The First Mobile Fleet would have to win the decisive victory without support.

THE FIRST MOBILE FLEET SORTIES

The initial appearance of TF 58 off the Marianas on June 11 surprised the Japanese. By the following day, however, Japanese air reconnaissance provided a fairly accurate depiction of TF 58's strength and location. By June 13, with the reported American shelling of targets on Saipan and Tinian and continuing air attacks on targets throughout the Marianas, American intentions were obvious. Toyoda ordered the Combined Fleet on alert for Operation *A-Go* and canceled Operation KON (a counterlanding on Biak Island that the Americans had invaded on May 27). Additional land-based air forces were ordered to the Marianas, and the First Mobile Fleet departed its anchorage at Tawi-Tawi Island in the Philippines at 1000 hours. Calculating the period of time required for a transit to Saipan, Toyoda tentatively set June 19 as the decisive battle day. After departing its anchorage, Ozawa's force moved to Guimaras Island in the Philippines where the First Mobile Fleet took on supplies from 1700 on June 14 until the next morning.

Having received reports of the American landing on Saipan early on June 15, Toyoda ordered *A-Go* to commence at 0717 hours that day. The First Mobile Fleet departed the Guimaras at 0900 and that evening entered the Philippine Sea through the San Bernardino Strait. The superbattleships *Yamato* and *Musashi* and other units from Operation KON were not with Ozawa's main body but were proceeding independently through the Philippine Sea. Upon entering the Philippine Sea, Ozawa headed southeasterly and at about 1700 on June 16 joined with *Yamato* and *Musashi*. Ozawa ordered the First Mobile Fleet to refuel, which took until late morning on June 17.

Ozawa enjoyed a major pre-battle advantage in intelligence. He was able to track TF 58 in general terms as it maneuvered off the Marianas and attacked Iwo Jima. The First Mobile Fleet maintained strict radio silence as it moved toward the Marianas, denying the Americans the best source of tracking the Japanese fleet until it came into air search range. The only information Spruance received on the approaching Japanese was from incomplete submarine sightings. As a result, Spruance was deprived of a clear picture of Ozawa's movements until June 19 when the First Mobile Fleet launched its first attacks. At 1300 hours on June 13, submarine *Redfin* provided the first confirmation that Ozawa was underway. The submarine issued a report of four battleships, six carriers, eight cruisers, and six destroyers heading north through the Sibutu Passage between Borneo and the Sulu Archipelago. Assuming this was the bulk of the First Mobile Fleet, Spruance calculated that the Japanese could not threaten the Marianas until June 17 at the earliest. Therefore, Spruance decided to go ahead with the scheduled June 15

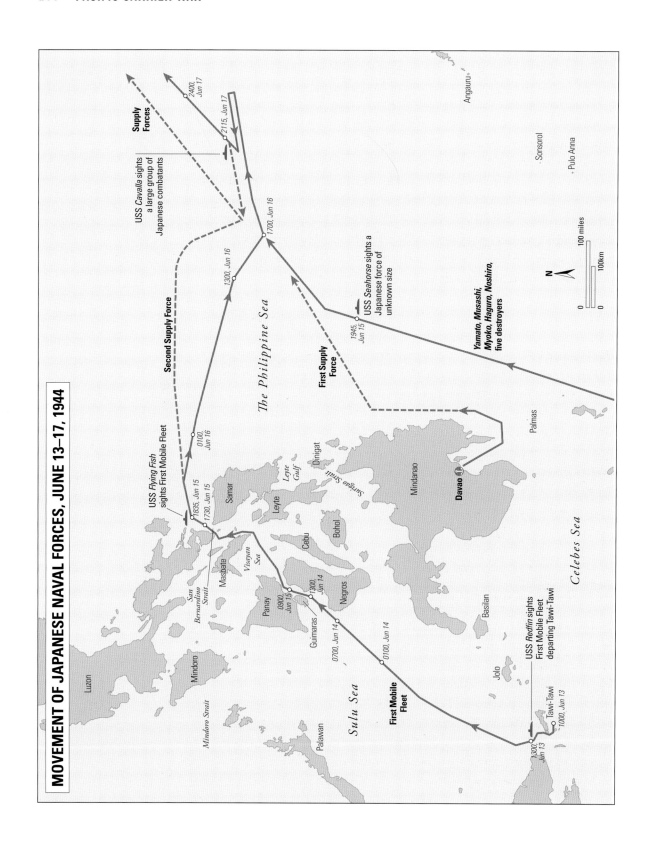

MOVEMENT OF JAPANESE NAVAL FORCES, JUNE 13–17, 1944

Supply
Forces

2400,
Jun 17

2115, Jun 17

USS *Cavalla* sights
a large group of
Japanese combatants

1700, Jun 16

1300, Jun 16

USS *Seahorse* sights a
Japanese force of
unknown size

1945,
Jun 15

**Yamato, Musashi,
Myoko, Haguro, Noshiro,
five destroyers**

The Philippine Sea

Second Supply Force

First Supply Force

USS *Flying Fish*
sights First Mobile Fleet

0100,
Jun 16

1835, Jun 15

1730, Jun 15

Samar

*Leyte
Gulf*

Dinigat

Mindanao

Palmas

Davao

Surigao Strait

Leyte

Cebu

Bohol

Masbate

*Visayan
Sea*

*San
Bernardino
Strait*

Panay

0900
Jun 15

1300,
Jun 14

Guimaras

Negros

0700, Jun 14

0100, Jun 14

Mindoro

Luzon

Mindoro Strait

Palawan

Sulu Sea

Jolo

Basilan

Celebes Sea

USS *Redfin* sights
First Mobile Fleet
departing Tawi-Tawi

**First Mobile
Fleet**

Tawi-Tawi

1000, Jun 13

1300,
Jun 13

Angauru

Sonsorol

Pulo Anna

N

100 miles

100km

0

0

landing on Saipan and the raids on Chichi Jima and Iwo Jima as long as the two participating carrier groups were in position off Saipan on the morning of June 18.

No further contact was gained on Ozawa's fleet until 1835 on June 15 when submarine *Flying Fish* reported a force including battleships and at least three carriers had passed through the San Bernardino Strait. The Japanese monitored the contact report so they knew they had been sighted. Submarine *Seahorse* sighted another Japanese force 200nm east-southeast of the Surigao Strait about an hour later. The composition of this force was unclear, but was thought to include battleships *Yamato* and *Musashi* plus escorts. However, *Seahorse* was not able to send her contact report until 0400 on June 16. In addition to the submarine sightings, a growing body of signals intelligence on June 15 indicated that a major Japanese fleet operation was underway.

While Spruance lacked a precise idea of Japanese movements and strength, Ozawa possessed a much better idea of TF 58's operations. Ozawa's staff arrived at a remarkably accurate assessment of TF 58's strength and Spruance's intentions. The Japanese believed TF 58 had 15 carriers – seven fleet and eight converted cruisers – which was spot-on. They assessed that only ten would leave Saipan and move to the west to a maximum distance of 300nm. They also correctly assessed that the Americans planned to cut off the Marianas from air and other reinforcement. Ozawa decided that he must bring the battle to a decisive phase as soon as possible. This meant that he had to maneuver in order to launch his massive air attacks on June 19 or possibly the day before depending on Spruance's movements. Ozawa planned intensive air reconnaissance, especially to his north, to avoid being surprised. Once TF 58 was located, the First Mobile Fleet would close the target to launch a series of massive strikes while being careful to remain out of range of an American counterstrike.

SPRUANCE PREPARES

With the approach of the First Mobile Fleet and a major carrier battle in the offing, Spruance prepared his forces for battle. On June 17 five heavy cruisers, three light cruisers, and 13 destroyers departed the invasion area to reinforce TF 58. This left seven battleships, three cruisers, and some 13 destroyers to provide fire support to the Marines ashore and for local defense of the beachhead. Spruance moved the invasion force well to the east of Saipan on June 18 with the exception of 17 Landing Ship Tanks and three other transports. The escort carriers accompanied the invasion force to provide air defense.

Mitscher was also preparing TF 58 for battle. On the afternoon of June 17, he ordered the formation of TG 58.7. This was the battle line comprising seven battleships, four heavy cruisers, and 13 destroyers. Although this reduced the antiaircraft power of each task group, it was accepted as it would be easier to form the battle line before the battle than during it. Both Spruance and Mitscher saw a major role for TG 58.7 either engaging Japanese surface forces should they accept battle or finishing off ships crippled from American air strikes. Mitscher also had to concentrate the dispersed task groups of TF 58, as TGs 58.1 and 58.4 were just returning from their excursion against Iwo Jima. He planned to have all four carrier task groups concentrated 150nm west of Saipan by noon on June 18. In the meantime, TGs 58.2 and 58.3 conducted searches 325nm to the west beginning on June 17 and found nothing. The only contact information provided to Spruance during daylight was a contact report from submarine *Cavalla* on one of Ozawa's tanker groups.

The first key moment in the battle came on the evening of June 17. At 2115 *Cavalla* sighted a large group of combatants zigzagging at high speed some 700nm west of Guam. Darkness precluded a definitive breakout of the ships, but the group included 15 ships and at least one carrier. Spruance and Mitscher did not receive *Cavalla*'s report until 0345 on June 18. Spruance could have used this priceless information in one of two ways – either advance during the night to engage the Japanese on June 18 with the possible advantage of surprise, or stay near Saipan and await the Japanese attack. Spruance's staff calculated that if the Japanese continued east at 19 knots, they would still be about 500nm from TF 58 by 0530 on June 18. This was well beyond American air search or strike range, but if TF 58 moved toward the contact it would be possible to engage the Japanese on the afternoon of June 18. Mitscher endorsed this aggressive option and even advocated a nighttime surface engagement.

The final decision belonged to Spruance, and his calculating mind had many problems with rushing TF 58 to the west. The biggest problem was that TF 58 was not yet concentrated. If Mitscher was released immediately, it would only be with two task groups and the battle line. This would offer the Japanese an opportunity to defeat TF 58 piecemeal. As for a night engagement, both Spruance and Vice Admiral Willis Lee, commander of the battle line, considered it too risky because of the IJN's proven night-fighting capabilities. Another factor weighing on Spruance was the captured Z Plan that called for flank attacks. This seemed like a realistic possibility since *Cavalla*'s report indicated a force of only 15 ships, which left the bulk of the Japanese fleet unaccounted for. After considering the options, at 2000 hours Spruance ordered TF 58 to change course toward Saipan instead of toward the Japanese. At 2130 he sent a message indicating his preference to fight a defensive battle on June 19. Mitscher tried to change Spruance's mind at about 2330 with a proposal to take TF 58 to the west so it could launch a strike on the Japanese the following morning. Spruance replied about an hour later with a firm denial.

MOVEMENT TO CONTACT

With Spruance having made his decision to fight a defensive battle, it was up to Ozawa to decide when the battle would start. As the First Mobile Fleet closed TF 58 on June 18, Ozawa received contact information from his search aircraft. During the morning hours floatplanes from Force C spotted six carriers from TF 58. During the afternoon search, aircraft from Carrier Division 1 flying out 420nm also spotted TF 58. The first report at 1514 hours referenced the detection of a task group with two carriers. Another search aircraft sighted a task group with an "unknown number of carriers" at 1600. The same aircraft issued another contact report an hour later and identified two task groups each with two carriers. All of these contacts were within the attack range of Ozawa's aircraft, but he decided not to launch strikes, as such a late launch would require a night recovery by pilots with little experience with night flying.

Rear Admiral Obayashi, the aggressive commander of Carrier Division 3, thought that a dusk attack could catch the Americans by surprise. With this in mind, he ordered a launch of 67 aircraft from carriers *Zuiho*, *Chitose*, and *Chiyoda* at 1637. While the launch was in progress and with 22 aircraft already airborne, Ozawa's orders, canceling any strike on June 18, arrived. Obayashi reluctantly aborted his dusk strike.

Though unable to initiate the battle on June 18, Ozawa would have been pleased with his overall position. His assessment of Spruance's intentions had proven accurate. The American commander was being cautious, which meant that Ozawa could maintain his position relative to TF 58 without fear of being attacked. His search aircraft detected no American activity to the north, so the threat of a flank attack had vanished. All that was left to do was to prepare a series of massive strikes for the next day. To maintain at least 400nm distance from TF 58, at 1540 Ozawa ordered a course change to the southwest. The First Mobile Fleet maintained this course until 1900 when it headed southeast at 16 knots. At 2100 Ozawa gave orders for the First Mobile Fleet's final attack approach. Force C headed due east to assume a lead position while Forces A and B headed south. At 0300 on June 19, all forces changed course to the northeast and increased speed to 20 knots.

Ozawa also took steps to coordinate his operations with the Base Air Force. An essential element of Operation *A-Go* was coordinated air strikes by carrier and land-based air forces. With his main air strike scheduled for the morning of June 19, Ozawa wanted to inform the Base Air Force commander, Rear Admiral Kakuta on Tinian, of his intentions. To do this Ozawa broke radio silence for the first time since leaving Tawi-Tawi. The transmission at 2020 was intercepted by

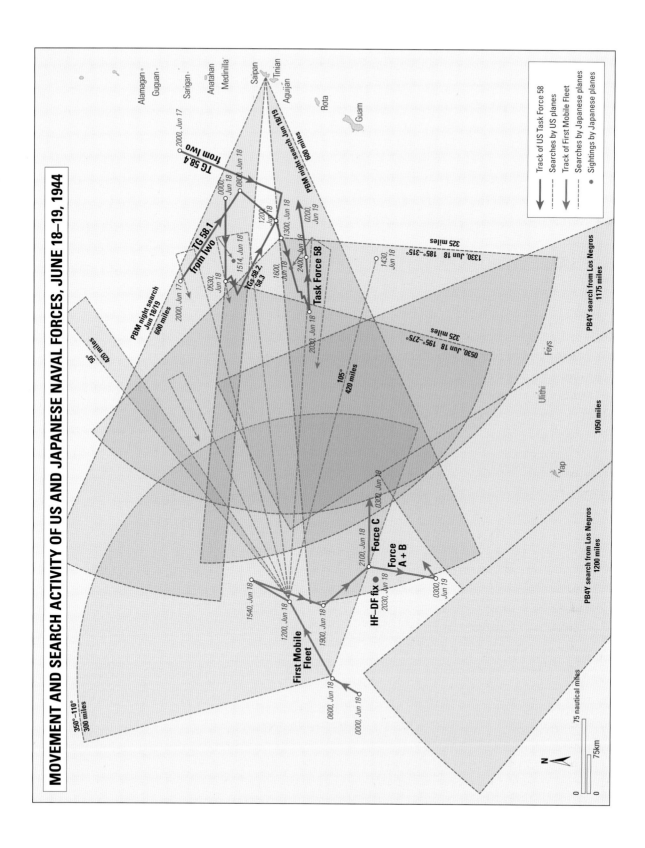

MOVEMENT AND SEARCH ACTIVITY OF US AND JAPANESE NAVAL FORCES, JUNE 18–19, 1944

the Americans and geo-located fairly accurately. Little did Ozawa know that such attention to coordinating his actions with Kakuta was unwarranted as the Base Air Force had already been neutralized. Kakuta's actions during the battle are difficult to explain. He issued a series of over-optimistic reports of the successes achieved by his aviators and failed to keep Ozawa informed of the true condition of the Base Air Force. Kakuta ordered the last 19 aircraft on Truk to move to Guam on June 19, which brought the total strength of Japanese aircraft in the Marianas to a mere 50. The Base Air Force would be unable to play a major role on June 19.

THE BATTLE BEGINS

The battle of the Philippine Sea was fought under clear weather conditions. The wind was from the east, forcing TF 58 to head away from the Japanese to conduct flight operations while the Japanese could advance toward their target while launching aircraft. Further, there was no chance of using weather for concealment. Ceiling and visibility were unlimited and the air temperature was in the mid-80s. Added to the clear conditions was the unusual creation of vapor trails by high-flying aircraft. During the battle some Japanese aircraft were spotted by American aviators at distances of up to 35nm.

TF 58 maintained course to the east until 0530 hours when it turned to the northeast to launch CAP, search, and antisubmarine patrols. Once the dawn launch was complete, TF 58 changed course to the west. The requirement to return to an easterly heading every time aircraft launched or recovered forced TF 58 to the east over the course of the day. In preparation for battle, Spruance deployed TGs 58.1, 58.3, and 58.2 in a line north to south. The center of each task group was 12–15nm from its neighbor and the battle line was positioned 15nm to the west of TG 58.3. The smallest task force, TG 58.4, was positioned north of the battle line. Each carrier task group deployed its carriers in the center of a circular formation some 4nm in diameter.

Spruance was well aware of the importance of land-based air power to the Japanese and took steps to suppress the airfields on Guam throughout the day. Beginning at 0530, Hellcats on CAP encountered Japanese aircraft from Guam. Japanese dive-bombers from Guam attacked destroyers of the battle line twice but inflicted no damage. At 0630 radar detected Japanese air activity over Guam and four Hellcats were sent to investigate. They found numerous Japanese aircraft taking off, which prompted a call for reinforcements. Beginning at 0807 and for the next hour, up to 33 Hellcats engaged Japanese aircraft over and near Guam. The Americans claimed 30 fighters and five bombers. This effectively removed the

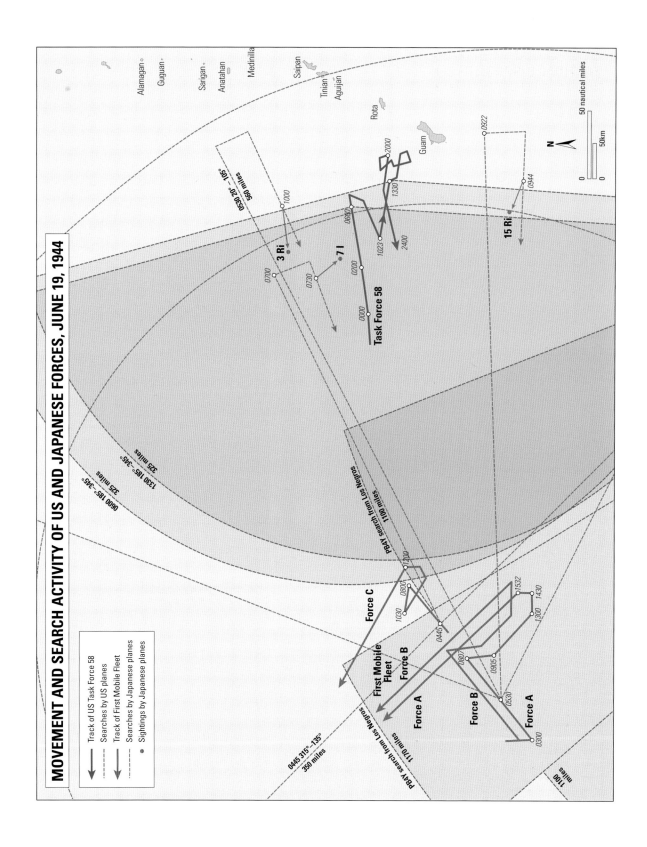

MOVEMENT AND SEARCH ACTIVITY OF US AND JAPANESE FORCES, JUNE 19, 1944

Track of US Task Force 58
Searches by US planes
Track of First Mobile Fleet
Searches by Japanese planes
Sightings by Japanese planes

50 nautical miles

50km

N

Alamagan
Guguan
Sarigan
Anatahan
Medinilla
Saipan
Aguijan
Tinian
Rota
Guam

0922
0944
15 Ri

2000
1330
0600
1023
2400
1000
3 Ri
7 I
0700
0730
0200
0000
0820 105°
560 miles
Task Force 58

PB4Y search from Los Negros
1100 miles

0600 185°–345°
325 miles
1330 185°–345°
325 miles

0445 315°–135°
350 miles

PB4Y search from Los Negros
1170 miles

1100 miles

1200
0800
1030
0445
0807
0905
0530
1552
1430
1300
0300

Force C
First Mobile Fleet
Force B
Force A
Force B
Force A

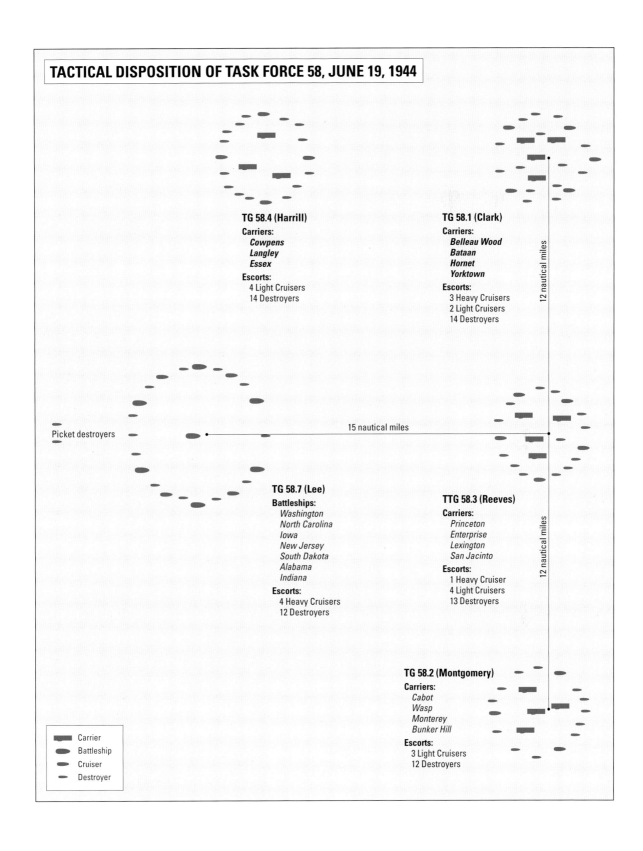

TACTICAL DISPOSITION OF TASK FORCE 58, JUNE 19, 1944

TG 58.4 (Harrill)
Carriers:
Cowpens
Langley
Essex
Escorts:
4 Light Cruisers
14 Destroyers

TG 58.1 (Clark)
Carriers:
Belleau Wood
Bataan
Hornet
Yorktown
Escorts:
3 Heavy Cruisers
2 Light Cruisers
14 Destroyers

12 nautical miles

15 nautical miles

Picket destroyers

TG 58.7 (Lee)
Battleships:
Washington
North Carolina
Iowa
New Jersey
South Dakota
Alabama
Indiana
Escorts:
4 Heavy Cruisers
12 Destroyers

TTG 58.3 (Reeves)
Carriers:
Princeton
Enterprise
Lexington
San Jacinto
Escorts:
1 Heavy Cruiser
4 Light Cruisers
13 Destroyers

12 nautical miles

TG 58.2 (Montgomery)
Carriers:
Cabot
Wasp
Monterey
Bunker Hill
Escorts:
3 Light Cruisers
12 Destroyers

Carrier
Battleship
Cruiser
Destroyer

ABOVE In this photograph a Hellcat from VF-1 on *Yorktown* prepares to take off on June 19. VF-1 was one of the most successful fighter squadrons during the battle. It submitted claims for 32 destroyed Japanese aircraft and five probable kills. (Naval History and Heritage Command)

RIGHT Condensation trails were prevalent on June 19, which aided the efforts of the Hellcats to intercept approaching Japanese aircraft. In this view, Hellcats from TG 58.2 produce condensation trails above a carrier. (Naval History and Heritage Command)

Base Air Force from playing any significant role in Ozawa's planned decisive air attacks. At 1000 all Hellcats over Guam returned to their carriers when radar detected large Japanese formations to the west of TF 58.

Flight activity by the First Mobile Fleet began at 0445 with the launch of search aircraft. The first group comprised 16 E13A floatplanes from the heavy cruisers and battleships of Force C. These aircraft reached the end of their search leg and headed back at about 0700. On their return track, one of the floatplanes spotted the battle line (TG 58.7) and TG 58.4. This detection was designated "7 I" by the Japanese. The second Japanese search was launched at 0515 and consisted of 13 Type 97s from the carriers and one floatplane from Force C. This search only managed to sight the picket destroyers deployed in advance of TG 58.7. Seven of the search aircraft were shot down with several being claimed by Hellcats from *Langley* of TG 58.4.

Based on contact 7 I, Ozawa began to launch his main attack. The first strike comprised aircraft from the three light carriers of Force C. A total of 69 aircraft were committed – 45 Zeros with bombs, 8 B6N2s with torpedoes, and an escort of 16 Zeros. When the strike was launched at 0830, Force C was some 300nm from TF 58.

TF 58 was ready and waiting. The first Japanese strike was detected by TG 58.7 at a distance of 125nm – more than enough time to prepare a hot reception. At 1023 Mitscher ordered every available Hellcat airborne. All airborne bombers on search and patrol missions were instructed to clear the area until the air battle was over. With the decks of the carriers clear, the Hellcats could return as necessary to rearm and refuel. Cycling the fighters in this manner kept as many Hellcats as possible airborne and at the disposal of the FDOs.

The approaching aircraft from Force C were designated Raid I by the Americans. The inexperienced aviators of Japanese Carrier Division 3 hesitated after closing to within 70nm of TF 58; at this point they began to orbit at 20,000 feet. This gave Mitscher more time to complete launching the Hellcats and gave the FDOs more time to get the fighters to their intercept altitudes of between 17,000 and 23,000 feet. The Hellcats from *Essex*'s VF-15 first spotted the incoming Japanese at 1035. The raid was arranged in two groups with escorting Zeros on each flank. About 50 Hellcats were involved in the initial intercept of Raid I including fighters from *Essex*, *Hornet*, *Bunker Hill*, and five light carriers. When the Hellcats tore into the Japanese formation, the escorting Zeros failed to protect the bombers and the bombers scattered, making them easy to pick off. The experienced pilots from VF-15 claimed 20 Japanese aircraft. Some 25 out of the 69 Japanese aircraft were destroyed in return for just three Hellcats lost in combat and a *Bunker Hill* Hellcat later forced to ditch.

This left some 40 Japanese aircraft. As the Japanese continued inbound, *Bunker Hill* Hellcats from VF-8 claimed another 16. The aircraft that survived intercept sighted TF 58.7 and began a series of uncoordinated attacks. Two bomb-carrying Zeros targeted *South Dakota* with one scoring a direct bomb hit. Shrapnel killed 27 men and wounded 23, but the ability of the battleship to steam and fight was unimpaired. Another Japanese aircraft scored a near miss on

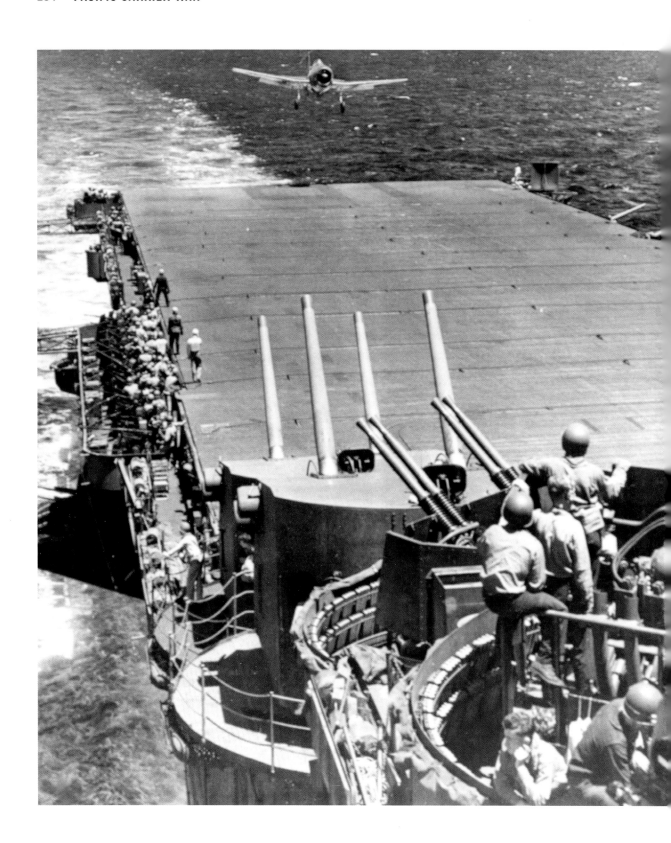

heavy cruiser *Minneapolis*, and a second barely missed heavy cruiser *Wichita*. Two TG 58.7 picket destroyers reported coming under attack but received no damage. As the last Japanese aircraft finished its attack and headed west, it was possible to take stock of the success of Raid I. No American carrier was attacked or even sighted, and the only bomb to strike a target caused no significant damage. Japanese records indicate that 42 aircraft were lost – eight Zeros, 32 Zero fighter-bombers, and two torpedo bombers. Hellcats accounted for most of the losses, with antiaircraft gunnery from TG 58.7 downing the rest.

Much better results were expected from Carrier Division 1 whose three fleet carriers carried the best-trained aviators in the First Mobile Fleet and constituted Ozawa's main punch. The first aircraft began launching at 0856, but this was disrupted at 0909 hours when *Taiho* came under attack by American submarine *Albacore*. The submarine was able to approach the carrier undetected and fired a full salvo of six torpedoes. One of *Taiho*'s dive-bombers saw the torpedoes heading for the ship and immediately dove into one to detonate it. This act of bravery did not prevent one of the torpedoes from hitting *Taiho* abreast the forward elevator. The ship's forward elevator had been raised for the launch; it was knocked out of alignment and fell several feet. Within 30 minutes damage control teams planked over the damaged elevator so that the launch could continue. This was only the beginning of the troubles for Ozawa's biggest attack. The attack originally consisted of 128 aircraft – 48 Zeros, 53 dive-bombers, and 27 B6N2s with torpedoes. In addition to the *Taiho* aircraft that dove into the torpedo, eight other aircraft developed engine trouble and were forced to return. When the attack group flew over Force C about 100nm east of Force A, it was engaged by antiaircraft fire. The friendly fire incident accounted for two aircraft shot down and damage to another eight, forcing them to return. Of the original 128 aircraft, just 109 were left to attack TF 58.

This large formation was detected by American radar at 1107 and designated Raid II. The detection distance of at least 115nm provided adequate time for another successful intercept. VF-15 was again the first to sight the Japanese. Twelve Hellcats led by *Essex*'s air group commander David McCampbell tore into the Japanese formation. McCampbell claimed three dive-bombers, and his wingman claimed another two. FDOs directed many other Hellcats to the scene and eventually about 70 Japanese aircraft were shot down. In addition to VF-15, VF-16 from *Lexington* claimed 22 Japanese aircraft without a loss; VF-1 from *Yorktown* scored heavily, and 12 *Bunker Hill* Hellcats claimed five kills. Light carriers *Bataan*, *Monterey*, and *Cabot* claimed ten, seven, and five Japanese aircraft, respectively.

Even with the tremendous execution recorded by the Hellcats, there were still over 30 Japanese aircraft headed for TF 58. Twenty were reported to be in three

OPPOSITE Of the 403 Hellcat sorties on June 19, 287 resulted in an engagement with a total of 548 Japanese aircraft. On this day, 13 Hellcats were lost to enemy aircraft, one to friendly antiaircraft fire, and six to operational causes. This view shows a Hellcat recovering aboard *Lexington*. (Naval History and Heritage Command)

ABOVE A Japanese D4Y1 dive-bomber from Raid II scores a near miss on *Bunker Hill*. The aircraft responsible can be seen on the left heading into the ocean without its tail. This was the closest the Japanese came to hitting an American carrier during the battle. The near miss on *Bunker Hill* killed three, wounded 73, damaged the port-side elevator, started several small fires, blew a Hellcat overboard, and damaged the hangar deck fuel system. (Naval History and Heritage Command)

RIGHT A group of D4Y1 dive-bombers avoided the CAP and attacked *Wasp* and *Bunker Hill* of TG 58.2. In this view, a Japanese bomb explodes off the starboard beam of *Bunker Hill*, too far away to do any damage. (Naval History and Heritage Command)

groups at 1145 hours, and these proceeded to make a series of uncoordinated attacks. Again, TG 58.7 absorbed the majority of these attacks. Picket destroyer *Stockham* reported coming under attack, but suffered no damage. Around noon the battleships of TG 58.7 came under attack. Two torpedo bombers attacked *South Dakota* with no success, and two more selected *Indiana* in the center of TG 58.7's formation as their target. One crashed into the beam of the heavily armored battleship at the waterline but caused little damage. Another torpedo bomber selected *Iowa* for attack but missed. At least two dive-bombers went after *Alabama*, but both missed their target.

A small number of Japanese aircraft launched the first attacks on American carriers during the battle. A group of six dive-bombers escaped the Hellcats and headed south until encountering TG 58.2. Four selected *Wasp* for attack; no hits

TOP LEFT A small number of Japanese aircraft from Raid II evaded the Hellcats and made attack runs on the carriers of TG 58.3. *Enterprise* is making high speed at the left of this view, and the carrier in the background is either *San Jacinto* or *Princeton*. Note the large 5-inch/38 shell bursts and the smaller 40mm bursts. (Naval History and Heritage Command)

MIDDLE LEFT A Japanese aircraft from Raid II is shot down over TG 58.3 just before noon. The light carrier is probably *Princeton*, which was subjected to an attack by three aircraft. (Naval History and Heritage Command)

BOTTOM LEFT TG 58.3 came under attack from several B6N torpedo bombers that avoided the American CAP. This photograph shows antiaircraft fire from *Enterprise* engaging the incoming Japanese aircraft. One B6N has just crashed into the ocean in the center of this view. The carrier at right is either *Princeton* or *San Jacinto*. (Naval History and Heritage Command) were scored, but one of the bombs detonated overhead, which rained shrapnel on the carrier's decks that killed one and wounded 12 crewmen. At 1203 the other two dove on *Bunker Hill*. They scored two near misses, causing minor damage and fires in addition to killing three and wounding 73 crewmen. Four of the attacking aircraft were destroyed by antiaircraft fire. Both carriers were able to continue flight operations. Six torpedo bombers were able to launch an attack against TG 58.3 that began minutes before noon. One selected *Enterprise* for its attentions but missed with its torpedo. Another three aimed their weapons at *Princeton*; all were destroyed by antiaircraft fire and none of their torpedoes found their mark.

Ozawa's main punch had come up empty. Of the 128 aircraft committed, 97 never returned to their carriers. Losses included 32 Zeros, 42 dive-bombers, and 23 B6N2s. Even more disappointing for the Japanese was the very small number of aircraft that succeeded in finding a carrier to attack. Carrier Division 1's attacks were scattered and uncoordinated, and the limited proficiency of the Japanese aviators resulted in not a single significant hit.

A third group of Japanese scout aircraft was launched at 0530 hours consisting of 11 D4Y dive-bombers from *Skokaku* and two E13A floatplanes from cruiser *Mogami*. These aircraft were assigned sectors 560nm to the east. Though Japanese search aircraft generally performed well during the battle, this search issued two erroneous contact reports that had a severe negative impact on the last two Japanese strikes. The first report was issued at 0945 of three carriers, five battleships, and ten other ships. This contact was designated "15 Ri." Unfortunately for the Japanese, the search plane crew forgot to correct for compass deviation, so the reported position of the contact was far to the south of TF 58's actual position. A second contact, designated "3 Ri," was reported at 1000. This contact was just to the northwest of contact 7 I and included one carrier, one light carrier, one battleship, and five destroyers. The reported position of 3 Ri was north of TF 58's actual position but may have represented an actual sighting of TG 58.4.

As the last two contacts were received by Ozawa, the third Japanese strike of the day was taking off from Carrier Division 2. The strike, designated Raid III by the Americans, comprised 47 aircraft including 15 Zeros, 25 Zeros with bombs, and seven B6N2s with torpedoes from *Junyo*, *Hiyo*, and *Ryuho*. The launch commenced at 1000 hours, and the strike departed with orders to attack the 7 I contact. En route to the target, the attack group received new orders to hit the 3 Ri contact, but this change was not received by the majority of the aircraft. Twenty-seven aircraft adhered to their original orders and flew to the reported 7 I contact location where they found nothing. After a search of the area found no potential targets, they returned to their carriers without loss. The remaining 20

THE BATTLE OF THE PHILIPPINE SEA

aircraft headed for the newer and more accurate 3 Ri contact. Upon arriving at the reported location, the Japanese spotted what they claimed were two battleships but continued to search for carriers. This search was unsuccessful, so at 1255 the group headed back to the location of the previously spotted battleships. Hellcats from *Hornet* and *Yorktown* were vectored to attack the wandering Japanese that were identified as 12–15 Zeros. The Americans claimed 14 aircraft destroyed, but actual Japanese losses were less than half that. A few of the Zeros found TG 58.4 and commenced an attack. Only one dropped its bomb that landed 600 yards from *Essex* at 1320. The offending Zero was shot down by Hellcats from *Langley*. This concluded the efforts of Ozawa's third strike. It inflicted no damage on the Americans, but 40 of the 47 aircraft survived to return to their carriers.

Ozawa still had uncommitted aircraft from Carrier Divisions 1 and 2. The final Japanese strike, totaling 82 aircraft mostly from Carrier Division 2, began launching at 1100 hours. Among the aircraft sent aloft were 30 Zero fighters, ten Zeros with bombs, 36 dive-bombers (27 Type 99s and nine D4Ys), and six B6N2s with torpedoes. All but the four Zeros and four B6N2s from *Zuikaku* were from the three carriers of Carrier Division 2. The strike was given orders to attack the 15 Ri contact. After arriving in the area of the non-existent contact, a search was unsuccessful in finding any targets. At this point the strike split into three groups. The largest, comprising 20 Zeros, 27 Type 99s, and two B6Ns, headed for Guam and was detected by TF 58 radar at 1449. Hellcats were vectored to intercept, including an initial group of 12 from *Cowpens* followed by over 40 more from five other carriers. The Japanese were caught at their most vulnerable as they were landing on Guam. In the ensuing massacre, 30 of the 49 Japanese aircraft were shot down. The remainder succeeded in landing, but either due to damage in the air or on the cratered runway, none flew again. Only two Hellcats were lost.

Another group of six Zeros and nine D4Y dive-bombers headed for the airfield on Rota but sighted TG 58.2 en route. The Japanese were initially detected on radar around 1330 at a distance of 134nm, so an intercept by the airborne CAP should have been a routine matter. However, on this occasion the CAP was ineffective because of a delay in identifying the contact as enemy and poor FDO work. The result was that the Japanese dive-bombers arrived over the carriers without interference and with one of the few chances during the battle to inflict real damage on TF 58. Six dive-bombers approached *Wasp* unmolested until they were engaged by antiaircraft fire just as they were dropping their bombs. The carrier's captain ordered a sharp turn to starboard and the nearest bomb hit the water 250 feet away from the ship. Antiaircraft fire accounted for several of the aircraft, with one crashing only 200 feet off *Wasp*'s port bow. At least one dive-bomber went after *Bunker Hill*. Before being shot down, it missed the carrier with its bomb by some 150 feet. Of the nine attackers, only one escaped. The third group of aircraft from Raid IV, consisting of the eight aircraft from *Zuikaku* and ten Zeros with bombs, opted to return to their carriers after finding nothing to attack. On their way home, the Japanese aircraft encountered two groups of *Lexington* scout aircraft consisting of four Avengers with two escorting Hellcats some 200nm west of Guam. The Zeros immediately attacked the outnumbered Americans, but the two Hellcats turned the tables and claimed six Japanese aircraft. At 1530 the same group of Japanese aircraft encountered two *Bunker Hill* aircraft on a search mission and shot both down. The fate of Ozawa's final strike was the most dismal of the four launched. Only nine of the 82 aircraft returned to their carriers while inflicting no damage on TF 58 and accounting for only a handful of American aircraft destroyed.

Throughout the day there was action in the air over Guam. Spruance was fearful that Ozawa would use Guam as a base for "shuttle bombing" so ordered sustained suppression of the airfields on the island. Action intensified whenever TF 58 dive-bombers and Avengers, ordered to steer clear of the air battle, dropped their ordnance on Guam. Just before noon, 15 *Yorktown* and 17 *Hornet* Helldivers bombed Orote Field. Another attack by Dauntlesses from *Lexington* and *Enterprise*, and nine Avengers from *Enterprise* with ten escorting Hellcats occurred at 1330. Later in the afternoon, Hellcats from *Bunker Hill* strafed the airfield and 11 Helldivers from *Essex* followed with bombs. The resultant poor condition of the airfield contributed to the loss of the 19 aircraft from Ozawa's final strike that attempted to land on Guam. The final action of the day occurred at 1845 when four Hellcats from *Essex* were jumped by a large number of Zeros. Three Hellcats were shot down. For the cost of six Hellcats and one Helldiver, the Americans prevented Japanese land-based aircraft from playing a significant role in the battle. The only Base Air Force aircraft to reach the area of TF 58 were six G4Ms and four D4Y dive-bombers that approached from the south at 1310 between Raid III and IV. Four Hellcats intercepted the Japanese and accounted for several aircraft. The raid never reached TF 58.

Hellcat pilots were the principal agent of the Japanese disaster on June 19. In this photograph, Lt Junior Grade Alexander Vraciu holds up six fingers to indicate the number of kills he recorded that day. He was assigned to VF-16 on *Lexington* and was one of six TF 58 pilots who claimed five or more kills on June 19 to become an ace in a single day. Vraciu went on to amass 19 kills, which made him the USN's fourth-highest ace. (Naval History and Heritage Command)

The other major events of June 19 were the actions of American submarines. *Cavalla*'s detection of Ozawa's fleet at 0730 on June 18 prompted orders to *Finback*, *Bang*, *Stingray*, and *Albacore* to move from their positions northwest of Saipan to new patrol areas 250nm to the south. The submarines were ordered to shoot first and send contact reports later. This change in operating area placed them right in the path of the First Mobile Fleet.

The first to strike was *Albacore*. As already mentioned, *Albacore* found herself in the middle of Carrier Division 1 as it was launching aircraft. By 0909, *Albacore*'s skipper was in position to fire a full torpedo spread at *Taiho*. One hit the ship on the forward side abreast the forward elevator. Besides jamming the elevator, the shock of the explosion cracked the forward aviation fuel tank. Damage control personnel made the fatal error of using the ship's ventilation system to spread fumes from the aviation fuel and the highly volatile Tarakan crude oil throughout the ship. This turned *Taiho* into a floating bomb. The inevitable occurred at 1532 when a massive explosion rocked the carrier, heaving up the flight deck and blowing holes in the hull. When the ship began to settle, Ozawa and his staff were evacuated by a destroyer. *Taiho* later sank, taking down 660 of her crew.

The second submarine to strike was *Cavalla*. At 1152 she spotted *Shokaku* recovering aircraft. *Cavalla*'s skipper made a skillful approach to close within 1,000 yards and fired a full salvo of six torpedoes. Three hit the carrier's starboard side with immediate and devastating effect. The stricken carrier listed to starboard as fires took hold on the hangar deck. The fires set off ordnance that cracked the forward fuel tank. Large explosions from escaping fuel vapors ensued and doomed the Pearl Harbor veteran. *Shokaku* sank suddenly by the bow at 1501, taking a heavy toll of 1,272 crewmen.

THE AFTERMATH OF JUNE 19

The events of June 19 were clearly a disaster for the Japanese, but the extent of the disaster remained opaque to Ozawa. The four strikes mounted by the First Mobile Fleet totaled 373 aircraft. Of these, a staggering 243 were lost. Total losses were even higher since nine aircraft were lost when *Shokaku* sank, another 13 went down with *Taiho*, and some 50 aircraft were lost from Guam. This brought total Japanese losses to about 315 aircraft. Hellcat pilots agreed that the caliber of their Japanese counterparts was low; Zeros displayed ignorance of sound tactics in favor of executing acrobatic maneuvers, and the Japanese bomber pilots were quick to break formation, making them easy targets. Some 296 Hellcats engaged the Japanese during the day with 14 lost in combat and another six lost to operational causes.

Ozawa was not aware of the full scope of this disaster. In his mind, there was cause for optimism since Japanese aviators reported four American carriers sunk and six damaged. Ozawa knew that few of his aircraft had returned to their carriers, but many of the missing aircraft could have recovered on Guam and Rota. The normal confusion of battle was heightened by the difficulty of exercising proper command and control using the limited communications facilities aboard cruiser *Haguro* to which Ozawa was forced to transfer after *Taiho*'s demise. The decisive battle was off to an uncertain start but was by no means lost. With this in mind, Ozawa ordered the First Mobile Fleet to the northwest at 1808 hours on June 19 to refuel the following day before renewing the battle.

The next morning, the First Mobile Fleet began refueling operations at 0920 hours. After three hours of confusion during which no progress was made, Ozawa canceled refueling operations. Ozawa and his staff transferred to *Zuikaku* at 1300. The communications facilities on the carrier provided Ozawa with a more accurate understanding of the results from June 19. The First Mobile Fleet was down to only 100 aircraft – 32 on *Zuikaku*, 46 on the three carriers of Carrier Division 2, and 22 on Carrier Division 3. Kakuta provided some false hope by reporting that some of the carrier aircraft had landed on Guam and that aircraft reinforcements were on the way for the Base Air Force. Ozawa decided to prolong the battle but did agree to delay the resumption of strikes until June 21.

Kurita advised retirement to escape any American counterstrike, but Ozawa was not convinced that the decisive battle was over. This stubbornness opened the First Mobile Fleet up to attack. At 1645 Japanese signals intelligence personnel informed Ozawa that American aircraft had sighted the First Mobile Fleet. Finally, aware that TF 58 had headed west and could be within striking range, Ozawa ordered his fleet to the northwest at 24 knots. Three carrier aircraft launched for an afternoon search found TF 58 at 1715, confirming that Spruance was headed west. However, by this time, the American counterstrike was already on its way.

TF 58 STRIKES

Throughout June 19, TF 58 had been forced to steam east to launch and recover aircraft. Following the recovery of all aircraft at 2000 hours, TF 58 headed west at 23 knots to close the distance to the First Mobile Fleet. Both Mitscher and Spruance were intent on striking the Japanese on June 20 with three carrier groups led by TG 58.7. TG 58.4 was detached to refuel and suppress Japanese air activity on Guam and Rota.

No strike could be launched until the First Mobile Fleet was located. Because the Japanese reverted to radio silence, and no information was forthcoming from

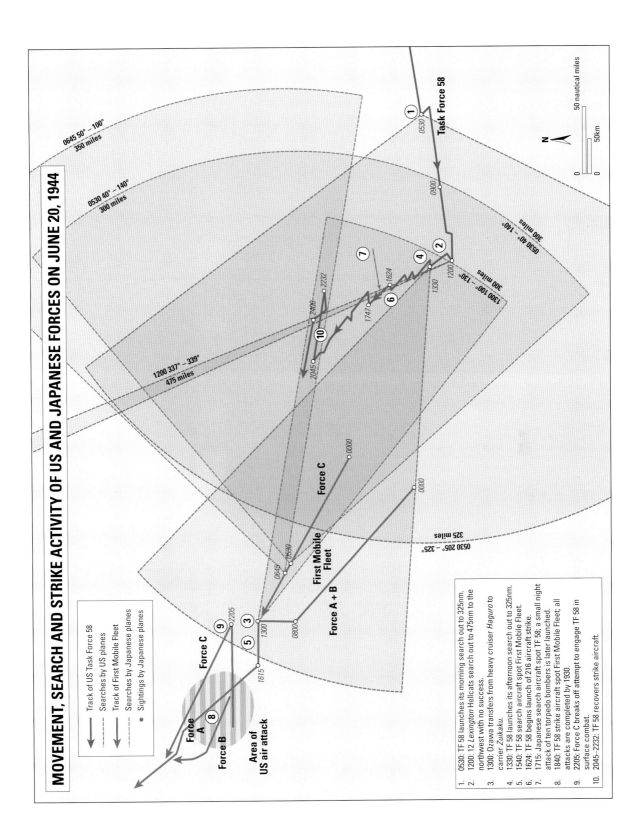

MOVEMENT, SEARCH AND STRIKE ACTIVITY OF US AND JAPANESE FORCES ON JUNE 20, 1944

Task Force 58

1 0530

0900

2 1200

0530 40° – 140°
300 miles

1300 100° – 130°
300 miles

0645 50° – 100°
350 miles

0530 40° – 140°
300 miles

1200 337° – 339°
475 miles

4

7

1624

6

1330

1747

2232

2400

10

2045

Force C

0000

First Mobile
Fleet

0000

0530

0645

0800

Force A + B

325 miles
0530 205° – 325°

9 2205

3

5 1300

1615

Force C

Force
A

Force B

Area of
US air attack

8

N

50 nautical miles

50km

0   50km
0

Legend:
Track of US Task Force 58
Searches by US planes
Track of First Mobile Fleet
Searches by Japanese planes
Sightings by Japanese planes

1. 0530: TF 58 launches its morning search out to 325nm.
2. 1200: 12 *Lexington* Hellcats search out to 475nm to the northwest with no success.
3. 1300: Ozawa transfers from heavy cruiser *Haguro* to carrier *Zuikaku*.
4. 1330: TF 58 launches its afternoon search out to 325nm.
5. 1540: TF 58 search aircraft spot First Mobile Fleet.
6. 1624: TF 58 begins launch of 216 aircraft strike.
7. 1715: Japanese search aircraft spot TF 58; a small night attack of ten torpedo bombers is later launched.
8. 1840: TF 58 strike aircraft spot First Mobile Fleet; all attacks are completed by 1930.
9. 2205: Force C breaks off attempt to engage TF 58 in surface combat.
10. 2045–2232: TF 58 recovers strike aircraft.

A formation of Hellcats, Dauntlesses, and Avengers forms up over *Lexington* on the afternoon of June 20. *Lexington*'s deckload strike consisted of 11 Hellcats, 16 Dauntlesses (one aborted), and six Avengers (armed with bombs, but one aborted after launch). Only *Lexington* and *Enterprise* from TG 58.3 still operated Dauntlesses. (Naval History and Heritage Command)

American submarines or from PBM flying boats operating from a tender off Saipan, TF 58 would have to find the Japanese itself. Mitscher needed location data on the Japanese as quickly as possible since the later in the afternoon, the more certain it would be that a strike would have to conduct a risky night recovery. At 0530 Mitscher launched the morning search that went out the usual 325nm. The search aircraft found nothing since the First Mobile Fleet was some 400nm distant. At about noon Mitscher approved a request to allow 12 Hellcats from *Lexington* flown by volunteers to fly out 475nm to the northwest. This effort also failed to find any sign of Ozawa.

The afternoon search launched at 1330 and again flew out the usual 325nm; it provided the break the Americans needed. The first American aviator to sight the First Mobile Fleet was an Avenger pilot from *Enterprise*. His initial contact report was issued at 1540, and just minutes later Mitscher informed Spruance that he was planning an all-out strike. With sunset at 1900, it was clear the strike would return after dark. The risk of launching a strike was further highlighted when the contact aircraft provided a corrected position which was actually 60nm further west. This placed the Japanese fleet 275nm from TF 58 – well past maximum strike range. Nevertheless, Spruance approved the strike since it looked like the only chance to hit the Japanese. Mitscher canceled the launch of the second deckload of strike aircraft after learning of the additional distance to the target.

A full deckload launch from 11 carriers began at 1624 and was completed in a record ten minutes. After 14 aircraft were forced to abort for various reasons, the strike consisted of 85 Hellcats (some carrying 500lb bombs), 77 dive-bombers (51 Helldivers and 26 Dauntlesses), and 54 Avengers (only 21 of which carried torpedoes; the rest carried four 500lb bombs). After a direct and uneventful flight, the lead aircraft spotted the First Mobile Fleet at 1840. No attempt was made to conduct a coordinated attack since the aircraft were at the end of their endurance, having flown almost 300nm and because there was only 20–30 minutes of daylight remaining. The ensuing attack was a chaotic brawl that was over in half an hour.

The First Mobile Fleet was not ready for the attack. Ozawa had ordered Force C, with the bulk of the heavy escorts, to assume its place in front of the carriers to act as a diversion and absorb the blow, but when the attack began Kurita's force was out of position. The entire First Mobile Fleet was headed northwesterly with Force C being the southernmost group, Force B in the center, and what was left of Force A to the north. The two supply groups were the farthest to the east, which made them the first Japanese force encountered by the Americans. Japanese radar detected the approaching raid at 1803, providing sufficient time to launch the 68 Zeros still available.

Force A contained *Zuikaku* which was the largest remaining Japanese carrier. The veteran carrier proved to be a difficult target with its CAP of 17 Zeros, ability to produce a large volume of antiaircraft fire, and adept maneuvering. Air groups from *Hornet*, *Yorktown*, and *Bataan* selected Ozawa's flagship for attack. The initial attacks were conducted by a total of 27 Helldivers from *Hornet* and *Yorktown*. Though the carrier was deluged with bombs and many hits were claimed, only a single 1,000lb bomb actually hit the carrier. Only four of the Avengers from *Hornet* carried torpedoes, and of these only two launched their weapons at the carrier; both missed. The ten bomb-carrying Hellcats from *Bataan* were also unsuccessful. American aviators reported large fires on the big carrier, but damage was not as great as it appeared. The single bomb that found its mark hit aft of the island and

The most valuable Japanese ship to come under attack on the early evening of June 20 was *Zuikaku*, which was the only remaining carrier of Force A. The carrier is shown taking a hard turn to starboard with several bomb splashes around her. Two escorting destroyers can also be seen. Although attacked by as many as 50 Avengers and Helldivers, *Zuikaku* suffered only a single bomb hit and survived. (Naval History and Heritage Command)

penetrated to the upper hangar deck where it started a fire among the few aircraft remaining. The aircraft had been defueled, so damage control teams were able to contain the fires and extinguish them. Before this success was apparent, an order to abandon ship was given and then quickly rescinded. *Zuikaku*'s speed was not impaired so she was able to escape and survived to fight again.

Force B, containing carriers *Hiyo*, *Junyo*, and *Ryuho*, was attacked by the most American aircraft. The Japanese CAP consisted of as many as 38 Zeros though the experience of the pilots varied wildly. Attacking Force B was *Lexington*'s strike group, Avengers from *Enterprise*, *Yorktown*, and *Belleau Wood*, and Hellcats from *Hornet* and *Yorktown* carrying 500lb bombs. The two biggest carriers, *Hiyo* and *Junyo*, received the most attention. All but three of *Lexington*'s 14 Dauntless dive-bombers dove on *Junyo* followed by a glide-bomb attack from six Avengers with bombs. At 1904, one or two bombs hit the carrier's island, and as many as six near misses created minor flooding. Overall damage was light, but 53 crewmen were killed. *Ryuho* came under heavy attack, but also escaped after all bombs and torpedoes aimed against her failed to find their target. Among the attackers were five Avengers from *Enterprise* with bombs; eight hits were claimed, but only slight damage was caused by near misses. Five Avengers from *Yorktown* attacked with torpedoes; two hits were claimed, but again all weapons missed. The carrier also survived attacks from six *Enterprise* Dauntlesses and Hellcats from *Hornet*.

Junyo and *Hiyo* were converted passenger liners with a relatively slow top speed, poor maneuverability, and little ability to take damage. These vulnerabilities proved fatal for *Hiyo*. The carrier left the formation to launch two B6N2s to lay a smoke screen and had not yet returned to the formation when the American

BELOW Force C was targeted by 28 USN strike aircraft. Only the *Chiyoda* group came under attack, and the Americans scored only one direct hit and a single damaging near miss against the light carrier. In this view *Chiyoda* maneuvers in the middle left portion of the photo while two large escorts can be seen at right. A destroyer maneuvers in the lower center of the photo. (Naval History and Heritage Command)

BELOW RIGHT This photo from a *Bunker Hill* aircraft shows Force C under attack. The ship in the lower part of the photo is battleship *Haruna* or *Kongo*, both of which were assigned to escort *Chiyoda*. The carrier is visible on the upper right. (Naval History and Heritage Command)

strike arrived. Three *Lexington* Dauntlesses opened the attack with a bomb that hit the foremast and exploded above the bridge, resulting in heavy casualties to bridge personnel. Another bomb, possibly from one of six *Enterprise* Dauntlesses, hit the flight deck. Four *Belleau Wood* Avengers armed with torpedoes conducted an anvil attack and succeeded in placing one torpedo in the vicinity of *Hiyo*'s starboard engine room. This was the only torpedo hit scored by the Avengers during the entire attack, but it proved fatal for the largely unprotected carrier. Flooding created an immediate list and, after the port engine stopped, the ship went dead in the water. A large explosion amidships was recorded at 1917 hours that caused a large fire fed by leaking aviation fuel. The conflagration led to multiple explosions, and the order to abandon ship was given. The carrier sank stern first at 2032 with 35 officers and 212 enlisted men still aboard. Leaking fuel vapors were the likely source of the initial large explosion that led to the ship's loss. If so, the same cause accounted for all three Japanese carriers lost in the battle. The two remaining carriers of Carrier Division 2 survived the battle with only 16 Zeros and one B6N2 remaining.

Force C was attacked by a total of 42 aircraft from *Bunker Hill*, *Monterey*, and *Cabot*. Kurita had arranged his force into three groups with several escorting battleships or heavy cruisers protecting each of the three light carriers. Only the southernmost group with *Chiyoda*, escorted by battleships *Haruna* and *Kongo* and several other ships, was attacked. The *Zuiho* and *Chitose* groups were untouched. The Japanese had 13 Zeros on CAP, but these waited until after the American aircraft had dropped their weapons to launch a series of ineffective attacks. None of *Bunker Hill*'s Helldivers were able to score a hit against the wildly maneuvering *Chiyoda*. Next to attack were the bomb-carrying Avengers from *Monterey* and *Cabot*. The only 500lb bomb to hit *Chiyoda* came from a *Monterey* aircraft; the bomb struck the flight deck aft and resulted in 20 dead, 30 wounded, and two aircraft destroyed. The ensuing fire was quickly extinguished, and damage was minimal. The best chance to cripple *Chiyoda* was from the torpedoes carried aboard eight Avengers from *Bunker Hill*. Five of the Avengers went after the light carrier, and two hits were claimed, but actually all weapons missed. Several of the American aircraft were forced to select secondary targets. Two Avengers from *Cabot* hit *Haruna* with a 500lb bomb that penetrated her stern and flooded the steering compartment. The battleship's speed was reduced, and 15 crewmen were killed and 19 wounded. Heavy cruiser *Maya* suffered a near miss that caused minor flooding.

The leader of *Wasp*'s attack group, with his fuel running low, decided to attack one of the supply groups in the hopes that sinking the oilers would impede the withdrawal of the First Mobile Fleet. Nine of the 12 Helldivers and seven Avengers attacked the tankers; *Genyo Maru* and *Seiyo Maru* were damaged and later scuttled. Fleet oiler *Hayasui* was also hit by a bomb and saw two near misses, but the crew put the fire out and the ship survived.

TF 58's series of hectic and uncoordinated attacks against the First Mobile Fleet produced disappointing results. Aside from the disjointed nature of the attacks, the low level of damage was attributable to the lack of practice against naval targets and the determined defense by the Japanese. If more than 21 Avengers had been armed with torpedoes, greater damage would almost certainly have been inflicted. As it was, the single torpedo that did find its mark produced the most important damage of the attack accounting for *Hiyo*. The biggest disappointment for the Americans was the escape of *Zuikaku*. The light damage to *Zuikaku*, *Junyo*, and *Chiyoda* was remarkable given the number of bombs directed at them and served as additional proof of the difficulty of killing large ships with bombs alone. In addition to the damage to fleet units, the Japanese also suffered heavy aircraft losses on June 20. They began the day with 100 aircraft available and ended the day with 35. Most of the losses were probably exacted from the large number of Zeros sent aloft on CAP and subsequently shot down by Hellcats. In comparison, American aircraft losses were light during the actual attack. Seventeen aircraft were lost – six Hellcats, five dive-bombers, and six Avengers. Only six were lost to antiaircraft fire with the balance being dispatched by Zeros on CAP.

This is another view of Force C under attack taken by an aircraft from *Bunker Hill*. Heavy cruiser *Maya* or *Chokai* is the ship in the lower right of the photograph while in the center right is *Chiyoda* surrounded by bomb splashes. Several things are noteworthy in this photograph. Note the small number of antiaircraft fire bursts above the formation and compare it to the much heavier volume of American antiaircraft fire evident in many other photographs. Note also that the ships are maneuvering independently under attack rather than maintaining formation to provide antiaircraft protection for the carrier. The circular evasion tactic of the Japanese is also evident in this view. (Naval History and Heritage Command)

With their attack concluded at dusk, the American aviators faced a trip of between 240 and 300nm back to TF 58 on a dark night. Mitscher ignored the potential threat of Japanese air and submarine attacks and ordered his ships to use illumination beyond the normal landing lights on each carrier deck to guide his appreciative aviators home. The first returning aircraft arrived at 2045, and for the next almost two hours a chaotic scene played out as the increasingly desperate aviators looked for somewhere to land before their fuel was

Chiyoda was hit by one bomb that started a fire in the hangar deck, which can be seen on this photograph near the stern of the carrier. (Naval History and Heritage Command)

exhausted. Any pretense of order was forgotten, and soon aircraft were ordered to land on any flight deck in sight. Almost half of the returning aircraft failed to find their parent ship. At the conclusion of this drama, another 82 aircraft (17 Hellcats, 42 dive-bombers, and 23 Avengers) were missing. Combined with the 17 aircraft lost in combat, almost half of the attacking aircraft were lost. Heavy aircraft losses could be replaced, but aircrew were more precious. Aboard the missing aircraft were some 170 pilots and aircrewmen. After an intensive search and rescue effort over the course of several days, only 16 pilots and 33 aircrewmen remained unaccounted for.

After the two damaged tankers were scuttled, none of Ozawa's ships were left behind as the First Mobile Fleet retired to the northwest. Toyoda issued orders to break off the battle at 2046. The shattered First Mobile Fleet arrived at Okinawa in the afternoon of June 22 with only 35 aircraft and 12 floatplanes remaining. Spruance and Mitscher were disappointed with the results of the dusk attack and were unsure whether any Japanese cripples remained to be finished off. TF 58 maintained course to the west, more in the hope of finishing off any Japanese cripples than in catching Ozawa's fleet. On the morning of June 21, Mitscher launched a full deckload strike to fly out 300nm to attack anything in sight. Since the First Mobile Fleet was some 360nm distant, the strike made no contact and returned. With no chance of catching Ozawa and no cripples to destroy, Spruance ordered the chase abandoned at 2030 hours on June 21. Twenty minutes later, TF 58 reversed course, bringing the battle to an end.

CHAPTER 9
CONCLUSION AND ANALYSIS

THE LAST CARRIER ENCOUNTER

After the battle of the Philippine Sea, the Fast Carrier Task Force changed its designation to TF 38 and acquired a new commander – William F. Halsey. With 17 fleet and light carriers at his disposal, Halsey began the task of reducing Japanese air power in the Western Pacific in preparation for the invasion of the Philippines. Leaving Eniwetok on August 28, Halsey led his carriers to conduct strikes against the Palau Islands, Mindanao Island in the southern Philippines, and the Visayan Islands in September. So weak was Japanese opposition that Halsey proposed the date for the invasion of the Philippines be advanced – an idea soon endorsed by the Joint Chiefs of Staff. TF 38 then fought a major air-sea battle off Taiwan between October 10 and 20 during which Japanese land-based air power suffered a major defeat.

The Japanese correctly assessed that the Philippines were the next American target. Defending them was going to be difficult as there was insufficient time to rebuild the Mobile Fleet, and land-based air power was negligible after Halsey's rampage in September and October. Toyoda devised a desperate plan in which the remainder of Ozawa's carrier force would lure the aggressive

Halsey away from the Philippines to allow Kurita to take a large force of battleships and cruisers into Leyte Gulf to attack the invasion force. This plan was ill-conceived in several important ways, but it did set the stage for the last carrier encounter of the war. Though American and Japanese carriers faced one another for the last time during the battle of Leyte Gulf, it would be grandiose to characterize it a carrier battle.

By the time the Americans landed on Leyte Island on October 20, Toyoda had already set his plan into motion. Kurita's force departed its base near Singapore on October 18, and Ozawa's carriers departed Japan two days later. For this operation Ozawa's force consisted of veteran *Zuikaku*, light carriers *Zuiho*, *Chitose*, and *Chiyoda*, and 12 escorts, two of which were battleships converted into hybrid carriers by having a small flight deck installed on their stern to operate a small air group of floatplanes. The total number of aircraft embarked on Ozawa's four carriers was 116 – comparable to the aircraft onboard a single Essex-class carrier.

On October 24 Kurita's force prepared to transit the Sibuyan Sea on its way to Leyte. To give Kurita any chance of reaching its target, Ozawa had to execute his decoy mission quickly and effectively. Even at this point of the

ABOVE In the battle of the Sibuyan Sea, superbattleship *Musashi* was the focus of relentless American air attacks. For more than five hours on October 24, the ship was struck by between 11 and 15 torpedoes and as many as 16 bombs. By this point in the war, the Fast Carrier Task Force could destroy even the most heavily armored ship, primarily because the Avenger had a fully functional torpedo. This is *Musashi* maneuvering during the attack. (Naval History and Heritage Command) war, Japanese carriers were still superior to their American counterparts in reconnaissance operations. Ozawa's search aircraft gained contact on TF 38 at 0820 on October 24, and his entire force closed to within 210nm of TF 38 just before noon to launch a strike. Despite his best efforts to create a suitable decoy, Ozawa's force was not spotted until 1640.

The final Japanese carrier strike of the war was launched at 1145 hours on October 24 and directed at TG 38.3 off eastern Luzon Island. TG 38.3 was also subjected to three attacks from Japanese land-based aircraft during the day. One D4Y dive-bomber got through the CAP and hit light carrier *Princeton*. The ship later sank, making her the first non-escort carrier sunk since *Hornet*'s loss in October 1942, and the last fast carrier sunk during the war. The 50 aircraft from Ozawa's carriers that attacked TG 38.3 were not even recognized by the Americans as having come from Japanese carriers. Fourteen of the attacking Japanese aircraft were shot down in exchange for no American losses. Only three aircraft from the Japanese strike force returned to their carriers; the other 34 recovered at various land bases.

As TG 38.3 dealt with Japanese air attacks, TF 38's main operation during the day was delivering a series of air attacks against Kurita's force as it transited east. This series of air attacks was one of the largest air-sea battles in history. The 29 ships of Kurita's force were subjected to a total of 259 sorties from TF 38. The Americans inflicted serious damage on Kurita by sinking the superbattleship *Musashi* and forcing a heavy cruiser to return to Singapore. The overall damage to Kurita's force was minimized by *Musashi* absorbing the attention of the majority of American pilots and taking at least 11 and maybe as many as 15 torpedoes along with 16 bomb hits.

The last strikes ever launched from carriers against other carriers at sea occurred the following day. Thinking he had crippled Kurita's force, Halsey steamed north to attack Ozawa's force with the entirety of TF 38. Ozawa had accomplished his mission of drawing Halsey away from Leyte, but the cost was high. Halsey threw 527 sorties against Ozawa's force in six strikes. The first strike was detected by *Zuikaku*'s radar some 108nm distant. The Japanese CAP consisted of only 13 Zeros, and was quickly brushed aside. The first strike hit *Zuikaku* with three bombs and one torpedo, but her experienced damage control teams successfully fought the fires and corrected the list. *Chitose* was quickly sunk and went down with 904 crewmen. *Chiyoda* was severely damaged and awaited her fate at the hands of American surface ships later that afternoon. The third American air strike brought *Zuikaku*'s illustrious career to an end. The carrier took six torpedoes and four bombs that brought her to a halt, started extensive fires, and created a heavy list.

Zuikaku later capsized with heavy loss of life. Some two hours after Zuikaku went down, she was joined by Zuiho.

Despite Kurita's attack against a force of American escort carriers off Samar Island on October 25 that sank several American ships including one escort carrier, the battle of Leyte Gulf was the death knell of the Imperial Navy. Aside from the sortie of superbattleship Yamato to Okinawa in early April 1945, the IJN's remaining ships were almost all hunted down and sunk in various ports in Japan before war's end. By the time of the Japanese surrender, only carriers Hosho, Junyo, Ryuho, and Amagi (a fleet carrier laid down in 1942 based on the design of Hiryu) were still afloat.

Ozawa's carrier force paid a heavy price for accomplishing its decoy mission at Leyte Gulf. All four Japanese carriers were sunk in the action off Cape Engano on October 25. This view shows Zuikaku and an Akizuki-class destroyer under attack. Light carrier Zuiho is visible in the background. (Naval History and Heritage Command)

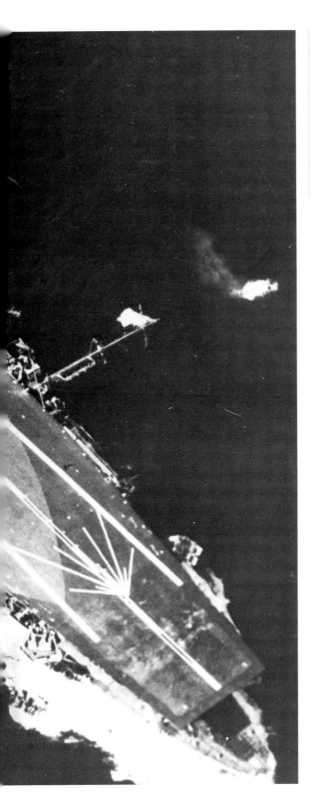

LEFT This iconic photograph shows *Zuiho* under attack by aircraft from *Enterprise* on October 25. After participating in three previous carrier battles, *Zuiho*'s luck ran out at Cape Engano. (Naval History and Heritage Command)

FOLLOWING PAGES Cape Engano was also the death knell of *Zuikaku*, which was present at every carrier battle of the war except for Midway. She was also the last remaining Japanese carrier from the Pearl Harbor attack. In this view, *Zuikaku*'s crew salutes as the Japanese national ensign is lowered. The ship sank shortly thereafter with the loss of 843 men. (Naval History and Heritage Command)

After Leyte Gulf, the Fast Carrier Task Force played a central role in the closing months of the war. From October 1944 the fast carriers faced a new threat just as deadly as the Japanese carrier force at its peak. The new threat was attacks by suicide aircraft that challenged American fleet air defense capabilities like nothing before. It proved impossible to provide the carriers with an air-tight defense from suicide aircraft, but those few aircraft that penetrated the CAP and antiaircraft fire lacked the penetrative power to sink large warships. In 1944 kamikazes hit Essex-class carriers six times, but none were seriously damaged. One Independence-class light carrier was hit by a suicide aircraft but also survived. The threat was even greater in 1945, with fleet carriers being hit ten times with one nearly sinking. One light carrier was also hit in 1945 but survived. In spite of the kamikaze threat, the fast carriers were always able to accomplish their missions. After the battle of Leyte Gulf they operated off the Philippines for an extended period. During the Okinawa campaign, the carrier force operated for more than 70 days within range of conventional and suicide attack from Japanese air bases on Kyushu, but still maintained control of the seas and the airspace around Okinawa. By war's end, kamikaze aircraft had sunk 47 USN ships and damaged more than 270 others, and were responsible for approximately 8,000 American deaths. Strategically, the kamikazes failed to curtail Fast Carrier Task Force planning and operations.

During the final campaign in 1945, the fast carrier force conducted strikes along the entire length of the Japanese Home Islands. TF 58 with 11 fleet and five light

RIGHT While operating off the Philippines, the Fast Carrier Task Force experienced its first kamikaze attacks on October 29, 1944. The following month, on November 25, the Japanese hit both *Intrepid* and *Essex* on the same day. This view shows the impact of a D4Y on *Essex*. Despite the heavy explosion, *Essex* suffered little structural damage and was repaired within two weeks at the fleet anchorage at Ulithi. (Naval History and Heritage Command)

carriers attacked the Tokyo area for the first time on February 16–17. From a launch point only 60nm off Honshu, over 1,000 offensive sorties were flown on the first day and almost 1,400 on the second. The carriers returned just over a week later to pound Tokyo again. From March until early June, the fast carriers focused on striking Kyushu in support of the invasion of Okinawa. Back under Halsey's command, TF 38 hit Tokyo in July and then struck targets on the northern island of Hokkaido. On July 24–25, the fast carriers conducted a total of 2,018 offensive sorties against naval targets in the Kure area, virtually annihilating the remainder of the Imperial Navy. In comparison, at the height of its powers the *Kido Butai* managed 343 sorties at targets on Hawaii to open the war.

In the final phase of the naval campaign against Japan, TF 38 launched nearly 4,000 sorties against the Home Islands in August 1945. Halsey hit Tokyo for the final time on August 13 before the Japanese government announced it had accepted surrender terms. For Operation *Olympic*, the projected invasion of Kyushu, there would have been two Fast Carrier Task Forces with a total of 15 fleet and seven light carriers together with five British fleet and four light carriers. Over the course of the war, the USN's carrier force had grown from three single-carrier groups making weak raids on the fringes of the Japanese empire into a strategic weapon.

PACIFIC CARRIER BATTLES – AN ANALYSIS

The popular vision of the Pacific War is of wide-ranging carrier task groups on both sides conducting sweeping attacks with all other naval components playing supporting roles. This notion aside, it is fair to characterize the Pacific War as a carrier war. This was certainly the case during the last half of the war. But for the first part Japanese and American carriers lacked the power and logistical support to generate strategic effects. As envisioned by Yamamoto, the opening strike on Pearl Harbor by the *Kido Butai* with its six fleet carriers was to be a decisive operation with strategic implications, but instead of giving Japan strategic leverage over the United States, it was an undeniable strategic disaster for Japan.

The *Kido Butai* was also not the only reason for Japan's initial wartime successes. Land-based air power spearheaded the Japanese advance in Southeast Asia. When Japanese carriers faced American carriers in the Coral Sea and at Midway, they were checked and then defeated for the first time. When the *Kido Butai* spearheaded a strategic operation in the Central Pacific, it fought unsupported and was defeated. In the second half of 1942, the

BELOW OPPOSITE After supporting the invasion of the Philippines in October during which it defeated the IJN's last major operation at the battle of Leyte Gulf and contended with a constant threat of Japanese land-based aircraft which included the first use of suicide aircraft, the Fast Carrier Task Force (redesignated TF 38 as part of the Third Fleet) went to Ulithi Atoll for a short rest period. This scene of naval power was captured at Ulithi on December 8, 1944 and includes (from front to back) Essex-class carriers *Wasp*, *Yorktown*, *Hornet*, *Hancock*, and *Ticonderoga*. (Naval History and Heritage Command)

FOLLOWING PAGES The IJN's last major operation after Leyte Gulf was the sortie of superbattleship *Yamato* and nine escorts to attack the American fleet off Okinawa in April 1945. In a series of attacks on April 7, *Yamato* was sunk by between nine and 12 torpedoes and seven bombs. The pointless sacrifice included the loss of over 3,000 men from her crew. This is *Yamato* maneuvering early in the attack as a bomb explodes off her port beam. (Naval History and Heritage Command)

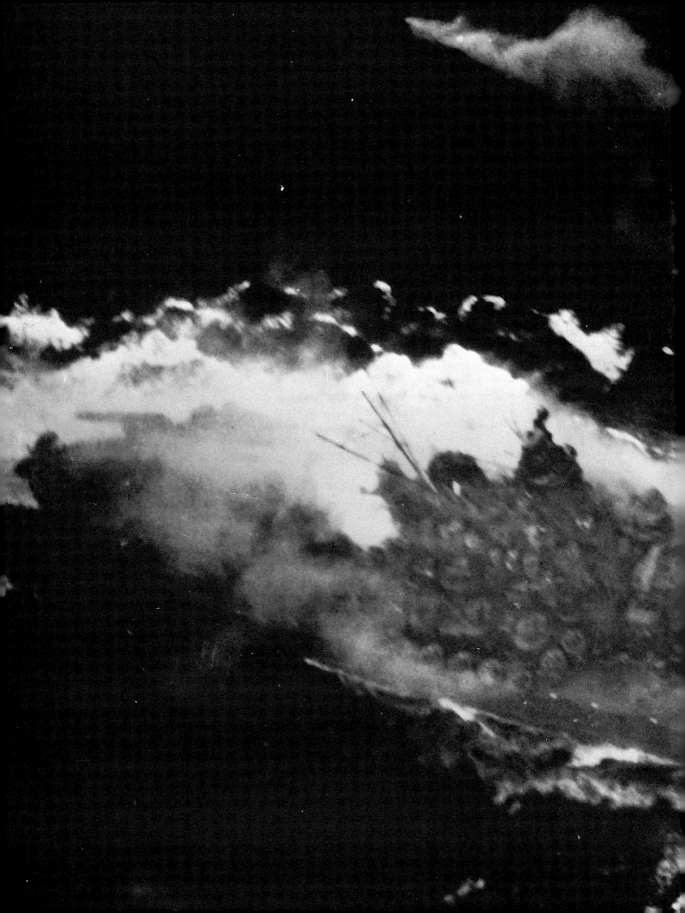

Kido Butai fought the USN's carrier force to a standstill in two carrier battles but proved unable to stop the American advance. This was a turning point since the Japanese carrier force (including its pool of experienced aviators) was gutted in the process and was not committed again until mid-1944.

A strong carrier force was a vital component to Japan's defensive strategy in 1944. But by the time the IJN was forced on the strategic defensive, the power of its carrier force had waned to the point where it was unable to support Japanese island garrisons under attack. Despite two more attempts to fight a decisive battle at the battles of Philippine Sea and Leyte Gulf, the IJN's carrier force was unable to exert any real influence over the outcome of either encounter. It was wholly impotent for the last nine months of the war.

The USN adopted the carrier as centerpiece of the fleet much earlier than the IJN. Since the USN spent the majority of the

ABOVE Two *Lexington* SB2C-3 Helldivers fly over TF 58 on February 16 or 17, 1945 en route to the first carrier raid on the Japanese capital since the Doolittle Raid in April 1942. Over the course of two days, TF 38 conducted some 2,400 offensive sorties against targets in the Tokyo area. (Naval History and Heritage Command)

OPPOSITE In July 1945 Halsey's Third Fleet conducted a series of attacks to finish off the IJN's remaining large units at Kure naval base. This photo is from July 28 and shows *Amagi* in the center which was attacked on July 24 and left heavily damaged but still afloat. The carrier capsized the next day as a result of her cumulative damage. The July 28 attack focused on *Katsuragi*, shown upper left. The ship was hit by at least one bomb but emerged seaworthy and was used postwar as a repatriation ship. (Naval History and Heritage Command)

war on the offensive, it was imperative that it master carrier operations and warfare and develop the Fast Carrier Task Force into a true power projection weapon. The Americans were able to do this by combining an unparalleled level of production in ships and aircraft with technology that vastly improved fleet air defenses, making the carrier force more survivable. All this was supported by an impressive commitment to fleet logistics that made the carrier force capable of sustained power projection. This combination simply overwhelmed the IJN.

After stopping the Japanese advance in 1942, American carriers made the Japanese defensive concept of forming a defensive cordon and forcing the Americans to mount costly attacks against it irrelevant. The USN massed carriers and sea power at selected key locations and then isolated and overwhelmed the Japanese defenders. The only Japanese hope of reversing the tide was by using their carrier fleet to relieve their besieged garrisons. By this time the IJN's carriers were outmatched numerically and technologically.

The true power of the Fast Carrier Task Force was displayed during the last year of the war. After smashing the Japanese fleet at Leyte Gulf, the American carriers overcame another deadly threat in the form of suicide aircraft. The ability of the Fast Carrier Task Force to endure the kamikaze threat allowed it to mount a crippling blockade of Japan and made it a war-winning strategic weapon.

Each of the carrier battles of 1942 demonstrated common characteristics, and these themes were almost all still in play during the single-carrier battle of 1944.

Key Factors in Pacific War Carrier Battles		
CHARACTERISTIC	IJN	USN
Strategic leadership and planning		X
Operational leadership		X
Intelligence		X
Tactical reconnaissance	X	
Strike doctrine	X	
Pilot training and tactics	X	
CAP doctrine		X
Antiaircraft capabilities		X
Integration of technology		X
Note: X indicates area of superiority		

As the table indicates, the Japanese excelled at the tactical aspects of carrier warfare. These strengths resulted in excellent reconnaissance operations (with the salient exception of Midway), consistent strike coordination, and coordinated strike tactics with a powerful torpedo bomber that provided a consistent ship-killing capability. While excellent at offensive operations, defensively the IJN's carrier force exhibited poor fleet air defense capabilities resulting from ineffective CAP tactics and weak antiaircraft defenses. Both the strengths and weaknesses of the IJN's carrier force reflected the priorities of the IJN in general.

The Americans excelled at the operational and strategic aspects of carrier warfare. Fleet air defense was also a strength, primarily because of the fragility of Japanese strike aircraft and the Americans' ability to develop and rapidly deploy improved technology. Offensively, the USN's carrier force displayed an inability to coordinate strikes driven by single air group tactics and communications problems, and ineffective torpedo bombers and/or torpedoes that created a reliance on dive-bombers for offensive punch.

Scouting was an important priority for both sides and both usually devoted considerable resources to it. However, gathering information from scouting aircraft is only a step in the intelligence cycle. Analyzing the information and successfully communicating it to decision-makers is key. At Coral Sea, the Japanese failed to take advantage of invaluable scouting information on May 6 and were prevented from taking advantage of even better scouting information the next day through an incredible sequence of communications problems that prevented them from springing a trap on the unsuspecting Fletcher. The battle could easily have been a Japanese version of Midway with the Japanese playing the role of ambusher due to the incomplete intelligence provided to Fletcher. Coral Sea was the first carrier battle, so it was marked by information gathering and dissemination errors on both sides.

Midway was the only carrier battle in which an ambush was successfully executed. This was primarily due to Japanese arrogance and overconfidence that led to a fatal lack of emphasis on reconnaissance. Had the *Kido Butai* taken scouting more seriously, it would have negated the American edge in strategic intelligence and may have created a battle in which Nimitz's carriers were destroyed. Without doubt, Midway is the most famous naval battle of the Pacific War. In spite of its heavy losses at Midway, the *Kido Butai* was rebuilt and went on to fight two more battles in 1942, including its only victory over the American carrier force.

The Guadalcanal campaign included two of the five carrier battles of the Pacific War. These two clashes, the battle of the Eastern Solomons and the battle of Santa Cruz, are somewhat overlooked compared to Coral Sea and Midway, but they helped determine which side would dominate the waters around Guadalcanal and were important steps in the neutralization of the Imperial Navy's carrier force. Nagumo retained command of the carriers for both battles and was overly cautious on both occasions. The battle of the Eastern Solomons was the most tentative of any of the carrier battles and was therefore the most indecisive.

Santa Cruz is perhaps the most interesting of any of the carrier battles. The trends discussed above were clearly evinced and reached their zenith at this battle. The Japanese took the lessons from Midway and applied them well. A critical mistake at Midway was their inattention to scouting. Japanese searches were effective at Santa Cruz, with the Americans admitting that the performance of Japanese scout aircraft was superior to their own. Japanese CAP tactics were refined with fighters positioned at various altitudes. Even so, it is important to note that the Japanese CAP was unable to seriously disrupt an American strike group that found the Japanese carriers. The effectiveness of Japanese antiaircraft fire was marginal, so the best protection from air attack remained adept evasive maneuvering. Greater attention to damage control and improved damage control procedures were evident and these saved *Shokaku* from destruction. The Japanese tactic of using the Vanguard Force as an advanced screen for the carriers also proved successful and was noted in favorable terms by American after-action reports. In the next carrier battle, the Americans used the same tactic but with greater effectiveness.

The American carrier force took a beating at Santa Cruz and barely escaped total destruction. The most controversial decision of the battle was Halsey's failure to cancel his orders for Kinkaid to move north of the Santa Cruz Islands. Halsey's plan called for the sweep north of the Santa Cruz Islands only in the absence of enemy carriers. Even after it was obvious that Nagumo's carriers were in the area, Halsey let the operation proceed. Though he clearly underestimated the degree of risk, Halsey was guilty of sending his only two carriers beyond the range of effective support from land-based aircraft to fight a Japanese carrier force twice as large. This was Halsey at his impulsive worst, but it was not the last time during the war he would take risks to engage the Japanese carrier force.

At the tactical level, Santa Cruz was the worst performance by an American carrier force during the war. There were several reasons for this, including flawed doctrine, persistent communications problems, the poor level of training of *Enterprise*'s new air group, and a series of questionable decisions by Kinkaid. The American inability to coordinate air strikes was on full display with the result being a series of piecemeal attacks mostly against secondary targets. Most damning was the fact that only ten of 75 strike aircraft attacked a Japanese carrier. Defensively, the Americans performed better but there were still problems. The performance of TF 61's FDO was considered ineffective from Halsey on down. A major factor in this regard was inadequate warning due to radar problems on the carriers. After-action reports indicated that instead of intercepts taking place at the desired 20nm from the carriers, they were occurring only a few miles away, which gave the Wildcats insufficient time to destroy approaching Japanese formations. Santa Cruz was the last time in the war that Japanese carrier aviators caused serious damage to an American carrier task force.

In the final carrier battle of the war, the IJN suffered a decisive defeat at the battle of the Philippine Sea. Of the nine Japanese carriers present, three were sunk, and two more were damaged. Of the 400 carrier aircraft available to Ozawa at the start of the battle, only 35 remained on June 21. Toyoda's decisive battle had been fought and lost. The failure of the decisive naval battle led to the fall of Saipan and was followed by the invasion of the remainder of the Marianas. This constituted a clear turning point for Japan as the horrors of war would soon be visited on the Home Islands in the form of B-29 raids.

Of all the carrier battles, the outcome of the battle of the Philippine Sea was the most predictable. The Japanese had given great thought to Operation *A-Go*, but its pillars were unsteady at best and already in a state of collapse at worst. The plan was predicated on the massive application of air power, carrier and land-based, but this is where the Japanese were weakest. The Base Air Force was unable to perform adequate reconnaissance, which allowed the Americans to achieve operational and tactical surprise. The lack of operational warning caught the Base Air Force out of position and gave the First Mobile Fleet a late start. Even more disastrous for the Japanese, the Base Air Force could not conduct successful attacks against TF 58, which meant the First Mobile Fleet had to engage a full-strength American carrier force. Even though Ozawa maneuvered successfully to launch his full air strength at TF 58, his massive first strike did not provide victory as it had in 1942. Confident in his ability to defeat a Japanese first strike, Spruance fought a defensive battle. While that was a recipe for disaster in 1942, by 1944 the combination of poor Japanese aircrew training and American radar-directed fighter intercepts made even a large Japanese strike ineffective. It should be noted that the air battle of June 19 still gave the Japanese opportunities to strike blows at TF 58. Several small groups of Japanese aircraft broke through the CAP to deliver attacks on American carriers. Had their skills been better, particularly in delivering torpedo attacks that had been deadly to USN carriers in 1942, the cost to TF 58 would have been higher.

Of the two main antagonists, Ozawa fought the more intelligent battle. He correctly assessed that Spruance's cautious nature meant he would not venture far from Saipan. This critical insight allowed the First Mobile Fleet to launch four strikes that would have been fatal to an American carrier task force in 1942. However, the Japanese failed to recognize the degree to which carrier warfare had changed by 1944. For example, the Japanese were unaware of the USN's use of radar-directed CAP that doomed large-scale high-altitude attacks. It did not matter how skillfully Ozawa handled his fleet since he lacked the means to deal serious blows to TF 58. Even if a few of the Japanese aircraft that penetrated TF 58's CAP had scored hits, the outcome of the battle would not have changed. The one fault Ozawa displayed during the battle was a readiness to accept the gross overestimation of successes reported by Kakuta's Base Air Force and his own carrier aviators.

Spruance was the clear winner of the battle, losing only 130 aircraft and 76 aviators while crippling the First Mobile Fleet. However, his decisions can be criticized as he was outmaneuvered by Ozawa and never able to bring the overwhelming power of TF 58 to bear. The first key juncture was Spruance's decision not to move west on the night of June 18–19. This lack of aggression meant that TF 58 would fight a defensive battle on June 19 and have difficulty in launching offensive strikes on June 20. Spruance made his decision based on the paramount importance he placed on the security of the amphibious operation against Saipan. He was convinced that the Japanese would attempt to draw him to the west and then conduct a flanking attack on the amphibious force off Saipan. The captured Z Plan and the pattern of Japanese movements on June 17–18 provided the groundwork for this assessment. In fact, Spruance fundamentally misjudged Japanese intentions since Ozawa aimed to destroy TF 58 instead of attacking the landing force. The defensive plan that Spruance settled on could have been disastrous as he was exposing his carriers to attack without any guarantee of being able to strike back. At no other carrier battle of the war did a commander adopt such an approach. Only the marked disparity between the skill of American and Japanese aviators prevented this strategy from backfiring. Spruance understood that his aviators were better, but nobody could have foreseen that Japanese aviators would be totally ineffective in their attacks on June 19.

Spruance's fear that the Japanese could slip around TF 58 and attack the invasion force was not only incorrect, it was misplaced. He had already taken the precaution of moving the invasion force 200nm east of Saipan, and even after TF 58's screen was reinforced with combatants from the invasion force, significant USN forces remained to protect the beachhead. Any major Japanese flanking attack against the invasion force was very unlikely to succeed in the face of TF 58's ability to scout large swaths of ocean and then launch powerful strikes. Spruance was thinking as a surface warfare officer instead of the commander of the world's most powerful carrier strike force with the ability to strike targets hundreds of miles away.

Spruance's incomplete victory still eliminated the Japanese carrier force as a factor for the remainder of the war. The fact that six of Ozawa's carriers escaped with empty decks was of little consequence. But the echoes of Philippine Sea resonated beyond June 1944. The "disappointing" American victory at Philippine Sea surely influenced Halsey's decision just a few months later to make destruction of the Japanese carriers his paramount objective. Even more lasting was the Imperial Navy's assessment that large-scale conventional air attacks against the American fleet were pointless. This realization forced the adoption of suicide attacks that presented American carriers with their most difficult challenge of the war.

Though it is somewhat superficial to compare losses, totaling the losses for each side for the five Pacific War carrier battles is illustrative. During these battles, the IJN lost nine carriers and the USN only three. Aircraft losses were also lopsided, with Japanese losses nearing 900 compared to American losses of approximately 450. From an operational perspective, the Japanese were not able to achieve their operational objectives in any of the five carrier battles; the Americans were able to do so in all five. From this perspective, the Pacific War's carrier battles were a key component of the American victory in the war.

BIBLIOGRAPHY

Aiken, David, "Torpedoing Pearl Harbor," *Military History*, December 2001

Aiken, David, "Ghosts of Pearl Harbor," *Flight Journal*, June 2007

Bicheno, Hugh, *Midway*, Cassell and Company, London, 2001

Bullard, Steven (translator), *Japanese Army Operations in the South Pacific Area*, Australian War Memorial, Canberra, 2007

Cressman, Robert J., et al., *A Glorious Page in Our History*, Pictorial Histories Publishing Company, Missoula, Montana, 1990

De Virgilio, John, "Japanese Thunderfish," *Naval History*, Winter 1991

Dickson, W.D., *The Battle of the Philippine Sea*, Ian Allan, London, 1975

Dillon, Katherine and Goldstein, Donald, ed., *The Pearl Harbor Papers: Inside the Japanese Plans*, Brassey's, Washington, DC, 1993

Dillon, Katherine and Goldstein, Donald, ed., *The Pacific War Papers: Japanese Documents of World War II*, Potomac Books, Washington, DC, 2004

Dull, Paul, *A Battle History of the Imperial Japanese Navy*, Naval Institute Press, Annapolis, 1978

Evans, David, ed., *The Japanese Navy in World War II*, Naval Institute Press, Annapolis, 1986

Foreign Histories Division, General Headquarters Far East Command, *Japanese Monograph No. 90, The "A-Go" Operations May–June 1944*, Tokyo, 1950

Foreign Histories Division, General Headquarters Far East Command, *Japanese Monograph No. 91, The "A-Go" Operations Log Supplement: May–June 1944*, Tokyo, 1950

Foreign Histories Division, General Headquarters Far East Command, *Japanese Monograph No. 117, Outline of Third Phase Operations (February 1943 to August 1945)*, Tokyo, 1950

Frank, Richard B., *Guadalcanal*, Random House, New York, 1990

Fuchida, Mitsuo and Okumiya, Masatake, *Midway*, Naval Institute Press, Annapolis, 1955

Hammel, Eric, *Guadalcanal: The Carrier Battles*, Crown Publishers, New York, 1987

Hammel, Eric, *Carrier Strike*, Pacifica Press, California, 1999

Isom, Dallas Woodbury, *Midway Inquest*, Indiana University Press, Bloomington, Indiana, 2007

Kawasaki, Manabu, *A New View of the Battle of Philippine Sea*, Dainihon Kaiga, Tokyo, 2007

Lord, Walter, *Day of Infamy*, Henry Holt and Company, New York, 2001

Lundstrom, John B., *The First Team*, Naval Institute Press, Annapolis, 1984

Lundstrom, John B., *The First Team and the Guadalcanal Campaign*, Naval Institute Press, Annapolis, 1994

Lundstrom, John B., *Black Shoe Carrier Admiral*, Naval Institute Press, Annapolis, 2006

McGovern, Terrance and Williford, Glen, *Defenses of Pearl Harbor and Oahu 1907–50*, Osprey, Botley, 2003

Millot, Bernard, *The Battle of the Coral Sea*, Ian Allan, London, 1974

Morison, Samuel Eliot, *The Rising Sun in the Pacific, 1931–April 1942* (Volume III of *The History of United States Naval Operations in World War II*), Little, Brown and Company, Boston, 1975

Morison, Samuel Eliot, *Coral Sea, Midway and Submarine Actions May 1942–August 1942* (Volume IV of *The History of United States Naval Operations in World War II*), Little, Brown and Company, Boston, 1975

Morison, Samuel Eliot, *The Struggle for Guadalcanal* (Volume V of *The History of United States Naval Operations in World War II*), Little, Brown and Company, Boston, 1975

Morison, Samuel Eliot, *New Guinea and the Marianas March 1944–August 1944* (Volume VIII of *The History of United States Naval Operations in World War II*), Little, Brown and Company, Boston, 1975

Morison, Samuel Eliot, *Leyte: June 1944–January 1945* (Volume XII of *The History of United States Naval Operations in World War II*), Little, Brown and Company, Boston, 1975

Parshall, Jonathan and Tully, Anthony, *Shattered Sword*, Potomac Books, Washington, DC, 2005

Peattie, Mark, *Sunburst: The Rise of Japanese Naval Air Power, 1909–1941*, Naval Institute Press, Annapolis, 2001

Prange, Gordon, *At Dawn We Slept*, McGraw-Hill, New York, 1981

Prange, Gordon, *Miracle at Midway*, McGraw-Hill, New York, 1982

Prange, Gordon, *December 7, 1941: The Day the Japanese Attacked Pearl Harbor*, Wings Books, New York, 1991

Reynolds, Clark, *The Fast Carriers*, Naval Institute Press, Annapolis, 1992

Smith, Peter C., *Midway: Dauntless Victory*, Pen and Sword, Barnsley, 2007

Tillman, Barrett, *Clash of the Carriers*, NAL Caliber, New York, 2005

United States Fleet, *Battle Experience: Supporting Operations for the Capture of the Marianas Islands (Saipan, Guam, and Tinian) June–August 1944*, 1944

Vego, Milan, *Major Fleet-versus-Fleet Operations in the Pacific War, 1941–1945*, Naval War College Press, Newport, 2014

Willmott, H.P., *The Barrier and the Javelin*, Naval Institute Press, Annapolis, 1983

Willmott, H.P., *Pearl Harbor*, Sterling Publishing Co, New York, 2001

Willmott, H.P., *The Battle of Leyte Gulf*, Indiana University Press, Bloomington, 2005

Y'Blood, William T., *Red Sun Setting*, Naval Institute Press, Annapolis, 1981

Zimm, Alan, *The Attack on Pearl Harbor: Strategy, Combat, Myths, Deceptions*, Casemate, Havertown, Pennsylvania, 2011

OVERLEAF A F6F-3 Hellcat of Fighting Squadron Sixteen (VF-16) aboard USS *Lexington* gets the OK for take-off, November 23, 1943. (US Navy Official)

INDEX